WORDS AND THEIR USES,

PAST AND PRESENT.

A STUDY OF THE ENGLISH LANGUAGE.

BY

RICHARD GRANT WHITE.

THIRD EDITION, REVISED AND CORRECTED.

BOSTON:
HOUGHTON, MIFFLIN AND COMPANY.
The Riverside Press, Cambridge.
1880.
LONDON: TRÜBNER & CO.

AFTERTHOUGHTS AND FOREWORDS

TO THE PRESENT EDITION.

IN preparing a new edition of this book I have sought help and taken hints from every criticism of it that I have seen ; and I heard of none that I did not try to find if it was not at hand. Whoever attempts to correct the faults of others in any respect, may expect severe treatment at the hands of the very men whom he would serve; and if his efforts are directed to their use of language, he may reasonably look forward to walking, sitting, and sleeping upon pen-points for a while. Wherefore I have been very pleasantly surprised that of the much that has been written about this book, so little, comparatively, was disparaging. In only one quarter have I found reason to complain of unfairness, or even of a captious spirit, while the general tone of my critics, public and private, has been that of thankfulness for a real service. But I have tried not to allow myself to be led by the favorable judgement of my critics into the belief that I could disregard the strictures of my censors.

In many passages of the book slight changes have been made ; upon matters of fact and of opinion a few important modifications will be found ; one new chapter has been added. The sum of these alterations and corrections will, I hope, be regarded as such an improvement of the book as will make it more worthy of the attention which it has received. The most of these changes would have been made

o whether my book has any value, let time dei
'hat I have written cannot bear criticism, it is w
ought to die. It will soon disappear into the li
gs forgotten; and the less that is said about
:r. Any disparagement of the "scholarship"
: gives me little concern. It is altogether fr
ose. Whatever value I hoped these desultory
ld have, depends in the least that is possible u
ling, real or supposed, of the author. If I hi
tation of that sort, it is not of my seeking. N
a the consideration due to a philologist. For
ilogist is a man who, horsed upon Grimm's law,
:vasive syllable over umlauts and ablauts into the
ing recesses of the Himalayas; and I confess that
linguistic Nimrod. I have joined a little in tha
like the Frenchman who, after one day of " *le*
i the soil of *perfide Albion*, being summoned nex
for another run, cried "Vot, do they make h
s?" and turned his aching bones to rest, I soon
left the field to bolder spirits and harder riders

philological. The few suggestions which I have made in etymology I put forth with no affectation of timidity, but with little concern as to their fate." It is upon this ground, humbler or higher, that in good faith I take my stand, and it is only this that I profess to be able to maintain.

Besides the topics of taste and reason in the use of language, there are two to which I have ventured direct attention. Upon one of these my position (as to which I have no vague notion, but a settled conviction) is that in the development of language, and in particular of the English language, reason always wins against formal grammar or illogical usage, and that the "authority" of eminent writers, conforming to, or forming, the usage of their day, while it does absolve from the charge of solecism those who follow such example, does not completely justify or establish a use of words inconsistent with reason, or out of the direction of the normal growth of language. In other words, I believe, assert, and endeavor to maintain that in language, as in morals, there is a higher law than mere usage, which, in morals as in language, makes that acceptable, tolerable, and even proper in one age, which becomes intolerable and improper in another ; that this law is the law of reason, toward a conformity to which usage itself is always struggling, and, although constantly hindered and often diverted, winning its way, little by little, not reaching, yet ever nearing an ever-receding goal. To assault any position of mine, which is not itself taken upon the ground of usage, by bringing up the "authority," that is the mere example, of eminent writers, is at once to beg the question at issue. It may be said, and is said, that in language usage is both in fact and of right the final law and the ground of law. But with any one who takes that for granted I cannot argue. We do not approach each other near enough for collision. We are as widely separated as two theological disputants would be, one of whom was a Protestant, and the other a Papist who set up as an axiom the divine establishment and perpetual infallibility of the Romish Church. He assumes and starts from the very point that I dispute.

That language has in all respects a normal growth, and that passing deviations from that normality are not to be defended and accepted without question on the ground that mere eminent usage justifies such irregularities, I do verily believe. And upon this point of so-called irregularity, it seems to me that the remarks made by Helfenstein in the introduction to his examination of the anomalous verbs, are of even wider application :

" Under this head we range all those verbs which in their inflexional forms show certain peculiarities so as to require separate treatment as a class of their own. We avoid the term irregular, for it is high time that this designation, which cannot but convey erroneous notions, should disappear from the terminology of grammarians. There is nothing irregular in these verbs, and nothing irregular in language generally. Every phenomenon is founded upon a law; it is not the product of haphazard or of an arbitrary will. Where the law has not yet been discovered, it remains the noblest task of linguists to strive after its discovery and elucidation. What as yet evades explanation may be left standing over as a fact which is sure to find some day sufficient illustration from other corollary facts grouped around. But we must do away once and for all with all notions of irregularity, and therefore drop the term which keeps such notions alive."—*Comparative Grammar of the Teutonic Languages*, p. 499.

I cannot believe that the arbitrary and capricious usage of a clique or a mere generation of writers is such a "phe nomenon" as Helfenstein regards as "founded upon a law, when he declares that there is nothing irregular in language generally.

And as to the weight of authority which is claimed for eminent writers, I cannot see why the endowment of creative genius should, or that it does, insure to its possessor a greater certainty of correctness in the use of language than may go with the possession of inferior powers. To admit that would oblige us to accept Chaucer as a higher authority than Gower, Spenser as higher than Sidney, Lyly than Ascham, Shakespeare than Jonson, Pope than Addison, Scott than Hallam, Byron than Southey, Carlyle than Landor or Macaulay, Dickens than Helps.

Upon the second of the topics to which I have referred, that English is to all intents and purposes a grammarless tongue, and therefore has a superiority over all others, I shall let what I have said stand without further argument, only calling to my support this passage from Sidney's "Apologie for Poetrie," which when I wrote before I had utterly forgotten. Speaking of English, he says:

"I know some will say it is a mingled language. And why not so much the better, taking the best of both the other? Another will say that it wanteth Grammer. Nay truly it hath that praise that it wanteth not [i. e., does not need] Grammer: for Grammer it might have, but it needes it not; being so easie of it selfe, and so voyd of those cumbersome differences of Cases, Genders, Moodes, and Tenses, which I think was a peece of the Tower of Babilon's curse, that a man should be put to schoole to learne his mother tongue. But for the uttering sweetly and properly the con-

ceits of the minde, which is the end of speech, that hath it
equally with any other tongue in the world : and is parti-
culerly happy in compositions of two or three words together
neere the Greeke, far beyond the Latine : which is one of
the greatest beauties can be in a language."

What Sidney saw, and thus with sweet dogmatism set
forth, I have but endeavored to illustrate and to establish.

Why I have been called upon to write this book is still
not easy for me to understand. For it is the result of
questions submitted to me from correspondents in all parts
of the country upon the subject of which it treats, although
I can hardly pretend to have made a special study of language—no other, in fact, than was part and parcel of
studies in English literature generally, and particularly that
of the Elizabethan period. But as these questions were
speered at me, I thought it would be pleasant and profitable
to answer them in the articles which have been gathered into
this volume. Let me say to my correspondents and readers
that if any of them hope to acquire a good style, or to
"learn to write," by reading such books as this, or even by
the study of grammar and rhetoric, as I have reason to fear
that some of them do, they will be grievously disappointed.
That acquisition comes only through native ability and general culture. No man ever learned to win the ear of the
public by studies of this nature. Those who write what is
read with pleasure and profit, do not get their power or
learn their craft from dictionaries, grammars, or books on
rhetoric. The study of language must be pursued for its
own sake. It has only a place, although a high one, in that
general culture which gives mental discipline and makes the
accomplished man. He who cannot write with clearness
and force without troubling his soul about pronouns and

prepositions, syntax and definitions, may better change his pen for a hoe and his inkstand for a watering-pot, and give his days and nights to market-gardening; an occupation equally honorable with literature, and, I can assure him, far more profitable, no less to the world at large than to the individual. With which counsel I bid my readers farewell.

To James Russell Lowell.

When your forefather met mine, as he probably did, some two hundred and thirty or forty years ago, in the newly laid out street of Cambridge (and there is reason for believing that the meeting was likely to be about where Gore Hall now stands), yours might have been somewhat more grimly courteous than he doubtless was, had he known that he saw the man one of whose children in the eighth generation was to pay one of his, at the same remove, even this small tribute of mere words; and mine might have lost some of his reputation for inflexibility had he known that he was keeping on his steeple-crown before him without whom there would be no "Legend of Brittany," no "Sir Launfal," no "Commemoration Ode," no "Cathedral," no "Biglow Papers," — without whom our idea of the New England these men helped to found would lack, in these latter days, some of the strength and the beauty which make it worthy of our respect, our admiration, and our love, — and without whom the great school that was soon set up where they were standing, to be the first and ever the brightest light of learning in the land, would miss one of its most shining ornaments.

We may be sure that both these honored men spoke English in the strong and simple manner of their time, of which you have well said that it was "a diction which we should be glad to buy back from desuetude at almost any cost," and which

TO JAMES RUSSELL LOWELL.

you have done so much to illustrate, to perpetuate, and to enrich. I have as little faith as I believe you have in the worth of a school-bred language. Strong, clear, healthy, living speech springs, like most strong, living things, from the soil, and grows according to the law of life within its seed. But pruning and training may do something for a nursery-bred weakling, and even for that which springs up unbidden, and grows with native vigor into sturdy shapeliness. It is because you have shown this in a manner which makes all men of New England stock your debtors, and proud of their indebtedness, that at the beginning of a book which seeks to do in the weakness of precept what you have done by the strength of example, I acknowledge, in so far as I may presume to do so, what is owing to you by all your countrymen, and also record the high respect and warm regard with which I am, and hope ever to be,

Faithfully your friend,

RICHARD GRANT WHITE.

New York, *August* 3, 1870.

(a)

PREFACE.

————◆◆————

THE following pages contain the substance of the articles which appeared in The Galaxy in the years 1867, 1868, and 1869, under the title now borne by this volume. Some changes in the arrangement of the subjects of those articles, some excisions, and a few additions, have been made; but after reading, with a willingness to learn, nearly all the criticisms with which I was favored, I have found reason for abandoning or modifying very few of my previously expressed opinions.

The purpose of the book is the consideration of the right use and the abuse of words and idioms, with an occasional examination of their origin and their history. It is occupied almost exclusively with the correctness and fitness of verbal expression, and any excursion into higher walks of philology is transient and incidental.

Soon after taking up this subject I heard a story of a professor at Oxford, who, being about to address a miscellaneous audience at that seat of learning, illustrated some of his positions by quotations in the original from Arabic writers. A friend venturing to hint that this

3

might be caviare to his audience, he replied, "O, everybody knows a little Arabic." Now, I have discovered that everybody does not know a little Arabic; and more, that there are men all around me, of intelligence and character, who, although they cannot be called illiterate, — as peasants are illiterate, — know so very little of the right use of English, that, without venturing beyond the limits of my own yet imperfect knowledge of my mother tongue, I might undertake to give the instruction that I find many of them not only need, but desire.

The need is particularly great in this country; of which fact I have not only set forth the reasons, but have endeavored to explain them with such detail as would enable my readers to see them for themselves, and take them to heart, instead of merely accepting or rejecting my assertion. Since I first gave these reasons in The Galaxy, they have been incidentally, but earnestly and impressively, presented by Professor Whitney in his book on Language and the Study of Language. Summing up his judgment on this point, that eminent philologist says, "The low-toned party newspaper is too much the type of the prevailing literary influence by which the style of speech of our rising generation is moulding. A tendency to slang, to colloquial inelegances, and even vulgarities, is the besetting sin against which we, as Americans, have especially 'to guard and to struggle."

What Professor Whitney thus succinctly declares, I have endeavored to set forth at large and to illustrate. Usage in the end makes language; determining not

only the meaning of words, but their suggestiveness,
and also their influence. For the influence of man
upon language is reciprocated by the influence of language upon man; and the mental tone of a community
may be vitiated by a yielding to the use of loose, coarse,
low, and frivolous phraseology. Into this people fall
by the mere thoughtless imitation of slovenly exem-
plars. A case in point — trifling and amusing, but not,
therefore, less suggestive — recently attracted my attention. Professor Whitney mentions, as one of his many
illustrations of the historical character of word-making,
that we put on a "pair of *rubbers*," because, when
caoutchouc was first brought to us, we could find no
better use for it than the rubbing out of pencil-marks.
But overshoes of this material are not universally called
"rubbers." In Philadelphia, with a reference to the
nature of the substance of which they are made, they
are called "gums." A Philadelphia gentleman and
his wife going to make a visit at a house in New
York, where they were very much at home, he entered
the parlor alone; and to the question, "Why, where
is Emily?" answered, "O, Emily is outside cleaning
her gums upon the mat;" whereupon there was a
momentary look of astonishment, and then a peal of
laughter. Now, there is no need whatever of the use
of either of the poor words *rubbers* or *gums* in this
sense. The proper word is simply *overshoes*, which
expresses all that there is occasion to tell, except to
a manufacturer or a salesman. There is neither necessity nor propriety in our going into the question of the
fabric of what we wear for the protection of our feet.

and of saying that a lady is either rubbing her rubbers or cleaning her gums on the mat ; no more than there is in our saying that a gentleman is brushing his wool (meaning his coat), or a lady drying her eyes with her linen (meaning her handkerchief). Language is generally formed by indirect and unconscious effort; but when a language is subjected to the constant action of such degrading influences as those which threaten ours, it may be well to introduce into its development a little consciousness. The difference between saying, He donated the balance of the lumber, and He gave the rest of the timber, is perhaps trifling; but man's language, like man himself, grows by a gradual accretion of trifles, and the sum of these, in our case, is on the one hand good English, and on the other bad. Therefore they are not unworthy of any man's serious attention.

Language is rarely corrupted, and is often enriched, by the simple, unpretending, ignorant man, who takes no thought of his parts of speech. It is from the man who knows just enough to be anxious to square his sentences by the line and plummet of grammar and dictionary that his mother tongue suffers most grievous injury. It is his influence chiefly which is resisted in this book. I have little hope, I must confess, of undoing any of the harm that he has done, or of plucking up any monstrosity which, planted by him, has struck root into the popular speech; particularly if it seems fine, and is not quite understood by those who use it.

Transpire and *predicate* — worthy pair — will be used, I fear, the one to mean happen, and the other found;

things will continue *to be being done*, and the gentle-manly barkeeper of the period will call his grog-shop a *sample-room*, notwithstanding all that I have said, and all that abler men and better scholars than I am may say, to the contrary. But, although I do not expect to purge away corruption, I do hope to arrest it in some measure by giving hints that help toward wholesome-ness.

This book may possibly correct some of the pre-vailing evils against which it is directed; but I shall be satisfied if it awakens an attention to its subject that will prevent evil in the future. Scholars and philolo-gists need not be told that it is not addressed to them; but neither is it written for the unintelligent and entirely uninstructed. It is intended to be of some service to intelligent, thoughtful, educated persons, who are in-terested in the study of the English language, and in the protection of it against pedants on the one side and coarse libertines in language on the other.

On the etymology of words I have said little, because little was needed. The points from which I have re-garded words are in general rather those of taste and reason than of history; and my discussions are philo-logical only as all study of words must be philological. The few suggestions which I have made in etymology I put forth with no affectation of timidity, but with little concern as to their fate. Etymology, which, as it is now practised, is a product of the last thirty years, fulfils toward language the function which the antiquarian and the genealogist discharge in the making of the world's history. The etymologist of the present day follows, as he should follow, his word up step by step through the written records of past years, until he finds its origin in the fixed form of a parent language. The disappearance of every letter, the modification of every sound, the introduction of every new letter, must be accounted for in accordance with the analogy of the language at the period when the change, real or supposed, took place. Thus etymology has at last been placed upon its only safe bases, — research and comparison, — and the origin of most words in modern languages is as surely determinable as that of a member of any family which has a recorded history.

I have only to add here that in my remarks on what I have unavoidably called, by way of distinction, British English and " American " English, and in my criticism of the style of some eminent British authors, no insinuation of a superiority in the use of their mother tongue by men of English race in " America " is intended, no right to set up an independent standard is implied. Of the latter, indeed, there is no fear. When that new " American " thing, so eagerly sought, and hitherto so vainly, does appear, if it ever do appear, it will not be a language, or even a literature.

———

This book was prepared for the press in the autumn of 1869. An unavoidable and unexpected delay in its appearance has enabled me to add a few examples in illustration of my views, which I have met with since that time; but it has received no other additions.

R. G. W.

New York, *July* 8, 1870.

CONTENTS.

(9)

CHAPTER VIII.

CHAPTER IX.

CHAPTER X.

CHAPTER XI.

CHAPTER XII.

CHAPTER XIII.

APPENDIX.

WORDS AND THEIR USES.

"They be not wise, therefore that say, what care I for man's wordes and utterance, if hys matter and reasons be good? Such men, say so, not so much of ignorance, as eyther of some singular pride in themselves, or some speciall malice of other, or for some private and parciall matter, either in Religion or other kynde of learning. For good and choice meates, be no more requisite for helthy bodyes, than proper and apt wordes be for good matters, and also playne and sensible utterance for the best and deepest reasons : in which two poyntes standeth perfect eloquence, one of the fayrest and rarest giftes that God doth geve to man."

Ascham's Scholemaster, fol. 46, ed. 1571.

"Seeing that truth consisteth in the right ordering of names in our affirmations, a man that seeketh precise truth had need to remember what every name he useth stands for, and to place it accordingly, or else he will find himselfe entangled in words as a bird in lime-twiggs. The more he struggles the more belimed."

Hobbes's Leviathan, I. 4.

"F. Must we always be seeking after the meaning of words?

"H. Of important words we must, if we wish to avoid important error. The meaning of these words especially is of the greatest consequence to mankind, and seems to have been strangely neglected by those who have made most use of them."

Tooke, Diversions of Purley, Part II., ch. 1.

"Mankind in general are so little in the habit of looking steadily at their own meaning, or of weighing the words by which they express it, that the writer who is careful to do both will sometimes mislead his readers through the very excellence which qualifies him to be their instructor ; and this with no other fault on his part than the modest mistake on his part of supposing in those to whom he addresses himself an intellect as watchful as his own."

Coleridge, The Friend, II., 2d Landing Place.

CHAPTER I.

INTRODUCTION.

ONE of the last judgments pronounced in philology is, that words are merely arbitrary sounds for the expression and communication of ideas; that, for instance, a man calls the source of light and heat the sun, because his mother taught him so to call it, and that is the name by which it is known to the people around him, and that if he had been taught in his childhood, and by example afterwards, to call it the moon, he would have done so without question. But this truth was declared more than two hundred years ago by Oliver Cromwell in his reply to the committee that waited upon him from Parliament to ask him to take the title of king. In the course of his refusal to yield to their request, he said, —

"Words have not their import from the natural power of particular combinations of characters, or from the real efficacy of certain sounds, but from the consent of those that use them, and arbitrarily annex certain ideas to them, which might have been signified with equal propriety by any other."

Thus mother wit forestalled philological deduction; but the reasoning would be weak that found in the fact that language is formed, on the whole, by consent and custom, an argument in favor

of indifference as to the right or wrong of usage.
For, although he was so earnestly entreated thereto,
and although it would have obviated some difficulty
in the administration of the government, Cromwell, notwithstanding his opinion as to the arbitrary
meaning of words, refused to be called a king, because *king* meant something that he was not, and
had associations which he wished not to bring up.
And although to the individual words are arbitrary,
to the race or the nation, they are growths, and are
themselves the fruit and the sign of the growth of
the race or the nation itself. So words have, like
men, a history, and alliances, and rights of birth,
and inherent powers which endure as long as they
live, and which they can transmit, although somewhat modified, to their rightful successors.

But although most words are more immutable,
as well as more enduring, than men are, some of
them within the memory of one generation vary
both in their forms and in the uses which they serve,
doing so according to the needs and even the
neglect of the users. And thus it is that living
languages are always changing. Spoken words
acquire, by use and from the varying circumstances
of those who use them, other and wider significations than those which they had originally; inflections are dropped, and construction is modified,
its tendency being generally towards simplicity.
Changes in inflection and construction are found not
to be casual or capricious, but processes according
to laws of development; which, however, as in the
case of all laws, physical or moral, are deduced from
the processes themselves. The apparent operation

of these laws is recognized so submissively by some philologists that Dr. Latham has propounded the dogma that in language whatever is, is right; to which he adds another, as a corollary to the former, that whatever was, was wrong. But even if we admit that in language whatever is — that is, whatever usage obtains generally among the people who speak a language as their mother tongue — is right, that is, fulfils the true function of language, which is to serve as a communication between man and man, it certainly therefore follows that, whatever was, was also right; because it did, at one time, obtain generally, and did fulfil the function of language.

The truth is, that, although usage may be compulsory in its behests, and thus establish a government *de facto*, which men have found that they must recognize whether they will or no, in language, as in all other human affairs, that which is may be wrong. There is some other law in language than the mere arbitrary will of the users. Language is made for man, and not man for language; but yet no man, no number of men, however great, can of purpose change the meaning of one monosyllable. For, unless the meaning of words is fixed during a generation, language will fail to impart ideas, and even to communicate facts. Unless it is traceable through the writings of many generations in a connected course of normal development, language becomes a mere temporary and arbitrary mode of intercourse; it fails to be an exponent of a people's intellectual growth; and the speech of our immediate forefathers dies upon their lips, and is forgotten. Of such misfortune there is, however, not the remotest probability.

The recognition of the changes which the English language has been undergoing from the time when our Anglo-Saxon, or rather our English forefathers, took possession of the southern part of Britain, is no discovery of modern philology. The changes, and the inconvenience which follows them, were noticed four hundred years ago by William Caxton, our first printer — a "simple person," as he describes himself, but an observant, a thoughtful, and a very intelligent man, and one to whom English literature is much indebted. He was not only a printer, but a writer; and as a part of his literary labor he translated into English a French version of the Æneid, and published it in the year 1490. In Caxton's preface to that book is a passage which is interesting in itself, and also germane to our subject. I will give the passage entire, and in our modern orthography : —

"And when I had advised me in this said book, I deliberated and concluded to translate it into English, and forthwith took a pen and ink and wrote a leaf or twain, which I oversaw again to correct it; and when I saw the fair and strange terms therein, I doubted that it should not please some gentlemen which late blamed me, saying, that in my translations I had over-curious terms which could not be understonden of common people, and desired me to use old and homely terms in my translations; and fain would I satisfy every man; and so to do, took an old book and read therein; and certainly the English was so rude and broad that I could not well understand it. And also my Lord Abbot of Westminster did shew to me of late certain evidences written in old English, for to reduce it into our English now used, and certainly it was written in such wise that it was more like Dutch than English. I could not reduce ne bring it to be understonden. And certainly our language now used varyeth far from what was used and spoken when I was born. For we Englishmen ben born under the domination of the Moon, which is never steadfast, but ever wavering, waxynge one season and waneth and decreaseth another season, and that common English that is spoken in one Shire varieth from another. Insomuch that in my days it happened that certain merchants were in a ship in Tamis [Thames] fer to have sailed over the sea into Zealand, and for lack of wind they tarried at Forland, and went to land for to refresh them. And one of them named Sheffield, a mercer, came into an house and axed for meat, and specially he axed for eggs. And the good wife answered that she could speak no French; and the merchant was angry; for he also could speak no French, but would have had the eggs, and she understood him not. And then at last another said that he would have *eyren*; then the good wife said that she understood him well. Lo, what should a man in these days write? *eggs* or *eyren?* Certainly it is hard to please every man, because of diversity and change of language. For in these days every man that is in any reputation in this country will utter his communication and matters in such manner and terms that few men shall understand them; and some honest and great clerks have been with me and desired me to write the most curious terms that I could find. And thus between plain, rude, and curious, I stand abashed."

My chief purpose in giving this passage in our regulated spelling is, that the reader may notice how entirely it is written in the English of to-day. Except *axed*, which we have heard used ourselves, and *eyren*, which Caxton himself notices as obsolete, *ben*, *ne*, and *understonden*, are the only words in it which have not just the form and the meaning that we now give to them; and but for these five words and a little quaintness of style, the passage in its construction and its idiom might have been written yesterday. And yet the writer was born in the reign of Henry IV., and died a hundred years before Shakespeare wrote his first play. He says, too, in another part of his preface, that he wrote in

2

the idiom and with the vocabulary in use among educated people of his day, in "Englishe not over rude," on the one hand, "ne curyous," that is, affected and elaborately fine, on the other. If the changes in language which took place during his life were as great as he seems to have thought them, if they were as great as those with which in the present day we seem to be threatened, certainly the period intervening between the time which saw him a middle-aged man and now — four hundred years — seems by contrast to have been one of almost absolute linguistic stagnation. This, however, is mere seeming. The period of which Caxton speaks was one in which the language was crystallizing into its present form, and becoming the English known to literature; and changes then were rapid and noticeable. The changes of our day are mostly the result of the very superficial instruction of a large body of people, who read much and without discrimination, whose reading is chiefly confined to newspapers hastily written by men also very insufficiently educated, and who are careless of accuracy in their ordinary speaking and writing, and ambitious of literary excellence when they make any extraordinary effort. The tendency of this intellectual condition of a great and active race is to the degradation of language, the utter abolition of simple, clear, and manly speech. Against this tendency it behooves all men who have means and opportunity to strive, almost as if it were a question of morals. For there is a kind of dishonesty in the careless and incorrect use of language.

Purity, however, is not a quality which can be accurately predicated of language. What the phrase so often heard, "pure English," really means, it would, probably, puzzle those who use it to explain. For our modern tongues are like many buildings that stand upon sites long swept over by the ever-advancing, though backward and forward shifting tide of civilization. They are built out of the ruins of the work of previous generations, to which we and our immediate predecessors have added something of our own. This process has been going on since the disappearance of the first generation of speaking men; and it will never cease. But there will be a change in its mode and rate The change has begun already. The invention of printing, the instruction of the mass of the people, and the ease of popular intercommunication, will surely prevent any such corruption and detrition of language as that which has resulted in the modern English, German, French, Spanish, and Italian tongues. Phonetic degradation will play a less important part than it has heretofore played in the history of language. Changes in the forms, and variation in the meanings of words will be slow, and if not deliberate, at least half conscious; and the corruptions that we have to guard against are chiefly those consequent upon pretentious ignorance and aggressive vulgarity.

It may be reasonably doubted whether there ever was a pure language two generations old; that is, a language homogeneous, of but one element. All tongues known to philology show, if not the min-gling in considerable and nearly determinable pro-

portions of two or three linguistic elements, at least
the adoption and adaptation of numerous foreign
words. English has for many centuries been far
from being a simple language. Chaucer's "well
of English undefiled" is very pleasant and wholesome drinking; but, pronouns, prepositions, conjunctions, and "auxiliary" verbs aside, it is a mixture
in which Normanized, Gallicized Latin is mingled
in large proportion with a base of degraded Anglo-
Saxon. And yet the result of this hybridity and
degradation is the tongue in which Shakespeare
wrote, and the translators of the Bible, and Milton,
and Bunyan, and Burke, and Goldsmith, and Irving,
and Hawthorne; making in a language without a
superior a literature without an equal.

But the presence in our language of two elements, both of which are essential to its present
fulness and force, no less than to its fineness and
flexibility, does not make it sure that these are of
equal or of nearly equal importance. Valuable as
the Latin adjuncts to our language are, in the
appreciation of their value it should never be forgotten that they are adjuncts. The frame, the
sinews, the nerves, the heart's blood, in brief, the
body and soul of our language is English; Latin
and Greek furnish only its limbs and outward
flourishes. If what has come to us through the
Normans, and since their time from France and
Italy and the Latin lexicon, were turned out of our
vocabulary, we could live, and love, and work, and
talk, and sing, and have a folk-lore and a higher
literature. But take out the former, the movement
of our lives would be clogged, and the language

would fall to pieces for lack of framework and foundation, and we could do none of those things. We might teach in the lecture-room, and formulate the results of our work in the laboratory, but we should be almost mute at home, and our language and our literature would be no more ours than it would be France's, or Spain's, or Italy's.

To the Latin we owe, as the most cursory student of our language must have observed, a great proportion of the vocabulary of philosophy, of art, of science, and of morals; and by means of words derived from the Latin we express, as it is assumed, shades of thought and of feeling finer than those of which our simple mother tongue is capable. But it may at least be doubted whether we do not turn too quickly to the Latin lexicon when we wish a name for a new thought or a new thing, and whether out of the simples of our ancient English, or Anglo-Saxon, so called, we might not have formed a language copious enough for all the needs of the highest civilization, and subtle enough for all the requisitions of philosophy. For instance, what we call, in Latinish phrase, remorse of conscience, our forefathers called againbite of inwit; and in using the former we express exactly the same ideas as are expressed by the latter. As the corresponding compounds and the corresponding elements have the same meaning, what more do we gain by putting together *re* and *morse*, *con* and *science*, than by doing the same with *again* and *bite*, *in* and *wit*? The English words now sound uncouth, and provoke a smile, but they do so only because we are accustomed to the Latin derivatives.

No advantage seems likely to be pleaded for the use of the latter other than that they produce a single impression on the mind of the English-speaking man, causing him to accept *remorse* and *conscience* as simple words, expressing simple things, without the suggestion of a biting again and an inner witting.   But it may first be doubted whether this thoughtless, unanalytic acceptance of a word is without some drawback of dissipating and enfeebling disadvantage; and next, and chiefly, it may be safely asserted that the English compounds would produce, if in common use, as single and as strong an impression as the Latin do.   Who that does not stop to think and take to pieces, receives other than a single impression from such words as *insight* (bereaved twin of *inwit*), *gospel, falsehood, worship, homely, breakfast, truthful, boyhood, household, brimstone, twilight, acorn, chestnut, instead, homestead*, and the like, of which our common current English would furnish numberless examples?

In no way is our language more wronged than by the weak readiness with which many of those who, having neither a hearty love nor a ready mastery of it, or lacking both, fly to the Latin tongue or to the Greek for help in the naming of a new thought or thing, or the partial concealment of an old one, calling, for instance, nakedness nudity, and a bathing-tub a lavatory.   By so doing they help to deface the characteristic traits of our mother tongue, and to mar and stunt its kindly growth.

No one denies — certainly I do not deny — the value of the Latin element of our modern English in the expression of abstract ideas and general notions

It also gives amplitude, and ease, and grace to a language which without it might be admirable only for compact and rugged strength. All which being granted, it still remains to be shown that there is not in simple English — that is, Anglo-Saxon without inflections — the power of developing a vocabulary competent to all the requirements of philosophy, of science, of art, no less than of society and of sentiment. I believe that pure English has, in this respect at least, the full capacity of the German language. Nevertheless, one of the advantages of English over German, in form and euphony, is in this very introduction of Anglicized Latin and Greek words for the expression of abstract ideas, which re lieves us of such quintuple compounds, for instance, as *sprachwissenschaftseinheit*. With the expression of abstract ideas and scientific facts, however, the Latinization of our language should stop, or it will lose its home character, and kin traits, and become weak, flabby, and inflated, and thus, ridiculous.

One of the changes to which language is subject during the healthy intellectual condition of a people, and in its progress from rudeness to refinement, is the casting off of rude, clumsy, and insufficiently worked-out forms of speech, sometimes mistakenly honored under the name of idioms. Speech, the product of reason, tends more and more to conform itself to reason; and when grammar, which is the formulation of usage, is opposed to reason, there arises, sooner or later, a conflict between logic, or the law of reason, and grammar, the law of precedent, in which the former is always victorious. And this has been notably the case in

the history of the English language. Usage, therefore, is not, as it is often claimed to be, the absolute
law of language; and it never has been so with any
people — could not be, or we should have an example of a language which had not changed from
what it was in its first stage, if indeed under such a
law there could be a first stage in language. Horace, indeed, in a passage often quoted, seems to
have accepted usage as the supreme authority in
speech:—

> "si volet usus,
> Quem penes arbitrium est, et jus, et norma loquendi."

But if this dictum were unconditional, and common
usage were the absolute and rightful arbiter in all
questions of language, there would be no hope of
improvement in the speech of an ignorant and
degraded society, no rightful protest against its mean
and monstrous colloquial phrases, which, indeed,
would then be neither mean nor monstrous; the
fact that they were in use being their full justification. The truth is, however, that the authority of
general usage, or even of the usage of great writers, is not absolute in language. There is a misuse
of words which can be justified by no authority,
however great, by no usage, however general.

And, as usage does not justify that which is essentially unreasonable, so in the fact that a word or
phrase is an innovation, a neologism, there is nothing whatever to deter a bold, clear-headed thinker
from its use. Otherwise language would not grow.
New words, when they are needed, and are rightly
formed, and so clearly discriminated that they have
a meaning peculiarly their own, enrich a language;

while the use of one word to mean many things, more or less unlike, is the sign of poverty in speech, and the source of ambiguity, the mother of confusion. For these reasons the objection on the part of a writer upon language to a word or a phrase should not be that it is new, but that it is inconsistent with reason, incongruous in itself, or opposed to the genius of the tongue into which it has been introduced. Something must and surely will be sacrificed in language to convenience; but too much may be sacrificed to brevity. A periphrasis which is clear and forcible is not to be abandoned for a shorter phrase, or even a single word, which is ambiguous, barbarous, grotesque, or illogical. Unless much is at stake, it is always better to go clean and dry-shod a little way about than to soil our feet by taking a short cut.

For two centuries and a half, since the time when King Lear was written and our revised translation of the Bible made, the English language has suffered little change, either by loss or gain. Excepting that which was slang, or cant, or loose colloquialism in his day, there is little in Shakespeare's plays which is not heard now, more or less, from the lips of English-speaking men; and to his vocabulary they have added little except words which are names for new things. The language has not sensibly improved, nor has it deteriorated. In the latter part of the last century it was in some peril. We ran the risk, then, of the introduction of a scholarly diction and a formal style into our literature, and of a separation of our colloquial speech, the language of common folk and common needs,

from that of literary people and grand occasions.
That danger we happily escaped, and we still speak
and write a common, if not a homogeneous language, in which there is no word which is excluded
by its commonness or its meanness from the highest
strain of poetry.

Criticism, however, is now much needed to keep
our language from deterioration, to defend it against
the assaults of presuming half-knowledge, always
bolder than wisdom, always more perniciously in-
trusive than conscious ignorance. Language must
always be made by the mass of those who use
it; but when that mass is misled by a little learning, — a dangerous thing only as edge tools are
dangerous to those who will handle them without understanding their use, — and undertakes to
make language according to knowledge rather than
by instinct, confusion and disaster can be warded
off only by criticism. Criticism is the child and
handmaid of reflection. It works by censure; and
censure implies a standard. As to words and the use
of words, the standard is either reason, whose laws
are absolute, or analogy, whose milder sway hinders
anomalous, barbarous, and solecistic changes, and
helps those which are in harmony with the genius of
a language. Criticism, setting at nought the assumption of any absolute authority in language,
may check bad usage and reform degraded custom. It may not only resist the introduction of that
which is debasing or enfeebling, but it may thrust
out vicious words and phrases which through carelessness or perverted taste may have obtained a
footing. It is only by such criticism that our lan-

guage can now be restrained from license and preserved from corruption. Criticism cannot at once with absolute and omnipotent voice, banish the bad and establish or introduce the good; but by watchfulness and reason it may gradually form such a taste in those who are, if not the framers, at least the arbiters, of linguistic law, that thus, by indirection finding direction out, it may insure the effectual condemnation of that which itself could not exclude.

Until comparatively late years language was formed by the intuitive sense of those who spoke it; but now, among highly civilized peoples, the element of consciousness is entering into its production. If consciousness must be present, it should be, at least in the last resort, the consciousness of trained and cultivated minds; and such consciousness is critical, indeed is criticism. And those who feel the need of support in giving themselves to the study of verbal criticism may find it in the comfortable words of Scaliger the younger, who says, "The sifting of these subtleties, although it is of no use to machines for grinding corn, frees the mind from the rust of ignorance, and sharpens it for other matters." * And it may reassure us to remember that, in the crisis of the great struggle between Cæsar and Pompey, Cicero, being then in the zenith of his power, turned aside, in a letter to Atticus upon weighty affairs of state, to discuss a point of grammar with that eminent critic.

* Harum indagatio subtilitatum, etsi non est utilis ad machinas farinarias conficiendas, exuit animum tamen inscitiæ rubigine, acuit-que ad alia.

CHAPTER II.

NEWSPAPER ENGLISH. BIG WORDS FOR SMALL THOUGHTS.

SIMPLE and unpretending ignorance is always respectable, and sometimes charming; but there is little that more deserves contempt than the pretence of ignorance to knowledge. The curse and the peril of language in this day, and particularly in this country, is, that it is at the mercy of men who, instead of being content to use it well according to their honest ignorance, use it ill according to their affected knowledge; who, being vulgar, would seem elegant; who, being empty, would seem full; who make up in pretence what they lack in reality; and whose little thoughts, let off in enormous phrases, sound like fire-crackers in an empty barrel.

> How I detest the vain parade
>   Of big-mouthed words of large pretence!
> And shall they thus thy soul degrade,
>   O tongue so dear to common sense!
> Shouldst thou accept the pompous laws
>   By which our blustering tyros prate,
> Soon Shakespeare's songs and Bunyan's saws
>   Some tumid trickster must translate
>
> Our language, like our daily life,
>   Accords the homely and sublime
> And jars with phrases that are rife
>   With pedantry of every clime.

For eloquence it clangs like arms,
  For love it touches tender chords,
But he to whom the world's heart warms
  Must speak in wholesome, home-bred words.

To the reader who is familiar with Beranger's "Derniers Chansons" these lines will bring to mind two stanzas in the poet's "Tambour Major," in which he compares pretentious phrases to a big, bedizened drum-major, and simple language to the little gray-coated Napoleon at Austerlitz — a comparison which has been brought to my mind very frequently during the writing of this book.

It will be well for us to examine some examples of this vice of language in its various kinds; and for them we must go to the newspaper press, which reflects so truly the surface of modern life, although its surface only.

There is, first, the style which has rightly come to be called newspaper English, and in which we are told, for instance, of an attack upon a fortified position on the Potomac, that "the thousand-toned artillery duel progresses magnificently at this hour, the howling shell bursting in wild profusion in camp and battery, and among the trembling pines." I quote this from the columns of a first-rate New York newspaper, because the real thing is so much more characteristic than any imitation could be, and is quite as ridiculous. This style has been in use so long, and has, day after day, been impressed upon the minds of so many persons to whom newspapers are authority, as to language no less than as to facts, that it is actually coming into vogue in daily life with some of our people. "Not long ago

my attention was attracted by a building which I
had not noticed before, and, stepping up to a policeman who stood hard by, I asked him what it was.
He promptly replied (I wrote down his answer
within the minute), "That is an institootion inaugurated under the auspices of the Sisters of Mercy,
for the reformation of them young females what
has deviated from the paths of rectitood." It was
in fact an asylum for women of the town; but my
informant would surely have regarded such a description of it as inelegant, and perhaps as indelicate. True, there was a glaring incongruity between the pompousness of his phraseology and his
use of those simple and common parts of speech,
the pronouns; but I confess that, in his dispensa-
tion of language, "them" and "what" were the
only crumbs from which I received any comfort.
But could I find fault with my civil and obliging
informant, when I knew that every day he might
read in the leading articles of our best newspapers
such sentences, for instance, as the following? —

"There is, without doubt, some subtle essence permeating
the elementary constitution of crime which so operates that
men and women become its involuntary followers by sheer force
of attraction, as it were."

I am sure, at least, that the policeman knew better what he meant when he spoke than the journalist did what he meant when he wrote. Policeman
and journalist both wished not merely to tell what
they knew and thought in the simplest, clearest
way they wished to say something elegant, and
to use fine language; and both made themselves
ridiculous. Neither this fault nor this complaint is

new; but the censure seems not to have diminished
the fault, either in frequency or in degree. Our
every-day writing is infested with this silly bombast, this stilted nonsense. One journalist, reflecting upon the increase of violence, and wishing to
say that ruffians should not be allowed to go armed,
writes, "We cannot, however, allow the opportunity to pass without expressing our surprise that the
law should allow such abandoned and desperate
characters to remain in possession of lethal weapons." *Lethal* means deadly, neither more nor less;
but it would be very tame and unsatisfying to use
an expression so common and so easily understood.
Another journalist, in the course of an article upon
a murder, says of the murderer that a policeman
went to his residence, and there secured the clothes
that he wore when he committed the murderous
deed; and that, being found in a tub of water,
they were so smeared by blood as to incarnadine
the water of the tub in which they were deposited.
To say that the policeman went to the house or
room of the murderer, and there found the clothes
he wore when he did the murder, which were so
bloody that they reddened the water into which
they had been thrown, would have been far too
homely."

But not only are our journals and our speeches
to Buncombe infested with this big-worded style,
the very preambles to our acts of legislature, and
the official reports upon the dryest and most matter-
of-fact subjects, are bloated with it. It appears in
the full flower of absurdity in the following sentence,
which I find in the report of a committee of the

legislature of New York on street railways. The
committee wished to say that the public looked upon
all plans for the running of fast trains at a height
of fifteen or twenty feet as fraught with needless
danger; and the committee man who wrote for
them made them say it in this amazing fashion: —

"It is not to be denied that any system which demands the
propulsion of cars at a rapid rate, at an elevation of fifteen or
twenty feet, is not entirely consistent, in public estimation, with
the greatest attainable immunity from the dangers of transpor-
tation."

Such a use of words as this indicates only the
lack as well of mental vigor as of good taste and
of education on the part of the user. "O," said
a charming, highly-cultivated, and thorough-bred
woman, speaking, in my hearing, of one of her
own sex of inferior breeding and position, but who
was making literary pretensions, and with some
success so far as notoriety and money were concerned, — "O, save me from talking with that woman! If you ask her to come and see you, she
never says she's sorry she can't come, but that
she regrets that the multiplicity of her engagements precludes her from accepting your polite
invitation."

The foregoing instances are examples merely of
a pretentious and ridiculous use of words which is
now very common. They are not remarkable for
incorrectness. But the freedom with which persons who have neither the knowledge of language
which comes of culture, nor that which springs
spontaneously from an inborn perception and mastery, are allowed to address the public and to speak

for it, produces a class of writers who fill, as it is unavoidable that they should fill, our newspapers and public documents with words which are ridiculous, not only from their pretentiousness, but from their preposterous unfitness for the uses to which they are put. These persons not only write abominably in point of style, but they do not say what they mean. When, for instance, a member of Congress is spoken of in a leading journal as "a sturdy republican of progressive integrity," no very great acquaintance with language is necessary to the discovery that the writer is ignorant of the meaning either of *progress* or of *integrity*. When in the same columns another man is described as being "endowed with an impassionable nature," people of common sense and education see that here is a man not only writing for the public, but actually attempting to coin words, who, so far as his knowledge of language goes, needs the instruction to be had in a good common school. So, again, when another journal of position, discoursing upon convent discipline, tells us that a young woman is not fitted for "the stern amenities of religious life," and we see it laid down in a report to an important public body that, under certain circumstances, "the criminality of an act is heightened, and reflects a very turgid morality indeed," it is, according to our knowledge, whether we find in the phrases "stern amenities" and "turgid morality" occasion for study or food for laughter.

Writing like this is a fruit of a pitiful desire to seem elegant when one is not so, which troubles many people, and which manifests itself in the use

3

of words as well as in the wearing of clothes, the
buying of furniture, and the giving of entertain-
ments; and which in language takes form in words
which sound large, and seem to the person who
uses them to give him the air of a cultivated man,
because he does not know exactly what they mean.
Such words sometimes become a fashion among
such people, who are numerous enough to set and
keep up a fashion; and they go on using them to
each other, each afraid to admit to the other that
he does not know what the new word means, and
equally afraid to avoid its use, as a British snob is
said never to admit that he *is* entirely unacquainted
with a duke. Our newspapers and reviews are
haunted now by two words of this sort—*normal*
and *inaugurate*. In the North American Review
itself (I name this review because of its very high
literary position—a position higher now than ever
before) a writer is permitted to say that, "This idea
[that of a ship without a bowsprit] was doubtless
a copy of the model inaugurated by Mr. E. K.
Collins, founder of the Collins line of American
Ocean Steamships." The writer meant invented
or introduced; and he might as well have written
about the President of the United States being invented on the 4th of March, as of inaugurating
the model of a ship. But ere long we shall probably have the milliners inaugurating their bonnets,
and the cooks making for us normal plum-puddings
and pumpkin pies. But *normal* and *inaugurate*,
and a crowd of such big words, are now used as
Bardolph uses *accommodated*, which, being approved by Mr. Justice Shallow as a good phrase.

he replies, "By this day I know not the phrase ; but
I will maintain the word with my sword to be a
soldier-like word, and a word of exceeding good
command.   Accommodated ; that is, when a man
is, as they say — accommodated ; or, when a man
is — being — whereby — he may be thought to be
accommodated ; which is an excellent thing."

There is no telling to what lengths this desire to
speak fine will lead.   It breaks out very strongly
with some people in the use of *have* and *were*.
They have taken into their heads a hazy notion
of the superior elegance of those words — as to the
latter from having heard it used by persons who are
precise as to their subjunctive mood ; how as to the
former I cannot conjecture.   So, some of them,
when they wish to be very fine indeed, say, " I were
going to Europe last fall, but were prevented by
the multiplicity of my engagements," leaving *was*
in the company of plain and simple folk.   I was
witness to a characteristic exhibition of this kind of
pretence.   With two or three friends I called on
business at the house of a very wealthy man in the
Fifth Avenue, whom I had never met before, and
who has since gone to the place where "all good
Americans go when they die."   He proposed that
we should ride with him to the place to visit which
was the object of our gathering, and he stepped out
to give some orders.   As the carriage came to the
door, he reëntered the parlor, and approaching our
group, revolving his hands within each other, as if
troubled by a consciousness, partly reminiscence,
that they needed washing, he said with a little
smirk, "Gentlemen, the carriage have arrived."

We stood it, as sober as judges; but one of us soon made an execrable pun, which afforded opportunity for laughter, in which our host, as ignorant of a play upon words as of the use of them, heartily joined. Now, that man, if he had been speaking to his wife, would have called out, " Sairy Ann, the carriage has come," and have rivalled Thackeray or Hawthorne in the correctness of his English.

We are suffering now, and shall suffer more hereafter, from the improper use of words, in a very important point, to wit, the drafting of our laws. When the Constitution of the United States was framed, the language of the instrument was considered with great care. Each paragraph, after having been discussed in committee and in full convention, and its purport clearly determined, was submitted to the revision of a committee on style, and it was not adopted until it had received the sanction of that committee. Hence it is that there is hardly a passage in the whole Constitution the meaning of which can be doubted; the disputes about the Constitution being, almost without exception, not as to what it provides, but as to the effects of its provisions. But as to most of the laws passed nowadays, both in the State and national legislatures, it would puzzle those who do not know the purpose of their framers, to discover it from their language; and when the present generation of politicians has passed away, these laws, if they last until that time, will bear any construction that any court, or any majority of any Congress, chooses to put upon them; which, perhaps, in the view of the latter, will be an

advantage. Some of the laws passed in the last
two sessions of Congress have little more coherence
or consistency than some of MotherGoose's rhymes.
But passing by such laws as touch great questions
of public policy, and as to which, therefore, it might
be unreasonable to expect our present legislators to
express themselves with clearness and propriety,
take, for example, the following section of a bill
brought into the legislature of New York in regard
to the metropolitan police : —

"SECTION 16. The Board of Metropolitan Police is hereby
authorized, in their discretion, to pay out of the Police Life Insurance Fund an amount, not exceeding three hundred dollars,
to the members of the force who may be disabled while in the
discharge of their duties. In cases of death by injuries received
while discharging their duties, the annuities shall be continued
to the widow, or children, or both, as the Board may deem best.
The Board of Metropolitan Police is hereby constituted Trustees
of the Life Insurance Fund."

Laying no stress upon such English as "the
board *is* authorized in *their* discretion," and "the
board *is* constituted *trustees*," let us try to find out
what it is that the board is authorized to do. It is
"to pay an amount not exceeding three hundred
dollars to the members of the force who may be
disabled while in the discharge of their duties."
That is, unmistakably, according to the language
used, to pay three hundred dollars to all the members of the force who may be so injured. This
seems rather a small provision for the purpose in
view ; as to which there is still further uncertainty.
For who are all the members of the force, for whom
this provision is made? All who are injured during
the existence of the board? So the law says, and

there is not a word, expressed or implied, to the contrary. And how much is to be paid to each member? There is not a word definitely to show. But in the next sentence, which oddly says that, "In case of death by injuries received while discharging *their* duties, the annuities shall be continued to the widows or children or both," the word *annuities* gives us a hint as to the meaning of the law, but no more. Yet it is safe to say that this section, which so completely fails to express a simple intention as to the payment of money that any construction of it might be plausibly disputed, was supposed by its framers to mean what it does mean in the corrected form following; in which it would have been written by any tolerably well-instructed person — any person of sufficient intelligence and education to be intrusted with the writing of an official letter — much more the drafting of a law.

"The Board of Police is hereby authorized in *its* discretion to pay out of the Police Life Insurance Fund an amount not exceeding three hundred dollars, *annually*, to *every member* of the force who may be disabled while in the discharge of *his* duties. In cases of death *from* injuries received *in the discharge of duty*, the annuities shall be *paid* to the widow or the children *of the deceased member*, or *to* both, as the Board may deem best. The Board of Metropolitan Police is hereby constituted the *Trustee* of the Police Life Insurance Fund."

There are laws of the United States, enacted within the last four years, and which must come up before the courts, and finally before the Supreme Court, as the ground of the decision of important questions, which are not a whit more explicit or coherent than this example of the style of late New York legislation.

Language being perverted in this country chiefly in consequence of the wide diffusion of very superficial instruction among a restless, money-getting, and self-confident people, although the daily press is the chief visible corrupter of our speech, it must be admitted that the latter cause of degradation is itself the consequence of the former. Our newspapers do the harm in question through their advertisements as well as through their reports, their correspondence, and their leading articles; and it would seem as if, in most cases, the same degree of knowledge of the meaning of words and of their use prevailed in all these departments. The style and the language of their advertisements and their reading matter generally indicate the careless confidence of a people among whom there is little deference, or reference, to standards of authority. Competent as some of our editors are, none of our newspapers receive thorough editorial supervision. What is sent to them for publication would be generally judged by a low standard; and of even that judgement the public too frequently has not the benefit. As to advertisements, every man of us deems himself able to write them, with what reason we shall soon see; while in England the writing of even these is generally committed to persons who have some knowledge of English and some sense of decorum. But here, the free, independent, and intelligent American citizen produces advertisements in which sense and decorum are set at naught with an absoluteness that speaks more for his freedom and his independence than for his intelligence. To pass his ordinary performances under censure would be trivial, if not superfluous; there is, however, a variety of his species, who is not unworthy of attention, because he is doing much to debauch the public mind — injuring it morally as well as intellectually. This is the sensation advertiser, who sometimes is a publisher, sometimes a perfumer; at others he sells fire-safes, bitters, sewing-machines, buchu, houses and lands, piano-fortes, or clothes-wringers. But whatever his wares, his English is generally vile, and his tone always nauseous. Here follows a specimen of the sort of riff-raff of language that he produces. It is actually a part of a long advertisement of a "real estate agent," which appeared in a leading paper in the interior of New York : —

"I am happy to inform my friends especially and the public generally, that I have entered upon the new year "as sound as a nut." My ambition is at bulkhead; my best efforts shall be devoted to the public. I am willing to live on crumbs and small fishes, and let others take the loaves and sturgeon. I am still dealing largely in Real Estate. Encouraged by success in the past, I shall buckle on the harness in the future. Therefore "come unto me" and I will "see" what I can do for you. I am too modest to speak, even in a whisper, in my own behalf, but I am willing the public should speak in "thunder tones." . . . Any man who really wants to buy a farm, small or large, I can suit him; also cheap houses and lots; also cheap vacant lots. . . . I am also looking after the soldier's interest. Let their widows, orphans, parents, etc., also the poor maimed soldiers, "come unto me" for pensions, bounties, etc., for they have my deep-bosomed sympathies. I have a very cheap house, barn and very large lot, with trees, and splendid garden land, some ten rods deep, to sell at a low figure "Come and see."

This gentleman, whose "ambition is at bulkhead," by which, if he meant anything, he possibly meant at flood-tide, who tells any man who wants to buy a farm that he can suit him, also cheap houses and lots, who advertises his deep-bosomed sympathies, who calls garden-land splendid, and who interlards his hideous attempt at humorous humbug with phrases quoted from the tenderest and most impressive passages of the Gospels, may, nevertheless, be a decent sort of person outwardly, and a shrewd man of business. Still, although we may be obliged to put a murderer out of the way as we would a wild beast, the murderer might be a much more tolerable sort of person in daily life, and work less *diffusive* evil than this advertiser. He is sure to do some harm, and if he should be a successful man, as he probably will be, he can hardly fail to do a great deal. For he will then have the more imitators. He is even now the representative of a class of men which increases among us year by year — men whose chief traits are greed and vulgarity, who often get riches, and whose traits, when riches come, are still greed and vulgarity, with the addition of purse-pride and vanity. Such advertising as his is a positive injury to public morals and public taste; and it is much to be desired that it could be excluded from all respectable newspapers. But of course this is as impossible as it would be to exclude rude, ill-mannered people from a hotel. Our only remedy is in the diffusion of a knowledge of the decencies of language and of intercourse.

As a general rule, the higher the culture, the simpler the style and the plainer the speech. But it is equally true that, for rudeness and positive coarseness in the use of language, as well as for affectation and pretence, we must look to our public

representatives, to the press, and to the members of
our various legislative bodies. Here, for instance,
is a paragraph from a grave and very earnest
leading article upon the currency, which recently
appeared in one of the foremost newspapers in
the country. The subject of the paragraph is a
Treasury note.

"The United States paid it out as money, and received for it
nearly or quite as much value as though it had been a half
eagle. We came honestly by it and we want it paid. Yet, if
we were to call on Mr. Sub-Treasurer Van Dyke and ask him to
fork over a half eagle and take up the rag, he would politely but
firmly decline."

A little racy slang may well be used in the course
of one's daily talk; it sometimes expresses that
which otherwise would be difficult, if not impossible, of expression. But what is gained in this case
by the use of the very coarse slang "fork over"
and "take up the rag"? What do these phrases
express that is not quite as well conveyed in the
words cash the note, and pay the note in gold? It
is quite impossible to believe that this offence was
committed in ignorance, and equally so, I hope,
that it was affected with the purpose of writing down
:o the level of a certain class of readers — a trick
which may win their present favor, but which, in
the end, they are sure to resent. It is rather to be
assumed that this phraseology was used only with
that careless indifference to the decencies of life and
of language which some journalists mistake for
smartness.

Such a use of language as that which has just
been made the subject of remark, although common

in our newspapers, in Congress, in our State legislatures, and even in the pulpits of certain religious denominations, is not a national peculiarity. On the contrary, there are, probably, more people in this country than in any other to whom such a style of writing and speaking is a positive offence. But the wide diffusion of just so much instruction as enables men to read their newspapers, write their advertisements, and keep their accounts, and the utter lack of deference to any one, or of doubt in themselves, which political equality and material prosperity beget in people having no more than such education, and no less, combine to produce a condition of society which brings their style of speech, as well as their manners, much more to the front, not to say to the top, than is the case in other countries.

CHAPTER III.

BRITISH ENGLISH AND "AMERICAN" ENGLISH.

IT has been frequently asserted by British critics that even among the best educated people and the very men of letters in the United States, the English language is neither written nor spoken with the clearness and strength and the mastery of idiom that are common among the people of Great Britain. Boucher, in his "Glossary," speaks of "Americans" as "making all the haste they can to rid themselves of the [English] language;"* and Dean Alford makes a like charge in a passage of his "Queen's English," which, no less for its reasoning than for its assertions, deserves entire reproduction. It would be ruthless to mar so complete and so exquisite a whole.

"Look, to take one familar example, at the process of deterioration which our Queen's English has undergone at the hands of the Americans. Look at those phrases which so amuse us in their speech and in their books; at their reckless exaggeration and contempt for congruity; and then compare the character and history of the nation — its blunted sense of moral obligation and duty to man, its open disregard of conventional right, where aggrandizement is to be obtained; and I may now say its reckless and fruitless maintenance of the most cruel and unprincipled war in the history of the world."

* Quoted from Schele de Vere. Boucher's "Glossary" which, was designed as a supplement to Johnson's Dictionary, I have not read

Some of our own writers, blindly following, I think, blind British guides, have been misled into the expression of like opinions. Mr. Lowell, in the preface to his second series of the "Biglow Papers," makes this damaging admission :—

"Whether it be want of culture, for the highest outcome of culture is simplicity, or for whatever reason, it is certain that very few American writers and speakers wield their native language with the directness, precision, and force that are as common as the day in the mother country."

Speaking upon the careful observation of several years, I cannot admit the justice of this self-accusation; and I must express no little surprise at the lack of qualification and reserve in Mr. Lowell's language, which I can account for only by supposing that his opinion was formed upon an insufficient examination of this subject. It is true that the writers and speakers of that very large class among us who are neither learned nor unlearned, and who are, therefore, on the one hand without the simplicity that comes of culture, and on the other incapable of that unconscious, intuitive use of idiom which gives life and strength to the simple speech of very humble people, do, most of them, use language awkwardly, and as if they did not feel at home in their own mother tongue. If it were not so this book would lack one reason of its being. But I do not hesitate to say that British writers, not of the highest grade, but of respectable rank, are open to the same charge; and, moreover, that it is more generally true with regard to them than with regard to writers of the same position in the United States.

Mr. Marsh, in the last of his admirable "Lectures on the English Language," expresses an opinion which, on the whole, is more nearly like that which I have formed than Mr. Lowell's, not to say Dean Alford's. But Mr. Marsh himself has this passage : —

"In general, I think we may say that, in point of naked syntactical accuracy, the English of America is not at all inferior to that of England; but we do not discriminate so precisely in the meaning of words; nor do we habitually, either in conversation or in writing, express ourselves so gracefully or employ so classic a diction as the English. Our taste in language is less fastidious, and our licenses and inaccuracies are more frequently of a character indicative of a want of refinement and elegant culture than those we hear in educated society in England."

But here Mr. Marsh himself indicates the point of my objection to all these criticisms. He compares our average speech with that of educated society in the mother country. By such a comparison it would be strange if we did not suffer. The just and proper comparison would be between the average speech of both countries, or between that of people of equal culture in both.

Among living writers few have easier mastery of idiomatic English than Mr. Lowell himself; and setting aside peculiar gifts, as imagination, fancy, humor, many New England men of the present generation and of that which is passing away are of his school, if not of his form. There have been abler statesmen and more accomplished lawyers, but has this century produced anywhere a greater rhetorical master of English than Daniel Webster? While Hawthorne lived, — and his grave is not yet as green as his memory, — was there a

British writer who used with greater purity or more plastic power the language that we brought with us from the old home? Our very kinsmen themselves, proud in their possession of the old homestead, the plate, the books, and the portraits, made no such pretension; but they settled the question for their own minds, by saying that Hawthorne "was not really an American writer." And Hawthorne's case is not singular in this respect. The "Saturday Review," in an article upon what it calls "American Literature," recently said, —

"There is very little that is American about American books, if we except certain blemishes of style and a certain slovenliness of grammar and clumsiness of expression derived from the colonial idioms of the country; and *these are wanting in the best American writers.* Longfellow, Motley, Prescott, Washington Irving *are only English writers who happen to print in America.* Poe's eccentricities are rather individual than national. Cooper is American in little but his choice of subjects."*

And not long ago the London "Spectator," which ought to have known better, declared that it is not among the eminent historians, poets, and essayists of America that we must look for American style, but to the journalists, politicians, and pamphleteers. A more ingenious way of establishing a point to one's own satisfaction than that adopted by both these British critics could not be devised. *Proposition:* The "American" style is full of blemishes; it is slovenly in grammar and clumsy in expression. *Reply:* But here are certain historians, novelists, poets, and essayists, who are the standard writers of "America," and in whose style

* I am glad to read this about Cooper. I shall fight with no one for possession of his literary fame.

the blemishes in question, as you yourself admit,
"are wanting." *Rejoinder:* But these are not
"American" writers. They are English writers
who happen to print in "America." The "American" writers in "America" are those only who
have the blemishes in question. Q. E. D. What
a bewitching merry-go-round such reasoning is!
And so perfect! It stops exactly at the point from
which it started.

Without picking out my examplars, I will take
up the last two books by British authors that I have
read for pleasure — both by men of note — Mr.
John Forster's "Arrest of the Five Members," and
Mr. Froude's "History of England," and turning to
passages which I remember noticing amid all my
interest in the narratives themselves, I quote; and
first from Forster : —

"Since his coming to town he had been greatly pleased to
observe a very great *alteration* of the affections of the city *to
what they had been* when he went away." — p. 21.

This is not English, or at least it is English
wretchedly deformed and crippled. If the affections of the city were altered to what they were
when the person spoken of went away, it is implied
that there had been two changes during his absence,
one from the condition in which he left the city, and
one again to that in which he left it. We have to
guess that the writer meant that the person in question observed a very great change in the affections
of the city since he went away. The blunder in
the bungling phrase "alteration of the affections to
what they had been," which is a variety of the
phrase "different *to*," is peculiarly British.

The faults in the two following passages are such as are found in the writings of natives of both countries : —

"Nor was it possible that Charles himself should have *drawn* any other construction *from* it. [*Anglice*, put any other construction upon it.]" — p. 23.

"Captain Slingsby wrote, with an alarm which he hardly *attempts* [*Angl.*, attempted] to conceal, of the *displays of manifestations* of feeling *from* the city." — p. 28.

Could the reverse of directness and precision, to say nothing of force, have more striking example than such a phrase as "the displays of manifestations of feeling from the city"? which we may be sure any intelligent and passably educated Yankee lad would change into "manifestations of feeling by [or in] the city." Now let us turn to Froude, whose slips will be pointed out almost without remark : —

"She [Elizabeth] gave him to understand that her course was chosen at last; she would accept the Archduke, and would be all *which* [*Angl.*, that] the Emperor could desire." — Vol. VIII., c. 10.

"The English Admiral was scarcely in the Channel *than* he was driven [*Angl.*, before he was driven] by a gale into Lowestoft Roads, and was left there for a fortnight motionless." — Vol. VII., c. 3.

"A husband, on receiving news of the sudden and violent death of a lady in whom he had so near an interest, might have been expected *to have at least gone* [*Angl.*, might have been expected at least to go] in person to the spot." — Vol. VII., c. 4.

"The Pope might succeed, and most likely would succeed at last in reconciling Spain; and experience proved that England lay *formidably* open [*Angl.*, perilously or alarmingly open] to attack." — Vol. III., c. 14.

"At eight o'clock the advance began to move, each division being attended by one hundred and twenty outriders to keep stragglers *into* line [*Angl.*, in line.]" — Vol. III., c. 15.

"If the tragedy of Kirk n Field had possessed a claim *for* notice [*Angl.*, to notice] on the first of these grounds," etc. — Vol. IX., c. 13, p. 1.

4

" Elizabeth regarded this unfortunate woman with *a* detestation *and* contempt beyond *what* she had felt at the worst times for Mary Stuart. [*Angl.*, with far greater detestation and contempt than she had ever felt for Mary Stuart.]" — *Ibid.*, p. 21.

" — and those who were apparently as guilty as Bothwell himself were yet assuming an attitude *to* him [*Angl.*, toward him] at one moment of cringing subserviency [a writer of Mr. Froude's grade should have said " subservience "], and at the next of the fiercest indignation." — *Ibid.*, p. 26.

" — and had Darnley proved the useful Catholic *which* the Queen intended him to be, they would have sent him to his account with as small compunction *as Jael sent the Canaanite captain*, or they would have blessed the arm that *did it with as much eloquence as Deborah.*" — *Ibid.*, c. 14, p. 127.

Here, to get at the writer's meaning from what he has written, we must ask, How small compunction did Jael send the Canaanite captain? and, What degree of eloquence did the arm attain that did *it* with as much as Deborah? What was it? and how much eloquence is Deborah? The sentence is so marked with slovenliness of grammar and clumsiness of expression, it is so lacking in directness, precision, and force, that it can be bettered only by being almost wholly re-written. We are all able to guess, but only to guess, that what Mr. Froude means is, that the persons of whom he speaks would have sent Darnley to his account with as little compunction as Jael felt when she sent the Canaanite captain to his, or would have blessed with the eloquence of Deborah the arm that did their pleasure. The blundering construction of which this last passage furnishes such a striking example is of a kind frequently met with in British writers of a rank inferior to Mr. Froude's; but it is rarely found in "American" books or even in "American" newspapers. From Mr. Froude I shall further

select only the three following passages; the first
containing a misuse of *would* and *which* — test
words as to the mastery of idiom — the second a
specimen of French English, and the third combining a misapplication of words with a miscon-
struction of the sentence : —

"The Bishop of Ross undertook that his mistress *would* do
anything *which* [*Angl.*, should do anything that] the Queen
of England and the nobility desired." — Chap. XVII., p. 432.

"Hepburn of Bolton, one of the last of Bothwell's servants
who had been brought to trial, spoke distinctly *to have* seen
[*Angl.*, of having seen] one of them." — Chap. XV., p. 199.

"Edward IV., when he landed at Ravenspurg, and Elizabeth's
grandfather before Bosworth Field had *fainter grounds to anticipate* success than *the party who was* now preparing to snatch
England out of the hands of revolution, and restore the ancient
order in Church and State." — Chap. XVII., p. 73.

A man may be said to have grounds on which to
rest hope of success, or anticipation of success ; or
even, perhaps, grounds of anticipating success ; and
those grounds may be strong or weak, sufficient or
insufficient ; but such a phrase as "fainter grounds
to anticipate success," in its misuse of the infinitive,
must be pronounced slovenly, and in its vague,
groping way of handling a metaphor so common
as to be almost an idiom, clumsy. But how much
worse than this is the succeeding phrase, "the party
who was now preparing, etc."! It would have
been easy, it seems, to write "the party *which* was
now preparing," or, "the party who *were* now preparing." and to one of these forms Mr. Froude
must change his sentence if he wishes it to be English ; unless, indeed, he means to speak of the
Duke of Norfolk (the head of the revolution in
question) as a very dangerous "party."

Turning to the books and papers lying on my table, I find two novels by British authors of well-deserved repute.

Mr. Trollope's "Phineas Finn" is full of examples of the following affected and inverted construction : —

"He felt that she moved him — that she made him acknowledge to himself how great would be the pity of such a failure *as would be his*." — Chap. LXIX.

"— one who had received so many of her smiles *as had Phineas*." — Chap. LXXII.

The same writer, in the following sentence, falls in with a vulgar perversion of *aggravate*, using it in the sense of irritate, worry : —

"This arose partly from a belief that the quarrel was final, and that therefore there would be no danger in *aggravating* Violet by this expression of pity." — Chap. LXXIII.

Mr. Charles Reade's last novel furnishes in only one of its monthly parts the following sentences : —

"Well, farmer, then *let's you* and *I* go [*Angl.*, let's go, or let you and me go] by ourselves."—*Put Yourself in his Place*, Chap. X.

"And while he hesitated, the lady asked him *was he* come [*Angl.*, if he was, or, if he had, come] to finish the bust."—*Ibid.*

"Ere he thoroughly *recovered the shock* [*Angl.*, recovered from the shock] a wild cry arose."—*Ibid.*

Mr. Reade is one of the most vivid and dramatic of modern novelists; but are these examples of the directness, precision, and force, and the mastery of idiom, which are "as common as the day in the mother country"?

Taking up the last London "Spectator,"— a paper of the very highest rank, — I find this sentence in

a careful, critical review of Lightfoot's " Saint Paul's
Epistle to the Galatians : " —

"But we must return to the Galatians. We are called on to
believe that the inspiration of this letter *derives* from a wholly
different source *than does* that of the apostles. [*Angl.*, is derived from a source wholly different from that of the apostles.]"

In the same copy of the "Spectator," I also find the
following amazing sentences among the quotations
from " Select Biographical Sketches," by William
Heath Bennett. The passage relates to the last
known instance of the infliction of ecclesiastical
penance in England, which took place in 1812.

" She was herself a pauper, and her father also, but who had
managed to contribute to her maintenance in jail from the
charity of others. This sentence of penance, although pronounced in general terms, her friends could never obtain from
the ecclesiastical authorities how it was to be complied with, except that she was to appear in a white sheet in the church with
a burning candle in her hand, and repeat some formula pre-
scribed by the old law."

The reviewer quotes other passages which support his opinion that the style of this book is slipshod and often ungrammatical. But the author
is a barrister at law, and might reasonably be
expected to write intelligibly, if not elegantly. Had
he been, however, not a British, but an "American"
lawyer, the "Spectator" and the "Saturday Review," the Dean of Canterbury (and shall we say
Mr. Lowell?) would have pronounced his style not
slipshod and ungrammatical, but "American" — in
a certain slovenliness of manner and clumsiness of
expression, and in a lack of precision, distinctness,
and force, that are as common as the day in the
mother country. How common they are the reader

is now, perhaps, better prepared to say than he was
before he began to read this chapter. For the passages above quoted are selected from many that
were open to like censure; and they were chosen
less because of the gravity of their offences against
the laws of the English language than because they
were impressive examples of the lack of the very
qualities which, Mr. Lowell tells us, are so common
in England, and the lack of which the "Saturday
Review," Dean Alford, and all of their sort will
have it, are the peculiar, the distinguishing traits
of those writers whom they call "American." And
these passages were not sought out, it should be
remembered; nor are they, most of them, taken
from the writings of inferior men. They lay in the
way of every-day reading, and are from books and
papers of high rank in contemporary British literature. Yet I venture to say that it would be difficult
to find in the writings of "American" authors and
journalists of corresponding position passages in
which mastery of idiom, directness, precision, and
force are as conspicuously absent. Let us, for one
more example in point, turn to a British author of
less repute than Mr. Forster, or Mr. Froude, or Mr.
Charles Reade, but of respectable standing, and
turn to him merely because he may reasonably be
taken as a fair example of the British writer of
average literary ability and culture, and because
the passage which I shall quote is one of two or
three which I noticed while consulting the work
from which it is taken — the well-known Natural
History by the Rev. J. G. Wood, M. A., F. L. S.,
etc., etc.

"All external objects are, in their truest sense, visible embodiments or incarnations of divine ideas, which are roughly sculptured in the hard granite that underlies the living and breathing surface of the world above; pencilled in delicate tracery upon each bark-flake that encompasses the trunk-tree, each leaf that trembles in the breeze, each petal that fills the air with fragrant effluence; assuming a living and breathing existence in the rhythmic throbbings of the heart-pulse that urges the life-stream through the body of every animated being; and attaining their greatest perfection in man, who is thereby bound by the very fact of his existence to outspeak and outact the divine ideas, which are the true instincts of humanity, before they are crushed or paralyzed by outward circumstances. . . . Until man has learned to realize his own microcosmal being, and will himself develop and manifest the god-thoughts that are continually inbreathed into his very essential nature, it needs that the creative ideas should be incarnated and embodied in every possible form, so that they may retain a living existence upon earth."

Any Yankee of ordinary sense and moderately cultivated taste would set this passage down as a fine specimen of stilted feebleness — in its style a very travesty of English. But it was written by a clergyman of the English church, a graduate of one of the universities, a man who has attained some distinction as a naturalist, and who has half a score of letters after his name. The truth is, that when the English of British authors is spoken of, it is not that of such writers as Mr. Wood, but that of — well, of such as Forster and Froude? — let us rather say of such as Macaulay, Thackeray, Helps, and George Eliot, as Johnson, Burke, Hume, Gibbon, Goldsmith and Cobbett. But when British critics speak of the English of "American" writers, they leave out Irving, Prescott and Motley, Hawthorne, Poe and Longfellow, as we have seen, and others less known, like Lowell, Story, and Howells,

who write in the same idiom; and they look for
"American" writers, not even among our thorough-
ly-educated men of letters of the second or third
rank, but to newspapers, written generally by men
of average common-school education, little training,
and no gift of language, and for the heterogeneous
public of the large cities of a country in which every
other Irish hackman and hodman keeps not only
his police justice, but his editor. That there are
journalists in this country whose English is irreproachable, no one competent to speak upon this
subject will deny. But they are they who will
admit most readily the justice of these strictures.

Upon the vexed question whether, on the whole,
English is better spoken throughout the United
States than throughout Great Britain, I do not deem
myself competent to express a decided opinion; but
of this I feel sure — that of the mother tongue common to the people of both countries, no purer form is
known to the Old England than to the New. If in
an assemblage of a hundred educated, well-bred
people, one half of them from London, Oxford, and
Liverpool, and the other from Boston, New York,
and Philadelphia (and I have more than once been
one of a company so composed, although not so
large), a ready and accurate phonographer were to
take down every word spoken during an evening's
entertainment, I feel quite sure that it would be impossible to distinguish in his printed report the speech
of the Britons from that of the "Americans," except
by the possible occurrence of acknowledged local
slang, or by the greater prevalence among the former or the latter of peculiar words, or words used in

peculiar senses, which would be acknowledged to
be incorrect as well by the authorities of the party
using them as by those of the other party. In brief,
their spoken language, reproduced instantly in writing, could be distinguished only by some confessed
license or defect, peculiar to one country, or more
prevalent there than in the other. And I am strongly inclined to the opinion that, the assemblage being
made up of educated and well-bred persons, there
would be somewhat more slang heard from the British than from the "American" half of the company,
and also a greater number of free and easy deviations from correct English speech, according to
British as well as "American" authority. The
standard in both countries is the same.

But although the written speech of these people
would be to this degree indistinguishable, an ear at
all nice in its hearing would be able to separate the
sheep from the goats by their bleat. The difference
would be one not of pronunciation (for the standard
of pronunciation is also the same in both countries,
and well-educated people in both conform to it with
like habitual and unconscious ease), but of pitch
of voice, and of inflection. Among those of both
countries who had been from their birth accustomed
to the society of cultivated people, even this distinction would be made with difficulty, and would,
in many cases, be impossible. But the majority of
one half hundred could thus be distinguished from
the majority of the other; and the superiority would
be greatly on the side of the British fifty. The
pitch of the British Englishman's voice is higher
and more penetrating than the American English-

man's, and his inflections are more varied than the
other's, because they more frequently rise. The
voice of the former is generally formed higher in
the throat than that of the latter, who speaks from
the chest with a graver monotone. Thackeray and
Goldwin Smith are characteristic examples on the
one side, Daniel Webster and Henry Ward Beecher
on the other. The distinction to a delicate ear is
very marked; but other difference than this of pitch
and inflection there is none whatever. Pronunciation is exactly the same. And even in regard to
pitch and inflection, there is not so much difference
between the average British Englishman of culture
and the average American Englishman of like training, as there is between the Yorkshireman and the
Norfolkman; and there is very much more difference
between the pronunciation and the idiom of the
two latter than there is between the speech of any
two men of the same race born and bred, however
remotely from each other, in this country.

In imagining my assemblage by which to test
speech and language, I have left altogether out of
mind those people who, in one country, would, for
instance, deal hardly with the letter *h*, or turn the
g in "nothing" to *k*, and the *v* in "veal" to *w*,*
although this class includes, as I have noticed, and
as Dean Alford confesses, some clergymen of the
Church of England; and, in the other, those who
speak with a nasal twang, although this class in-

---

* Theodore Hook thus wittily illustrated this peculiar mispronunciation:—

"With Cockney gourmands great's the difference whether
    At home they stay or forth to Paris go;
For as they linger here or wander thither,
    The flesh of calves to them is *weal* or *wees*."

cludes, as we all know, some persons of similar position in "America." The point is, that those who would be regarded, in their own country, as among the best speakers and writers, conform to precisely the same standard of language in all particulars. From the speech of these the variations in both countries, but chiefly in England, are manifold. It is in these variations, degraded or dialectic, that local, or what may be called national, peculiarities appear. But, in judging of the degree of purity in which our mother tongue is preserved by our British kinsmen, we must judge only by those among them whose speech they themselves regard as pure. To do otherwise would be manifestly unfair. And in trying ourselves upon this point we must be careful to form our opinion by a like rule of evidence; otherwise we may find ourselves condemning the nation upon the language of a man who, fifteen or twenty years ago, was an oysterman or a bartender, and who, since that time, has added much to his possessions, but nothing to his general knowledge or his right use of language—a change which, however profitable and pleasant it may be to his children, seems in him deplorable.

Dean Alford makes merry over a story of an "American friend" who ventured to speak, in England, of the "strong English accent" which he heard around him. The dean evidently thinks that this is quite as if an Englishman were to go to France, and tell the people there, in the "French of Stratford at Bow," that they spoke with a strong French accent. It is nothing of the sort. An educated Genevan Frenchman, for instance, visiting Paris,

and offended, — as well he might be, — by the accent of the mass of the people around him, might
complain of the strong Parisian accent with which
they spoke; and this case would correspond to that
which the Dean of Canterbury has cited.   Should it
happen, however, I doubt if a French dignitary of
the church would flout the objection on the ground
that Paris is in France and Geneva in Switzerland;
for he would know, as a general truth, that language belongs to race, not to place, and as a particular fact, that the best French is spoken at
Geneva.

The English accent which Dean Alford's "American" friend noticed with implied disapproval, —
although common, and even general, among South
Britons (it rarely taints North British speech), — is
not heard among cultivated people, or approved by
any authority on either side of the water.   It can
be described, I think, so that Dean Alford himself,
and most of his friends and neighbors, — certainly
the best bred and educated among them, — would
recognize it in the description.   One of the persons
in question asking, for instance, for a glass of ale,
would pronounce *glass* with the broad *ah* sound of
a, to rhyme with *pass*, and *ale* as one syllable with
the first or name sound of *a*, so as to rhyme with
male and *sail*.   So would every Yankee of like
culture.   But let our Very Reverend and accomplished censor kindly take a well-bred mouthful of
finely-mashed potato, and after chewing it a deco-
rous while, say, just as he is about swallowing it,
"a *gloss* of *ayull;*" he and the friends around him
will then hear a striking example of what his

"American" friend called English spoken with an
English accent, but which he should have called
English with a South British accent. Now, according to my observation, no man whom the Dean of
Canterbury would accept as a speaker of pure English says, with thick utterance, "a gloss of ayull;"
and yet thousands of his countrymen do speak
thus. But with social refinement and mental cul-
cure this peculiarity of British English passes gradually away, until among the best bred and best
educated people it vanishes, and is heard no more
than it, or a nasal twang, is heard under similar
circumstances here.

One trait of English spoken with a South British
accent was thus whimsically contrasted with the
pure English accent by "Punch," a few years ago.
The value of the illustration is not affected by the
fact that the pronunciation in question was that of a
foreign word. The true pronunciation of the name
of the Italian hero of the day was mooted, and
"Punch" decided that it should be,—

> "Garibaldi when duchesses gave him a *bal*,
> Garibawldi when up goes the shout of the people."

The distinction thus so daintily and humorously
drawn is one that, with opportunity, no quick and
sensitive ear could fail to notice. The strong tendency of the uncultivated South Briton is to give
to the broad *a*, not the sound of *ah* from the chest,
which is heard in the mouths of educated persons in
Old and in New England, but a thick *aw*, formed
in the upper part of the throat. The low and
lower-middle class London man calls Garibaldi
Gawribawldi, or, rather, *Gorribawldi*. But if the

Yankee, in a similar condition of life, deviates from the true *Gahribahl*di, he will make the vowel shorter and thinner, pronouncing it as in "palace"— *Gärry-bäl*di. The thick, throaty pronunciation of the broad *a* is a British peculiarity; but while it is heard in the mouths of so many persons that it divides with the "exhasperated" *h* the honor of the chief distinction of English spoken with a British accent, it is as little prevalent as the extinction or superfluous utterance of the latter letter is among the best speakers in England, or as a nasal twang, *aout* for "out," and *tew* for "too" are among cultivated people in New England. Among British Englishmen few but those who to a good education unite the very highest social culture are perfectly free from both these traits of English as spoken with a British accent.

It may here be pertinently remarked that the pronunciation of *a* in such words as *glass, last, father*, and *pastor* is a test of high culture. The tendency among uncultivated persons is to give *a* either the thick, throaty sound of *aw* which I have endeavored to describe, or, oftenest, to give it the thin, flat sound which it has in "an," "at," and "anatomy." Next to that tone of voice which, it would seem, is not to be acquired by any striving in adult years, and which indicates breeding rather than education, the full, free, unconscious utterance of the broad *ah* sound of *a* is the surest indication in speech of social culture which began at the cradle.

CHAPTER IV.

STYLE.

ACCURACY of expression is the most essential element of a good style; and inaccurate writing is generally the expression of inaccurate thinking. But when men have shown that their thought is important, it is ungracious and superfluous to hunt down their *ifs* and *ands*, and arraign their pronouns and prepositions. This remark would apply to some of the criticisms in the previous chapter, if their special purpose were left out of consideration.

Style, according to my observation, cannot be taught, and can hardly be acquired. Any person of moderate ability may, by study and practice, learn to use a language according to its grammar. But such a use of language, although necessary to a good style, has no more direct relation to it than her daily dinner has to the blush of a blooming beauty. Without dinner, no bloom; without grammar, no style. The same viand which one young woman, digesting it healthily and sleeping upon it soundly, is able to present to us again in but a very unattractive form, Gloriana, assimilating it not more perfectly in slumbers no sounder, transmutes into charms that make her a delight to the eyes of every

beholder.   That proceeding is Gloriana's physio-
logical style.   It is a gift to her.   Such a gift is
style in the use of language.   It is mere clearness
of outline, beauty of form and expression, and has
no relation whatever to the soundness or the value
of the thought which it embodies, or to the importance or the interest of the fact which it records.
Learned men, strong and subtle thinkers, and
scholars of wide and critical acquaintance with
literature, are often unable to acquire even an ac-
ceptably good, not to say an admirable, style; and,
on the other hand, men who can read only their
own language, and who have received very little
instruction even in that, write and speak in a style
that wins or commands attention, and in itself gives
pleasure.   Of these men John Bunyan is, perhaps,
the most marked example.   Better English there
could hardly be, or a style more admirable for every
excellence, than appears throughout the writings
of that tinker.   No person who has read "The
Pilgrim's Progress" can have forgotten the fight
of Christian with Apollyon, which, for vividness of
description and dramatic interest, puts to shame all
the combats between knights and giants, and men
and dragons, that can be found elsewhere in romance or poetry; but there are probably many who
do not remember, and not a few perhaps who, in
the very enjoyment of it, did not notice, the clearness, the spirit, the strength, and the simple beauty
of the style in which that passage is written.   For
example, take the sentence which tells of the beginning of the fight: —

"Then Apollyon straddled quite over the whole breadth of the way, and said, I am void of fear in this matter: prepare thyself to die; for I swear by my infernal Den that thou shalt go no further; here will I spill thy soul."

A man cannot be taught to write like that; nor can he by any study learn the mystery of such a style.

Style, however, although it cannot be taught, is, to a certain extent, the result of mental training. A man who would write well without training, would write, not more clearly or with more strength, but with more elegance, if he were educated. But he will profit little in this respect by the study of rhetoric. It is general culture — above all, it is the constant submission of a teachable, apprehensive mind to the influence of minds of the highest class, in daily life and in books, that brings out upon language its daintiest bloom and its richest fruitage. So in the making of a fine singer: after the voice has been developed, and the rudiments of vocalization have been learned, further instruction is of little avail. But the frequent hearing of the best music, given by the best performers, the living in an atmosphere of art and literature, will develop and perfect a vocal style in one who has the gift of song; and for any other, all the instruction of all the musical professors that ever came out of Italy could do no more than teach an avoidance of positive errors in musical elocution. But, after all, the student's style may profit little by his acquirements.

Unconsciousness is one of the most important conditions of a good style in speaking or in writing. There are persons who write well and speak ill;

others who write ill and speak well; and a few who
are equally excellent as writers and speakers.   As
both writing and speaking are the expression of
thought through language, this capacity for the one,
joined to an incapacity for the other, is naturally the
occasion of remark, and has, I believe, never been
accounted for.   I think that it will be found that
consciousness, which generally causes more or less
embarrassment of one kind or another, is at the
bottom of this apparent incongruity.   The man who
writes in a clear and fluent style, but who, when he
undertakes to speak, more than to say yes or no,
or what he would like for dinner, hesitates, and
utters confusion, does so because he is made self-
conscious by the presence of others when he speaks,
but gives himself unconsciously to the expression
of his thought when he looks only upon the paper
on which he is writing.   He who speaks with ease
and grace, but who writes in a crabbed, involved
style, forgets himself when he looks at others, and
is occupied by himself when he is alone.   His consciousness, and the effort that he makes, on the one
hand to throw it off, and on the other to meet its
demands upon him, confuse his thoughts, which
throng, and jostle, and clash, instead of moving
steadily onward with one consent together.

Mere unconsciousness has much to do with the
charming style of many women's letters.   Women's
style, when they write books, is generally bad with
all the varieties of badness; but their epistolary
style is as generally excellent in all the ways of excellence.   A letter written by a bright, cultivated
woman, — and she need not be a highly educated,

or a much instructed woman, but merely one whose intercourse is with cultivated people, — and written merely to tell you something that interests her and that she wishes you to know, with much care about what she says, and no care as to how she says it, will, in twelve cases out of the baker's dozen, be not only irreproachably correct in expression, but very charming. Some literary women, though few, are able to carry this clear, fluent, idiomatic English style into their books. Mrs. Jameson, Charlotte Brontë, and perhaps George Eliot (Miss Evans), are prominent instances in point. Mrs. Trollope's book, "The Domestic Manners of the Americans," which made her name known, and caused it to be detested, unjustly, in this country,* is written in this delightful style — easy-flowing and clear, like a beautiful stream, reflecting from its placid surface whatever it passes by, adding in the reflection a charm to the image which is not in the object, and distorting only when it is dimpled by gayety or crisped by a flaw of satire or a ripple of humor. It is worth reading only for its style. It may be studied to advantage and emulated, but not imitated; for all about it that is worthy of emulation is inimitable. Mr. Anthony Trollope's mastery of our language is inherited; but he has not come into possession of quite all the maternal estate.

For at least a hundred years the highest reputa-

* Unjustly, because all of Mrs. Trollope's descriptions were true to life, and were evidently taken from life. She, however, described only that which struck her as peculiar; and her acquaintance with the country was made among the most uncultivated people, and chiefly in the extreme South-west and West, thirty-five years ago; which was much like going into "the bush" of Australia ten years ago. With society in New York, Boston, and Philadelphia Mrs. Trollope was charmed; but of it she, apparently for that reason, says comparatively little.

tion for purity of style in the writing of English prose has been Addison's. Whether or not he deserves, or ever did deserve, the eminence upon which he has been placed, he certainly is one of the most elegant and correct writers of the last century. Johnson's formal and didactic laudation, with which he rounds off his criticism of this author, "whoever wishes to attain an English style, familiar but not coarse, and elegant but not ostentatious, must give his days and nights to the volumes of Addison," has been worth a great deal to the booksellers, and has stimulated the purchase of countless copies of "The Spectator," and, let us hope, the perusal of not a few. But in the face of so weighty a judgment, let us test Addison, not merely by comparison with other writers, but by the well-established rules of the language, and by those laws of thought the governing power of which is admitted in every sound and educated intellect, and to which every master of style unconsciously conforms. Seeing thus what manner of man he is who has been held up to three generations as the bright exemplar of purity, correctness, and grace in English style, we may intelligently determine what we can reasonably expect of the great mass of unpretending writers in our hard-working days.

I have been led to this examination by recently reading, for the first time, the "Essay upon the Pleasures of the Imagination," which runs through ten numbers of the "Spectator,"* and which is one of Addison's most elaborate performances. Bishop Hurd says of it, in his edition of this author's writ-

* Nos. 411 to 421.

ings, that it is "by far the most masterly of all Mr.
Addison's critical works," and that "the style is
finished with so much care as to merit the best
attention of the reader."

The first number of the Essay appeared on Saturday, June 21, 1712, with a motto from Lucretius,
which intimates that Mr. Addison broke his own
path across a trackless country to drink from an
untasted spring.* This should excuse some deviation from the line of our now well-beaten road of
criticism; but there are other errors for which it is
no apology. The first sentence tells us that "our
sight is the most perfect and delightful of all our
senses." A careless use of language, to begin with;
for sight is not more perfect than any other sense.
Perfect hearing is just as perfect as perfect sight;
that is, it is simply perfect. But passing by this as
a venial error, we find the third sentence beginning
thus : —

"The sense of feeling can indeed give us a notion of extension,
shape, and all other ideas that enter at the eye, except colours."

Now, we may be sure that Addison did not mean
to say what he does say — that the sense of feeling
can give us the notion of ideas, and that colors are
an idea. His meaning, we may be equally sure
was this : The sense of feeling can indeed give us
a notion of extension *and of* shape, and *every* other
idea that can enter at the eye, except *that of color*.
A little farther on we find this explanation of the
subject of his Essay : —

* "Avia Pieridum peragere loca, nullius ante
Trita solo: juvat integros accedere fonteis.
Atque haurire."

" — so that by the pleasures of imagination or of fancy (which I shall use promiscuously), I here mean such as arise from visible objects."

Here the strange confounding of imagination with fancy — faculties which had been clearly distinguished a hundred years before the time of Addison — first attracts attention. But not insisting upon that mistake, let us pass on to learn immediately that he means to use the pleasures of those faculties promiscuously. But he manifestly intended to say that he would use the words *imagination* and *fancy* promiscuously. The confusion in his sentence is produced by his first mentioning the faculties, and then using *"which"* to refer, not to the faculties, but to the words which are their names. Again he says, —

" — but we have the power of retaining, altering, and compounding those images which we have once received into all the varieties of picture and vision that are most agreeable to the imagination."

Did Addison mean that we have the power of " retaining images into " all the varieties of picture, and so forth? Certainly not; although that is what he says. Here again is confusion of thought. He groups together and connects by a conjunction three verbs, — *retain, alter,* and *compound,* — only two of which can be united to the same preposition. This fault is often committed by writers who do not think clearly, or who will not take the trouble to perfect and balance their sentences by repeating a word or two, and by looking after the fitness of their particles. What Addison meant to say was, — but we have the power of retaining those images *which*

we have once received, and of altering and compounding *them* into all the varieties of picture,
and so forth. A few lines below we find this
sentence : —

"There are few words in the English language which are employed in a more loose and uncircumscribed sense than those of
the fancy and imagination."

The confusion here is great and of a very vulgar
kind. It is produced by the superfluous words
"those of the." Addison meant to say— in a more
loose and uncircumscribed sense, not than the words
of the fancy and imagination, but than *fancy* and
imagination. In the same paragraph which furnishes the foregoing example, the writer says, "I
divide these pleasures in two kinds." It is English
to say, I divide these pleasures *into* two kinds. The
next paragraph opens thus : —

"The pleasures of the imagination, taken in their full extent,
are not so gross as those of sense, nor so refined as those of the
understanding."

Here again is confusion produced by a careless
use of language — careless even to blundering.
Addison did not mean to speak of *taking pleasures*,
either of the imagination, the sense, or the understanding. If he had written — The pleasures of
imagination, *regarded*, or *considered*, in their full
extent, are not so gross, and so forth — he would
have uttered what the whole context shows to have
been his thought. The next paragraph makes the
following assertions in regard to what is called a
man "of polite imagination :" —

"He meets with a secret refreshment in a description, and
often feels a greater satisfaction in the prospect of fields and

meadows than another does in the possession. It gives him, indeed, a kind of property in everything he sees, and makes the most rude and uncultivated parts of Nature administer to his pleasures; so that he looks upon the world, as it were, in another light, and discovers in it a multitude of charms that conceal themselves from the generality of mankind."

The first of these sentences is imperfect. We may be sure that the writer means that his man of polite imagination feels a greater satisfaction in the prospect of fields and meadows than another does in the possession *of them*. But he does not say so. Nor by any rule or usage of the English language are the preposition and pronoun implied or understood; for the sentence might just as well end — "than another does in the possession *of great riches*." And what does the author mean by saying that his politely imaginative man looks upon the world "in another light"? Another than what? No other is mentioned or implied. The writer was referring to an idea which he had in mind, but which he had not expressed; and we can only guess that he meant — another light than that in which the world is regarded by men of impolite imagination. The same sort of confusion appears in the first sentence of the very next paragraph : —

"There are, indeed, but very few who know how to be idle and innocent, or have a relish of pleasures that are not criminal; every diversion they take is at the expense of some one virtue or another."

Here, in the first place, by neglecting to repeat *who*, Addison says that there are very few men who know how to have a relish of pleasures that are not criminal; whereas, he manifestly meant to say that there are very few who know how to be idle and

innocent, or *who* have a relish of pleasures that are
not criminal. But the chief blunder of the sentence
is in its next clause. Who are "they" who are said
to take every diversion at the expense of some virtue? According to the writer's purpose, "they" has
really no antecedent. Its antecedent, as the sentence stands, is, "very few who know how to be idle
and innocent;" but these, the writer plainly means
to say, are they who do *not* take their diversion at the
expense of some virtue. By "they" Addison meant
the many from whom he had in his own mind separated the very few of whom only he spoke; and
he thus involved himself and his readers in a confusion which is irremediable without a recasting of
his sentence. All these marked faults of style —
faults which are not examples of mere inelegance,
but of positively bad English and confused thought
— occur within three duodecimo pages. It might
possibly be suggested that perhaps Addison wrote
this particular number of "The Spectator" when
the usual mellowness of his style had been spirited
into his brain.* But, on the contrary, similar examples of slovenly writing may be found all through
those charming "Spectators" to which Johnson
refers us as models of English style. Let us see.
Here is the third sentence in "Spectator" 405, a
musical criticism apropos of Signor Nicolini's sing-
ing; for Addison, as well as Guizot, wrote art
criticisms for the daily press.

* Bishop Hurd says of this Essay, "Some inaccuracies of expression have, however, escaped the elegant writer; and these, as we go along, shall be pointed out."
But it is important to our purpose to mention that not one of the inaccurate and confused passages noticed above is pointed out by the editor, who calls attention to but
one or two trifling lapses in mere elegance of expression.

"I could heartily wish there was the same application and
endeavours to cultivate and improve our church-musick as have
been lately bestowed on that of the stage."

It would not be easy to construct an intelligible
sentence, without burlesque, that would be more
blundering than this one is. To begin: "I could
heartily wish" is nonsense. A man wishes, or he
does not wish. But to pass by this feeble and
affected phrase, which is too commonly used, the
writer wishes that there "*was* the same application
and endeavors," etc., "as *have been*," etc. He says
neither "was" and "has been," nor "were" and
"have been." He should have used the plural form
of each verb, of course; but he contrived to get into
his sentence all the errors of which it was capable.
Besides, the use of the pronoun "*that*" is extremely
awkward, even if, indeed, it be correct. For,
as the sentence stands, "that" refers to "church
music," and the writer really speaks of the endeavors
which have been bestowed "on the church music of
the stage." He should have written either — church
music and stage music, or music of the church and
that of the stage; of which constructions the latter
is the better. The sentence may, therefore, be
correctly written (it cannot be made graceful or
elegant) thus: I heartily wish that there were the
same application and endeavors to cultivate and improve the music of the church as have lately been
bestowed on that of the stage.

In "Spectator" No. 381 is the following sentence: —

"The tossing of a tempest does not discompose him, which
he is sure will bring him to a joyful harbour."

The use of *which* in this sentence is like that which Mr. Dickens has so humorously caricatured in the speech of Mrs. Gamp; indeed, the sentence is almost in her style, or that of her invisible gossip, Mrs. Harris. Addison meant to say — The tossing of a tempest does not discompose him *who* is sure *that it* will bring him to a joyful harbor.

In this sentence, from "Spectator" No. 21, *venture* is used for *allow*: —

" — as a man would be well enough pleased to buy silks of one whom he would not venture to feel his pulse."

And what shall be said of the correctness of a writer who couples the separative *each* with the plural *are*, as Addison does in the following passage from "Spectator" No. 21?

" When I consider how *each* of these professions *are* crowded with multitudes that seek their livelihoods in them," etc.

That slovenly writing is the birth-form of careless thinking, could hardly be more clearly shown than by the following example, from "Spectator" No. 111: —

"That cherubim which now appears as a god to a human soul knows very well that the period will come above in eternity, when the human soul shall be as perfect as he himself now is; nay, when she shall look down upon that degree of perfection as much as she now falls short of it."

If Addison did not know that *cherubim* was the plural of *cherub*, and that he should have used the latter word, there is at least no excuse for the last clause of the sentence, which is chaotic. He would have expressed his meaning if he had written — Nay, when she shall look down upon that degree of perfection as much as she now *looks up to* it; or, better — Nay, when she shall *find herself as much above* that degree of perfection as she now falls short of it.

With two more examples I must finish this array. Speaking of Sir Andrew Freeport, Addison says, —

" — but in the temper of mind *he was then*, he termed them mercies, favours of Providence, and blessings upon honest industry." — *Spectator*, No. 549.

Explaining a pasquinade, he writes, —

" This was a reflection upon the Pope's sister, who, before the promotion of her brother, was in those circumstances *that Pasquin represented her*." — *Spectator*, No. 23.

It would be superfluous either to point out or to correct the gross errors in these passages — errors which are worthy of notice as examples of blunders peculiarly British in character. Errors of this kind are not unfrequently met with in the writing or the speech of the middling folk among our British cousins at the present day; but on this side of the water they seldom occur, if ever. Our faults are of another sort; and they appear in the casual writings of inferior journalists, who produce at night what must be printed before morning, or in those of authors who attain not even to local reputation. It would be difficult to match with examples from American writers of even moderate distinction such sentences as the following, which appear in Brougham's appreciation of Talleyrand : —

" Among the eminent men who figured in the eventful history of the French revolution was M. Talleyrand; and whether in that scene, or in any portion of modern annals, we shall in rain look for one who represents a more interesting subject of history."

What a muddle of thoughts and words is here! Talleyrand figured in the French revolution, not in the history of that event. It may be correctly said of him that he *figures* in the history of the French revolution; but whether this is what Brougham meant to say, the latter clause of the sentence makes it impossible to discover. For there "*scene*," which refers to the event itself, and "*annals*," which refers to the record of events, are confounded; and we are finally told that a man who figured in an eventful history represents an interesting subject of history! Within a few lines of this sentence we have the one here following : —

"He sided with the revolution, and continued to act with them, joining those patriotic members of the clerical body who gave up their revenues to the demand of the country, and sacrificed their exclusive privileges to the rights of the community."

With whom did Talleyrand continue to act? What is the antecedent of "*them*"? It has none. It refers to what is not expressed, and, except in the mind of the writer, not understood — the revolutionary clergy; and I have quoted the whole of the sentence, that this might appear from its second clause. And yet Henry Brougham was one of the men who achieved the splendid early reputation of the "Edinburgh Review."

But to what conclusion are we tending? If not only Brougham's but Addison's sentences thus break down under such criticism as we apply to the exercises of a school-boy, — Addison, of whose style we are told by Johnson, in Johnsonian phrase, that

... principal writer of "The Spectator,"
although he may have been without either
...osity or elaboration, he was also quite a...
... often without both purity and exactness.
...aults of style as those which are above po...
...n the writings of Addison are not to be...
...believe, in Shakespeare's prose, in Bacon...
...Milton's; but they do appear in Dryden's...
...will be looked for in vain, if I may trust m...
...ory, in the works of Goldsmith, Johnson,...
...Gibbon, Hallam, Jeffrey, Macaulay, Irvin...
...cott, Ruskin, Motley, and Hawthorne. A...
...appearing at a time when English literature...
...very low ebb, made an impression wh...
...writings would not now produce, and won...
...ation which was then his due, but which h...
...urvived his comparative excellence. Char...
...he gentle flow of his thought, — which, neith...
...or strong, neither subtle nor struggling w...
...ostacles of argument, might well flow ea...
...y his lambent humor, his playful fancy (...
...ry slenderly endowed with imagination),...
...ealthy tone of his mind, the writers of...

and refinement. But, as a writer of English, he is
not to be compared, except with great peril to his
reputation, to at least a score of men who have
flourished in the present century, and some of whom
are now living. And from this slight examination
of the writings of him whom the world has for so
long accepted as the acknowledged master of English prose, and who attained his eminence more by
the beauty of his style than the value of the thought
of which it was the vehicle, we may learn the true
worth and place of such criticisms as those which
have preceded these remarks. Their value is in
their fitness for mental discipline. Their place is
the class-room.

CHAPTER V.

MISUSED WORDS.

THE right use of words is not a matter to be left to pedants and pedagogues. It belongs to the daily life of every man. The misuse of words confuses ideas, and impairs the value of language as a medium of communication. Hence loss of time, of money, and sore trial of patience. It is significant that we call a quarrel a misunderstanding. How many lawsuits have ruined both plaintiff and defendant, how many business connections have been severed, how many friendships broken, because two men gave to one word different meanings! The power of language to convey one man's thoughts and purposes to another, is in direct proportion to a common consent as to the meaning of words. The moment divergence begins, the value of language is impaired; and it is impaired just in proportion to the divergence, or to the uncertainty of consent. It has been told, as evidence of the richness of certain Eastern languages, that they have one thousand words, more or less, for the sword, and at least one hundred for the horse. But this, unless the people who use these languages have a thousand kinds of swords and a hundred kinds of horses, is no proof of wealth in that which makes

the real worth of language. A highly civilized
and cultivated people having a language adequate
to their wants will be rich in words, because they
will need names for many thoughts, and many
acts, and many things. Parsimony in this respect
is a sign, not of prudence, but of poverty. Juli-
ana, passing her honeymoon in the cottage to
which her ducal bridegroom leads her, flouts his
assurance that the furniture is useful, with the reply, conveying a sneer at his supposed poverty,
"Exceeding useful; there's not a piece on't but
serves twenty purposes." So, when we find in a language one word serving many needs, we may be
sure that that language is the mental furniture of
an intellectually rude and poverty-stricken people.
The Feejee islanders ate usually pig, but they
much preferred man, both for his flavor and his
rarity ; and as we call pig prepared for table pork,
and deer in a like condition venison, so those poor
people called their loin or ham "short pig," and
their daintier human haunch or saddle "long pig."
Archbishop Trench, assuming that there was in the
latter name an attempt at a humorous concealment
of the nature of the viand to which it was applied,
finds in this attempt evidence of a consciousness of
the revolting character of cannibalism. But this
seems to be one of those pieces of fanciful and over-
subtle moral reflection which, coming gracefully
enough from a clergyman, have added to the popu-
larity of Trench's books, although hardly to their
real value. The poor Feejeeans called all meat
pig, distinguishing two sorts only by the form of the
animal from which it was taken, merely because of

the rude and embryotic condition of their language,
just as a little child calls all fur and velvet "pussy-
cat." The child knows as well as its mother that
her muff or her gown has not four legs, claws,
whiskers, and a tail; and it has no purpose of
concealing that knowledge. But its poverty of
language enables it to speak of the muff and the
velvet gown only by a name which expresses (to
the child) the quality which the muff, the gown,
and the animal have in common.

A neglect to preserve any well-drawn distinction
in words between thoughts or things is, just so far,
a return toward barbarism in language. In the
London "Times's" report of the revolting scene in
front of the gallows on which Muller (he who killed
a fellow-passenger in a railway carriage) was
hanged, it was said that many of the spectators,
knowing that if they would get a good place they
must wait a long while to see the show, came provided with "jars of beer." Now, we may be sure
that there was not a jar in all that crowd. A jar,
which is a wide-mouthed earthen vessel without a
handle, would be a very unsuitable and cumbrous
vessel on such an occasion and in such a place;
and besides, beer is neither kept in jars, nor drunk
from them. The "Times's" reporter, who is said
to have been, on this occasion, a man of letters of
some reputation, meant, doubtless, tankards, pots,
jugs, or pitchers. Of household vessels for containing fluids we have in English good store of
names nicely distinctive of various forms and uses;
and there seems to be a chance that we shall lose
some of them, through either the ignorance or the

indolence of writers and speakers like the Times's
reporter. It is not long since every lady in the
land had, as Gremio said that Bianca should have,
"basins and ewers to lave her dainty hands,"
although not of gold, as that glib-tongued lover
promised. But now we are all, with few exceptions, content to use a bowl and pitcher. The
things are the same, only they are handsomer; but
we have, many of us at least, given up the distinction between bowl and basin, and common pitcher
and ewer, and so far we have retrograded in civil-
ity. Some British writers and speakers say "a
basin of bread and milk." We may be sure they
mean a bowl, for a basin is an uncomfortable vessel
to eat from. But if they mean a bowl, they should
say a bowl; for although we have dropped *por-
ringer* except in poetry (yet there are men living
who, in their childhood, have talked of porringers
as well as eaten out of them), we may as well try
to preserve some distinction between the names of
our domestic utensils, unless, emulating the simplicity of the Feejeeans in their short pig and long
pig, we call them all, for example, cup, and say
short cup, long cup, high cup, low cup, big cup,
little cup, deep cup, shallow cup.

Our British kinsmen have, during the last fifty
or perhaps hundred years, fallen into the use of a
peculiar misnomer in this respect. They, without
exception, I believe, talk of the water jug and the
milk-jug, meaning the vessels in which water and
milk are served at table. Now, those vessels are
not jugs, but pitchers. A jug is a vessel having a
small mouth, a swelling belly, and a small ear or

handle near the mouth; and this, we know, is never used at table: a pitcher is a vessel with a wide mouth, a protruding lip, and a large ear; and this we know that they, as well as we, do use at table for milk and for water. The thing has had the name for centuries. Hence the old saying that Little pitchers (not little jugs) have great ears Little pitchers, from the physical necessity of their shape and proportion, must have great ears; little jugs may have ears in proportion to their size. This word, by the by, is the best test, if indeed it is not the only sure test, of the nationality of a cultivated man of English blood, — for as to the uncultivated, no nice test is needed. *Been* and *bin*, *sick* and *ill*, *drive* and *ride*, a quarter *to* twelve and a quarter *of* twelve o'clock, rail*way station* and rail*road depot*, even pitch and inflection of voice, may fail to mark the distinction; but if a man asks for the milk-jug, be sure that he is British bred; if for the milk-pitcher, be equally sure that he is American.* But perhaps some people are quite indifferent whether or no it is said that they sip their coffee out of a jar, drink their beer from a vase, and put their flowers into a jug. Such readers will not be at all interested in the following remarks upon the misuse of certain English words. It is not my purpose in these remarks to notice

* As to the use of *ill* for *sick*, and *drive* for *ride*, see pages 192, 196. Since this passage was written, I have had a remarkable confirmation of its truth in the language of a lady born and bred in London, who spoke, with entire unconsciousness of her excellence, the most beautiful English I ever heard even among her countrywomen, however high their breeding or their culture — beautiful in idiom, in pronunciation, in enunciation, and in quality and inflection of voice. She, being entirely ignorant of any question upon these points, and thoughtless about her speech, said, "I have been sick with a cold;" "I have enjoyed the ride" (in a carriage); but even she asked the servant to bring "a jug of water."

slang, but I shall notice cant. Between the two, although they are often confounded, there is a clear distinction.

Slang is a vocabulary of genuine words or unmeaning jargon, used always with an arbitrary and conventional signification, and generally with humorous intent. It is mostly coarse, low, and foolish, although in some cases, owing to circumstances of the time, it is racy, pungent, and pregnant of meaning. Cant is a phraseology composed of genuine words soberly used by some sect, profession, or sort of men, in one legitimate sense, which they adopt to the exclusion of others as having peculiar virtue, and which thereby becomes peculiar to themselves. Cant is more or less enduring, its use continuing, with no variation of meaning, through generations. Slang is very evanescent. It generally passes out of use and out of mind in the course of a few years, and often in a few months.

ABORTIVE. — A ridiculous perversion of this word is creeping into use through the newspapers. For example, I read in one, of large circulation and high position, that "a young Spaniard yesterday abortively seized two pieces of alpaca." That is abortive which is untimely in its birth, which has not been borne its full time; and, by figure of speech, anything is abortive which is brought out before it is well matured. A plan may be abortive, but an act cannot. It would be a great waste of time to notice such ludicrous writing as that above quoted, were there not among journalists, and generally among that vast multitude who think it fine to use a word which they do not quite understand, a tendency to the use of *abortion* to mean failure in all its kinds and all its stages.

ADOPT. — A very strange perversion of this word from its true meaning prevails among some un-lettered folk, generally of Irish birth, whose misuse of it is daily seen in the Personal Advertisements in the New York "Herald." Thus, "Wanted to Adopt — A beautiful and healthy female infant." The advertisers mean that they wish to have the children mentioned in their advertisements *adopted*. In speaking of the transaction, their phrase is that the child is "adopted out," or, that such and such a woman "adopted out" her child. The perversion, it may be said inversion, of this word, is worth no-ticing because upon the misuse of *adopt* in these advertisements, travellers and foreign writers have founded an argument against the reproductive pow-er of the European races in this country. From the many advertisements "Wanted to Adopt," it has been inferred that the advertisers were childless and hopeless of children; how unjustifiably will appear by the following example, which appeared a few days ago : —

"A lady having two boys would like to adopt one. Inquire for two days at 228 Sullivan Street."

This lady, quite surely an Irish emigrant peasant woman, wished to rid herself of one of her children.

AFFABLE. — A use of this word, which has a very ludicrous effect to those for whom it has the signification given to it by the best English usage, is becoming somewhat common in newspaper cor-respondence and accounts of what are therein called "receptions" and "ovations." It means, literally, ready to speak, easily approachable in conversation. But by the usage of the best writers and speakers, and by common consent, it has been limited to the expression of an easy, courteous, and considerate manner on the part of persons of superior position to their inferiors. A king may be affable, as Charles II. was to his attendants; and so may a nobleman be to a laborer. Dr. Johnson at the height of his career might have been affable to a penny-a-liner, but he wasn't. General Washington was not affable, but Aaron Burr was. Milton calls Raphael "the affable archangel," and makes Adam say to him, as he is about departing heavenward, —

> "Gentle to me and affable hath been
> Thy condescension, and shall be honored ever
> With grateful memory."

But in "American" newspapers we now read of affable hotel-keepers and affable steamboat captains; and we are told that Mrs. Bullions, at her "elegant and *recherché* reception," although moving in a blaze of diamonds, tempered by a cloud of *point de Venise* lace, was "very affable to her guests." Far be it from me to suppose that there may be a difference between a hotel-keeper and an archangel, or to hint that the true sense of this word may be preserved in this usage by there being the same distance between a steamboat captain and a reporter that there was between Raphael and Adam. That suggestion is made by the reporters themselves. Perhaps this usage is one of the signs of the levelling power of democracy, and affability is about passing away among the vanished graces.

AGGRAVATE is misused by many persons ignorantly, and, in consequence, by many others thoughtlessly, in the sense of provoke, irritate, anger. Thus: He aggravates me by his impudence — meaning he angers me: Her martyr-like airs were very aggravating — the right word being *irritating.* The following example is from an elaborate article in the critical columns of a newspaper of high pretensions: "This lovely girl, so different in her naïve ways and lady-like carriage from all her homely surroundings, puzzles Felix, aggravates him, and finally leads him into attempting to infuse more of seriousness into her nature." The writer meant that Esther provoked or irritated Felix. Her conduct and bearing called forth, *i. e.,* pro-voked, certain action on his part. *Aggravate* means merely to add weight to. Injury is aggravated by the addition of insult. Thus, in Howell's Letters (sec. V. 12): "This [opposition] aggravates a grudge the French king hath to the duke for siding with the Imperialists." An insult may be aggravated by being offered to a man who is courteous and kindly, as it may be palliated by being offered to a brute and a bully. But it is no more proper to say in the one case that the person is aggravated, than in the other to say that he is palliated.

ALIKE is very commonly coupled with *both* in a manner so unjustifiable and so inconsistent with reason as to make the resulting phrase as gross a bull as was ever perpetrated. For example: "Those two pearls are both alike." This is equal to the story of Sam and Jem's resembling each other very much, particularly Sam. When we say of two objects that they are alike, we say that they are like each other — that is, simply, that one is like the other. For the purpose of comparing one with the other, they must be kept in mind separate; but by using *both*, we compare them as two together, not separately one with the other. *Both* means merely, and only, the two together. Etymologically it means the two two, and it corresponds to the French phrase *tous les deux*. Of two objects we may say that both are good, and that they are equally good; but not that both are equally good, which we do say if we say that both alike are good. The authority of very long and very eminent usage can be brought in support of *both alike;* but this is one of those points upon which such authority is of no weight; for the phrase is not an idiom, and it is at variance with reason. The error is more and other than pleonastic or than tautological. It is quite like that which I heard from a little girl, — a poor street waif, — who told a companion that she "had two weenie little puppy-dogs at home, and they were both brothers."

ALLUDE is in danger of losing its peculiar significaction, which is delicate and serviceable, by being used as a fine-sounding synonyme of *say* or *mention.* The honorable gentleman from the State of Kokeeko, speaking of the honorable gentleman from the same State, denounces him as a drunken vagabond and a traitor to his party. The latter rises and says that his colleague has alluded to him in terms just fit for such a scoundrelly son of a poorhouse drab to use, but that he hurls back the honorable gentleman's allusions, and so forth, and so

forth. The spectacle is a sad one to gods and men,
and also to all who have respect for the English
language. For whatever may have been the case
with the other words, *allude* and *allusion* were used
in their Kokeekokian, certainly not in their English,
sense. *Allude* (from *ludo, ludere*, to play) means
to indicate jocosely, to hint at playfully, and so to
hint at in a slight, passing manner. Allusion is
the by-play of language. "The Round Table"
having said, some months ago, that a certain article in "The Galaxy" was "respectably dull," the
writer thereof amused himself by turning off for
the next number the following epigram :—

> "Some knight of King Arthur's, Sir Void or Sir Null,
> Swears a trifle I wrote is respectably dull.
> He is honest for once through his weakness of wit,
> And he censures a fault that he does not commit ;
> For he shows by example — proof quite unrejectable —
> That a man may be dull *without* being respectable."

Here the journal in question is not mentioned, but
it is alluded to in the first line in such a manner that
any person acquainted with the press of New York
could not doubt as to the one intended.

ALLOW.—A western misuse of this word is creeping eastward; and sometimes, owing to the elevat-
ing effect of suddenly acquired wealth, is heard in
fashionable if not cultivated circles. It is used to
mean say, assert, express the opinion. *E.g.* "He
was mightily took with her, and allowed she was
the handsomest lady in Muzzouruh." We may
allow, or admit, that which we have disputed, but
of which we have been convinced; or we may
allow certain premises as the basis of argument;
but we assert, not allow, our own opinions.

ANIMAL.— It would seem that man is about to be deprived of the rank to which he is assigned by Hamlet — that of being the paragon of animals. Man, like the meanest worm that crawls, is an animal. His grade in the scale of organic life makes him neither the more nor the less an animal. And yet many people affect to call only brutes animals. Is this because they are ashamed of the bond which binds them to all living creatures? Do they scorn their poor relations? On this supposition Mr. Bergh might account for that lack of sympathy, the absence of which causes the cruelty of some men to their dumb fellow-beings, were it not that in past days, when no one had thought of taking man out of the animal kingdom, brutes were more hardly treated than they are now. Mr. Bergh's society — like that in London, of which it is a copy — is called The Society for the Prevention of Cruelty to Animals. It is in reality a society for the prevention of cruelty to brutes; for the animal that suffers most from cruelty — man — appears not to be under the shield of its protection.

ANTECEDENTS.—The use of this word as in the question, What do you know of that man's antecedents? is not defensible, except upon the bare plea of mutual agreement. For in meaning it is awkward perversion, and in convenience it has no advantage. *Antecedent*, an adjective, meaning going before, might logically be used as a substantive, to mean those persons or things which have preceded any person or thing of the same kind in a certain position. Thus the antecedents of General Sherman in the generalship of the army of the

United States are General Washington, General
Scott, and General Grant. There are also the
substantive uses of the word in grammar, logic, and
mathematics. But to call the course of a man's life
until the present moment *his antecedents* is nearly as
absurd a misuse of language as can be compassed.
And it is a needless absurdity. For if, instead of,
What do you know of his antecedents? it is asked,
What do you know of his previous life? or, better,
What do you know of his past? there is sense instead of nonsense, and the purpose of the question
is fully conveyed.

APT. — This little word, the proper meaning of
which it is almost impossible to express by definition
or periphrasis, is in danger of losing its fine sense,
and of being degraded into a servant of general
utility for the range of thought between *liable* and
likely. I have before me a letter published by a
woman of some note, who, asking for contributions
to her means of nursing sick and wounded soldiers,
says that anything directed to her at a certain place
"will be apt to come." The blunder is amusing. I
have no doubt it provoked many smiles; and yet
how delicate is the line which divides this use of the
word from the correct one! To say that a package
will be apt to come, is inadmissible ; but to say that
it would be apt to miscarry, would provoke no remark. This lady meant that the packages would
be likely to come. Her error was of the same sort
as that of the member from the rural districts, who,
driving into a village, called out to a person whom
he met, "I say, mister, kin yer tell me where I'd
be liable to buy some beans?" A man is liable to

that to which he is exposed, or obliged, or subject; but he is not liable to act. He is liable to take cold, to pay another man's debts, or to incur his wife's displeasure. He is liable to fall in love; but, unless he is a very weak brother, he is not liable to be marry. Aptness and liability both express conditions — one of fitness and readiness, the other of exposure — inherent in the person or thing of which they are predicated. A man may be liable to catch the plague or to fall in love, and yet not be apt to do either. For manhood's sake we would not say of any man that he is liable to be married; yet, under certain circumstances, most men are apt to be married; and having done so, a man is liable, and may be apt, to have a family of children. Shakespeare makes Julius Cæsar say of Cassius,—

> "I fear him not;
> Yet if my name were liable to fear,
> I do not know the man I should avoid
> So soon as that spare Cassius."

Cæsar might have said, "if I were liable to fear" as well as "if my name were liable." He could have said, "if I were apt to fear," but not, "if my name were apt to fear."

ARTIST is a much abused word, and one class of men misuse it to their own injury, — the painters, — who seem to think that *artist* is a more dignified name than *painter*. But *artist* has been beaten out so thin that it covers almost the whole field of human endeavor. A woman who turns herself upside down upon the stage is an artist; a cook is an artist; so is a barber; and Goldsmith soberly calls a cobbler an artist. The word has been so pulled and hauled that it is shapeless, and has no peculiar fitness to any craft or profession; its vagueness deprives it of any special meaning. Its only value now is in the acknowledgment of the expression of an æsthetic purpose, or, rather, of any excellence beyond that which is merely utilitarian. The painters say that they assume it lest they should be confounded with house-painters. The excuse is as weak as water. If they are liable to such confusion, or fear it, so much the worse for them. Leonardo, Raphael, Michael Angelo, Correggio, Titian, were content to be called painters. True, *they were* decorative house-painters. But the same name satisfied Rubens, Vandyke, Reynolds, and Stuart, who did not paint houses.

BALANCE, in the sense of rest, remainder, residue, remnant, is an abomination. Balance is metaphorically the difference between two sides of an account — the amount which is necessary to make one equal to the other. It is not the rest, the remainder. And yet we continually hear of the balance of this or that thing, even the balance of a congregation or of an army! This use of the word has been called an Americanism. But it is not so: witness this passage from "Once a Week:" —

"Whoso wishes to rob the night to the best advantage, let him sleep for two or three hours, then get up and work for two hours, and then sleep out the balance of the night. Doing this, he will not feel the loss of the sleep he has surrendered."

BOUNTIFUL. — This word is very generally misused both in speech and in writing. The phrase, a bountiful dinner, a bountiful breakfast, or, to be fine, a bountiful repast, is continually met with in newspapers, wherein we also read of bountiful receipts at the box-offices of theatres, and even, in a leading article of a journal of the first class now before me, of "bountifully filled hourly trains."

This use of the word altogether perverts and degrades it from its true meaning, which is too valuable to be lost without an effort for its preservation. Bountiful applies to persons, not to things, and has no reference to quantity; although quantity in benefits received is often the consequence of bountifulness in the giver. Lady Bountiful was so named because of the benefits she conferred. But the things that she gave — the food and clothing — were not bountiful. A breakfast or dinner which is paid for by those who eat it, has no relations of any kind to bounty; but it may be plentiful; and if it is given in alms or in compliment, it will be plentiful because the giver is bountiful. The repasts, collations, and banquets, above referred to, were plentiful; the receipts at the theatres large; and the trains well filled or crowded.

BRING, FETCH. — The misuse and confusion of these two words, which are so common, so rooted for centuries in the deep soil of our vernacular, would indicate a very great unsettling of the foundations of our language, were it not that the perversion is confined almost entirely to cities. You will hardly find an English or a Yankee farmer who is content to speak his mother tongue as his mother spoke it, who, without taking thought about it, does not use these words as correctly as persons bred in the most cultivated society. But people filled with the consciousness of fine apparel are heard saying to their shop boys, "Go to such or such a place, and bring this parcel with you; and, say! you may fetch that other one along." Now, *bring* expresses motion toward, not away. A boy is properly told to take his books to school, and to bring them home. But *at* school he may correctly say, I did not bring my books. *Fetch* expresses a double motion — first from and then toward the speaker. Thus, a gardener may say to his helper, "Go and bring me yonder rake;" but he might better say, "Fetch me yonder rake," *i. e.*, go and bring it. And so we find in our English Bible (Acts xxviii. 13), "and from thence we fetched a compass;" *i. e.*, we went out, around, and back, making a circuit. The distinction between *bring* and *fetch* is very sharply drawn in the following passage. (1 Kings xvii. 11.) "And as she was *going* to *fetch* it, he called to her and said, *Bring me*, I pray thee, a morsel of bread." From this usage of these words there is no justifiable variation. The slang phrase — "a fetch" — is hardly slang, for it expresses a venture, *i. e.*, a metaphorical going out to bring something in.

CALCULATE. — A very common misuse of this word should be corrected. I do not mean that of which the gentleman from the rural districts' is guilty when he cahlc'lates he kin do a pooty good stroke of work for himself when he gets into the Legislatur, but that which prevails much more widely, and among people who think no evil of their English, and who would say, for instance, that the nomination of Mr. Greeley to the Presidency was calculated to deprive the Democrats of the votes of the Free Traders. It was calculated to do no such thing. Who needs to be told that no such object entered into the calculations of the leading Democrats? But this use of the word has even the very high authority of Goldsmith to support it : —

"The only danger that attends the multiplicity of publications is, that some of them may be *calculated* to injure rather than benefit society." — *Citizen of the World*, Letter XXIV.

Now, *calculate* means to compute, to reckon, to work out by figures, and, hence, to project for any certain purpose, the essential thought expressed by it, in any case, being the careful adjustment of means to an end. But Goldsmith did not mean that the authors of the books he had in mind intended to injure society, and wrote with that end in view. He did mean that these books might contain something that would do society an injury. *Calculate*, used in this sense, is only a big, wrongful pretender to the place of two much better words — *likely* and *apt*. Goldsmith meant to express a fear that the books in question were likely to injure society; and whether Mr. Greeley's nomination was likely to cost his party the Free trade vote, is matter of opinion; but whether it was calculated to do so, is not.

CALIBRE is used with a radical perversion of its meaning by many persons who should know better. As, for instance, —

"She has several other little poems of a much higher calibre than that." — *London Spectator*, February 20, 1869.

The writer of this sentence might as well have said, a broader altitude, a bulkier range, or a thinner circumference. Calibre is the measure of the mass contained or containable in a cavity; *e. g.*, the

7

calibre of a bullet or a brain, and hence of a gun or a skull. Therefore its metaphorical use is for the expression of capacity, and its proper augmentatives are of expansion, not of height or depth.

CAPTION. — The affectation of fine, big-sounding words which have a flavor of classical learning has had few more laughable or absurd manifestations than the use of *caption* (which means seizure, act of taking), in the sense, and in the rightful place, of *heading*. In our newspapers, even in the best of them, it is too common. This monstrous blunder was first made by some person who knew that *captain* and *capital* expressed the idea of headship, but who was sufficiently ignorant to suppose that *caption*, from its similarity in sound to those words, had a kindred meaning. But *captain* and *capital* are from the Latin *caput*, a head; and *caption* is from *capio*, I seize, *captum*, seized. Language rarely suffers at the hands of simple ignorance; by which indeed it is often enriched and strengthened; but this absurd misuse of *caption* is an example of the way in which it is made mere empty sound, by the pretentious efforts of presuming half-knowledge. *Captivate* — a word closely connected with *caption* — once, indeed, its relative verb — is, on the other hand, an interesting example of the perfectly legitimate change, or limitation, which may be made by common consent in a word's meaning. *Captivate* means primarily to seize, to take captive, and, until within a few years, comparatively, it was used in that sense. But within the last two generations it has been so closely limited to the metaphorical expression of the act of charming by beauty of person and insnaring by wiles and winning ways, that it seems very strange to read in one of Washington's letters that "our citizens are frequently captivated by Algerine pirates."

CATCH is very generally misused for reach, get to, overtake. Many persons speak of catching a car. If they reach the car, or get to it, it being at the station, or if, it being in motion, they overtake it or catch up with it, they may catch some person who is in it, or they may catch scarlet fever from some one who has been in it. But they will not catch the car.

CHARACTER, REPUTATION. — These words are not synonymes; but they are too generally used as such. How commonly do we hear it said that such or such a man "bore a very bad character in his vicinity," the speaker meaning that the man was of bad repute in his neighborhood! We know very little of each other's characters; but reputations are well known to us, except our own. *Character*, meaning first a figure or letter engraved, means secondarily those traits which are peculiar to any person or thing. Reputation is, or should be, the result of character. Character is the sum of individual qualities: reputation, what is generally thought of character, so far as it is known. Character is like an inward and spiritual grace, of which reputation is, or should be, the outward and visible sign. A man may have a good character and a bad reputation, or a bad character and a good reputation; although, to the credit of human nature, which, with all its weakness, is not ignoble, the latter is more common than the former. Coleridge uses *character* incorrectly when he says (Friend I. 16), "Brissot, the leader of the Gironde party, is entitled to the character of a virtuous man." Sheridan errs in like manner in making Sir Peter Teazle say, as he leaves Lady Sneerwell's scandalous coterie, "I leave my character behind me." His reputation he left, but his character was always in his own keeping.

CHASTITY. — Priestcraft and asceticism have caused a confusion of this word with *continence* — a confusion which has lasted for centuries, and may yet last for many generations. Even such a priest-hater as Froude says of Queen Catharine that she was invited to take the vows, and enter what was called the *religio laxa* — a state, he adds, "in which she might live unencumbered by obligation, except the easy one of chastity." Does Mr. Froude mean that Catharine would have been more chaste as a secular nun than she was as Henry's wife? that a man is to look upon his mother or his wife as less chaste than his maiden aunt? He, of course, meant no such absurdity; he merely fell in with a bad usage. He should have said, except the easy obligation of continence. Chastity is a virtue. Continence, under some circumstances, is a duty, but is never a virtue, it being without any moral quality whatever.

CITIZEN is used by some writers for newspapers with what seems like an affectation of the French usage of *citoyen* in the first Republic. For instance: "General A is a well-known citizen, and responsible for these grave charges;" or, "Several citizens carried the sufferer to a drug store on the next

block." A citizen is a person who has certain political rights, and the word is properly used only to
imply or suggest the possession of these rights. The
sufferer was cared for by several persons, by-stand-
ers, or passengers, some or all of whom might have
been aliens. The writer might as well have said
that the sufferer was carried off by several church
members or several Free Masons.

CLARIONET and VIOLINCELLO are constantly used
for *clarinet* and *violoncello*. There was a stringed
instrument which has long been disused, and
which was called the *violone*. It was large, and
very different from the *violino*. A small instrument of the kind was made, and called the *violoncello* (*cello* being an Italian diminutive); and this,
somewhat modified, is the modern instrument of
that name. *Violincello* would be the name of a
little violin; whereas a *violoncello* is four times as
large as a violin. A similar contraction of word
and thing has given us *clarinet* (*clarinetto*) from
clarino.

CONSIDER is perverted from its true meaning by
most of those who use it. Men will say that they
do not consider a certain course of conduct right or
politic — that they do not consider Mr. So-and-So
a gentleman — and even that they do not consider
gooseberry tart equal to strawberry short-cake.
Now, *considere* (the infinitive of *consido*) on which
consider is formed, means to sit down deliberately,
to dwell upon, to hold a sitting, to sit in judgement;
and hence *consider*, by natural process came to
mean, to ponder, to contemplate. And there seems
to have been more than a mere happy fancy in the

notion, now abandoned, that *consider* was from *con.*
with, and *sidera*, the stars, and meant to take counsel with the stars, to peer into the future by watch-
ing the heavens. A court reserves its opinion
that it may consider a question which it sometimes
has for weeks under consideration. A business
man asks until to-morrow to consider your proposition, and meantime he ponders it, *i. e.*, weighs it
carefully, ruminates upon it. A man whose ability,
character, or position gives weight to his opinion, is
a man of consideration, because what he says is
worthy to be considered; and whatever is large
enough or strong enough to deserve serious attention is considerable. All this fine and useful sense
of the word is lost by making it a mere synonyme
of *think*, *suppose*, or *regard*.

CONSUMMATE. — Of all the queer uses of big
words which are creeping into vogue, the use of
this word, both in speech and in the newspapers, to
express the performance of the marriage ceremony,
is the queerest. For instance, I heard a gentleman
gravely say to two ladies, "The marriage was consummated at Paris last April." Now, consumma-
tion is necessary to a complete marriage; but it is
not usually talked about openly in general society.
The gentleman meant that the ceremony took place
at Paris.

COUPLE. — Although the misuse of this word is
very common, and of long standing, the perversion
of meaning in the misuse is so great that it cannot
be justified, even by time and custom. It is used
to mean simply two; as, for instance, "A couple
of ladies fell upon the ice yesterday afternoon.'

"Five workingmen, stimulated by the prospect of a couple of small money prizes, offered by an enterprising local firm, delivered speeches," etc. — " *Pall Mall Gazette*," March 6, 1869. Why people should use these three syllables, *couple of*, to say incorrectly that which one syllable, *two*, expresses correctly, it is hard to tell. It would be quite as correct in the above examples to say, a brace of ladies, and more surely correct to say a pair of prizes. For a couple is not only two individuals who are in a certain degree, at least, equal or like, *i. e.*, a pair, but two that are bound together by some close tie or intimate relationship; who, in brief, are coupled. Two railway cars are bound together by the coupling; a man and a woman are made a couple by the bond of sexual love, which even the legal bond of marriage cannot accomplish; for a man and his wife may be separated, and be no longer a couple. Twins, even, are not a couple, but a pair. In *couple*, which is merely the Latin *copula* Anglicized, this idea of copulative conjunction is inherent. So William Lilly, in his "Short Introduction of Grammar," defines *jugum* as "a yoke, or a yoke of oxen, that is, a couple." It is as incorrect and as absurd to speak of a couple of ladies, or a couple of prizes, as of a couple of earthquakes or a couple of comets.

CONVENE is much perverted from its true meaning by many people who cannot be called illiterate. Thus: The President convened Congress. *Convene* (from *con* and *venio*) means to come together. The right word in this case is *convoke*, which (from *con* and *voco*) means to call together. The President convokes Congress in special session, and then Congress convenes. *Convene* is misused in the Constitution of the United States itself, which is singularly free from errors in the use of language.

CRIME. — The common confusion of the words *crime*, *vice*, and *sin*, is probably due, in a great measure, to a failure to distinguish the things. The distinction was long ago made, although hardly with sufficient exactness. Crime is a violation of the law of a particular country. What is crime in one country may not be crime in another; what is crime in one country at one time may not be crime in the same country at another time. Sin is the violation of a religious law, which may be common to many countries, and yet be acknowledged by only a part of the inhabitants of any one. What is sin among Jews or Mohammedans is, in some cases, not sin among Christians, and *vice versa*. Vice has been defined as a violation of the moral law; but to make this definition exact in terms and universal in application, a consent as to the requirements of the moral law is necessary. Vice is a course of action or habit of life which is harmful to the actor or wrongful to others. The viciousness of an act is quite irrespective of the country, or the creed of the person who commits it, or of the people among whom it is committed. That which is criminal may be neither sinful nor vicious; that which is sinful, neither criminal nor vicious; and that which is vicious, neither criminal nor sinful. Thus, smuggling is a crime, but neither a sin nor a vice; covetousness and blasphemy are sins and vices, but not crimes; gambling is a crime and a vice, but not a

sin; idleness is vice, but, in itself, neither sin nor
crime; while theft is criminal, sinful, and vicious.
The magnitude of the wrong in some acts raises
them above or sinks them below the level of vice.
Murder is not a vice. It would not be well to speak
of Herod's slaughter of the innocents as a vicious
or even a very vicious act. The idea of continuity,
or of possible continuity, of a habit of action is
conveyed in the word vice. Filial disrespect is vicious; but the same cannot be said of parricide; for
although parricide is filial disrespect carried to the
extreme, it cannot become a habit, because a man
can have but one father and one mother.

DECIMATED. — The learned style of that eminent
and ambitious writer, the War Correspondent, has
brought this word into vogue since the Rebellion,
but with a sense somewhat different from that in
which it was used by his guide and model, Caius
Julius Cæsar. After the battle on the Rapidan, or
the Chattanooga, he — I do not mean the greater of
the two eminent persons, and probably the former
will admit that C. J. Cæsar was the more distinguished even as a writer upon military affairs —
used to say, in his fine Roman style, that the army
was "awfully decimated," as in one of the many
instances before me: "The troops, although fighting bravely, were terribly decimated, and gave
way." Old Veni-vidi-vici would tell him that he
might as well have written that the troops were
terribly halved or frightfully quartered. When a
Roman cohort revolted, and the revolt was put
down, a common punishment was to decimate the
cohort — that is, select every tenth man, *decimus*,

by lot, and put him to death. If a cohort suffered in battle so that about one man in ten was killed, it was consequently said to be decimated. But to use decimation as a general phrase for great slaughter is simply ridiculous. The exact equivalent of this usage would be to say, The troops were terribly tithed.

DEFALCATION is misused on all sides and every day in the sense of default or defaulting. *Defalcation* is the noun of the verb *defalcate*, which means to lop off, and so to detract from. Congress might defalcate the tariff, and the defalcation might be large or small; but it would not be a default. A default might be made by any officer intrusted with the collections of the customs duties. If he should not pay these into the treasury, he would default, *i. e.*, fail in his duty, and be a defaulter; but he would not defalcate, or would his act be a defalcation.

DIRT means filth, and primarily filth of the most offensive kind. A thing that is dirty is foul. The word has properly no other meaning. And yet some women, intelligent and well educated, say that they like to ride on "a dirt road." They mean a ground road, an earth road, a gravel road, or, in general terms, an unpaved road. *Dirt* is used by some persons as if it meant earth, loam, gravel, or sand; and we sometimes hear "clean dirt" spoken of. There is no such thing.

DIVINE. — The use of this adjective as a noun, meaning a clergyman, a minister of the gospel, is supported by long usage and high authority. In "Richard III." Buckingham points out to the Mayor of London the hypocritical Gloster "meditating with two deep divines." Chaucer calls the priest Calchas a divine. Yet I cannot but regard this use of the word as at variance with reason, as fantastic and extravagant. Think it over a little, and say it over a few times — a divine, *a* divine — meaning a sort of man! It might be more blasphemous to leave out the article, and call the man divine; but would it be quite as absurd? This use of this adjective as a noun has a parallel in the calling philosopher "a philosophic," which is done in a newspaper article before me; in the more common designation of a child as "juvenile," and even of books for children as "juveniles;" in the phrase "an obituary," meaning an obituary article; and in the name "monthly," which is sometimes given to a literary magazine; all of which are equally at variance with reason and with good taste. In either case the thing is deprived of its substantive name, and designated by an unessential, accidental quality.

DOCK is by many persons used to mean a wharf or pier; thus: He fell off the dock, and was drowned. A dock is an open place without a roof, into which anything is received, and where it is enclosed for safety. A prisoner stands, or used to stand, in the dock at his trial. A ship is taken into a dock for repairs. The Atlantic Dock is properly named. The shipping around a city lies at wharfs and piers, but goes into docks. A man might fall into a dock; but to say that he fell off a dock is no better than to say that he fell off a hole.

DRESS has the singular fortune of being misused by one sex only. By town-bred women, both in Great Britain and the United States, and by that very large and wide-spread rural class who affect town-bred airs, *dress* is used for *gown;* and thus woman, in a very unhousewifely way, takes from one good servant half his rights, and throws another out of place entirely, thereby leaving herself short-handed. The radical idea expressed in the word *dress* is, right; and *dress,* the verb, means, simply, to set right, to put in order. A captain of infantry orders his company to dress to the right — that is, to bring themselves into order, into line, by looking to the right. The kitchen dresser is so called because upon it dishes are put in order. As to the body, dress is that which puts it in order, in a condition comfortable and suitable to the circumstances in which it is placed. *Dress* is a general term, including the entire apparel, the under garments as well as the outer. No man thinks of calling his coat or his waistcoat his dress, more than of so calling his shirt or his stockings. But women do so call the gown; and thus they use a word which is a vague, general term, and is applicable to all apparel, and belongs to men as much as to women, instead of one which means exactly that which they wish to express — a long outer garment, extending from the shoulder below the knee. *Frock,* sometimes used for *gown,* is properly of more limited application, although it belongs both to masculine and feminine attire. The origin of the perversion is probably untraceable, except by the aid of some woman of close observation and reflection, who is old enough to have been brought up to say *gown.* Such a person might be able to tell us how and why, in a little more than a generation, this word has come to bĕ thus perverted by her sex only.

EDITORIAL. — An unpleasant Americanism for *leader* or *leading article*, which name is given to the articles in newspapers upon the leading topics of the day. These articles are not generally written by the editor of the paper, although he is responsible for them; but so is he for the other articles, and for the correspondence. And even were the case otherwise, *leader* or *leading article* would, none the less, be a good descriptive name for them, and *editorial* would be poor, both for its meagre significance, and for its conversion of an adjective, not signifying a quality, as *good* or *ill*, into a noun.

ESQUIRE. — An attempt to deprive any citizen of this democratic republic of his right to be called an esquire by his friends and all his correspondents, would be an outrage upon our free institutions, and perhaps treason to the natural rights of man, whatever they may be. Upon this subject I confess myself fit only to be a learner; but I have yet to discover what a man means when he addresses a letter to John Dash, Esq. (who is in no manner distinguished or distinguishable from other Dashes), except that Mr. Dash shall think he means to be polite.

EVACUATE. — This word is often subjected to the same kind of ill treatment from which *leave* suffers. Thus: General Pemberton expects to evacuate to-morrow about nine A. M.; or, The enemy evacuated last night. *Evacuate* does not mean to go away, but to make empty; and when the word is used in regard to military movements, evacuation is a mere consequence, result, or, at most, con-

comitant of the going away of the garrison. For
obvious reasons the mention of the place departed
from is in this case particularly necessary.

EVERY. — A gross misuse of this word has been
brought into vogue within the last few years on both
sides of the water — the first offenders having been
people who wished to be elegant, but who did not
know enough to be correct; the others being their
thoughtless followers. Thus, General Napier, writing to Disraeli from Abyssinia, said, "The men
deserve every praise;" "The Tribune" says that
"Congress has exercised every charity in its treatment of the President;" a manager is reported as
having said that as a certain actor has recovered
his health, he, the manager, "has every confidence
in announcing him"; and we see grateful people
acknowledging, in testimonials, that in their trouble
such or such a captain, or landlord, "rendered them
every assistance." This is absurdly wrong. *Every*
is separative, and can be applied only to a whole
composed of many individuals. Composed originally of the Anglo-Saxon *æfer*, ever, and *ælc*, each,
its course of descent has been *everælc*, *everilk*,
everich, *every*. It means each of all, not all in
mass. It cannot, therefore, be applied to that which
is in its very nature inseparable. The manager
might as well have said that he had multitudinous
confidence, as that he had every confidence. He
meant perfect or entire confidence; and the grateful
people, that the captain rendered them all possible
assistance. Such a sentence, too, as the following,
from the work of an admired British novelist, is
absurd: "Every human being has this in common."

All human beings might have something in common; but what every man has, he has individually for himself.

EXECUTED. — A vicious use of this word has prevailed so long, become so common, that, although it produces sheer nonsense, there is little hope of its reformation, except in case of that rare occurrence in the history of language, a vigorous and persistent effort on the part of the best speakers and writers and professional teachers toward the accomplishment of a special purpose. The perversion referred to is the use of *executed* to mean hanged, beheaded, put to death. Thus a well-known historian says of Anne Boleyn that "she was tried, found guilty, and executed;" and in the newspapers we almost always read of the "execution" of a murderer. The writers declare the performance of an impossibility. A law may be executed; a sentence may be executed; and the execution of the law or of a sentence sometimes, although not once in a thousand times, results in the death of the person upon whom it is executed. The coroner's jury, which sits in the prison-yard upon the body of a felon who has been hanged, brings in its formal verdict, "Execution of the law." To execute (from *sequor*) is to follow to the end, and so to carry out, and to perform; and how is it possible that a human being can be executed? A plea of metaphorical or secondary use will not save the word in this sense; for the law or a sentence is as much executed when a condemned felon is imprisoned as when he is put to death. But who would think of saying that a man was executed because he was shut up in the

State Prison? And even were it not so, how much
simpler and more significant a use of language to
say that a felon, or a victim of tyranny, had been
hanged, beheaded, shot, or generally, put to death,
than to say he was executed! of which use of this
word there is no justification, its only palliation being that afforded by custom and bad example.

EXEMPLARY. — Archbishop Trench has pointed
out that a too common use of this word makes it
"little more than a loose synonyme for *excellent.*"
Its proper meaning is, that which serves for an example. Cervantes' *Novelas exemplares* were so
called, because each of them furnished an example. The misuse of *exemplary* confines it to
examples that should be followed. But some examples are not to be followed. A man is hanged
for an example. Othello says, "Cassio, I'll make
an example of thee." The language would gain a
word by the restriction of *exemplary* to its proper
meaning. *Example* itself is too often loosely used
for *problem.* A problem often is an example of the
operation of a rule, but not always; and in any case
its exemplary is not its essential character.

EXPECT is very widely misused on both sides of
the water in the sense of suppose, think, guess.
E. g., "I expect you had a pretty hard time of it
yesterday." *Expect* refers only to that which is
to come, and which, therefore, is looked for (*ex,*
out, and *spectare,* to look). We cannot expect
backward.

EXPERIENCE. — Perhaps an objection to the use
of this word as a verb has no better ground than
that of taste or individual preference, which should

be excluded from discussions like the present; yet
I am inclined to make that objection very strongly. We are told, for instance, in a London newspaper of repute, that an Armenian archbishop
who penetrated into Abyssinia at the request of the
British authorities, " fell into the hands of some barbarous tribes of that district, from whom he is ex-
periencing very rough usage." He was receiving
or suffering rough usage; and although that was
part of his experience, he did not experience it.
Experience is the passing through a more or less
continuous course of events or trials. A man's experience is the sum of his life; his experience in any
profession, business, or condition of life, is the aggre-
gate of the observation he has had the opportunity of
making in that profession, business, or condition.
Experience should be a means of obtaining knowledge and understanding, but it is not so always.
Some men learn much by experience; most men,
very little; many, nothing. *Experience* is akin to
experiment, both being derived from the same Latin
word, *experior*, *experimentum*, the idea expressed
by which is trial. But experiment is voluntary trial,
experience involuntary. In experiment the trier is
an agent; in experience, an observer, and often a
sufferer. He not only tries, but is tried himself.
Natural science advances by experiments which are
undertaken by scientific men, and an experiment is
a positive fact, of which all men may avail themselves according to their knowledge and ability;
but experience is of little value except to him who
has passed through it. From the noun *experience* is
formed the participial adjective *experienced* (which
                             8

is not the perfect participle of a verb *experience*),
as *moneyed* from *money*, *landed* from *land*, *talented*
from *talent*, *casemated* from *casemate*, *battlemented*
from *battlement*. *Battlemented* is not a part of a
verb — *I battlement, thou battlementest*, etc.; or
talented from a verb — *I talent, thou talentest*, etc.
So an experienced man is a man of experience, not
one who has been experienced, *i. e.*, according to
the dictionaries, has been tried, proved, observed,
but one who has tried, has proved, has observed.
Of the use of *experience* as an active transitive verb,
I have been able to find, by diligent search, only
one example of any authority — the following, quoted
by Richardson from "The Guardian" — "the maxim of common sense — that men ought to form their
judgments of things unexperienced from what they
have experienced." The examples easiest to find
are such as the following, furnished by an incensed
farmer: "Wal, I'll be durned ef ever I exper'enced
sech a cussed cross-grained critter as that in all my
life;" the cross-grained creature which the speaker
experienced being a cow that kicked over the milk-
pail. That this is not an extreme case, take the
following examples in evidence — the first from the
London "Spectator," the second from "The Mark
Lane Express," two high-class British newspapers:
"The attempt to adapt ourselves by temporary ex-
pedients to a climate which we *experience* [to which
we are exposed] about once in twenty or thirty
years;" "The hay crop is one of the most deficient
experienced [that we have had] in many years."
Now, if we may experience a hot day, or experience
a hay crop, can we refuse to experience a cow,

without coming athwart the stupendous principle of equal rights for everybody and everything, and subjecting ourselves to discipline at the hands of Mr. Bergh's society? Let us bear, suffer, try, live through, endure, prove, and undergo; and from all this we shall gain experience and become experienced; but let us not experience either a hay crop, or a cow, nor indeed any other thing.

EXTEND. — The fondness for fine words leads lecture committees, and other like public bodies, to propose to "extend an invitation" to one distinguished man or other, instead of merely asking him, inviting him, or giving him an invitation; as, for instance, it was reported by telegraph that "an invitation had been extended to Reverdy Johnson" to dine with the Glasgow bailies; and in the dedication of a book of some ability, upon an important literary subject, the compliment is said to be paid "in remembrance of the kind interest extended to the author." An interest may be taken or shown in a man, or his labors; but to extend an interest is to make that interest larger. A man who has ten thousand dollars in a business, and puts in ten thousand more, extends his interest in that business. And, moreover, as *extend* (from *ex* and *tendo*) means merely to stretch forth, it is much better to say that a man put out, offered, or stretched forth his hand, than that he extended it. Shakespeare makes the pompous, pragmatical *Malvolio* say, "I extend my hand to him, thus;" but Paul "stretched forth the hand and answered for himself." This, however, is a question of taste, not of correctness.

FLY is very frequently misused for *flee*. It has

even been questioned whether there is a real difference between these two words. Certainly there is;
the distinction is valid and useful. *Flee* is a general
term, and means to move away with voluntary ra-
pidity; *fly* is of special application, and means to
move with wings, either quickly or slowly. True,
the words have the same original; but so have
sit and *set*, *lie* and *lay*. The needs of language,
guided by instinct, we know not exactly how, effected the distinction between these pairs of words,
and it has been confirmed by the usage of many
centuries. The similarity between the members of
each pair is so great, and they are so easily confused, that it is difficult to decide what was the usage
of any one of our older authors except in those cases
in which their works were very carefully printed
under their own eyes. The worth of the distinction
and the real difference involved in it will appear by
reading, instead of "Sisera lighted down off his
chariot and fled away on his feet," Sisera lighted
down off his chariot and *flew* away on his feet, or
for "the arrow that flieth by day," the arrow that
fleeth by day.

GET, one of the most willing and serviceable of
our vocal servants, is one of the most ill used and
imposed upon — is, indeed, made a servant of all
work, even by those who have the greatest retinue
of words at their command. They use the word
get — the radical, essential, and inexpugnable meaning of which is the attainment of possession by voluntary exertion — to express the ideas of possessing,
of receiving, of suffering, and even of doing. In
all these cases the word is misused. A man gets

riches, gets a wife, gets children, gets well (after
falling sick), and, figuratively, gets him to bed,
gets up, gets to his journey's end — in brief, gets
anything that he wants and successfully strives for.
But we constantly hear educated people speak of
getting crazy, of getting a fever, and even of getting
a flea on one. A man hastening to the train will
say that he is afraid of getting left, and tell you
afterward that he did or did not get left — meaning
that he is afraid of being left, and that he was or
was not left.

The most common misuse of this word, however,
is to express simple possession. It is said of a man
that he has got this, that, or the other thing, or that
he has not got it; what is meant being simply that
he has it, or has it not — the use of the word *got*
being not only wrong, but, if right, superfluous. If
we mean to say that a man is substantially wealthy,
our meaning is completely expressed by saying that
he is rich, has a large estate, or has a handsome
property. We do not express that fact a whit better
by saying that he has got rich, or has got a large
estate; we only pervert a word which, in that case,
is at least entirely needless, and is probably somewhat more than needless. For it is quite correct to
say, in the very same words, that by such and such
a business or manœuvre the man has gotten a large
estate. Possession is completely expressed by *have;*
get expresses attainment by exertion. Therefore
there is no better English than, Come, let us get
home; but to say of a vagrant that he has got no
home is bad. So we read, "Foxes have holes;
birds of the air have nests; but the Son of Man hath

not where to lay his head"—not, have got holes,
have got nests, hath not got where to lay his head.
The phrase, He got the property through his mother
or by his wife, is common, but it is incorrect. An
estate inherited is not gotten. The correct expression is, That property came to him through his
mother, or by his wife. This word has a very wide
range, but the boundaries which it cannot rightfully
pass are very clearly defined.

There is among some persons not uneducated or
without intelligence a doubt about the past participle
of *got*—*gotten*, which produces a disinclination to
its use. I am asked, for instance, whether *gotten*,
like *proven*, belongs to the list of "words that are
not words." Certainly not. *Prove* is what the
grammars call a regular verb; that is, it forms its
tenses upon the prevailing system of English verbal
conjugation, which makes the perfect tense in *ed*.
It is in this respect like *love*, the example of regular
verbal conjugation given in most grammars; and
we may as well say that Mary has *loven* John as that
John's love for Mary was not *proven*. But *get* is of
the irregular conjugation, in which the preterite
tense is formed by an internal vowel change, and the
past participle in *n*, with or without such vowel
change; thus—*get, gat, gotten*. The number of
these irregular verbs, having what is well called a
strong preterite, is large in our language, of which
they are a very fine and interesting feature, and one
that we should solicitously preserve with their original native traits unchanged. They are all pure English, and, if I remember rightly, nearly all of them
monosyllables. Such are *do, did, done; begin* [or

*gin] began, begun; spin, span, spun; slay, slew, slain;
fly, flew, flown; grow, grew, grown; eat, ate, eaten;
thrive, throve, thriven; shake, shook, shaken; speak,
spake, spoken; drink, drank, drunken; get, gat, gotten.*

There is and has long been, even among edu
cated people, a proneness to error in the use of
these strong verbs. A weak preterite is substi
tuted for the strong; the participle for the preterite
The former variation began so early, and became
so common in the last century, that it has been
assumed to indicate a tendency of the language.
Long ago it was noticed that the strong conjugation hardly holds it own, while all new verbs
are conjugated weak. But the confusion of preterite and participle cannot be even thus palliated. Thus Sterne says, "At the close of such
a folio as this, *wrote* for their sake." We can
forgive Yorick such errors as this, because of the
many charming pages that he has *written* for our
sake; but they were committed by hundreds of others
who have not his claims upon our forbearance. This
mistake, by the by, is rarely made by writers on
this side the water. Pope opens his "Messiah"
with an error of this sort, into which he frequently
falls.

> "Rapt into future times the bard *begun*:
> A virgin shall conceive and bear a son."

He should, of course, have written *began;* and if
the need of a rhyme were pleaded and admitted
as his excuse in this instance, it would not avail in
the following passage in his "Essay on Criticism,"
where—of all places!—he makes the blunder
at the beginning of a line, in the body of which

he weakens a preterite and an expression together : —

> "In the fat age of pleasure, wealth, and ease,
> *Sprung* [sprang] the rank weed, and *thriv'd* [throve] with
>   large increase."

Again, in the same poem, he has the following couplet, without the excuse of rhyme, making, indeed, the blunder in two words which would have rhymed as well if properly used : —

> "A second deluge learning thus o'er*run* [o'erran],
>   And the monks finished what the Goths *begun* [began]."

So Savage, in his "Wanderer," is guilty of the same fault, in mere wantonness, it would seem, or ignorance : —

> "From Liberty each nobler science *sprung* [sprang],
>   A Bacon brightened and a Spenser *sung* [sang]."

And Swift writes, "the sun has *rose*," "will have *stole* it," and "have *mistook*." For the sake of illustration, I cite the following instance of the right use of the strong preterite and past participle in the same sentence : —

> "A certain man made a great supper, and *bade* many; and
> sent his servant at supper-time to say to them that were *bidden*,
> Come, for all things are now ready." — *Luke* xiv. 17.

The confusion of the preterite and the past participle of *do*, which is so frequent among entirely illiterate people — He *done* it, for He did it, and He has *did* it, for He has done it — provokes a smile from those who themselves are guilty of exactly corresponding errors. For instance : He *begun* well, for He began well; His father had *bade* him to go home, for His father had bidden him go home; and The jury has *sat* a long while, for The jury has sitten a long while. Thus *got*, having by custom been poorly substituted for *gat*, so that we say He *got* away, instead of He gat away, many persons abbreviate *gotten* into *got*, saying He had *got*, for He had gotten; and hence the doubt whether *gotten* is not really, like *proven*, a word that is no word. But if *got* is the preterite of *get*, as *did* is of *do*, He had *got* is an error of the same class as He had *did*; and, on the other hand, if *got* is the past participle of *get*, as *done* is of *do*, He got is really no worse than He done — only more common among people of some education. Among such people we too often hear, He had *rode*, for He had ridden, and, perhaps, most frequently of all this class of errors, I had *drank*, for I had drunk, or (better) I had drunken, and I *drunk*, for I drank.

Contrary to common supposition, the irregularity of these strong verbs is not in their deviation from the weak form of conjugation — with the preterite in *ed* or *d*. They have merely a peculiar form of conjugation; and their inflections (so to speak of an internal change) are as systematic as those of the other and larger division of the same part of speech. The really irregular verbs are the strong which have acquired weak preterites. We have all of us laughed often enough at "First it blew, and then it snew, and then it thew, and then it friz." But if this were ever uttered in good faith (and it may have been so), it was the product of ignorance only as to the last word. *Snew* is the regular preterite of *snow*, the regular past participle of which is not *snowed*, but *snown*. *E. g.*, *grow, grew, grown; throw, threw, thrown; blow, blew, blown.* The preterite *snew* is to be

found in our early literature. Gower uses it, and
Douglas, in his translation of the Æneid, the maker
of the glossary to which (said in an old manuscript
note in my copy to have been John Urry) erroneously marks it as a Scotticism. Holinshed, noticing
an entertainment called *Dido*, given in the year
1583, says that in the course of it, "it *snew* an artificial kind of snow"; and in the account, given in
Sprott's "Chronicles," of the battle of Towton, we
find "and all the season it *snew*." It is only according to present usage that *snow* is an irregular verb;
and it is so because *snowed* is the vagary of some
man struggling long ago toward supposed regular-
ity. The regular conjugation of these verbs in *ow*
is to form the preterite in *ew* and the past participle
in *wn*; as *throw, threw, thrown*; and *snow, snowed,
snowed* is as irregular as *throw, throwed, throwed*
would be, or *blow, blowed, blowed*. But although
there is high authority for the phrase, "You be
blowed," I cannot but look upon it *quoad hôc* as a
corruption. *Show, sow,* and *mow* have been, like
snow, perverted from their regular conjugation.
The conjugation, according to the usage now in
vogue, is *show, showed, shown; sow, sowed, sown,*
and *mow, mowed, mown,* in which we have a preterite of one form of conjugation, and a past participle of another— a union of incongruity and irregularity quite anomalous. But the regular preterites
have not yet been quite ousted by the interlopers.
In some parts of England *mew* and *sew* are still
heard instead of *mowed* and *sowed*. In some parts
of New England, and notably in Boston, we still
hear from intelligent and not uneducated people,
He shew (pronounced *shoo*) me the way, which is

sneered at by persons who do not know that *shew* is the regular and *showed* an irregular preterite, the use of which is justified only by custom. The preterite *shew* occurs in the following interesting passage of the Wycliffite "Apology for the Lollards," written about A. D. 1375, in which there is the Anglo-Saxon preterite *strake*, of *strike :* —

"Sin Jeshu was temptid, he overcam hunger in desert, he despicid auarice in the hille, he strak ageyn veynglorie upon the temple ; that he *schew* to us that he that may ageynsey his womb [*i. e.*, deny his belly], and despice the goodis of this world and desire not veynglorie, he howith [*i. e.*, oweth, ought] to be maad Christ's vicar."

Although new verbs take the weak form, the deprived strong verbs have for two generations been reclaiming their own preterites. Some of the latter were nearly lost in the last century, when, for example, *shined* for *shone*, *drinked* for *drank*, *strived* for *strove*, *catched* for *caught*, *teached* for *taught*, and *beseeched* for *besought* were common.* And we have *digged* for *dug*, not only in the Bible and in Shakespeare, but earlier. Now good writers and speakers use the strong form of those verbs. The fact that some of them, like *teach* and *catch*, belonged in an earlier stage of the language to a mixed form of conjugation, which combined the vowel change of the strong with the terminal inflection of the weak, has no bearing on the tendency in question. It is not impossible that this restoration may go on. The participle *snown* will, I think, surely resume the place to which it has the same right as *flown* and *grown* have to theirs.

* " If parts allure thee, think how Bacon *shin'd*
　　The wisest, brightest, meanest of mankind."
　　　　　　　　　　　Pope. *Epistle IV.*

GRATUITOUS. — An affected use of this word has of late become too common. It is used in the various senses, unfounded, unwarranted, unreasonable, untrue, no one of which can be given to it with propriety. It is not thus used either by the cultivated, or by those who speak plain English in a plain way, they know not why or how, and who are content to call a spade a spade. *Gratuitous* means, without payment ; as, for instance, Professor A. delivered a gratuitous lecture. What meaning can it have, then, in a sentence like the following? "The assumption of Senator Fessenden, that a man who goes into a caucus and acts there is bound to vote in House or Senate in accordance with the decision of the caucus majority, is wholly gratuitous." It is not gratuitous ; it may be unwarranted, intolerable, unreasonable. But this word is supposed to mean something else, people don't know exactly what or why, and, therefore, because of this very ignorance, they use it. For, in language, the unknown is generally taken for the magnificent. True, dictionaries are found in which gratuitous is defined as meaning " asserted without proof or reason." But in a moment's reflection any intelligent person will see that *gratuitous* cannot mean asserted, in any manner. Dictionaries have come to be, in too many cases, the pernicious record of unreasonable, unwarranted, and fleeting usage.

GROW is even more perverted than *get* is, in vulgar use, although the misapplications of it are not so numerous. It properly means to increase, and expresses either enlargement or development. It is, on the contrary, widely used in the sense of

... or diminish. An acorn grows
... into a bird, a fish, or other ani-
... therefore normally come to be
... a passage from one state to another;
... to grow faint, to grow dark. But
... cannot be reasonably said to grow
... after the full, the moon grows smaller.
... diminishes; the opposite of growth. And
... even a change of condition is more
... expressed by *become* than by *grow*.

... I have heard objection made to the use
... "in the sense of avoid," which I notice
... such a criticism is a good example of
... treatment of language that would
... of all strength and flexibility. There is
... English than "I can't help it," which is a
... homely way of saying the matter is
... said. Aufidius, when he is told that
... of Coriolanus overshadows him, re-

> "I cannot help it now,
> ... by using means I lame the foot
> Of my design."

... of the word in this sense must be much
... Shakespeare's poetry. It is one of those
... matic uses of words (impossible in this
... French or Latin, for example) that are
... that should not be unsettled, that, in-
... be helped. There is no surer way to
... artificial style than the sitting in
... upon the use of words and phrases of
... growth, which are not at variance with
... have been used for centuries by

all sorts and conditions of men. A man who uses language as Sampson, the valiant retainer of the Capulet, bit his thumb, only when he has the law on his side, will soon come to write like an attorney drawing a lawpaper.

HELP MEET. — An absurd use of these two words, as if they together were the name of one thing — a wife — is too common. They are frequently printed with a hyphen, as a compound word; and there is your man who thinks it at once tender, respectful, biblical, and humorous to speak of his wife as his help-meet; and this merely because in Genesis we are told that woman was given to man as a help that was meet, fit, suitable for him. "I will make him an help meet for him;" not "I will make a helpmeet for him." Our biblical friend might as well call his "partner," his help-fit, or help-proper. That this protest is not superfluous, even as regards people of education, may be seen by the following sentence in a work — and one of ability, too — on the English language. "Heaven gave Eve, as a help-meet, to Adam." Here the hyphen and the change of the preposition from *for* to *to*, leave no doubt as to the nature of the blunder, which is lamentable and laughable. And yet Matthew Harrison, the author of the work in which it appears, is not only a clergyman of the Church of England, but Fellow of Queen's College, Oxford.

So a writer of some distinction in "The Galaxy," says, that "woman was designed by her Creator to be a helpmeet to man;" and we are told in a leading article in "The Tribune" on Mormon affairs, that "the saints have gone on with their wholesale marrying and sealing, and the head prophet has taken his forty-fifth help-meet."

HUMANITARIAN is very strangely perverted by a certain class of speakers and writers. It is a theological word; and its original meaning is, One who denies the godhead of Jesus Christ, and insists upon his human nature. But it is used by the people in question, whose example has infected others, as if it meant humane, and something more. Now, as the meaning of *humane* is recognizing in a common humanity a bond of kindness, good will, and good offices, it is difficult to discover what more *humanitarian*, if admitted in this sense, could mean. In brief, *humane* covers the whole ground, and *humanitarian*, used in the sense of widely-benevolent and philanthropic, is mere cant, the result of an effort by certain people to elevate and to appropriate to themselves a common feeling by giving it a grand and peculiar name. Mr. Gladstone uses this word correctly in the following passage, in which he is speaking of the Olympian system of theomythology set forth by Homer.

"Homer reflected upon his Olympos the ideas, passions, and appetites known to us all, with such a force that they became with him the paramount power in the construction of the Greek religion. This humanitarian element gradually subdued to itself all that it found in Greece of traditions already recognized, whether primitive or modern, whether Hellenic, Pelasgian, or foreign." — *Juventus Mundi*, Cl ap. VII. p. 181.

ICE-WATER, ICE-CREAM. — By mere carelessness in enunciation these compound words have come to be used for *iced-water* and *iced-cream* — most incorrectly and with a real confusion of language, if not of thought. For what is called ice-water is not made from ice, but is simply water iced, that is, made cold by ice; and ice-water might be warm, as snow-water often is. Ice-cream is unknown.

INAUGURATE is a word which might better be eschewed by all those who do not wish to talk high-flying nonsense, else they will find themselves led by bad examples into using it in the sense of begin, open, set up, establish. The Latin word, of which it is merely an Anglicized form, meant to take omens from the flight of birds and the inspection of their entrails and those of beasts, and hence was applied to the occasions at which such omens were chiefly sought. To inaugurate is to receive or induct into office with solemn ceremonies. The occasions are very few in regard to which it may be used with propriety. But we shall read ere long of cooks inaugurating the preparation of a dinner, and old Irish women inaugurating a peanut stand; as well these as inaugurating, instead of opening, a ball, or inaugurating, instead of setting up, or establishing, a business. Howells affords the following good example of the figurative use of the word: "To inaugurate a good and jovial year, I send you a morning's draught, viz., a bottle of metheglin."— *Letters*, IV. 41.

INITIATE is one of the long, pretentious words that are coming into vogue among those who would be fine. It means begin; no more, no less. It may be more elegant to say, The kettle took the initiative, than to use the homelier phrase to which our ears have been accustomed; but I have not been able to make the discovery. And I may as well here despatch a rabble of such words, all of kindred origin and pretentious seeming. Unless a man is a crown prince, or other important public functionary, it is well for him to have a house and a home, where he lives, not a place of *residence*, where he *resides*. From this let him and his household go to church or to meeting, if they like to do so; but let not the *inmates proceed* to the *sanctuary*. And if, being able and willing to do good, he gives something to the parson for the needy, let him send his cheque, and not *transmit* it. Let him oversee his household and his business, not *supervise* them. Let him reject, disown, refuse, or condemn what he does not like, but not *repudiate* it, unless he expects to cause shame, or to suffer it, in consequence of his action; and what he likes let him like or approve or uphold, but not *indorse;* and, indeed, as to indorsing, let him do as little of that as possible. I have come from pretension into the shop, and, therefore, I add, that if he is informed upon a subject, has learned all about it, knows it, and understands it, let him say so, not that he is *well posted* on it. He will say what he means, simply, clearly, and forcibly, rather than pretentiously, vulgarly, and feebly. It is noteworthy and significant that the man who will say that he is posted up on this or that subject, is the very one who will use such a foolish, useless, pretentious word as *recuperate*, instead of *recover*. Thus the Washington correspondent of a leading journal wrote that General Grant and Mr. Speaker Colfax expected to start for Colorado on the first of July, and that their trip is "for the sole purpose of recuperating their health." If the writer had omitted five of the eight words which he used to express the

Q

purpose of the travellers, and said the trip is "for health only," his sentence would have been bettered inversely as the square of the number of words omitted. But it will not do to be so very exacting as to ask people not to use many more words than are necessary, and so all that can be reasonably hoped for is, that *recuperate* may be shown to the door by those who have been weak enough to admit him. He is a mere pompous impostor. At most and best, *recuperate* means recover; not a jot more or less. *Recover* came to us English through our Norman-French kinsfolk, and sometime conquerors. It is merely their *recouvrer* domesticated in our household. They got it from the Latin *recuperare*. But why we should go to that word to make another from it, which is simply a travesty of *recover*, passes reasonable understanding. But I must have done with such minute and particular criticism of verbal extravagance, having written thus much only by way of suggestion, remonstrance, and illustration. It would be well if all such words as those of which I have just treated could be gathered under one head, to be struck off at a blow by those who would like to execute justice on them.

JEW. — A noteworthy objection has been made of late years by Jews to the common use of this designation. I remember two instances, in one of which the "Pall Mall Gazette" of London, and in the other the "New York Times," was taken to task for mentioning that certain criminals were Jews. In each case the same question was asked, in effect if not in words, Would you speak of the arrest of two Episcopalians, a Puseyite, three Presby-

terians, and a Baptist? and in each case there was
an apology made, and a promise given that the
"offence" should not be repeated. What offence
could be reasonably taken at this designation, it
would be difficult to discover. The Jews are a
peculiar people, who, in virtue of that strongly-
marked and exclusive nationality which they so
religiously cherish, have outlived the Pharaohs who
oppressed them, and who seem likely to outlive the
Pyramids on which they labored. And when they
are mentioned as Jews, no allusion is meant or made
to their faith, but to their race. A parallel case to
those complained of would be the saying that a
Frenchman or a Spaniard had committed a crime,
at which no offence is ever taken. A Jew is a Jew,
whether he holds to the faith of his fathers or leaves
it for that of Christ or of Mohammed. The complaint
rests on a confusion of the distinctions of race with
those of religion, owing to the fact that in this case the
boundaries of the race and the religion are almost
identical. But it is none the less confusion.

JEWELRY, as applied to trinkets and precious
stones, means, properly, jewels in general, not any
particular jewels. Its use in the latter sense is of
very low caste. Think of Cornelia pointing to the
Gracchi and saying, " These are my *jewelry;*" or
read thus a grand passage in the last of the Hebrew
prophets: " And they shall be mine, said the Lord
of Hosts, in that day when I make up my *jewelry !*"
The word is of very late introduction, not being in
Shakespeare, the Bible, Milton, or Johnson's Dictionary. Richardson's earliest authority for it is
Burke, who speaks of "the jewelry and goods of

India," where the two nouns are happily conjoined
For *jewelry*, like *goods*, is a general and somewhat
abstract term; and the frequent misapplication of
the former to particular articles of ornament is akin
to that of the latter to particular articles of dress,
which is pointed out on page 143. So Burke might
well have spoken of the spicery of India, but of the
spices, not the spicery, in a pudding. Jewelry is
the most important department at Tiffany's, but the
necklace, brooch, and earrings that a lady is wearing are not her jewelry, but her jewels. In brief,
such words as *spice* and *spicery*, *jewels* and *jewelry*
are not synonymes. They distinguish the particular from the general.

The termination *ry*, *ary*, or *ery* is of heterogeneous origin and of various and not easily determinable meaning. But neither its history nor its
meaning is to our present purpose; and of the
words which have this ending we are concerned
only with a class of about fifty nouns which express
primarily place, or condition, which is moral place.
Such are *belfry, library, bakery, slavery, beggary* and
the like. To this class *jewelry* belongs in one of
its senses, which may be that in which it was first
used. For the same or a similar difference obtains
between *jewelry*, jewels in general, and *jewelry*, a
place for jewels, that there is between *surgery*, an
art, and *surgery*, a place where the art is practised;
battery, the act of battering, and *battery*, a collection of battering engines; *gentry*, the condition of
gentleness in blood, and *gentry*, those who are in
that condition; *poultry*, fowls in general, and *poultry*,
the place where fowls are kept or sold. In which

sense *jewelry* was first used is not known; but as *pastry, confectionery*, and *shrubbery* were first used to express the place, the *locus in quo* of paste, confections, and shrubs, a like origin of *jewelry* is probable. This supposition receives support from the fact that the old French word *joyaulrie* was defined by Cotgrave, A. D. 1611, only as "the trade and mystery of jewelling." As *jewelry* is but an Anglicised form of *joyaulrie*, it seems likely that the former was brought in by the jewellers themselves; and that when written shop-signs took the place of symbols, *jewelry* was so used, meaning at first the art and mystery (as such words on signs do often now-a-days), but afterward by natural transition, a place where the art was practised and its productions were stored. Thence the transition would be natural to the meaning, a miscellaneous collection of such productions, or jewels in general, which, and not particular jewels, seems clearly to be its proper meaning. So we wear and use arms; but a place where arms are kept, and a collection of arms or arms in general, we call an armory.

KINSMAN. — For this hearty English word, full of manhood and warm blood, elegant people have forced upon us two very vague, misty substitutes — *relation* and *connection*. By the use of the latter words in place of the former, nothing is gained and much is lost. Both of them are very general terms. Men have relations of various kinds, and connections are of still wider distribution. Even in regard to family and friends, it is impossible to give these words exactness of meaning; whereas a man's kin, his kinsmen, are only those of his own blood. His cousin is his kinsman, but his brother-in-law is not. Yet *relation* is made to express both connections, one of blood, and the other of law. In losing *kinsman* we lose also his frank, sweet-lipped sister, *kinswoman*, and are obliged to give her place to that poor, mealy-mouthed, ill-made-up Latin interloper, *female relation*.

LEAVE. — This verb is very commonly ill used by being left without an object. Thus: Jones left this morning; I shall leave this evening. Left what? shall leave what? Not the morning or the evening, but home, town, or country. When this verb is used, the mention of the place referred to is absolutely necessary. To wind up a story with, "Then he left," is as bad as to say, then he sloped — worse, for *sloped* is recognized slang.

LIE, LAY. — There is the same difference between these two verbs that there is between *sit* and *set*. The difficulty which many persons find in using them correctly will be removed by remembering that *lay* means transitive action, and *lie*, rest. This difference between the words existed in the Anglo-Saxon stage of our language; *lay* being merely the modern form of *lecgan*, to put down, to cause to lie down, and so, to kill, — in Latin, *deponere, occidere*, — and *lie* the modern form of *licgan*, to extend along, to repose — in Latin, *occumbere*. *Lie* is rarely used instead of *lay*, but the latter is often incorrectly substituted for the former. Many persons will say, I was *laying* (lying) down for a nap: very few, She was *lying* (laying) down her shawl, or, He was lying down the law. The frequent confusion of the two verbs in this respect is strange; for almost every one of us heard them rightly used from the time when he lay at his mother's breast and until he outgrew the sweet privilege of lying in the twilight and hearing her voice mingle with his fading consciousness.

> "Hush, my babe, lie still and slumber."
> "Now I lay me down to sleep."

The tendency to the confusion of the two verbs may be partly due to the fact that the preterite of *lie* is *lay*.

> "In the slumbers of midnight the sailor boy *lay*;"

and that this expression of the most perfect rest is identical in sound with the expression of the most violent action.

> "*Lay* on, Macduff,
> And damn'd be he who first cries, Hold, enough!"

Even Byron uses *lay* incorrectly in "Childe Harold."

> "And dashest him again to earth — there let him lay."

The keeping in mind the distinction that *lay* expresses transitive action, and *lie* rest, as is shown in the following examples, will prevent all confusion of the two: —

I *lay* myself upon the bed (action). I *lie* upon the bed (rest).

I *laid* myself upon the bed (action). I *lay* upon the bed (rest).

I have *laid* myself upon the bed (action). I have *lain* upon the bed (rest).

A hen *lays* an egg (action). A ship *lies* at the wharf (rest). The murdered Lincoln *lay* in state (rest); the people *laid* the crime upon the rebels (action).

The need there is for these remarks could not be better shewn than by the following ludicrous passages in the Rules of the Senate and the Rules of the House of Representatives of the United States : —

"When a question is under debate, no motion shall be received but to adjourn, to *lie on the table*, to postpone indefinitely," &c. — *Senate Rule* 11.

"When a question is under debate, no motion shall be received but to adjourn, to *lie on the table*, for the previous question," &c. — *House Rule* 42.

And so it is all through the Manual. Now, considering the condition in which honorable gentlemen sometimes appear on the floor, if the rule had been "no motion shall be received but to lie under the table," the Manual would, in this respect, have been beyond censure. The correct uses of *lie* and *lay* are finely discriminated in the following passages from the Book of Ruth, one of the most beautiful and carefully written in our translation of the Bible : —

"And it shall be that when he *lieth* down, that thou shalt mark the place where he shall *lie*; and thou shalt go in and uncover his feet and *lay thee* down. And when Boaz had eaten and drunk, and his heart was merry, he went to *lie* down at the end of the heap of corn, and she came softly and uncovered his feet and *laid her* down. . . . and behold a woman *lay* at his feet. . . . *lie* down until the morning. And she *lay* at his feet until the morning." — Chap. III. 4, 7, 13, 14.

LIKE, AS. — The confusion of these two words, which are of like meaning, but have different functions, produces obscurity in the writing even of men who have been well educated. Of this I find an instructive and characteristic example in a London paper of high standing — "The Spectator." In an article supporting a remonstrance of the London gas-stokers against being compelled to work twelve hours a day for seven days of the week before huge fires in a temperature often of one hundred and eighty degrees, the writer, deprecating a strike by the stokers, goes on to say, "The Directors could fill their places in three hours from the docks alone; but that does not give them a right to use up Englishmen like Cuban planters." But how have directors of British gas companies the right to use up Cuban planters? and how could they use up Cuban planters? There are no answers to these inevitable questions, and the sentence as it stands is sheer nonsense. But a little thought discovers that what the writer meant to say was, that the directors had no right to use up Englishmen as Cuban planters use up negroes. His meaningless sentence was the result of the confusion of *like* and *as*, which is common with careless speakers. Thus, for instance, He don't do it like you do, instead of *as* you do. *Like* and *as* both express similarity, but the former compares things, the latter action or existence. We may say correctly, John is like James, and may express the same opinion by saying that John is such a man as James is. We may say, A's speech is like B's, or, A speaks as B does; but not A's speech is as B's, or, A speaks like B does. When *as* is correctly used, a verb is expressed or understood. The woman is as tall as the man, *i. e.*, as the man is. With *like*, a verb is neither expressed nor understood. He does his work like a man; not, like a man works.

LOAN is not a verb, but a noun. A loan is the completed act of lending, or is the thing lent. The word is the past participle of the Anglo-Saxon verb *lænan*, to lend, and therefore of course means lent. It may sound larger to some people to say that they loaned than that they lent a thousand dollars — more as if the loan were an important transaction; but that can be only because they are either ignorant or snobbish.

LOCATE is a common Americanism, insufferable to ears at all sensitive. If a gentleman chooses to say, "I guess I shall locate in Muzzouruh," meaning that he thinks he shall settle in Missouri, he has, doubtless, the right, as a free and independent citizen of the United States, to say so. Certainly *locate* and *Muzzouruh* should be left together; each in fit company. *Locate* is simply a big word for *place* or *settle;* and a man for whom those words are not ample enough, may correctly speak of locating himself, his family, or his business here or elsewhere. But *locate* without an object is suited to the use of those only who are too ignorant and too restless to settle anywhere.

LOVE and LIKE are now confused by many speakers, and even by some writers of education and repute. *Love* is often used for *like;* the latter not so often for the former. Both words express a pleasure in and a desire for the object to which they are applied; but *love* expresses this and something more — a devotion to it, an absorption in it, a readiness for sacrifice to obtain or to serve the beloved object. A man loves his children, his mother, his wife, his mistress, the truth, his country. But some men speak of loving green peas or apple pie, meaning that they have a liking for them. The dis-

tinction between the two words existed in the Anglo-Saxon stage of our language, and is one of great
value, as it enables us to discriminate between a
higher and lower preference, which differ in kind as
well as in degree. It gives us an advantage over
the French, for instance, who are obliged to use the
same word to express their affection for *La France*
and for *méringues à la crême*. We shall have
deteriorated, as well as our language, when we no
longer distinguish our liking from our loving.

MANUFACTURER is another one of the big words
that are now applied to little things. The village
shoemaker is disappearing, and shoes are made by
the hundred — not nearly so well as he used to make
them — by machinery in large factories, which have
come to be called manufactories, although manufacture is making by the hand. But although boots
are going out of fashion, one does not see a little
shoe-shop without the sign Boot Manufactory, and
the condescending announcement, Repairing done
with despatch — meaning that there shoes are made
and mended. It would be well, on the score of
comfort as well as of taste, if there were a little more
of the old skill in the gentle craft, and a little less
magniloquence. But all this is a concomitant of
"progress," and may be borne with equanimity
if the boot-manufacturer and repairer is a worthier
and a happier man than the old shoemaker and
mender.

MARRY. — There has been not a little discussion
as to the use of this word, chiefly in regard to public announcements of marriage. The usual mode
of making the announcement is — Married, John

Smith to Mary Jones. Some people having been
dissatisfied with this form, we have seen, of late
years, in certain quarters — Married, John Smith
with Mary Jones; and in others — John Smith *and*
Mary Jones. I have no hesitation in saying that
all of these forms are incorrect. We know, indeed,
what is meant by any one of them; but the same is
true of hundreds and thousands of erroneous uses of
language. Properly speaking, a man is not married to a woman, or married with her; nor are a
man and a woman married with each other. The
woman is married to the man. It is her name that
is lost in his, not his in hers; she becomes a member of his family, not he of hers; it is her life that
is merged, or supposed to be merged, in his, not his
in hers; she follows his fortunes, and takes his station, not he hers. And thus, manifestly, she has
been attached to him by a legal bond, not he to her;
except, indeed, as all attachment is necessarily mutual. But, nevertheless, we do not speak of tying
a ship to a boat, but a boat to a ship. And so long,
at least, as man is the larger, the stronger, the more
individually important, as long as woman generally
lives in her husband's house and bears his name, —
still more should she not bear his name, — it is the
woman who is married to the man. "*Nubo: viro
trador:* to be married to a man. For it is in
the woman's part only." *Lilly's Grammar.* — In
speaking of the ceremony it is proper to say that he
married her (*duxit in matrimonio*), and not that
she married him, but that she was married to him;
and the proper form of announcement is — Married,
Mary Jones to John Smith. The etymology of the

word agrees entirely with the conditions of the act which it expresses. To marry is to give, or to be given, to a husband, *mari*.

MILITATE is rarely misused, except that any use of it is misuse, and it belongs rather among words which are not words. It does not appear in Johnson's Dictionary, and it is of comparatively recent introduction. But it must have been creeping into newspaper use in Johnson's day, as it occurs in the following sentence of a passage quoted in the "Pall Mall Gazette," from the "St. James's Chronicle," of more than ninety years ago : —

"On Saturday, the Exhibition of the Royal Academy was opened for the first time, at the great room in Pall Mall. We are sorry to observe that though this institution has successfully militated against all others, and nearly swallowed them up, it seems to be on the decline."

What could be more absurd than the making of the Latin *milito* into an English word to take the place of *oppose, contend, be at variance with*, as, for instance, in the following extract from a report of the murder of a young lady in Virginia : —

"It was at first supposed that the lady had been thrown from her horse, and killed by being dragged along the ground. Several circumstances, however, militate against this supposition."

The absurdity is the greater because it is usually a supposition, or a theory, or something quite as incorporeal, that is *militated against*. The use of this word is, however, not a question of right or wrong, but one of taste. It belongs to a bad family, of which are *necessitate, ratiocinate, effectuate*, and *eventuate*, which, with their substantives, — *necessitation, ratiocination, effectuation*, and *eventuation* (which must be received with their parent verbs), —

should not be recognized as members of good English society. It is well in keeping for negro minstrels, in announcing their performances, to say, "The felicity will eventuate every evening."

OBNOXIOUS. — It were well if this word had stopped short of its last deflected meaning. An Anglicized form of the Latin *obnoxius*, its root is the verb *noceo*, to harm, hence *noxius*, harmful, and therefore *obnoxious* means, liable or exposed to harm. Until the close of the last century it was used in this sense only, as may be seen by reference to Richardson's Dictionary. Milton wrote in "Samson Agonistes" "obnoxious more to all the miseries of life," and Dr. Armstrong, in his "Art of Preserving Health," "to change obnoxious." But as a person who is obnoxious to punishment is supposed to be blameable, and as we affect that a blameable person is an offensive one, it has come to be used in the sense of offensive, particularly by those who do not know exactly what it does mean. We do not need both *offensive* and *obnoxious*, with but one meaning between them; but perhaps it is too much to hope that we may retain both, and restore to *obnoxious* its proper and useful signification.

OBSERVE. — This word, the primary meaning of which is to keep carefully, and hence to heed, has by an orderly and consistent deflection, come to mean also to keep in view, to follow with respect and deference, *e. g.*, "and let thine eyes observe my ways," and to fulfil and attend to with religious care, as to observe one's duties, to observe the Sabbath. But it is frequently used as a mere synonyme of *say*. This sense is not a derived or deflected sense, but

an extraneous one imposed upon the word by loose
usage. It is reached by uniting to the sense of
heeding or remarking, that of expressing what is
remarked, and then dropping the essential meaning
of the word in favor of that which has been imposed upon it. Used to mean heed, take note of,
keep in view, follow, attend to, fulfil, it does good
service. But in the sense of *say*, as, I observed to
him so and so, for, I said so and so to him, or,
What did you observe? for, What did you say? it
might better be left to people who must be very
elegant and exquisite in their speaking.

PARTIALLY is often used, and by educated people, for *partly*. Even Mr. Swinburne says, in his
interesting but somewhat strained and overwrought
book on William Blake, "If this view of the poem
be wholly or partially correct." But *partially*, the
adverb of *partial*, means with unjust or unreasonable bias. A view cannot be both correct and partial.
When anything is done in part, it is partly, not
partially, done. Both words are from one root;
but to confuse the two is to deprive us of the use
of one.

PARTOOK. — Say, that you *ate* your breakfast or
your dinner, not that you partook of some rolls and
butter and coffee, or of beef and pudding. Although,
if you are at breakfast when a friend comes in, you
may ask him, if you like the phrase, to sit down
·and partake of it, *i. e.*, take a part of it, share it
with you.

PARTY, ARTICLE, GOODS. — These shop words
should, in their shop sense, be left in the shop.
Mr. Bullions, in making a contract or going into

an "operation," is a party; but in his house or yours he is a person. Mrs. Bullions's Sevres vase, being on her cabinet, is no longer an elegant article, but a vase, more or less beautiful; and the material of her gown, having been honored by her possession, and shaped by her figure, is no longer goods. Mr. Sheldon's books, Mr. Low's tea, Mr. Stewart's silk, are their goods; but we neither read goods, nor drink goods; how, then, do we wear goods? Yet some people, and even women of some cultivation,— they who so rarely err in language, — will speak of the materials of their garments as goods. *Goods* means articles of personal property, regarded as property, not as personal appendages. Houses and lands are good, but not goods; nor are ships; but the cotton and the corn in the ships are goods: a stock in trade is goods; but a man's household gods are not his goods until he puts them into the market. And so Mrs. Bullions, when she is sold out, may rightly enumerate her gown among her goods, and her Sevres vase among her "articles of bigotry and virtue."

PATRON. — If you are in retail trade, don't call your customers your patrons, and send them circulars asking for a continuance of their patronage; unless you mean to say that they buy of you, not because they need what you have to sell, but merely to give you money, and that you are a dependant upon their favor. There is patronage in this country, both within and without the administration of government; and it does not imply loss of independence on the one side or arrogance on the other; but it does not consist in buying what one needs for one's own comfort or pleasure.

PELL-MELL. — This word or phrase implies a crowd and confusion (Fr. *mêlée*), and should never be applied, as it is by some speakers and some writers for the press, to an individual; as, for instance, in this sentence from a first-rate newspaper: " I rushed pell-mell out of the theatre." The writer might as well have said that he rushed out promiscuously, or that he marched out by platoons.

PERSUADED. — The use of this participle in the sense of convinced, cannot, I think, be justly condemned as vulgar or a solecism. The best usage is too strongly in its favor. "All the people will stone us, for they be persuaded that John was a prophet." *Luke* xx. 6. "I am persuaded that none of these things were hidden from him; for this thing was not done in a corner." *Acts* xxvi. 26. "This is the monkey's own giving out. She is persuaded I will marry her out of her own love and flattery, not out of my promise." *Othello* iv. 1. Nevertheless its use in this sense is a loss to the language. It deprives us of a word which expresses the result of influences gentler than those that produce conviction. A man is sometimes persuaded to act against his conviction. The root of the Latin word *suadeo*, from which the verb *persuade* is derived, has in it a suggestion of sweetness (*suavis*, sweet), hinting gentleness and allurement. *Suavium* means a sweet mouth, and so, a kiss. Women persuade when they cannot convince. It would be well if this tender and delicate sense of the word could be preserved.

PORTION is commonly misused in the sense of *part.* For instance, "A large portion of Broadway is impassable for carriages, on account of the snow and ice." A correct speaker would say, "A large part of Broadway," etc. A portion is a part set aside for a special purpose, or to be considered by itself.

PREDICATE.—Should I express to my own satisfaction the feeling which the frequent misuse of this word by people who use it because they do not know its meaning, excites in the bosoms of those who do know, and who, therefore, use it rarely, I might provoke a smile from my readers, and I certainly should smile at myself. If there is one verbal offence which more than any other justifies an open expression of contempt, it is when an honorable gentleman rises in his place and asks whether the honorable body of which he is a member "intends to predicate any action upon the statement of the honorable gentleman who has just sat down;" what he wishes to know being, if they mean to do anything or to take any steps about it, or found any action upon it. And so a well-known member of Congress addessed a letter to the New York "Times" in which he said, "You predicate an editorial on a wrong report of my speech in Brooklyn." Yet, perhaps, such a man does not forfeit all the consideration due to a vertebrate animal. *Predicate* means primarily to speak before, and, hence, to bear witness, to affirm, to declare. So the Germans call their clergymen *predicants*, because they bear witness to and declare the gospel. But in English, *predicate* is a technical word used by grammarians to express that element of the sentence which affirms something of the subject, or (as a noun) that which is affirmed. And thus action may be predicated *of* a body or an individual; but action predicated *by* a body *upon* circumstances or statements, is simple absurdity. Those persons for whom this distinction is too subtle had better confine themselves to plain English, and ask, What are you going to do about it? — language good enough for a chief justice or a prime minister.

PRESENT. — The use of this word for *introduce* is an affectation. Persons of a certain rank in Europe are presented at court; and the craving of every item of the sovereign people of this democratic republic to be presented at the Tuileries affords one of the greatest charms of the life of our minister resident near that court, and is the chief solace of his diplomatic labors. In France, every person, in being made acquainted with another, is presented, the French language not having made the distinction which is made in England between *present* and *introduce*. We present foreign ministers to the President; we introduce, or should introduce, our friends to each other. We introduce the younger to the older, the person of lower position to the person of higher, the gentleman to the lady — not the older to the younger — the lady to the gentleman. Yet some ladies will speak of being introduced to such and such a gentleman. Is this a revolutionary intimation that they set nothing by the deference which man in his strength and mastery and sexual independence pays to their weakness, their charms, and their actual or probable motherhood?

QUITE means completely, entirely, in a finished

icanism, *quite a number*, is unjustifiabl
a theatre may be quite full; and there
a pint in the cup, or quite a thousand p
theatre, and neither may be quite full.
is indefinite in its signification, and th
not be properly qualified by *quite*. Y
Hughes, whom we all think of as T
in his letter about the Oxford and Ha
race, spoke of "quite a number of you
cans."

RAILROAD DEPOT is the abominable
ally given in this country to a railway st
England they generally say *railway;* b
their companies are styled Railroad Comp
America the compound most in use is *ra*
we have the Erie Railway Company, an
like name. How the difference came abo
be difficult to discover; but *railway* is
right, and *railroad*, at least, measurab
A way is that which guides or directs
or that upon which anything moves or
Hence, we say that a ship, when she is

is always somewhat, and generally very much, wider
than the way. But the calling a way, a road, is a
venial offence compared to that of calling a station
a *dépôt*. Every *dépôt* is a station, although not in
all cases a passenger or even a freight station; but
very few stations are. *dépôts*. A *dépôt* is a place
where stores and materials are deposited for safe
keeping. A little lonely shanty, which looks like
a lodge outside a garden of cucumbers, a staging
of a few planks upon which two or three people
stand like criminals on the scaffold — to call such
places *dépôts* is the height of pretentious absurdity. But it is not less incorrect to give the same
name to the most imposing building which is used
merely as a stopping place for trains and passengers. *Station* means merely a standing, as in
the well-known passage in Hamlet, —

> "A station like the herald Mercury
> New-lighted on a heaven-kissing hill," —

and a railway station is a railway standing — a place
where trains and passengers stand for each other.
There is no justification whatever for calling such a
place a *dépôt*. And to aggravate the offence of so
doing as much as possible, the word is pronounced
in a manner which is of itself an affront to common sense and good taste — that is, neither *day-
poh*, as it should be if it is used as a French word,
nor *dee-pott*, as it should be if it has been adopted
as an English word. With an affectation of French
pronunciation as becoming as a French bonnet or
French manners to some of those who wear them,
it is called *dee-poh*, the result being a hybrid Eng-

lish-French monster, which, with the phrase of which it forms a part, should be put out of existence with all convenient despatch.

REAL ESTATE is a compound that has no proper place in the language of every-day life, where it is merely a pretentious intruder from the technical province of law. Law makes the distinction of real and personal estate; but a man does not, therefore, talk of drawing some personal estate from the bank, or going to Tiffany's to buy some personal estate for his wife; nor, when he has an interest in the national debt, does he ask how personal estate is selling. He draws money, buys jewels, asks the price of bonds. *Real estate*, as ordinarily used, is a mere big-sounding, vulgar phrase for houses and land, and, so used, is a marked and unjustifiable Americanism. Our papers have columns headed in large letters, "Real Estate Transactions," the heading of which should be Sales of Land.

RECOLLECT is used by many persons wrongly for *remember*. When we do not remember what we wish to speak of, we try to re-collect it. *Misrecollect* appeared in a leading article in the "Tribune" not long ago — a word hardly on a par with Biddy's *disremember*. We either can or cannot recollect what we do not at once remember. We cannot recollect amiss, unless it be that we recollect the facts, but not in their proper order.

RELIGION is constantly used as if it were a synonyme of *piety*, to the obliteration of a very important distinction in ethics, and the consequent misleading of many minds. Religion is a bond, according to which all who acknowledge it assume the performance of certain duties and rites having relation to a supreme being, or to a future state of existence, or to both. Piety is that motive of human action which has its spring in the desire to do good, in the reverence for what is good, and in the spontaneous respect for the claims of kindred or gratitude. There are many religions: there is but one piety. Judaism is a religion; Mohammedanism is a religion; Christianity has become a religion, within which are three religions, the Roman, the Greek, and the Protestant. And as to which of all these is the true religion, very different views are honestly held by Jews, Mohammedans, Roman Catholics, and Protestants, all of whom may be pious with the same piety. Socrates inculcated piety; but when, on his death-bed, with his last breath, he reminded his friend to sacrifice a cock to Æsculapius, he conformed to the rites of a religion for attempting to undermine which he was put to death. When Christ kept the Passover, he conformed to a right of Judaism into which he had been born and in which he had been bred. But he was put to death by the priests and the Pharisees chiefly because he taught the needlessness of that very religion. The Sermon in the Mount teaches not religion, but piety.

REMIT.—Why should this word be thrust continually into the place of *send?* In its proper sense, to send back, and hence to relax, to relinquish, to surrender, to forgive, it is a useful and respectable word; but why one man should say to another, I will remit you the money, instead of, I will send you the money, it would be difficult to say, did we not so frequently see the propensity of people to use a big word of which they do not know the meaning exactly, in preference to a small one that they have understood from childhood. This leads people, in the present instance, to speak even of sending remittances; than which it would be hard to find an absurder phrase. But it sounds, they think, much finer to say, My correspondents have not sent the remittances I expected, instead of, My friends have not sent me the money I looked for.

RESTIVE means standing stubbornly still, not frisky, as some people seem to think it does. A restive horse is a horse that balks; but horses that are restless are frequently called restive. Restiveness, however, is one sign of rebellion in horses. Thus Dryden (quoted by Johnson) : —

> "The pampered colt will discipline disdain,
> Impatient of the lash, and *restiff* to the rein."

Hence a misapprehension, by which those who did not understand the word, were led to a complete reversion of meaning.

REVEREND and HONORABLE. — The editor of a western newspaper has asked me the following question : "In speaking of a clergyman — not a Catholic or an Episcopalian — is it proper to say *the* Rev. John Jones, for instance, or, simply, Rev. John Jones? If it is proper to say *the* Rev. John Jones, why is it not proper to say *the* Captain Tom Robinson, or *the* General Robert Smith?"

The article is absolutely required. The sect to which the clergyman belongs does not affect the question. Between *Reverend* and *Captain* or *General* there is no analogy. The latter are names of offices; they are titles pertaining of right to the persons who hold those offices. *Reverend* is not the name of an office, nor is it a title, and it belongs to no one of right. Clergymen are styled Reverend by a courtesy which supposes that every man set apart for his special sanctity and wisdom as an example, a guide, and an instructor, is worthy of reverence. So members of Congress are styled Honorable, but by mere courtesy. But in Congress does a member ever rise and say, "I heartily agree with the views which honorable gentleman from —— has just laid before the House. Honorable gentleman could not have presented them with greater force or clearness"? The most unlettered and careless speaker in the House of Representatives would say *the* honorable gentleman. *Honorable* and *Reverend* are not even courtesy titles; they are adjectives, mere epithets applied at first (the one to men of importance, and the other to clergymen) with special meaning, but afterward from custom only. The impropriety of omitting the article can be clearly shown by a transposition of the epithet and the name, which does not affect the sense. For instance, Henry Ward Beecher, the Reverend; Charles Sumner, the Honorable; not Henry Ward Beecher, Reverend; Charles Sumner, Honorable. But the transposition which has this effect in the case of epithets has none in that of official titles; thus: Winfield Hancock, Major-General, Samuel Nelson, Judge, which, indeed, are very common modes of writing such names and titles. The omission of the article has been the cause of a misapprehension on the part of many persons as to the name of the ecclesiastical historian to whom we owe so much of our knowledge of our Anglo-Saxon forefathers in England. He was styled by his successors the Venerable Bede; but this having been written in Latin *Venerabilis Beda*, he has often been mentioned by British writers as Venerable Bede, which some readers have taken, as a whole, for his name. (I have more than once heard the question mooted among intelligent people.) He was merely called Bede, the venerable; but the Latin has no article; and hence the mistake of calling him Venerable Bede. We may correctly speak of a distinguished prelate who recently died as Bishop Hopkins, as the Right Reverend Bishop Hopkins, or as the Right Reverend John Henry Hopkins, Bishop (not *the* Bishop) of Vermont. But if we speak of the officer without mention of the individual, even although we give the courtesy epithet, we should use the article before the title, as, the Right Reverend the Bishop of Vermont; and so, in speaking of a military officer by name, the article is not admissible; but if we speak of the officer without mentioning the name, the article is required: thus, Major-General Meade, Commanding-in-Chief, but, the Major-General Commanding-in-Chief.

SAMPLE ROOM. — This confluent eruption has appeared on sign-boards all over New York during the last few years. Thus used, it means, not a room in which samples are displayed, but simply a place at which spirits and beer may be drunk at a bar, and is the fruit of a nauseous attempt to sweeten *bar-room*, *ale-house*, and *tavern*. Its history is a very disgusting one. It first appeared in small, shame-faced letters over the doors of partitions put up across the back part of certain so-called wholesale wine and liquor stores; and it told of men sponging up liquor by samples until it became necessary to say that if they "sampled" they must pay; and then of the self-styled wholesale wine merchant, who was above keeping a bar, finding that it was profitable as well as gentlemanly to ask acquaintances to "sample" his liquors; and of this sham's being kept up until it became necessary to hide the multitudinous "samplers" and the multifarious "sampling" from the public and the police by a screen or partition; and, finally, of the spread of this "gentlemanly" way of keeping a tippling house; so that the very sight of the word is enough to make one's gorge rise. Very worthy and well-behaved, and even intelligent, men do keep bars and taverns; but if they do, let them say so. When I see *sample-room* over a door, I feel a respect for a bar-room, and as if I could take to my heart a man who owns that he keeps a grog-shop.

SECTION. — An unpleasant Americanism for neighborhood, vicinity, quarter, region; as, for instance, our section, this section of country. It is western, of course, but has crept eastward against the tide. It is the result of the division of the unoccupied lands at the West, for purposes of sale, into sections based upon parallels of latitude and longitude. Emigrant parties would buy and settle upon a quarter-section of land; and they continued talking about their section even after they had homes, and neighborhoods, towns, villages, and counties; a fashion which, even with them, should have had its day, and in which they should not be imitated.

SIT (one of the verbs a confusion in the use of
parts of which has previously been remarked upon)
is confounded with another word, *set*, as most of my
readers well know. The commoner mistakes upon
this point I pass by; but some prevail among people who fancy that they are very exquisite in their
speaking. Most of us have heard and laughed at
the story of the judge who, when counsel spoke of
the setting of the court, took him up with, "No,
brother, the court sits; hens set." But I fear that
some of us have laughed in the wrong place. Hens
do not *set*; they sit, as the court does, and frequently
to better purpose. No phrase is more common than
"a setting hen," and none more incorrect. A hen
sits to hatch her eggs, and, therefore, is a sitting
hen. *Sit* is an active, but an intransitive verb —
a very intransitive verb — for it means to put one's
self in a position of rest. *Set* is an active, transitive verb — very active and very transitive — for it
means to cause another person or thing to sit, willy-
nilly. A schoolma'am will illustrate the intransitive
verb by sitting down quietly, and then the transitive
by giving a pupil a setting down which is anything
but quiet. This setting down is metaphorical, and
is borrowed from the real, physical setting-down
which children sometimes have, much to their astonishment. The principal parts of one of these
verbs are *sit, sat, sitten;* but of the other, the present, preterite, and the past participle are in form the
same, *set.* Many persons forget this, and use *sat*
as the preterite of *set*, thus: She *sat* her pitcher
down upon the ground. But as we read in our
translation of Matthew's Gospel (chap. xxi.), it was

that Christ should come "sitting upon ... and, therefore, his disciples took a colt and ... him thereon." On the other hand, some ... the preterite of *set* for that of *sit*, *e. g.*, ... and *set* down; while others have invented ... saving monosyllable for both these hard ... verbs. For instance, "I went to meet him ... office, sharp on time, and *sot* (sat) down and ... for him, and sot, and sot, and sot; and when ... in, he sot (set) me down that his time was ... because he'd sot (set) his watch that morning ... City Hall clock." I have heard the word ... by an estimable and not unintelligent mer-... As far as the poultry-yard is concerned, the ... sets the hen, but the hen *sits*. The use of ... word for the latter in this case is so com-... and I have heard it defended so stoutly by ... people, that I shall not only refer to ... dictionaries those of my readers who care to ... them, but cite the following examples in

... partridge *sitteth* on eggs and hatcheth them not, etc.
Jeremiah, xvii. 11. *Tr.* 1611.

... birds *sit* brooding in the snow.
Love's Labor's Lost, iv. 3.

Thou from the first
... present, and with mighty wings outspread,
Dove-like *sat'st* brooding on the vast abyss,
And mad'st it pregnant.
Paradise Lost, I. 21.

... the nominative in a sentence requiring *sit*
... the subject of the action, the word is *set*;
... nominative is not the subject, the word
... *sit*, which, like most of its kind, is su-

perfluous to those who can understand it, and useless to those who cannot.

Sit and *set*, unlike *lie* and *lay*, which have the
same relations with each other as the former have,
and are subject to a like confusion, have no tenses
or participles which are the same in form.

There is one peculiarity in the use of the two former which is worthy of attention. We say that a
man rises and sits; but that the sun rises and sets.
For this use of *set*, which has prevailed since English was a language, and from which it would
require an unprecedented boldness to deviate, there
is no good reason. It is quite indefensible. *Set*
is no part of the verb *sit;* and as to setting, the sun
sets nothing. For we do not mean to say that he
sets himself down — an expression which would not
at all convey our apprehension of the gradual descent and disappearance of the great light of the
world. If either of these words be used, we should,
according to reason and their meaning, say the sun
sits, the sun is sitting.

I had supposed that this application of the verb
set to the sinking of the sun was inexplicable as
well as unjustifiable, when it occurred to me that in
the phrase in question *set* might be a corruption of
settle. On looking into the matter, I found reason
for believing that my conjecture had hit the mark.
In tracing this corruption, it should be first observed
that the Anglo-Saxon has both the verb *sittan* (sit)
and *settan* (set). In coming to us, these words
have not changed their signification in the least;
they have only lost a termination. Indeed, it is only
the absence or the presence of this termination that

makes them in the one case English, and in the
other Anglo-Saxon. They have been used straight
on, with the same signification by the same race for
at least fifteen hundred years. But when that race
spoke Anglo-Saxon, they said, neither the sun sets
nor the sun sits, but the sun settles, and sometimes
the sun sinks; and his descent they called not sunset or the sun setting, but the sun settling. Thus
the passage in Mark's Gospel, i. 32, which is
given thus in our Bible, "And at even, when the
sun did *set*, they brought him all that were dis-
eased," etc., appears thus in the Anglo-Saxon version, "Soþlice ða hit was œfen geworden ða sunne
to *setle* eode." That is, Verily when it was evening made when the sun to settle went. In Luke's
account of the same matter our version has "Now
when the sun was *setting;* but the Anglo-Saxon
"Soþlice ða sunne *asah*"—Verily when the sun
sank down. And the Mæso-Gothic version has
"Miþþanei þan sagq sunno"—when the sun sagg-
ed, or sank down. In Genesis, xv. 17, "And it
came to pass when the sun went down," we have
again in the Anglo-Saxon version "þa þa sunne
eode to *setle*"—when the sun went to settle; and
in Deuteronomy, xi. 30, "by the way where the sun
goeth down," is in the Anglo-Saxon Bible "be þam
wege þe lið to sunnen *setlgange*"—by the way
that lieth to the sun settle-going, or settling; and
in Psalms, cxiii. 3, "From the rising of the sun
unto the going down of the same," in Anglo-Saxon
"From sunnan uprine oð to *setlgange*"—From sun's
uprising even to settle-going. The word *setl* in all
these passages, is not a verb, but a noun; and the

exact meaning in each case is that the sun was going seat-ward — toward his seat. All the stronger, therefore, is the conclusion that it is right to say that the sun sits or takes his seat, and wrong to say that he sets: the clear distinction between the two Anglo-Saxon verbs *sittan*, to sit, to go down, and *settan*, to place in a seat, to fix, being remembered.

This conclusion receives yet other support from the facts that, according to Herbert Coleridge's Glossary, *sunrising* appears in the English of the thirteenth century, but *sunset* is not found, and that in the passages above cited, and others in which the same fact is mentioned, the earlier English versions of the Bible do not use *set*. Wycliffe's, made about A. D. 1385, Tyndale's, A. D. 1536, Coverdale's, A. D. 1535, and the Geneva version A. D. 1557, have either "when the sun went down," or "when the sun was down." It is not until we reach the Rheim's version, A. D. 1582, that we find "in the evening, after sunset." But in Thomas Wilson's "Arte of Rhetorike," A. D. 1567 (first published in 1553), I find "All men commonly more rejoice in the sonne rising then thei do in the sonne setting" (fol. 35, *b*.). It would therefore seem as if the corruption of *setle* into *set* had been handed down through common speech, and perhaps by vulgar writers, from the time when our language passed from its Anglo-Saxon to its so-called early English period, but that *sunset* was not used by scholars until the middle of the sixteenth century.

I offer, not dogmatically, but yet with a great degree of confidence, this explanation of our singular use of the verb *set* to express the descent of the sun to the horizon; warning my readers at the same time that the definitions of *set* in dictionaries, as meaning to go down, to decline, to finish a course, all rest upon the presence, or rather the supposed presence, of this word in the old and common phrase *sunset*, which is really an abbreviation of *sun-settling*, the modern form of *sunnan-setlgang*.

SOCIABLE, SOCIAL. — We are in danger of losing a fine and valuable distinction between these words. This is to be deplored, and, if possible, prevented. The desynonymizing tendency of language enriches it by producing words adapted to the expression of various delicate shades of meaning. But the promiscuous use of two words each of which has a meaning peculiar to itself, by confounding distinctions impoverishes language, and deprives it at once of range and of power. The meaning of *sociable* is, fitted for society, ready for companionship, quick to unite with others — generally for pleasure. *Social* expresses the relations of men in society, communities, or commonwealths. Hence, social science. But there is no sociable science, although some French women are said to make *société* an art. A man who is an authority upon social matters may be a very unsociable person. Those who are inclined to like that strange kind of entertainment called a social surprise, the charm of which is in the going in large bodies to a friend's house unannounced and unexpected, should at least call their performance a sociable surprise; for it must be the crucial test of the sociability of him to whom it is administered. It may possibly tend to a pleas-

11

ant sociability among those whose taste it suits; but its social tendency is quite another matter.

SPECIAL is a much overworked word, it being loosely used to mean great in degree, also peculiar in kind, for the particular as opposed to the general, and for the specific as opposed to the generic. Sometimes it seems to express a union or resultant of all these senses. This loose and comprehensive employment of the word is very old, at least six hundred years; and yet it cannot but be regarded as a reproach to the language. But to point out the fault is easier than to suggest a remedy, other than the dropping of the first and third uses, in which it is at least superfluous.

SPLENDID suffers from indiscriminate use, as *awful* does, but chiefly on the part of those whom our grandfathers were wont to call, in collective compliment, the fair. A man will call some radiant beauty a splendid woman; but a man of any culture will rarely mar the well-deserved compliment of such an epithet by applying it to any inferior excellence. But with most women nowadays everything that is satisfactory is splendid. A very charming one, to whose self the word might have been well applied, regarded a friend of mine with that look of personal injury with which women meet minor disappointments from the stronger sex, because he did not agree, *avec effusion*, that a hideous little dog lying in her lap was " perfectly splendid; " and once a bright, intelligent being in muslin at my side predicated perfect splendor of a slice of roast beef which was rapidly disappearing before her, any dazzling qualities of which seemed to me to be due to her own

sharp appetite. The sun is splendid, a tiara of diamonds may be splendid, poetry may be metaphorically splendid. But all good poetry is not splendid;
for instance, Gray's "Elegy." The use of *splendid*
to express very great excellence is coarse.

STATE is much misused in the sense of say.
State, from *status*, perfect participle of the Latin
verb meaning to stand, means to set forth the condition under which a person, or a thing, or a cause,
stands. A bankrupt is called upon to state his condition, to make a statement of his affairs. But if a
man merely says a thing, do let us say merely that
he says it.

STORM is misused by many people, who say that
it is storming when they mean merely that it is
raining. A storm is a tumult, a commotion of the
elements; but rain may fall as gently as mercy.
There are dry storms. Women sometimes storm
in this way; with little effect, however, except upon
very weak brethren. But the gentle rain from a
fair woman's eyes, few human creatures, not of her
own sex, can resist. A dry storm not unfrequently
passes off in rain. Hence, perhaps, the confusion
of the two words.

TEA is no less or more than tea; and while we
call strong broth beef-tea, or a decoction of camomile flowers camomile tea, we cannot consistently
laugh at Biddy when she asks whether we will have
tay tay or coffee tay.

TRANSPIRE. — Of all misused words, this verb is
probably the most perverted It is now very commonly used for the expression of a mode of action
with which it has no relations whatever. Words

may wander, by courses more or less tortuous, so far from their original meaning as to make it almost impossible to follow their traces. An instance of this, well known to students of language, is the word *buxom*, which is simply bow-some or bough-some, *i. e.*, that which readily bows or yields, like the boughs of a tree. No longer ago than when Milton wrote, *boughsome*, which, as *gh* in English began to lose its guttural sound, — that of the letter *chi* in Greek, — came to be written *buxom*, meant simply yielding, and was of general application.

> " and, this once known, shall soon return,
> And bring ye to the place where thou and Death
> Shall dwell at ease, and up and down unseen
> Wing silently the buxom air." — *Paradise Lost*, II. 840.

But aided, doubtless, as Dr. Johnson suggests, by a too liberal construction of the bride's promise in the old English marriage ceremony, to be "obedient and buxom in bed and board," it came to be applied to women who were erroneously thought likely to be thus yielding ; and hence it now means plump, rosy, alluring, and is applied only to women who combine those qualities of figure, face, and expression. *Transpire*, however, has passed through no such gradual modification of meaning. It has not been modified, but forced. Its common abuse is due solely to the blunder of persons who used it although they were ignorant of its meaning, at which they guessed. *Transpire* means to breathe through, and so to pass off insensibly. The identical word exists in French, in which language it is the equivalent of our *perspire*, which also means to breathe through, and so to pass off insensibly. The Frenchman says, *J'ai beaucoup transpiré* — I have much perspired. In fact, *transpire* and *perspire* are etymologically as nearly perfect synonymes as the nature of language permits; the latter, however, has, by common consent, been set apart in English to express the passage of a watery secretion through the skin, while the former is properly used only in a figurative sense to express the passage of knowledge from a limited circle to publicity. Here follow examples of the proper, and the only proper or tolerable use of this word. The first, which is very characteristic and interesting, is from Howell's Letters : —

"It is a true observation that among other effects of affliction, one is to try a friend; for those proofs that were made in the shining, dazzling sunshine are not so clear as those which break out and transpire through the dark clouds of adversity." — L. 6, 55.

The next three, because I have had such frequent occasion to censure severely the general use of words in newspapers, I have pleasure in saying, are from the columns of New York journals : —

"Who the writer of this pamphlet was, who, four years before the great uprising in 1848, saw so clearly, and spoke so pointedly, has, to our knowledge, never transpired."

"After twelve o'clock last night it transpired that the Massachusetts delegation had voted unanimously in caucus to present the name of General Butler for Vice-President."

"It transpired Monday that the 'Boston Daily Advertiser' has been recently sold to a new company for something less than two hundred and fifty thousand dollars."

The following very marked and instructive example of the correct use of *transpire* is — marvellous to relate — from one of the telegrams of the Associated Press : —

"At a quarter past four o'clock Judge Fisher received a communication from the jury, and he sent a written reply. The subject of the correspondence has not transpired."

The next is from the London "Times:"—

"The Liberals of Nottingham, England, have selected Lord Amberley and Mr. Handel Cossham as their candidates. It has not yet transpired who the conservative candidate will be. The election, the first after the vote on the Reform bill, will be of great importance."

But the same number of the same paper furnishes, in the report of a speech by a member of Parliament (I neglected to note by whom), the following example of the misuse of the word in the sense of occur, take place. The insurrection in Jamaica was the subject of discussion.

"So that, notwithstanding that the population of the Island was 450,000, it was stated that only 1,500 voted for the members of the Legislature. The whole thing had culminated in the horrors and the atrocities which had lately transpired there, and which he was obliged to believe had thrown discredit upon the English government and the English character in every other country in the world."

So I find it said, in a prominent New York newspaper, that "the Mexican war transpired in the year 1847." The writer might as well — and, considering the latitude in which the battles were fought, might better — have said that the Mexican war perspired in the year 1847. The most monstrous perversion of the word that I have ever met with — than which it would seem that none could be more monstrous — is in the following sentences, the first and second from journals of the highest position, the last from a volume of which tens of thousands have been sold, and which aspires to the dignity of history:—

" Before this can be finished, years may transpire; indeed, it may take as long to complete the West Bank Island Hospital as it has taken to erect the new Court-house."

" The police drill will transpire under shelter to-day in consequence of the moist atmosphere prevailing."

" More than a century was allowed to transpire before the Mississippi was revisited by civilized man."

To any person who has in mind the meaning of the word, the idea of years and centuries and police drills transpiring, is ridiculous.

There is a very simple test of the correct use of *transpire*. If the phrase *take place* can be substituted for it, and the intended meaning of the sentence is preserved, its use is unquestionably wrong; if the other colloquial phrase, *leak out*, can be put in its place, its use is correct.

This is illustrated in the following sentence : —

"An important cabinet meeting was held to-day; but what took place did not transpire." *

* The writer of an article in the "Methodist Quarterly Review" thus boldly advocates the misuse of *transpire*, and flouts those who oppose it : —

" *We have as one word to express the regular coming into existence of an event.* . . . Now, there is a word which is fresh and clear, which is not very irrevocably appropriated to any other idea, and which by popular healthy instinct is aspiring to occupy the blank spot. The word is *transpire*. 'O, no,' exclaim the effeminates, 'that word must not designate the *taking place* of an event; it signifies *to become known*.' It is of no use to tell these imbeciles that the latter meaning is itself little known, little used, and little needed, while the want it is called to supply is a startling defect in the entire language. You may supply reasons, but you cannot supply brains. Your only method is to use the needed word in the needing place, and leave the shrieking pedant to his spasms."

To this the answer is, first, that *transpire* is misused to express not the regular coming into existence of an event, but the most hap-hazard accidents of daily life, as any one may see; next, the flat contradiction of the assertion that the meaning, to become known, is little known, little used, and little needed. Of the contrary, examples are given above, taken from newspapers of the day; and here follow others, recently taken from the minor news reports of two New York journals, the "Times" and the "Tribune," which, although they may sometimes have been written by imbeciles, it would seem are rarely or never from the pens of pedants : —

" Nothing new transpired concerning the steamer Euterpe yesterday. Workmen were engaged in filling her with a quantity of hay," &c.

THOSE SORT. — Many persons who should, and
who, perhaps, do, know better, are in the habit of
using this incongruous combination, *ex gr*., those sort
of men, instead of that sort of men. The pronoun
(so-called) belongs to *sort*, and not to *men*. It would
be as proper to say, those company of soldiers.

TRUISM is often used for *truth*, as if such use
were more elegant and scholarly; whereas it is the
reverse. For instance, take the following sentence
from a leading article in a high-class New York
newspaper : —

"That the rents charged for tenements on the lower part of
this island are higher than men of moderate means can afford
to pay, is a palpable truism."

It is no such thing. The writer meant to say that

"It transpires that the Gould-Fisk control of the Bank is not to be consummated
until January, although Jay Gould is already a director."

"Hannah Baker, a child nine years old, was kidnapped near her home, in Park
Avenue, by Catharine Turner, and taken to New York, where it transpired that the
child disowned the woman as her mother," &c.

"Soon after the funeral, however, it transpired that the supposed dead and buried
woman was alive and in good health, the fact being made certain to her daughters by
her actual, living presence."

And see the following passage from the very preamble to Resolutions passed at a
political meeting within the erudite precincts of Tammany Hall, on the evening of
March 29, 1870 : —

"Whereas, A call for a meeting of the General Committee, to be held in Tammany
Hall this evening, has been issued, having for its ostensible purpose the consideration
of measures of legislation relating to this city, but it has transpired that this movement
has originated with Mr. John Morrissey and his prominent associates," &c., &c.

The contemporary London press would also furnish numberless instances like the
following : —

"A meeting of the Tory party was called by Mr. Disraeli, on Wednesday, at Lord
Lonsdale's house. The meeting was fully attended, — Lord Stanley, however, being
absent, — and no report of its proceedings was allowed to transpire." — *Spectator*,
April 17, 1869.

A page of such examples might be taken even from newspapers published within a
week of the publication of the 'Methodist Quarterly's' assertion, quoted above. The
truth is, that this word seems to be used in its proper sense by all who know its
meaning, in which sense it is valuable, and occupies a place which can be filled by
no other

his proposition was plainly true; but to say so simply would have been far too simple a style for him. He must write like a moralist or a philosopher, according to his notion of their writing. A truism is a self-evident truth; *a* truth, not merely the truth in the form of a true assertion of fact. Thus: The sun is bright, is not a truism: it is a self-evident fact, but not a self-evident truth. But, All men must die, Youth is weak before temptation, are truisms; *i. e.*, self-evident, or generally admitted truths.

ULT., INST., PROX.— These contractions of *ultimo*, *instante*, and *proximo*, should be used as little as possible by those who wish to write simple English. It is much better to say *last month*, *this month*, *next month*. The contractions are convenient, however; and much must be sacrificed to convenience in the use of language. But from the usage in question a confusion has arisen, of which I did not know until I was requested to decide a dispute whether, in a letter written, for instance, on the 15th of September, "the 10th ult.," would mean the last 10th, *i. e.*, the 10th of September, or the 10th of the last month, *i. e.*, the 10th of August, and "the 20th prox." would mean the next 20th or the 20th of the next month, October. *Ult.* and *prox.* are contractions of *ultimo* and *proximo*, which are the ablative cases of *ultimus* and *proximus*, and mean, not the last and the next, but *in* the last and *in* the next —what? The last and the next month. *Ultimo* and *proximo* are themselves contractions of *ultimo mense*, in the last month, and *proximo mense*, in the next month; so that "the 10th ult." means the 10th day in the last month, and "the 20th

prox." the 20th day in the next month.   Instant is *instante mense*, the month now standing
before us.   We do a thing instantly, or on the instant, when we do it at the present moment, the
moment standing before us.   But I submit it to the
good sense of my readers that it is better to write
August 10th and October 20th, than to write 10th
ult. and 20th prox., and that it is nearly as expe-
ditious and convenient.

UTTER. — This word is merely *outer* in another
form.   The outer, or utter, darkness of the New
Testament is the darkness of a place completely
outside of the realm of light.   To utter is merely to
put out, to put forth, or outside of the person uttering.   Utter nonsense is that which is entirely outside
the pale of reason.   This outwardness is the essence
of the word in all its legitimate uses, and in all its
modifications.   But some people seem to think that
because, for instance, utter darkness is perfect darkness, and utter nonsense absolute nonsense, therefore utter means perfect, absolute, complete.   Thus,
in a criticism in a literary paper upon a great picture, it is said of the color that "the effect is that of
utter harmony;" and in one of Mrs. Edwards's
novels, she says of a girl and a man, "Nelly's
nature fitted into his nature utterly."   This is sheer
nonsense, unless we agree to deprive *utterly* of its
proper meaning, and make it do superfluous duty
as a mere synonyme of *complete* and *perfect*, which
would be by just so much to impoverish and confuse
our language.   The use of this word in the sense
of absolutely is not, however, of recent or of popular origin.   Witness the following examples : —

" Full cunningly these lords two he grette,
    And did his message, asking him anon
    If that they were broken, or aught wo begon,
    Or had need of lodesmen or vitaile,
    For socoure they shoulde nothing feile,
    For it was *utterly* the queenes will."
                Chaucer, Legend of Good Women, 1. 1460.

" It is not necessary that Traditions and Ceremonies be in all places *utterly* alike."
    Thirty-Nine Articles of the Church of England, Art. 34.

VENTILATE. — Many persons object to the use cf this word in the sense of to bring into discussion, on the ground that it is a neologism. This use, of course, is metaphorical; and while we may say that a man airs his notions at a public meeting or in a newspaper, I am not prepared to defend the good taste of saying that he ventilates them. But this use of *ventilate* is not a neologism, as appears by this passage in a state paper of the time of Henry the Eighth, quoted by Froude: "Nor shall it ever be seen that the king's cause shall be ventilated or decided in any place out of his own realm."

VERACITY. — It is newspaper English to say, as nowadays is often said, that a man is "a man of truth and veracity." *Veracity* is merely an Anglicized Latin synonyme of truthfulness. Truth *and* veracity is a weak pleonasm. But *veracity* is propery applied to persons, truth to things. A story is or is not true; a man is or is not veracious — if truthful is too plain a word. We may doubt the truth of a story because we doubt the veracity, or, better, the truthfulness, of the teller.

VICINITY. — This word is subject to no perversion of sense that I have observed; but it is very often incorrectly and vulgarly used without the possessive pronoun necessary to define it and cause it to express a thing instead of a thought. Thus : New York and vicinity, instead of New York and its vicinity. With equal correctness and good taste we might say, New York and neighborhood; which no one, I believe, would think of doing. This error has arisen from the frequent occurrence of such phrases as, this city and vicinity, *i. e.*, this city and this vicinity, *this* being understood. So we may say, this village and neighborhood. When a pronoun is used before a common noun, as, this town, this village, it need not be repeated after the conjunction which unites the noun to *vicinity*. But otherwise a pronoun is required before *vicinity*, just as one is before *neighborhood*, which, in most cases in which *vicinity* is used, is the better, as well as the shorter, word.

VULGAR, the primitive meaning of which is *common*, and which, from its frequent qualification of the conduct and the speech of the vulgar, came in natural course, to mean low, rude, impolite, is often misused in the sense of immodest. A lady not without culture said to another of a third, " She dresses very low ; but as she has no figure, it doesn't look vulgar ; " meaning, by the feminine malice of her apology, that it did not look immodest. The gown was perhaps low enough (at the top) to be vulgar, if material lowness were vulgarity ; but only that which is metaphorically low is vulgar.

WIDOW WOMAN. — Here is an unaccountable superfluity of words; for it would seem that the most ignorant of those persons who use the phrase must know that a widow is necessarily a woman.

It would be as well to say a female lady, or a she cow. The error is hardly worth this notice; but the antiquity of the word *widow* in exactly the same sense in which it is now used, the remoteness of its origin, and the vast distance which it has travelled through ages without alteration of any kind, — except as to the pronunciation of *v* and *w*, which are continually interchanging, not only in various languages but in the same language, — make it an unusually interesting word. How many thousand years this name for a bereaved woman has been used, by what variety of nations, and over what extent of the earth's surface, it would not be easy to determine. Our Anglo-Saxon forefathers used it a thousand years ago in England and in North Germany; they spelled it *widuwe* or *wudewe*. The Mæso-Goths, in the fourth century, for the same thing used the same word—*widowo*. But nearly a thousand years before that time it was used by the Latin people, who wrote it *vidua*. And yet again, a thousand years and more backward, on the slopes of the Himalayas a bereaved wife was called a widow; for in the Sanscrit of the Rig Veda we find the word *vidhavâ*.* Pronounce the *v* as *w*, and see how simply each stricken woman has taken this word from her stricken sister and passed it on from lip to lip as they were bearing our fathers in the weary pilgrimage of war and suffering through untold ages from what are now the remotest bounds of civilization. The Sanscrit *vidhavâ* is merely the

---

* I give this on the authority of Max Müller. My having in Sanscrit, like Orlando's beard, is a younger brother's revenue—what I can glean from the well-worked fields of my elders and betters.

word *dhavâ*, a man, and *vi*, without; so that the word at its original formation meant simply a woman left without a man, just as it does to-day; and it has remained all these ages materially unchanged both in sound and meaning.

Widow is one of the very few words of which the feminine form is the original; for owing to the traits, functions, and relations of the sexes, among no people would a peculiar name be first given to a man who was deprived of a woman. It would be only after the condition of widowhood had been long recognized, and conventional usages had narrowed and straitened the sexual relations, that it would enter the mind of a people to give *widow* its masculine companion-word. It must be admitted that in English this has been done clumsily. *Widower* is a poor word, which should mean one who widows, not who is widowed. Its etymology seems uncertain; for it can hardly be a modern form of *widuwa*, which is given by Morris (*English Accidence*, p. 82), but not by Bosworth, as the masculine of *widuwe*. But finely formed and touching as the original feminine word is, it was inevitable that the preposterousness of forming upon it a masculine counterpart should produce monstrosity. The same difficulty did not occur in Latin; for although it would seem that the word must have come into that language in its original feminine form, yet, as the Latin had gender, all that was necessary was to give *vidua* a masculine termination, and it became *viduus*, or a neuter, and it became *viduum*. It was an adjective in Latin, as doubtless it was first in Sanscrit, and it became a noun also, like many adjectives in most languages.

By metaphor it came to mean deprived, deprived
of anything.   But until recently *deprived* was given
in Latin lexicons as its primary meaning, and deprived of wife or husband was given as its secondary and dependent meaning,—preposterously, as
we have seen.   It must have been applied first to
women, then to men, and last to things in general,
which is the natural manner of growth in language.
Men do not conceive an abstract idea and then project their thoughts into infinite space in search of a
name for the new born ; but having names for particular and concrete objects, they transfer, modify,
and combine these names to designate new things
and new thoughts.*

WITNESS. — This word is used by many persons as a big synonyme of *see*, with absurd effect.
"I declare," an enthusiastic son of Columbia says,
as he gazes upon New York harbor, "this is the most
splendid bay I ever witnessed."   In which exclama-
tion, by the by, if the speaker has much acquaintance with bays, the taste is worthy of the English.
Witness, an English or Anglo-Saxon word, is from
witan, to know, and means testimony from personal knowledge, and so the person who gives such
testimony ; and hence the verb *witness*, to be able
to give testimony from personal knowledge.   A
man witnesses a murder, an assault, a theft, the
execution of a deed, or of the sentence of a felon.
He witnesses any act at the performance of which
he is present and observing.   "Bear witness,"

* In two out of seventy instances in the English Bible a widow is called a
widow woman ; the reason being, as I am informed by a friend who is, what I
am not, a Hebrew scholar, that in those cases the original reads " a woman a
widow."

say we, "that I do thus." But we cannot witness a thing : no more a bay or a range of mountains than a poodle dog or a stick of candy.

And yet, if mere ancient usage and high authority could justify any form of speech, this would not be without an approach to such justification, as will be seen by the following sentence in Wycliffe's "Apology for the Lollards : " —

"Forsoþ it is an horrible þing þat in sum kirkes is witnessid marchaundis to haue place." — p. 50, *Ed. Camd. Soc*

SQUEAMISH CANT.

Persons of delicacy so supersensitive that they shrink from plain words, and fear to call things by their names, who think evil of the mothers that bore them, and, if men, of the women who have brought them children, and who are so prurient that they prick up their ears and blush at any implied distinction of sex in language, even in the name of a garment, would do well to avoid the rest of this chapter, which cannot but give them offence. But that would leave me only the well-bred and modest among my readers; and they are they who least need counsel in the use of language.

CHEMISE. — How and why English women came to call their first under-garment a *chemise*, it is not easy to discover. For in the French language the word means no more or less than shirt, and its meaning is not changed or its sound improved by those who pronounce it *shimmy*. Of the two names *shirt* and *smock*, given at a remote period to this garment, the first was common, like *chemise* in

French, to both sexes; *e. g.*, the following passage from Gower's "Confessio Amantis:"—

> "Jason his clothes on him cast,
>   And made him redy right anon,
>   And she her *sherte* did upon
>   And cast on her a mantel close,
>   Withoute more, and than arose."

By common consent *shirt* came to be confined to the man's garment, and *smock* to the woman's, to express which it was generally, if not universally, used until the middle of the last century. It is now so used by some English women of high rank and breeding, and unimpeachable in propriety of conduct, while by the large majority it is now thought coarse — why, is past conjecture. The place of *smock* was taken and held for a time by *shift* — a very poor word for the purpose, the name of the act of changing being applied to the garment changed. As *smock* followed *shirt*, so *shift* has followed *smock;* and women have returned to *shirt* again, merely giving it its French name. From this it is more than possible that the granddaughters of those who now use it with no more thought that it is indelicate than *stocking*, may shrink as they now do from *smock* or *shift*, and for the same reason, or, rather, with the same lack of reason. Indeed, the history of our language gives us reason to believe that this will surely happen, unless good sense, simplicity, and real purity of thought should drive out the silly shame that seeks to hide its unnatural face behind a transparent veil of foreign making.

ENCEINTE. — The use of this French word by English-speaking folk to mean, with child, like tha

12

of *accouchement* for delivery, seems to me gross, prurient, and foolish.   Can there be a sweeter, purer
phrase applied to a woman, one better fitted to claim
for her tenderness and deference from every man,
than to say of her that she is with child?   What is
gained by the use of the French word, or of the round-
about phrase "in a delicate situation"?   Certainly
nothing is gained in delicacy by implying, as these
periphrastic euphemisms do, that her condition is indelicate.   Delicate health may be owing to various
causes; and yet even the phrase "in delicate health"
is used by many persons with exclusive limitation
to pregnancy or child-bearing.   There is about this
a cowardly, mean-minded shifting and shuffling
which is very contemptible.   Can there be in language anything purer and sweeter than the declara-
tion, "He shall tenderly lead all those that are with
young," or that, "Woe unto them that are with
child, and to them that give suck, in those days"?
As bad as *accouchement* is *confined*, used in a similar sense — worse, indeed; for the former does
mean a bringing to bed.   The use of this word is
carried by some persons to that pitch of idiocy that,
instead of saying of a woman that her child was
born at such or such an hour, — half past six, for
instance, — they will say that she was confined at
half past six; the fact being that she was confined,
and from the same cause, just as much a few hours
before, and would before some days afterward.
This esoteric use of this word is liable to ludicrous
and unpleasant consequences — like this.   A lady
was reading aloud in a circle of friends a letter just
received.   She read, "We are in great trouble.

Poor Mary has been confined"—and there she stopped; for that was the last word on a sheet, and the next sheet had dropped and fluttered away, and poor Mary, unmarried, was left really in a delicate situation until the missing sheet was found, and the reader continued—"to her room for three days, with what, we fear, is suppressed scarlet fever." The disuse of the verb *to child* has been a real loss to our language, with the genius of which it was in perfect harmony, while it expressed the fact intended to be conveyed with a simplicity and delicacy which would seem unobjectionable to every one, except those who are so superfinely and superhumanly shameful that they think it immodest that a woman should bear and bring forth a child at all. It might comfort them in the use of this word to remember that the French, which they regard as a language so much more refined than their own, has in constant use an exactly correspondent word,— *enfanter*. But that might lead them to say that yesterday Mrs. Jones enfanted.*

FEMALE. — The use of this word for *woman* is one of the most unpleasant and inexcusable of the common perversions of language. It is not a Briticism, although it is much more in vogue among British writers and speakers than among our own. With us *lady* is the favorite euphemism for woman. For every one of the softer and more ambitious sex who is dissatisfied with her social position, or uncertain of it, seems to share Mrs. Quickly's dislike of being called a woman. There is no lack of what is called authoritative usage during three centuries for this misuse of *female*. But this is one of those pe‑

* See Note at the end of this chapter.

versions which are justified by no example, however eminent. A cow, or a sow, or any she brute, is a female, just as a woman is; as a man is no more a male than a bull is, or a boar; and when a woman calls herself a female, she merely shares her sex with all her fellow-females throughout the brute creation.*

GENTLEMAN, LADY. — These words have been forced upon us until they have begun to be nauseous, by people who will not do me the honor of reading this book; so that any plea here for *man* and *woman* would be in vain and out of place. But I will notice a very common misuse of the former, which prevails in business correspondence, in which Mr. A. is addressed as Sir, but the firm of A. B. & Co. as Gentlemen. Now, the plural of *Sir* is *Sirs;* and if *gentleman* has any significance at all, it ought not to be made common and unclean by being applied to mere business purposes. As to the ado that is made about "Mr. Blank and lady," it seems to me quite superfluous. If it pleases any man to announce on a hotel book that his wife, or any other woman who is travelling under his protection, is a lady, a perfect lady, let him do so in peace. This is a matter of taste and habit. The world is wide, and the freedom of this country has not yet quite deprived us of the right of choosing our associates or of forming our own manners.

* The following whimsical fling at this squeamishness is from Graham's "Word Gossip," which has appeared since the publication of these chapters in their original form. Observe the implication that a young person must be of the female sex. This is a Briticism: —

"In the many surgings of the mighty crowd I had actually laboured to assist and protect two (I was going to say ladies, but ladies are grateful; I can't say young persons, for they weru't young; nor can I say women, for that is considered a slight; or females, for such persons are no longer supposed to exist) — well, two individuals of a different sex from my own." — p. 79.

LIMB. — A squeamishness, which I am really ashamed to notice, leads many persons to use this word exclusively instead of *leg.* A limb is anything which is separated from another thing, and yet joined to it. In old English *limbed* was used to mean joined. Thus, in the "Ancren Riwle," "Loketh that ye beon euer mid onnesse of herte *ilimed* togeder," *i. e.,* "Look that ye be ever with oneness of heart joined together." The branches of a tree have a separate individual character, and are yet parts of the tree, and thus are limbs. The fingers are properly limbs of the hand; but the word is generally applied to the greater divisions, both of trees and animals. The limbs of the human body are the arms and the legs; the latter no more so than the former. Yet some folk will say that by a railway accident one woman had her arms broken, and another her limbs — meaning her legs; and some will say that a woman hurt her leg when her thigh was injured. Perhaps these persons think that it is indelicate for a woman to have legs, and that therefore they are concealed by garments, and should be ignored in speech. Heaven help such folk; they are far out of my reach. I can only say to them that there is no immodesty in speaking of any part or function of the human body when there is necessity for doing so, and that when they are spoken of it is immodest not to call them by their proper names. The notion that by giving a bad thing a wrong or an unmeaning name, the thing, or the mention of it, is bettered, is surely one of the silliest that ever entered the mind of man. It is the occasion and the purpose of speech that make

it modest or immodest, not the thing spoken of, or
the giving it its proper name.

RETIRE. — If you are going to bed, say so,
should there be occasion. Don't talk about retir-
ing, unless you would seem like a prig or a prurient
prude.

ROOSTER. — A rooster is any animal that roosts.
Almost all birds are roosters, the hens, of course,
as well as the cocks. What sense or delicacy, then,
is there in calling the cock of the domestic fowl a
rooster, as many people do? The cock is no more
a rooster than the hen; and domestic fowls are no
more roosters than canary birds or peacocks. Out
of this nonsense, however, people must be laughed,
rather than reasoned.

NOTE (p. 179).—Southey uses the verb *to child* in "The Battle of Blenheim,"
one of the simplest and most popular of his poems.

"And many a childing mother died."

How much more truly decent and delicate this is than the following passage
from, I am sorry to say, the London "Medical Press:"
"For what female about legitimately to become a mother would desire to be
among strangers at such a time!"
That a physician, of all men, should call a wife near her delivery, or a married woman near childbirth, by such a sickening round-about phrase as "a
female about legitimately to become a mother!" But the extremity of this
nauseating nonsense was reached in a woman's letter which was produced in a
divorce case in some Western State. The wife, who was herself with child
when she was married, discovered, about six months afterwards, a letter addressed to her husband in a feminine hand, which she was dishonorable enough
to open and read. In it she found, as she deserved to find, this question:—
"Did you marry that child because she too was *en famille!*" As a combination of ignorant profession and prurient prudery, this is unsurpassable. *En
famille* means at home, without ceremony, in the family circle, domestic.
This poor creature thought she was elegantly using the French for that hideous
English phrase, "In the family way."

CHAPTER VI.

SOME BRITICISMS.

I HAVE heretofore designated the misuse of certain words as Briticisms. There is a British affectation in the use of a few other words which is worthy of some attention. And in saying that a form of English speech is of British origin, or is a Briticism, I mean that it has arisen or come into vogue in Great Britain since the beginning of the eighteenth century, when, by the union of England and Scotland (A. D. 1706-7), the King of England and of Scotland became King of the United Kingdom of Great Britain and Ireland, a British took the place of an English Parliament, and Englishmen became politically Britons. This period is one of mark in social and literary, as well as in political history. To us it is one of interest, because, about that time, although our political bonds were not severed until three quarters of a century latter, our absolute identity with the English of the mother country may be regarded as having ceased. For, after a moderate Jacobite exodus at the end of the seventeenth century, there was comparatively little emigration from the old England to the new. They change their skies, but not their souls, who cross the sea; and whatever the population of this country may become hereafter, it had remained, till within twenty-five years, as to race, an English people, just as absolutely as if our fathers had not left the Old Home. The history of England, of the old England, pure and simple, is our history. In British history we have only the interest of kinsmen; but the English language and English literature before the modern British period belongs to both of us, in the same completeness and by the same title — inheritance from our common fathers, who spoke it and wrote it, quickened by the same blood, on the same soil. And, in fact, the English of the period when Shakespeare wrote and the Bible was translated has been kept in use among people of education somewhat more in the new England than in the old. All over the country there are some words and phrases in common use, and in certain parts of New England and Virginia there are many, which have been dropped in British England, or are to be found only among the squires and farmers in the recesses of the rural counties. The forms of speech which may be conveniently called Briticisms, are, however, generally of later origin than the beginning of the British empire. They have almost all of them sprung up since about A. D. 1775.

As WELL. — This phrase is improperly used by some British writers in the sense of all the same. For instance, "Her aged lover made her presents, but just as well she hated the sight of him and the sound of his voice;" i. e., she hated him all the same. This misusage has yet no foothold here, although, owing to the influence of second-rate British novels, it begins to be heard.

AWFUL. — It would seem superfluous to say that *awful* is not a synonyme of *very*, were it not that the word is thus used by many people who should know better than to do so. The misuse is a Briticism; but it has been spreading here within the last few years. I have heard several educated English gentlemen speak in sober, unconscious good faith of "awfully nice girls," "awfully pretty women," and "awfully jolly people." That is awful which inspires or is inspired by awe; and in the line in the old metrical version of the Hundredth Psalm,

"Glad homage pay with awful mirth,"

Tate and Brady did not mean that we were to be awfully jolly, or very mirthful or gay, in our worship. Observe here, again, how misuse debases a good and much-needed word, and voids it of its meaning, by just so much impoverishing the language.

COMMENCE. — There is a British misuse of this word which is remarkably coarse and careless. British writers of all grades but the very highest will say, for instance, that a man went to London and commenced poet, or commenced politician. Mr. Swinburne says that "Blake commenced pupil;" and Pope, quoted by Johnson, —

"If wit so much from ignorance undergo,
Ah, let not learning too commence its foe."

A man may commence life as an author, or a politician, or he may commence a book, or any other task, although it is better to say he begins either. But it is either a state or an action that he commences. Commencement cannot be properly predicated of a noun which does not express the idea of continuance. It may be said that a woman commences married life, or that she commences jilting, but not that she commences wife, or commences jilt, any more than that she ends hussy.

DIRECTLY. — The radical meaning of this word is, in a right line; and hence, as a right line is the shortest distance between two points, it means at once, immediately. Its synonyme in both senses is a good English word, now, unhappily, somewhat obsolete—*straightway*. But John Bull uses *directly* in a way that is quite indefensible — to wit, in the sense of when, as soon as. This use of the word is a wide-spread Briticism, and prevails even among the most cultivated writers. For instance, in the London "Spectator" of May 2, 1867, it is said that "Directly Mr. Disraeli finished speaking, Mr. Lowe rose to oppose," etc. *Anglice*, As soon as Mr. Disraeli finished speaking, etc. It is difficult to trace by continuous steps the course of this strange perversion, for which there is neither justification nor palliation. A fortnight ago I should have said that it was unknown among speakers and writers of American birth; but since then I have read Mr. Howells's charming book, "Italian Journeys," than which I know no book of travel more richly fraught with pleasure to a gentle reader. And by a gentle reader I mean one who, like its author, can look not only with delight upon all that is beautiful and loveable, but with sympathy upon that which is neither beautiful nor loveable in the customs and characters of those who are strangers to him, whose ways of wickedness are not his ways, and whose follies are foreign to him, — one who can admire the boldness of an impostor, and see the humorous side of rascality. When a traveller sees with Mr. Howells's very human eyes, and writes with his graphic and humorous pen, — a pen that caricatures with a keenness to which malice gives no edge, — travelling with him on paper, which is generally either the dullest or the most frivolous of employments, is one of the most inspiriting, and not the least instructive. Mr. Howells's style, too, is so good, it shows such unobtrusive and seemingly unconscious mastery of idiomatic English, that I notice with the more freedom two or three lapses, one of which, at least, I attribute to the deleterious influences of foreign travel. I am sure that it was not in New England, and not until after he had been subjected to daily intercourse with British speakers and to the influence of British journals, that he learned to write such sentences as these : " Directly I found the house inhabited by living people, I began to be sorry that it was not as empty as the library and the street,' p. 30. "I was more interested in the disreputable person who mounted the box beside our driver directly we got out of our city gate," p. 218. Mr. Howells meant that *when* he found the house inhabited he began to be sorry, and that the interesting and disreputable person mounted his coach-box *as soon as* they got out of the gate. Mr. Howells is the first born and bred Yankee that I have known to be guilty of this British offence against the English language; and his example is likely to exert so much more influence than my precept, that, unless he repents, I am likely to be pilloried as his persecutor by the multitude of his followers. But I am sure that he will repent, and that, with the amiable

leaning toward iniquity which enables him to throw
so fresh a charm over the well-trodden ways of
Italy, he will even think kindly of the critic who
has put him upon the barb as if he loved him.

So sure am I of this, that, wishing to use him
again as an eminent example of error, I shall bring
forward two other faults which I have noticed in his
book, and in which he is not singular among Yankees. There is among some people a propensity,
which is of late growth, and is the fruit of presuming half-knowledge, to give to adjectives formed
participially from nouns, and to nouns used as adjectives, a plural form, the effect of which is laughably
pedantic, as all efforts to struggle away from simple
idiom to superfine correctness are apt to be. For
instance, the delicious confection, calf's-foot jelly,
is advertised in many confectionary windows as
calves'-feet jelly — the confectioners having been
troubled in their minds by the reflection that there
went more than one calf's foot to the making of
their jelly. So I once heard a richly-robed dame,
whose daughter, named after the goddess of wisdom, was suffering pangs that only steel forceps
could allay, say, with a little flourish of elegance,
that "M'nervy was a martyr to the teethache." And
could this gorgeous goddess-bearer doubt that she
was right, when she found Mr. Howells saying that
the peasants in Bassano return from their labor
"led in troops of eight or ten by stalwart, white-
teethed, bare-legged maids!" She would probably
be shocked by the bareness of the maidens' legs,
but she would glory in the multitudinous dental
epithet which Mr. Howells applies to them. But

because the most beautiful of the Nereides trips
through our memories as silver-footed Thetis, do
we, therefore, think of her as a unipede, a one-
legged goddess? How would it do for the Cambridge lads to translate, silver-*feeted* Thetis? And
if we have *calves'-feet* jelly, why must not we, *a
fortiori*, have *oysters*-pie and *plums*-pudding? and
if white-*teethed* maids, why not *teeth*-brushes? and,
above all, why do we commit the monstrous absurdity of speaking of the numberless human race
as mankind instead of *men*-kind? A noun used as
an adjective expresses an abstract idea; and when
by the introduction of the plural form this idea is
broken up into a collective multitude of individuals,
it falls ludicrously into concrete ruin.

A like endeavor toward precision has led some
folk to say, for instance, that a man was *on* Broad
way, or that such and such an event took place *on*
Tremont Street; and Mr. Howells countenances
this folly by writing, "There were a few people to
be seen *on* the street." Let him, and all others who
would not be at once childish and pedantic, say,
in the street, *in* Broadway, and not be led into the
folly of endeavoring to convey the notion that a man
was resting upon or moving over an extended surface between two lines of houses. A house itself is
in Broadway, not on it; but it may stand on the line
of the street; and an event takes place in a certain
street, whether the actors are on the pavement or on
the steps, or in the balcony of a house in that street,
or in the house itself. We are in or within a limited
surface, but on or upon one that is without visible
boundaries. Thus, a man is in a field, but on a

plain. Some generations, at least, will pass away before a man shall appear who will write plainer, simpler, or better English than John Bunyan wrote; and he makes Christian say, "Apollyon, beware what you do, for I am *in* the king's highway."

There is no telling into what absurdity these blind gropers after precision will stumble when we find them deep in such a slough as *written over the signature*, fancying the while that they stand on solid ground. A man's signature, we are told, is at the bottom of his letter, and therefore he writes over the signature! But — answering a precisian according to his preciseness — the signature was not there while the man wrote the letter; it was added afterward. How, then, was the letter written over the signature? This is the very lunacy of literalism. A man writes under a signature whether the signature is at the top, or the bottom, or in the middle of his letter. For instance, an old correspondent of the New York "Times" writes under the signature of "A Veteran Observer," and his letters, written *sub tegmine fagi*, are under the date of "The Beeches." And as they would be under that date whether it were written at the top, or, as dates often are, at the bottom of the letter, so they are under that signature, wherever on the sheet it may be signed. A soldier or a sailor fights under a flag, not, as Mr. Precisian would have it, because the flag is flying over his head, but because he is under the authority which that flag represents. Sometimes he does his fighting above the flag, as is often the case with sharpshooters in both army and navy; and Farragut, in the futtock shrouds of the "Hartford," fought the

battle of Mobile Bay as much under the United
States flag that floated ten or fifteen feet below him,
as if he had issued his orders from the bottom of the
hold. So writs are issued under the authority of a
court, although the seal and the signature which
represent that authority are at the bottom of the
writ; and a man issues a letter under his signature,
i. e., with the authority or attestation given by his
signature, whether the signature is at top or bottom.
The use of such a phrase as *over the signature* is
the sign of a tendency which, if unchecked, will
place our language under the formative influence.
not of those who act instinctively under guidance of
what we call its genius, or of scholars and men of
general culture, but of those who have least ability
to fashion it to honor — the literate folk who know
too much to submit to usage or authority, and too
little rightfully to frame usage or to have authority
themselves.

I shall notice only one other bad example set by
Mr. Howells, that in the phrase "when we came to
settle for the wine." He meant, to pay for the wine,
that and nothing more. To settle is to fix firmly,
and so, to adjust; and therefore the adjusting of
accounts is well called, by figure, their settlement.
But the phrase *to settle*, meaning to pay, had better
be left entirely to the use of those sable messengers,
rapidly passing away, who summon passengers on
steamboats to "step up to the cap'n's office and settle."
For accounts may be settled, that is, they may be
made clear and satisfactory, — as the passenger
wished his cup of coffee to be made when he called
upon the negro to take it to the captain's office and
have it settled, — and yet they may not be paid,

To settle your passage means, if it means anything, nothing more or less than to pay your fare;
and there is no reason whatever for the use of the
former phrase instead of the latter. It displaces
one good word, and perverts another; while the
use of *settle* without any object, which is sometimes
heard, as, Hadn't you better settle with me? is
hideous.

These four slips are notable as being all that I
remarked in reading "Italian Journeys" thoroughly
and carefully. There have been very few books,
if any, published on either side of the water, that
would not furnish more as well as greater opportunities to a carping critic.

DRIVE and RIDE are among the words as to which
there is a notable British affectation. According to
the present usage of cultivated society in England,
ride means only to go on horseback, or on the back
of some beast less dignified and comfortable, and
drive, only to go in a vehicle which is drawn by
any creature that is driven. This distinction, the
non-recognition of which is marked by cousin Bull
as an Americanism, is quite inconsistent with common sense and good English, and it involves absurd
contradictions. *Drive* comes to us straight from
the Anglo-Saxon: it means to urge forward, to
expel, to eject, and *Drift* is simply that which is
driven. There is no example of any authority
earlier than this century known to me, or quoted
by any lexicographer, of the use of *drive* with the
meaning, to pass in a carriage. Dr. Johnson gives
that definition of the word, but he is able to support
it only by the following passages from Shakespeare
and Milton, which are quite from the purpose : —

> "There is a litter ready: lay him out,
>   And *drive* toward Dover." — *King Lear*.

> "Thy foaming chariot wheels, that shook
>   Heaven's everlasting frame, while o'er the neck
>   Thou *drov'st* of warring angels disarrayed."
>   *Paradise Lost*.

In the first of these the person addressed is merely ordered to drive or urge forward his carriage to Dover; in the second, Jehovah is represented as urging the wheels of his war chariot over his fallen enemies. There is not a suggestion or implication of the thought that *drive* in either case means to pass in any way, or means anything else than to urge onward. Dr. Johnson might as well have quoted from the account in Exodus of the passage of the Red Sea, that the Lord took off the chariot wheels of the Egyptians, that "they drave them heavily." *Drive* means only to force on; but *ride* means, and always has meant, to be borne-up and along, as on a beast, a bird, a chariot, a wagon, or a rail. We have seen that Shakespeare, and Milton, and the translators of the Bible use *drive* in connection with *chariot* when they wish to express the urging it along; but when they wish to say that a man is borne up and onward in a chariot, they use *ride*.

"And Pharaoh made him [Joseph] to *ride* in the second chariot which he had." — *Genesis* xli. 43.

"And I will overthrow the chariots and those that *ride* in them; and the horses and their riders shall come down, every one by the sword of his brother." — *Haggai* ii. 22.

"So Jehu *rode* in a chariot, and went to Jezreel. . . . And the watchman told, saying, He came even unto them, and cometh not again; and the *driving* is like the *driving* of Jehu the son of Nimshi; for he *driveth* furiously." — *2 Kings* ix. 16, 20.

13

In these passages *drive* and *ride* are used in what is their proper sense, and has been since long before the days of the Heptarchy, and as they are used now in New England. And yet only a few days since, as I spoke of riding to a British friend, he said to me, pleasantly, but with the air of a polite teacher, "You use that word differently to what we do. We *ride* on horseback, but we *drive* in a carriage; now, I have noticed that you *ride* in a carriage." "The distinction seems to be, then," I replied, "that when you are on an animal, you ride, and when you are in a vehicle, you drive." "Exactly; don't you see? quite so." "Well, then" (we were in Broadway), "if you had come down from the Clarendon in that omnibus, you would say that you drove down, or, if you went from one place to another in a stage coach, that you drove there." "'M! ah! no, not exactly. You know one rides in a 'bus or a stage coach, but one drives in one's own carriage or in a private vehicle." I did not answer him. Our British cousins will ere long see the incorrectness of this usage and its absurd incongruity, and will be able to say, for instance, — for are they not of English blood and speech as well as we? — We all rode down from home in the old carryall to meet you, and John drove. But if they insist, in such a case, upon saying that they *all drove*, we shall have reason to suspect that there is at least the beginning of a new language, — the British, — and that the English tongue and English sense has fled to the Yankees across the sea.

RIGHT. — A Briticism in the use of this word is creeping in among us. It is used to mean obliga

tion, duty. On one of those celebrations of St.
Patrick's day in the city of New York, when, in
token of the double nationality of its governing
classes, the City Hall is decorated with the Irish
and the United States flag, and miles of men, each
one like the other, and all wearing stove-pipe hats
and green scarfs, are allowed to take possession of
its great thoroughfares, in acknowledgement of the
large share which their forefathers took for two
hundred and fifty years in framing our government
and establishing our society upon those truly Irish
principles of constitutional liberty and law which
are the glory and the safeguard of our country, and
in acknowledgement, also, of that devotion to the
great cause of religious freedom which brought
those Celtic pilgrims to our shores — on one of those
occasions I heard an alien creature, a Yankee, who
had presumed to drive out jauntily in a wagon on
that sacred and solemn day, and who ventured to be
somewhat displeased because he had been detained
three quarters of an hour lest he should break the
irregularity of that line, and interrupt his masters'
pleasure — I heard this Yankee say to the police-
men, as he saw the Fourth Avenue cars allowed to
pursue their course (probably because it was thought
they might contain some of the females of the dom-
inant race), "What do you stop me for? The cars
have as good a right to be stopped as the carriages."
This was unpleasant. That he should have stood
humbly before his masters, having put a ballot into
their hands with which to break his back, was a
small matter; but of his language he should have
been ashamed. He could not have spoken worse

English if he were a Cockney; and from some
Cockney he must have caught this trick, which,
common enough for a long while among British
speakers, and even writers of a low order, has been
heard here only within a few years. He meant that
carriages had as good *a right* as cars *to go on* without interruption, and that the cars had as much
obligation to stop as the carriages. A right is an
incorporeal, rightful possession, and, consequently,
something of value, which we strive to get and to
keep, except always when it is claimed from us in
the name of the patron saint Patrick, of the great
State and the great city of our country. Death is
the legal punishment of certain felonies. But we
do not speak of the murderer's right of being
hanged. Yet in case of a choice of two modes of
death, we should use the word, and speak, for instance, of the soldier's right to be shot rather than
hanged.

SICK and ILL are two other words that have been
perverted in general British usage. Almost all
British speakers and writers limit the meaning of
sick to the expression of qualmishness, sickness at
the stomach, nausea, and lay the proper burden of
the adjective *sick* upon the adverb *ill*. They sneer
at us for not joining in the robbery and the imposition. I was present once when a British merchant,
receiving in his own house a Yankee youth at a
little party, said, in a tone that attracted the attention of the whole room, " Good evening! We
haven't seen you for a long while. Have you been
seeck" (the sneer prolonged the word), "as you
say in your country?" "No, thank you," said the

other, frankly and promptly, "I've been *hill*, as they say in yours." John Bull, although he blushed to the forehead, had the good sense, if not the good nature, to join in the laugh that followed; but I am inclined to think that he never ran another tilt in that quarter. As to the sense in which *sick* is used by the best English writers, there can be, of course, no dispute; but I have seen this set down in a British critical journal of high class as an "obsolete sense." It is not obsolete even in modern British usage. The Birmingham "Journal" of August 29, 1869, informs its readers that, "The Sick Club question has given rise to another batch of letters from local practitioners of medicine;" Mrs. Massingberd publishes "Sickness, its Trials and Blessings" (London, 1868); and a letter before me, from a London woman to a friend, says, "I am truly sorry to hear you are so very sick. Do make haste and get well." One of Matthew Arnold's poems is "The Sick King in Bokara," in which are these lines:

> "O, King thou know'st I have been sick
> These many days, and heard no thing."

British officers have sick leave; British invalids keep a sick bed, or a sick room, and so forth, no matter what their ailment. No one of them ever speaks of ill leave, an ill room, or an ill bed. Was an Ill Club ever heard of in England? The incongruity is apparent, and it is new-born and needless. For the use of *ill* — an adverb — as an adjective, thus, an ill man, there is no defence and no excuse, except the contamination of bad example.

STOP for *stay* is a Briticism; *e. g.*, "stop at 'ome." To stop is to arrest motion; to stay is to remain where motion is arrested. "I shall stop at the Clarendon," says our British friend — one of the sort that does not "stop at 'ome." And he will quite surely stop there; but after he has stopped, whether he stays there, and how long, depend upon circumstances. A railway train stops at many stations, but it stays only at one.

NASTY. — This word, at best not well suited to dainty lips, is of late years shockingly misused by British folk who should be ashamed of such defiled English. Thus we read in the Saturday Review or the Spectator of Mr. Disraeli's or Mr. Bernal Osborne's making "a nasty retort:" meaning that the rejoinder was ill-natured or irritating. And in Miss Broughton's last novel, "Good-bye, Sweetheart," the same misuse occurs in more than one passage. For example:

"Fiddlesticks," replies Scrope, brusquely, "a man to throw a girl over to whom he is passionately attached, because she says a few nasty things to him ; more especially (smiling a little maliciously) when she has got into a habit of saying nasty things to everybody." *Part* 2, *Chap.* 9.

Miss Broughton reproduces the daily talk of the cultivated people for whom she writes. But could there be better reason for a man's throwing a girl over than her saying nasty things? For hardly three other English words are so nearly the same in meaning as *dirty, filthy,* and *nasty ;* of which the last expresses the greatest offence to all the senses — the quality and condition of moist and generally ill-smelling filth. This slangy misuse of the word is rarely or never heard in the United States.

CHAPTER VII.

WORDS THAT ARE NOT WORDS.

WHAT is a word? Every one knows. The most ignorant child, if it can speak, needs no definition of *word*. Probably no other word in the language is so rarely referred to in dictionaries. Until I began to write this chapter, and had framed a definition of *word* for myself, I had never seen or heard one, that I remember. Yet, if any reader will shut this book here, and try to tell exactly what a word is, and write down his definition before he opens the book again, he may find that the task is not so easy as he may have supposed it to be. Dr. Johnson's definition is, "a single part of speech," at the limited view and schoolmasterish style of which we may be inclined at first to smile. Richardson's first definition is, "anything spoken or told." But this applies equally to a speech or a story. His second is, "an articulate utterance of the voice," which is really the same as Worcester's, "an articulate sound." But this will not do; for *baclomipivit* is an articulate sound, but it is not a word, and I hope never will be one in my language; and *I* and *you* are not articulate sounds, and yet they are words. Webster's definition is, —

"An articulate or vocal sound, or a combination

of articulate and vocal sounds, uttered by the human voice, and by custom expressing an idea or ideas.'

Here plainly, fulness and accuracy of definition have been sought, but they have not been attained. The definition, considering its design, is superfluous, inexact, and incomplete. The whole of the first part of it, making a distinction between articulate and vocal sounds, and between such sounds and a combination of them, is needless and from the purpose. The latter part of the definition uses *custom* vaguely, and in the word *idea* fails to include all that is required.

A word is, an utterance of the human voice which in any community expresses a thought or a thing. If there is a village or a hamlet where *ao* expresses I love, or any other thought, and *babo* means bread, or anything else, then for that community *ao* and *babo* are words. But words, generally, are utterances which express thoughts or things to a race, a people. Custom is not an essential condition of wordship. Howells, in one of his letters (Book I. Letter 12), says of an Italian town, "There are few places this side the Alps better built and so well *streeted* as this." *Streeted* was probably never used before, and has probably never been used since Howells used it, two hundred and forty years ago. But it expressed his thought perfectly then to all English-speaking people, and does so now, and is a participial adjective correctly formed. It is unknown to custom, but it has all the conditions of wordship, and is a much better English word than very many in "Webster's Dictionary." And, after all, Johnson's definition covers the ground. We must dismiss from our minds our grammar-class notion of a sort of things, prepositions, nouns, adverbs, and articles, the name of which is part-of-speech, and think of a single part of speech. Whatever is a single part of any speech is a word.

But as there are books that are not books, so there are words that are not words. Most of them are usurpers, interlopers, or vulgar pretenders; some are deformed creatures, with only half a life in them; but some of them are legitimate enough in their pretensions, although oppressive, intolerable, useless. Words that are not words sometimes die spontaneously; but many linger, living a precarious life on the outskirts of society, uncertain of their position, and a cause of great discomfort to all right thinking, straightforward people.

These words-no-words are in many cases the consequence of a misapprehension or whimsical perversion of some real word. Sitting at dinner beside a lady whom it was always a pleasure to look upon, I offered her a croquette, which she declined, adding, in a confidential whisper, "I am Banting." I turned with surprise in my face, (for she had no likeness to the obese London upholsterer,) and heard the *naif* confession that she lived in daily fear lest the polished plumpness which so delighted my eye should develop into corpulence, and that therefore she had adopted Banting's system of diet, the doing of which she expressed by the grotesque participle *banting*. She was not alone in its use, I soon learned. And thus, because a proper name happened to end in *ing*, it was used as a participle formed upon the assumed verb *bant*.   In fact, I have since that time often heard intelligent women, speaking without the slightest intention of pleas- antry, and in entire simplicity and unconsciousness, say of one or another of their friends, "O, she *bants*," or "She has *banted* these two years to keep herself down." The next edition of "Webster's Dictionary" will probably contain a new verb — *Bant*, to eschew fat-producing food.

Another example of this mode of forming words is afforded by the following political advertisement, which I found in a Brooklyn newspaper:—

"Notice. — I am intercessed by Mr. —— and certain of his friends to withdraw my claims for the supervisorship of this Ward. I have only to say to the citizens of the 13th that I run for the office upon the recommendation and support of many influential citizens, amounting to me as much as is claimed by the so-called regularly nominated candidate. I shall run for the office as Democratic Supervisor, despite intercessions or browbeating, and if elected shall make it my sole duty to attend to the inter ests of property-holders and rights of the country.

J——S K——G."

I have given the advertisement entire, because it shows that the writer is a man of intelligence and some education; and yet such a man not only sup- poses that *intercession* means simply entreaty, — losing sight entirely of the vicarious signification which is its essential significance (its primitive meaning being, going between), — but that it is from a verb *intercess;* or else he boldly forms *in- tercess* from *intercession*, and uses it apparently without the least hesitation or compunction. His honesty of purpose should win him forgiveness for less venial errors; but at this rate, and with this style of word-formation, where shall we stop? For *intercess*, although it is yet rather raw and new, is as good a word as others which are in not infrequent use among people of no less intelligence and general information than his. In this chapter some of these words will be examined, and also some others against which purism has raised objections which do not seem to be well taken.

A DJECTIVES are used as substantives with clearness and force when they thus give substantive form to an abstract quality, as, Seek the good, eschew the evil; the excellent of the earth; speak well of the dead. But the use of the adjective part of a compound-designating phrase as a noun is to be avoided upon peril of vulgarity and absurdity, and generally produces a word-no-word of the most monstrous and ridiculous sort. For example, a large gilded sign in Wall Street announces that Messrs. A & B are "Dealers in Governments;" but if any gentleman in want of the articles should step in and ask to be supplied with a republic and two monarchies, he would then probably learn that Messrs. A & B dealt not in governments, but in government securities. In like manner the editor of a Southern paper, carried out of the orbit of high journalistic reserve by the attractions of two ladies unknown to fame, begins thus an article in their glory : —

"For the first time during the existence of this paper we notice a theatrical representation editorially. We generally leave that matter to our locals; but really the Worral sisters —— ! "

What "a local" is might well puzzle any reader who had not the technical knowledge that would enable him to see that it is "short" for *local re-porter*, itself an incorrect name for a reporter of local news. Beguiling the time by reading the ad-vertising cards in a railway station where I awaited a belated train, my eye was caught by the following sentence in one of them : —

"The Southern States is without exception the most com-plete six-hole premium ever made."

What a premium was I knew, but a six-hole pre-mium, and, still more, a complete six-hole premium, was beyond the range even of my conjecture, un-less, perhaps, it might be a flute given as a reward of merit. But, reading farther, I found that the advertisers called public attention not only to their Southern States, but to their "Dixie for wood, with extended fire-box. A perfect premium!" This, and the wood-cut of a cooking stove, led me step by step to the apprehension of the fact that these in-ventors in language, as well as in household articles, had produced a utensil for the kitchen, which, hav-ing received a premium for it, they called, rightly enough, their premium stove; and that thereafter they called their stoves, and perhaps all other good stoves, if any others than theirs could be good, *pre-miums*, and consequently the best and largest of them all a complete six-hole premium. The height of absurdity which they thus reached is a sufficient warning, without further remark, against the sub-stantive use of adjectives of which they furnished so bewildering an example.

AUTHORESS, POETESS. — These words and oth-ers of their sort have been condemned by writers for whose taste and judgement I have great respect; but although the words are not very lovely, it would seem that their right to a place in the language cannot be denied. The distinction of the female from the male by the termination *ess* is one of the oldest and best-established usages of English speech. *Mistress*, *goddess*, *prioress*, *deaconess*, *shepherdess*, *heiress*, *sempstress*, *traitress* are examples that will occur to every reader. Sir Thomas Chaloner, in his translation of Erasmus's " Praise of Folly " (an excellent piece of English) makes a feminine noun, and a good one, by adding *ess* to a verb — *foster*.

" Further, as concernyng my bringynge up, I am not envious that Jupiter, the great god, had a goat to his *fostress*."

Gower says that Clytemnestra was " of her own lord *mordrice*." Fuller uses *buildress* and *intrudress*, Sir Philip Sidney *captainess*, Holland (Plutarch) *flattress*, Sylvester *soveraintess*, and Ben Jonson *victress*. And could we afford to lose Milton's

" Thee, *chauntress*, oft the woods among
I woo, to hear thy even song " ?

Indeed, these examples and this defence seem quite superfluous. There can be no reasonable objection made, only one of individual taste, to *actress*, *authoress*, *poetess*, and even to *sculptress* and *paintress*.

DONATE. — I need hardly say, that this word is utterly abominable — one that any lover of simple honest English cannot hear with patience and without offence. It has been formed by some presuming and ignorant person from *donation*, and is

much such a word as *vocate* would be from *voca-
tion*, *orate* from *oration*, or *gradate* from *grada-
tion*; and this when we have *give*, *present*, *grant*,
confer, *endow*, *bequeath*, *devise*, with which to
express the act of transferring possession in all its
possible varieties. The first of these will answer
the purpose, in most cases, better than any one of
the others, and *donation* itself is not among our
best words. If any man thinks that he and his gift
are made to seem more imposing because the latter
is called a donation, which he donates, let him
remember that when Antonio requires that the
wealthy Shylock shall leave all he dies possessed
of to Lorenzo and Jessica, he stipulates that "he
do record a gift" of it, and that Portia, in consequence, says, "Clerk, draw a deed of gift;" and
more, that the writers of the simplest and noblest
English that has been written called the Omnipotent "the Giver of every good and perfect gift."
But there are some folk who would like to call
him the Great Donater because he donates every
good and perfect donation. If they must express
giving by an Anglicized form of the Latin *dono*, it
were better that they used *donation* as a verb. So
Cotton writes (Montaigne's Essays, I. 359), "They
used to collation between meals." This is better
than "They used to collate between meals."

ENQUIRE, ENCLOSE, ENDORSE. — These words
have been condemned by some writers on the
ground that they are respectively from the Latin
inquiro, *includo*, and *in dorsum*, and should, therefore, be written *inquire*, *inclose*, and *indorse*. This
is an error. They are, to be sure, of Latin origin

but remotely; they come to us directly from the old French *enquerre*, *enclos*, and *endorser*. For centuries they appear in our literature with the prefix *en*. That Johnson gives this class of words with the prefix *in* must be attributed to a tendency, not uncommon, but not healthy, to follow words of Norman or French origin back to their Latin roots, and to adopt a spelling in conformity to these, in preference to that which pertains to them as representatives of an important and inherent element in the formation of the English language. The best lexicographers and philologists now discourage this tendency, and adhere to the forms which pertain to the immediate origin of derived words. But it must be confessed that the class of words in question is notably defiant of analogy, and very much in need of regulation. For instance, *enquire*, *enquiry*, *inquest*, *inquisition*. No one would think of writing *enquest* and *enquisition*. The discrepancy is of long standing, and must be borne, except by those who choose to avoid it by writing *inquire* for the sake of uniformity; condemnation of which may be left to purists.

ENTHUSED. — This ridiculous word is an Americanism in vogue in the southern part of the United States. I never heard or saw it used, or heard of its use, by any person born and bred north of the Potomac. The Baltimore "American" furnishes the following example of its use: —

"It seems that this State, so quickly *enthused* by the generous and loyal cause of emancipation, has grown weary of virtuous effort, and again stands still."

I shall not conceal the fact that the following

defence might be set up, but not fairly, for *en-thuse*. Ενθουσιασμος (*Enthousiasmos*) was formed by the Greeks from ενθους (*enthous*), a contracted form of ενθεος (*entheos*), meaning in or with God, *i. e.*, divinely inspired. From the Greek adjective *enthous*, an English verb, *enthuse* might be properly formed. But, with no disrespect to Southern scholarship, we may safely say that *enthuse* was not made by the illogical process of going to the Greek root of a Greek word from which an English noun had already been formed. It was plainly reached by the backward process of making some kind of verb from the noun *enthusiasm*, as *donate* was formed from *donation*. If our Southern friends must have a new word to express the agitation of soul to which this one would seem to indicate that they are peculiarly subject, let them say that they are *en-thusiasmed*. The French, who have the word *en-thousiasme*, have also the verb *enthousiasmer*, and, of course, the perfect participle *enthousiasmé*, en-thusiasmed, which are correctly formed. But while we have such words as *stirred, aroused, inspired, excited, transported, ravished, intoxicated*, is it worth while to go farther and fare worse for such a word as *enthused*, or even *enthusiasmed?*

&c. &c. — This convenient sign is very frequently read "and so forth, and so forth ;" and what is worse, many persons who read it properly, *et cetera*, regard it and use it as a more elegant equivalent of "and so forth;" but it is no such thing. *Et cetera* is merely Latin for *and the rest*, and is properly used in schedules or statements after an account given of particular things, to include other things too unimportant and too numerous for particular mention. But the phrase *and so forth* has quite another meaning, *i. e.*, and as before so after, in the same strain. It implies the continuation of a story in accordance with the beginning. Sometimes the story is actually continued in the relation, at other times it is not. Thus we may say, And so forth he told him — thus and so; or, after the relation of the main part of a story we may add, And so forth; meaning that matters went on thereafter as before. This phrase is one of the oldest and most useful in the language. Gower thus used it in his "Confessio Amantis," written nearly six hundred years ago : —

> " So as he mighte [he] tolde tho [then]
>   Unto Ulixes all the cas,
>   How that Circes his moder was,
>   *And so forth* said him every dele
>   How that his moder grete him wele."

FELLOWSHIP used as a verb (for example, "An attempt to *disfellowship* an evil, but to *fellowship* the evil-doer ") is an abomination which has been hitherto regarded as of American origin. It is not often heard or written among people whose language is in other respects a fair example of the English spoken in "America ; " but Mr. Bartlett justly says in his "Dictionary of Americanisms " (a useful and interesting, although a very misleading book), that it "appears with disgusting frequency in the reports of ecclesiastical conventions, and in the religious newspapers generally." The conventions, however, and the newspapers are those of the least educated sects. To this use of *fellowship* it would be a perfect parallel to say that,

14

fifteen years ago, the monarchs of Europe would n
kingship with Louis Napoleon.   There is no excu
of need for the bringing in of this barbarism.   *Fi*
low, like *mate*, may be used as a verb as well as
noun; and it is as well to say, I will not fellow wi
him, as I will not mate with him.   The authority
eminent example is not needed for such a use of *fi*
low; but those who feel the want of it may find
in Shakespeare's plays and in "Piers Ploughmar
Vision" by referring to Johnson's and Richardso
dictionaries, in both of which *fellow* is given as
verb.   Words ending in *ship* express a conditi
or state, and *fellowship* means the condition or st
of those who are fellows, or who fellow with ea
other.   But the use of this word as a verb did r
begin in "America;" witness the following p
sages from the "Morte d'Arthur:—

"How Syr Galahad faught wyth Syr Tristram, and h
Syr tristram yelded hym and promysed to *felaushyp* with lan
lot."

"And, sire, I promyse you, said Sir Tristram, as soone a
may I will see Sir launcelot, and *enfelaushyp* me with hym,
of alle the knyghtes of the world I moost desyre his felaushi
        "*Morte d'Arthur*," Ed. Southey, Vol. I. pp. xix. 287

This was written A. D. 1469, and the verbs *f*
lowship and *enfellowship* were reprinted in
editions, notwithstanding numerous and importa
modernizations and corrections of the text, down
that of 1634, which Mr. Wright has made t
basis of his excellent edition of 1858.   If the wo
could be justified by origin and use, is has the
of sufficient antiquity and high authority.   A
as to its being an Americanism, it was in u
like many other words, so-called, before Columb

set sail on the voyage that ended in the unexpected discovery of the new continent.

FORWARD, UPWARD, DOWNWARD, TOWARD, and other compounds of *ward* (which is the Anglo-Saxon suffix *weard*, meaning in the direction of, over against), have been written also *forwards*, *upwards*, and so forth, from a period of remote antiquity, extending even to the Anglo-Saxon form of the language. But there seems hardly a doubt that the *s* is a corruption as well as a superfluity. The weight of the best usage is on the side of the form without the *s*. "Speak to Israel that they go *forward*." (Exodus xiv. 15.) "For we will not inherit with them on yonder side Jordan, or *forward*; because our inheritance is fallen to us on this side Jordan *eastward*." (Numbers xxxii. 19.) No reason can be given for using *forwards* and *backwards* which would not apply to *eastwards* and *westwards*, which no one thinks of using. Granting that both forms are correct, the avoiding of the hissing termination, which is one of the few reproaches of our language, is a good reason for adhering to the simple, unmodified compound in *ward*.

GENT and PANTS. — Let these words go together, like the things they signify. The one always wears the other.

GUBERNATORIAL. — This clumsy piece of verbal pomposity should be thrust out of use, and that speedily. While the chief officers of States are called governors, and not gubernators, we may better speak of the governor's house and of the governor's room, than of the gubernatorial mansion and the gubernatorial chamber; and why that which

relates to government should be called gubernatorial rather than governmental, except for the sake
of being at once pedantic, uncouth, and outlandish,
it would be hard to tell.

HYDROPATHY. — This word, and *electropathy*,
and all of the same sort, should also be scouted out
of sight and hearing. They are absolutely without meaning, and, in their composition, are fine
examples of pretentious ignorance. Hahnemann
called the system of medicine which he advocated,
homœopathy, because its method was to cure disease by drugs which would cause a like (*omoios*)
disease or suffering (*pathos*). The older system
was naturally called by him (it was never before
so called by its practisers) allopathy, because it
worked by medicines which set up an action counter
to, different from (*allos*), the disease. These are
good technical Greek derivatives. And by just as
much as they are good and reasonable, are *hydropathy* and *electropathy* bad and foolish. Why
should water-*cure* be called water-*disease?* why
electric-cure, electric-disease? The absurdity of
these words is shown by translating them. They
are plainly sprung from the desire of those who
practise the water-cure and the electric-cure to be
reckoned with the legitimate *pathies*. And the
"hydropathists" and "electropathists" are not alone.
I saw once, before a little shop with some herbs in
the window, a sign which ran thus : —

INDIAN
OPATHIST.

I was puzzled for a moment to divine what an
opathist might be. But, of course, I saw in the

next moment that the vender of the herbs in the little shop, thinking that his practice had as good a right as any other to a big name, and deceived by the accent which some persons give to *homæopathy* and *allopathy*, had called his practice Indian-Opathy, and himself an Indian-Opathist. He was not one whit more absurd than the self-styled "hydropathist" and "electropathist." As great a blunder was made by an apothecary, who, wishing to give a name to a new remedy for cold and cough, advertised it widely as *coldine*. Now, the termination *ine* is of Latin origin, and means having the quality of; as *metalline*, having the quality of metal; *alkaline*, having the quality of alkali; *canine* having the qualities of a dog; *asinine*, those of an ass. And so this apothecary, wishing to make a name that would sound as fine as *glycerine*, and *stearine*, and the like, actually advertised his remedy for a cold as something that had the quality of a cold. The rudest peasants do better than that by language, for they are content with their mother tongue. A gentleman who was visiting one of the remotest rural districts of England, met a bare-footed girl carrying a pail of water. Floating on the top of the water was a disc of wood a little less in diameter than the rim of the pail. "What's that, my lass?" he asked. "Thot?" (with surprise) ; "why, thot's a *stiller*." It was a simple but effective contrivance for stilling the water as it was carried. The word is not in the dictionaries, but they contain no better English. It is only when men wish to be big and fine, to seem to know more than they do know, and to be something that they are not, that they make such absurd words as *hydropathy*, *electropathy*, *indianopathy*, and *coldine*.

Ize and Ist, two useful affixes for the expression of action and agency, are often ignorantly added when they are entirely superfluous, and when they are incongruous with the stem. They are Greek terminations, and cannot properly be added to Anglo-Saxon words. *Ist* is the substantive form, *ize* the verbal. Among the monsters in this form none is more frequently met with than *jeopardize* — a foolish and intolerable word, which has no rightful place in the language, although even such a writer as Charles Reade thus uses it : —

"He drew in the horns of speculation, and went on in the old, safe routine; and to the restless activity that had jeopardized the firm succeeded a strange torpidity."

Certain verbs have been formed from nouns and adjectives by the addition of *ise*, or properly *ize*; as, for example, *equal*, *equalize*; *civil*, *civilize*; *patron*, *patronize*. But *jeopardize* has no such claims to toleration or respect. It is formed by adding *ize* to a *verb* of long standing in the language, and which means to put in peril; and *jeopardize*, if it means anything, means nothing more or less.

Experimentalize is a word of the same character as the foregoing. It has no rightful place in the language, and is both uncouth and pretentious. The termination *ize* is not to be tacked indiscriminately to any word in the language, verbs and adverbs as well as adjectives and nouns, for the purpose of making new verbs that are not needed. It has a meaning, and that meaning seems to be continuity of action; certainly action, and action which is not momentary. Thus, *equalize*, to make equal; *naturalize*, to make as if natural; *civilize*, to make civil; so with *moralize*, *legalize*, *humanize*, etc. But the people who use *experimentalize*, use it in the sense, to try experiments. *Experiment*, however, is both noun and verb, and will serve all purposes not better served by *try* and *trial*.

Controversialist, *conversationalist*, and *agriculturalist*, too frequently heard, are inadmissible for reasons like to those given against *experimentalize*. The proper words are *controvertist*, *conversationist*, and *agriculturist*. The others have no proper place in the English vocabulary.

The ridiculous effect of the slang words *shootist*, *stabbist*, *walkist*, and the like, is produced by the incongruity of adding *ist* to verbs of Teutonic origin. *Er*, the Anglo-Saxon sign of the doer of a thing, is incorrectly affixed to such words as *photograph* and *telegraph*, which should give us *photographist* and *telegraphist*; as we say, correctly, *paragraphist*, not *paragrapher*; although the latter would have the support of such words as *geographer* and *biographer*, which are firmly fixed in the language.

PETROLEUM. — This word may be admitted as perfectly legitimate, but it is one of a class which is doing injury to the language. *Petroleum* means merely rock oil. In it the two corresponding Latin words, *petra* and *oleum*, are only put together; and we, most of us, use the compound without knowing what it means. Now, there is no good reason, or semblance of one, why we should use a

pure Latin compound of four syllables to express
that which is better expressed in an English one of
two.   The language is full of words compounded
of two or more simple ones, and which are used without a thought of their being themselves other than
simple words — *chestnut, walnut, acorn, household,
husbandman, manhood, witchcraft, shepherd, sher-
iff, anon, alone, wheelwright, toward, forward,*
and the like.   The power to form such words is an
element of wealth and strength in a language : and
every word got up for the occasion out of the Latin
or the Greek lexicon, when a possible English compound would serve the same purpose, is a standing
but unjust reproach to the language — a false im-
putation of both weakness and inflexibility.   The
English *out-take* is much better than the Latin
compound by which it has been supplanted — *except.*   And why should we call our bank-side towns
riparian?   In dropping *wanhope* we have thrown
away a word for which *despair* is not an equivalent; and the place of *truth-like,* or *true-seeming*
would be poorly filled by the word which some very
elegant people are seeking to foist upon us — *vrai-
semblable.*   If those who have given us *petroleum*
for *rock-oil* had had the making of our language in
past times, our evergreens would have been called
sempervirids.

PRACTITIONER is an unlovely intruder, which has
slipped into the English language through the physician's gate.   We have no word *practition* to be
made a noun of agency by the suffix *er* or *ist.*
But either *practitioner* or *practitionist* means only
one who practises, a practiser.   Physicians speak of

their practice, and of the practice of medicine, and in the next breath call a medical man a practitioner. The dictionary-makers give *practise* as the stem of *practitioner* — it is difficult to see why. The word is evidently the French *praticien*, which has been Anglified first by distortion, and then by an incongruous addition, in the hope of attaining what was unattainable — a word meaning something bigger and finer than is meant by the simple and correct form *practiser*.

PRESIDENTIAL. — This adjective, which is used among us now more frequently than any other not vituperative, laudatory, or boastful, is not a legitimate word. Carelessness or ignorance has saddled it with an *i*, which is "on the wrong horse." It belongs to a sort of adjectives which are formed from substantives by the addition of *al*. For example, *incident, incidental; orient, oriental; regiment, regimental; experiment, experimental.* When the noun ends in *ce*, euphony and ease of utterance require the modification of the sound of *al* into that of *ial*; as *office, official; consequence, consequential; commerce, commercial.* But we might as well say *parential, monumential,* and *governmential,* as *presidential.* The proper form is *presidental,* as that of the adjectives formed upon *tangent* and *exponent* is *tangental* and *exponental. Presidential, tangential,* and *exponential* are a trinity of monsters which, although they have not been lovely in their lives, should yet in their death be not divided.

Tangential and *exponential,* it is plain, were incorrectly made up by some mathematician; and mathematicians, however exact they may be in their scientific work, are frequently at fault in their formation of words and phrases. These words and *presidential* are the only examples of their kind which have received the recognition, and have been stamped with the authority, even of dictionary-makers; which recognition and stamp of authority mean simply that the dictionary-makers have found the words somewhere, and have added them to the heterogeneous swarm upon their pages. Euphony, no less than analogy, cries out for the correct forms, *presidental, tangental,* and *exponental.* The rule of analogy is far from being absolute; but if analogy may not be reasoned from in etymology (although not always as the *ultima ratio*), language must needs be abandoned to the popular caprice of the moment, and we must admit that, in speech, whatever is, at any time, in any place, among whatever speakers, is right.

The phrase *presidential campaign* is a blatant Americanism, and is a good example of what has been well styled * "that inflamed newspaper English which some people describe as being eloquence." Is it not time that we had done with this nauseous talk about campaigns, and standard-bearers, and glorious victories, and all the bloated army-bumming bombast which is so rife for the six months preceding an election? To read almost any one of our political papers during a canvass is enough to make one sick and sorry. The calling a canvass a campaign is not defensible as a use of

* In "The Nation," a paper which is doing much, I hope, at once to sober and to elevate the tone both of our journalism and our politics.

metaphor, because, first, no metaphor is called for,
and last, this one is entirely out of keeping.   We
could do our political talking much better in simple
English.   One of the great needs of the day, in regard to language, is the purging it of the prurient
and pretentious metaphors which have broken out
all over it, and the getting plain people to say plain
things in a plain way.   An election has no manner
of likeness to a campaign or a battle.   It is not
even a contest in which the stronger and more dex-
terous party is the winner: it is a mere comparison,
a counting, in which the bare fact that one party is
the more numerous puts it in power, if it will
only come up and be counted; to insure which,
a certain time is spent by each party in belittling
and reviling the candidates of its opponents, and in
magnifying and lauding its own; and this is the
canvass, at the likening of which to a campaign
every honest soldier might reasonably take offence.
The loss of an election is sure to be attributed to various causes by the losers; but the only and the simple and sufficient cause is, that more men chose to
vote against them than with them; and as to the
why of the why, it is either conviction, or friendship, or interest, with which all the meeting and
parading, and bawling and shrieking, of the previous three or four months has nothing whatever to
do.   It will be well for the political morality and
the mental tone of our people when they are brought
to see this matter as it is, simply of itself; and one
very efficient mode of enabling them to do so, would
be for journals of character and men of sense to
write and speak of it in plain language, calling a

spade a spade, instead of using " that inflamed En
lish " which is now its common vehicle, and which
so contagious and so corrupting :—so contagious, a
so corrupting, indeed, that I am not fond enough
hope that anything said here, even were it said w
more reason and stronger persuasion than I can u
will unsettle any fixed habit of speech in my rea
ers. I merely tell them what, in my judgment,
is right and best to say, knowing in my heart,
the while, that they, or most of them, will go
speaking as they hear those around them speak,
they will act as they see those around them actin
People do not learn good English or good manne
by verbal instruction received after adolescenc
Every man is like the apostle Peter in one r
spect—that his tongue bewrays him.

PROVEN, which is frequently used now by la
yers and journalists, should, perhaps, be rank
among words that are not words. Those who u
it seem to think that it means something more,
other, than the word for which it is a mere Lov
land Scotch and North of England provincialis
Proved is the past participle of the verb *to pro*
and should be used by all who wish to spe
English.

RELIABLE. — Before giving our attention dire
ly to this word, it will be well to consider wh
might be said in favor of one which has som
what similar claims to a place in the language
undisfellowshipable. We have seen that the verb
fellowship has the " authority " of ancient and disti
guished usage. Now, if we can fellowship with
man, we may disfellowship with him ; and if a m

whom we may rely upon is a reliable man, a man
whom we can disfellowship with is disfellowshipa-
ble, and one whose claims upon us are such that we
cannot disfellowship with him is undisfellowshipable.
I admit that I can discover no defect in this reasoning
if the premises are granted. If mere ancient and
honorable use authorizes a word, the verb *to fellowship* — as, I would fellowship with him — has un-
deniable authority; and no reason which can be
given for calling a man who may be relied upon
reliable will fail to support us in calling a man who
can be fellowshipped with fellowshipable. It may,
however, be urged, — and I should venture to take
the position, — that the mere use of a word, or a collocation of syllables with an implied meaning, whatever the eminence of the user, is not a sufficient
ground for the reception of that word into the recognized vocabulary of a language. For instance,
the word *intrinsecate* is used by Shakespeare himself : —

> "Come, mortal wretch,
> With thy sharp tooth this knot intrinsecate
> Of life at once untie." — *Ant. and Cleop.*, V. 2.

This may have been a superfluous attempt to An-
glicise the Italian *intrinsecare*, or, as Dr. Johnson
suggested, an ignorant formation between *intricate*
and *intrinsical*. But notwithstanding the eminence
of the user, it has no recognized place in the language, and is one of the words that are not words.

Reliable is conspicuous among those words.
That it is often heard merely shows that many persons have been led into the error of using it; that
other words of like formation have been found in

the writings of men of more or less note in literature merely shows that inferior men are not more incapable than Shakespeare was of using words ignorantly formed by the union of incongruous elements. Passing for the present the words which are brought up to support *reliable* by analogy (on the ground, it would seem, unless they themselves can be sustained by reason, that one error may be justified by others), let us confine our attention to that one of the group, which, being oftenest heard, is of most importance.

Probably no accumulation of reason and authority would protect the language from this innovating word (which is none the worse, however, because it is new) ; for to some sins men are so wedded that they will shut their ears to Moses and the prophets, and to one risen from the dead. Previous writers have well remarked that it is anomalous in position and incongruous in formation; that adjectives in *able*, or its equivalent, *ible*, are formed from verbs transitive, the passive participle of which can be united with the meaning of the suffix in the definition of the adjective. For example, *lovable*, that may be loved; *legible*, that may be read; *eatable*, that may be eaten; *curable*, that may be cured, and so forth; that *reliable* does not mean that may be relied, but is used to mean that may be relied *upon*, and that, therefore, it is not tolerable. The counter-plea has been, until recently, usage and convenience. But the usage in question has been too short and too unauthoritative to have any weight; and convenience is not a justification of monstrosity, when the monstrosity is great, offensive, and of degrading influence, and the convenience so small as to be inappreciable. But it has been recently urged, with an air of pardonable triumph, that the rule of formation above mentioned has not prevailed in our language, as is shown by the presence in it of long-established adjectives, bearing with them the weight of all possible authority; for instance, *laughable*, which does not mean that may be laughed, but that may be laughed *at*. Here the case has rested; and if this argument could not be overthrown, the question would have been decided by it, and the use of *reliable* would be a matter of individual taste. But the argument goes too far, because those who used it did not go far enough. *Comfortable* does not mean that may be comforted, but that has or that gives comfort; *forcible*, not that may be forced, but that is able to force; *seasonable*, not that may be seasoned, but that is in season, in accord with the season; *leisurable*, that has leisure; *fashionable*, that has fashion. The suffix *able*, in Latin *abilis*, expresses the idea of power,[*] and so of capacity, ability, fitness. It may be affixed either to verbs or to nouns; and of adjectives in this class not a few are formed upon the latter. In the examples above it is affixed to nouns. Now, *laugh* is a noun, and *laughable, marriageable, treasonable, leisurable, objectionable*, and *companionable* are in the same category. *Laughable* does, in effect, mean that may be laughed at, as *objectionable* means, in effect, that may be objected to; but neither must therefore be regarded as formed from the verb by which each may be defined. Finally, the

[*] See Tooke's "Diversions of Purley," Vol. II. p. 502.

fact is that, excepting a comparatively few adj
tives in *able* or *ible* thus formed upon nouns,* ev
one of the multitudinous class of adjectives form
by this suffix — a class which includes about n
hundred words — is formed upon a verb transiti
and may be defined by the passive participle.   Th
afford, therefore, no support to the word *relial*
because we cannot rely anything.

Professor Whitney, in his book on "The Stu
of Language," a work combining knowledge a
wisdom in a greater degree than any other of
kind in English literature, gives some attention
the word in question, but contents himself w
setting forth the arguments for and against it, wi
out summing up the case and passing judgeme
Among the reasons in its favor he mentions "t
enrichment of the language by a synonyme, whi
may yet be made to distinguish a valuable sha
of meaning; which, indeed, already shows sight
doing so, as we tend to say 'a *trustworthy* witne
but '*reliable* testimony.'"

This is plausible, but only plausible; and it h
been well answered by an able pupil of Profess
Whitney's, and one worthy of his master,† as f
lows : —

"A little examination will show that there is no case at all
the word in question.   There is really no tendency whatev
in common speech, to differentiate the two words in the sen
named, for *reliable* is, in a large majority of cases, applied
persons.   Nor, if there were such a tendency, would it add an
thing to the language, any more than to devise two disti
verbs meaning *believe*, the one to express believing a man, t
other, believing what he says."

* No small proportion of them is cited above.   Many which have no proper p
in the language are to be found in dictionaries.
† Mr. Charlton Lewis in "The Evening Post" of March 6, 1869.

Of the common use of *reliable*, I met with the following amusing and illustrative example in the Paris correspondence of the London "Star." The Prince and Princess Christian, arriving at the French capital, had been compelled, for want of better carriage, to visit Trianon in a cab. Whereupon a quarter of a column of British astonishment and disgust, closing with this paragraph: —

"I do the justice to the Prefect to assert that a telegram despatched on the party leaving Paris would have secured the presence of a more reliable vehicle than a hackney cab at the Versailles station."

Here our word is put to fitting service in contrasting a reliable vehicle with an unreliable cab. And here is yet another instance in which the word appears suitably accompanied. The sentence is from the prospectus of "The Democrat," published by the gentleman known as "Brick Pomeroy."

"Politically it will be Democratic, red-hot and reliable."

The red-hot and reliable democracy of Mr. "Brick Pomeroy's" paper and the unreliable cab at Versailles are well consorted.

Of the few words which may be, and some of which have been, cited in support of *reliable*, here follow the most important — the examples of their use being taken from Richardson's Dictionary: —

Anchorable. "The sea, everywhere twenty leagues from land, is *anchorable.*" — *Sir T. Herbert.*

Complainable. "Though both be blamable, yet superstition is less *complainable.*" — *Feltham.*

Disposable. "The office is not *disposable* by the crown." — *Burke.*

Inquirable. "There may be many more things *inquirable* by you." — *Bacon.*

15

Of these passages, the first affords an example of the improper use of words properly formed; the second, of unjustifiable formations, like *reliable*. A vessel may be anchorable; a sea cannot be so: neither a superstition nor anything else can be complainable, although it may be complained of. Herbert and Feltham could go astray in the use of *anchorable* and *complainable*, as Shakespeare could in that of *intrinsecate*. The other two words could be accepted as of any weight upon this question only through ignorance both of their meaning and their history. *Dispose* does not need *of* to complete its transitive sense; and the preposition has been added to it in common usage quite recently — long after *disposable* came into the language. Richardson affords the following examples in point: —

> "Sens God seeth everything out of doutance,
> And hem disposeth through his ordinance."
>
> *Chaucer.*
>
> "But God, who secretly disposeth the course of things."
>
> *Tyndal.*

And to this day we say that people dispose (not dispose of) themselves in groups to their liking, as Spenser said: —

> "The rest themselves in troupes did else dispose."
>
> *Faerie Queene,* II. 8.

And accordingly Prynne, a careful writer, who lived two hundred years before Burke, says of the realm of Bohemia, "most of the great offices of which realme are hereditary, and not disposable by the king."

Inquirable, as used by Bacon, means, not that may be inquired into, but that may be inquired, *i. e.,* asked. It is simply equivalent to *askable*. In the sense of inquired into it would not be admissible, and no recent examples of its use, or of its use in that sense, are cited by Richardson.

Available— the word which seems most to support *reliable*, because it is surely formed upon the verb *avail*, and because, although we may say of a thing that it avails much or it avails nought, we cannot say it may be availed — is itself unavailable to the end for which it is cited. For *avail* itself is an anomalous and exceptional word in the manner of its use. It means to *have* value, effect, worth, power. Yet we say, both, It avails little, and He avails himself of it; both, Of what avail was it? and It was of no avail, as we say, Of what worth was it? and It was of no worth. But we cannot, or do not, speak of the avail of anything, as we speak of the worth of any thing. *Avail*, both as verb and substantive, was used absolutely by our early writers in the sense of value, and *available* — *i. e.*, that may be valued — came into the language under those circumstances.

Unrepentable, which is used by Pollok, a writer of low rank and no authority, has been cited in support of *reliable*. But there is no verb *unrepent;* nor is there any instance known of the use of the adjective *repentable*. And although examples are numerous of the use in the Elizabethan period of *repent* absolutely, without *of*,[*] yet we read in our English Bible not of a repentance not repentable, but of "a repentance not to be repented of."

* See Mrs. Clarke's "Concordance to Shakespeare."

Accountable and *answerable* are, like *availabl*
anomalous, self-incongruous, and exceptionab
Accountable is used to mean, not that may be a
counted for, but that may be held to account; b
answerable is used to mean both that may be a
swered (in which it is not a counterpart of *reliab*
and, that may be held to answer; while *unaccou*
able is used only to mean that cannot be accou
ed for, and *unanswerable*, only that cannot be a
swered.   These adjectives are out of all keeping

These are all the instances of adjectives in
which are worthy of attention in the considerati
of this formation; and we have seen that none
them support the use of the affix with a verb
pendent and intransitive, like *rely*.   If there w
a noun *rely*, upon that we might form *reliable*,
companionable has been formed on *companion*, a
dutiable on *duty*.   Unless we keep to this law
formation, there is no knowing where we may fi
ourselves — stranded, it may be, on some such ro
as a grievable tale, an untrifleable person, or a we
able tragedy.   For instance, *reliable* has been f
lowed into the world by a worthy kinsman, *liveal*
in the phrase "a liveable house," which we
only hear now sometimes, but even see in pri
although it has not yet been taken into the dicti
aries.   See, for example, the following passa
from a magazine of such high and well-deserve
reputation as "Macmillan's:" —

"In the first place, we would lay down as a fundamental pi
ciple in furnishing, that the end in view should be to mak
house or a room cheerful, comfortable, and liveable.   We
liveable, because there are so many which, though handson
furnished, are dreary in the extreme, and the very thought
living in them makes one shudder."

Now, a life is liveable, because a man may live a life, as he can be himself; but a house cannot be lived any more than a pea-jacket. Either may be lived in, according to the liver's fancy. Let us not, through mere sloth and slovenliness, give up for such a mess as *reliable* our birthright in a good word and a good phrase for a man who is trustworthy, and whose word may be relied upon.

PREVENTATIVE, CASUALITY, receive a passing notice, only because they are heard so often instead of *preventive, casualty*. They ought to be, but I fear that they are not, evidences of an utter want of education and of a low grade of intelligence.

RESURRECTED. — This amazing formation has lately appeared in some of our newspapers, one of them edited by a man who has been clerk of the Senate, another, one of the most carefully edited journals in the country. For example : —

"The invention described in yesterday's Times, and displayed on Saturday at Newark, by which a person who may happen to be buried alive is enabled to resurrect himself from the grave, may leave some people to fancy there is actual danger of their being buried alive."

A weekly paper, of some pretensions, now extinct, described Thomas Rowley as a priest whose writings Chatterton "professed to *resurrect* in the form of old, stained, moth-eaten manuscripts."

What is this word intended to mean? Possibly the same act which people who speak English mean when they say that Lazarus was raised from the dead. The formation of *resurrect* from *resurrection* is just of a piece with the formation of *donate* from *donation*, *intercess* from *intercession*. But it is

somewhat worse; for *resurrected* is used to me
raised, and *resurrection* does not mean raising,
rising.   Thus we speak of the raising of Lazar
but of the resurrection of Christ; of God's raisi
the dead, but of the resurrection of the dead.

SIS, SISSY.—The gentlemen who, with aff
tionate gayety and gay affection, address v
young ladies as Sis or Sissy, indulge themsel
in that captivating freedom in the belief that th
are merely using an abbreviation of *sister*.   Th
are wrong.   They doubtless mean to be frat
nal, or paternal, and so subjectively their not
is correct.   But *Sis*, as a generic name for a you
girl, has come straight down to us, without
break of a day, from the dark ages.   It is a m
abbreviation or nickname of *Cicely*, and appe
all through our early literature as *Cis* and *Cis*
It was used, like *Joan* and *Moll*, to mean
young girl, as *Rob* or *Hob*, the nicknames
Robert, were applied in a general way to
young man of the lower classes.

> "Robert's esteemed for handling flail,
>   And Ciss for her clean milking-pail."
>   *The Sarah-ad.*, 1742, p. 5.

SHAMEFACED, as every reader of Archbish
Trench's books on English knows, is a mere c
ruption of *shamefast*, a word of the *steadfast* s
The corruption, doubtless, had its origin in a mis
prehension due to the fact that *fast* was pronoun
like *fac'd*, with the name sound of *a*, which led to
supposition that *shamefast* was merely an irregu
spelling of *shamefaced*.   To a similar confusion
words pronounced alike we owe the phrase "

worth a damn," in which the last word represents *water-cress.* The Anglo-Saxon name of the cress was *cerse;* and this, by that transposition of the *r* so common in the earlier stages of our language, and which gave us *bird* for *brid,* and *burn* for *bren,* became *cres.* But for a long time it retained its original form; and a man who meant to say that anything was of very little value, said sometimes that it was not worth a rush, and others that it was not worth a cerse, or kerse. For example (one of many), see this passage of "Piers Ploughman's Vision:"—

> Wisdom and wit now
> Is noght worth a *kerse,*
> But if it be carded with coveitise,
> As clotheres kemben his wolle."

Identity of sound between two words led to a misapprehension which changed the old phrase into "not worth a curse;" and a liking for variety, which has not been without its influence, even in the vocabulary of oaths and objurgations, led to the substitution to which we owe "not worth a damn." But for one variety of this phrase, which is peculiar to this country, and which is one of its very few original peculiarities, "not worth a continental damn," I am at a loss to assign a source; except that it may be found in that tendency to vastness of ideas, and that love of annexation of which we are somewhat justly accused, and which crops out even in our swearing.

STAND-POINT. — To say the best of it, this is a poor compound. It receives some support, but not full justification, from the German *stand-punkt,* of

which, indeed, it is supposed to be an Angliciz
form, first used by Professor Moses Taylor. Gra
ing for the moment that *stand-point* may be accept
as meaning standing-point, and that when we sa
from our stand-point, we intend to say from the po
at which we stand, what we really mean is, fro
our *point of view*, and we should say so.   Perip
rasis is to be avoided when it is complicated
burdensome, but never at the cost of correctnes
and periphrasis is sometimes not only stronge
because clearer, than a single word, but more e
gant.   *Stand-point*, whatever the channel of
coming into use, is of the sort to which the vulg
words *wash-tub*, *shoe-horn*, *brew-house*, *cook-sto*
and *go-cart* belong, the first four of which a
merely slovenly and uncouth abbreviations of *was*
ing-tub, *shoeing-horn*, *brewing-house*, and *cookin*
stove, the last being a nursery word, a counterp
to which would be *rock-horse*, instead of *rockin*
horse.   Compounds of this kind are properly form
by the union of a substantive or participle, us
adjectively, with a substantive ; and their meani
may be exactly expressed by reversing the position
the elements of the compound, and connecting the
by one of the prepositions *of*, *to*, and *for*.   Thu
death-bed, bed of death ; *stumbling-block*, blo
of stumbling ; *turning point*, point cf turnin
play-ground, ground for play ; *dew-point*, point
dew ; *steam-boat*, boat for or of steam (*bateau de*
peur) ; *starvation-point*, point of starvation ; *hor*
trough, trough for horses ; *rain-bow*, bow of rai
bread-knife, knife for bread ; *house-top*, top of hous
dancing-girl, girl for dancing ; and *standing-poi*

point for or of standing; and so forth. But by no
contrivance can we explain *stand-point* as the point
of, or to, or for, stand.

TELEGRAM. — This word, which is claimed as
an "American" production, has taken root quickly,
and is probably well fixed in the language. It is
both superfluous and incorrectly formed; but it is
regarded as convenient, and has been allowed to
pass muster. *Telegraph* is equally good as a verb
expressing the act of writing, and as a noun expressing the thing written. This is according to a
well-known analogy of the language. But they
who must have a distinct etymology for every word
may regard *telegraph*, the verb, as from γραφειν
(*graphein*) = to write, and the noun as from the
Greek noun γραφη (*graphē*) = a writing. In *monograph*, *epigraph*, and *paragraph*, the last syllable
in like manner represents γραφη (*graphē*) ; in *monogram*, *epigram*, and *diagram* the last syllable
represents γραμμα (*gramma*) = an engraved character, a letter.* This distinction, remembered, will
prevent a confusion which prevails with many
speakers as to certain words in *graph* and *gram*.
A monograph is an essay or an account having a
single subject; a monogram, a character or cipher
composed of several letters combined in one figure ;
an epigraph is an inscription, a citation, a motto ;
an epigram, a short poem on one subject. The
confusion of these terminations has recently led
some writers into errors which are amazing and

* Γραφμα, litera, scriptum ; (1) librum ; (3) scriptum quodcunque ut tabulæ publicæ
legæ, libri rationum, &c., et *in plurali* ; (4) epistola, literæ ; (5) literæ, doctrina ;
(6) acta publica, tabulæ ; (7) chirographum.
  Γραφη, scriptura, scriptio ; (2) pictura ; (3) accusatio. — *Hederici Lexicon.*

amusing. We have had *photogram* proposed, and
stereogram, and — Cadmus save us ! — *cablegram*,
not only proposed, but used. Finally, to cap the
climax of absurdity, some ingenious person, encouraged by such example, proposes *thalagram* as " fully
expressive and every way appropriate," because
thalassa is the Greek for sea, and *gramma* the Greek
for letter, and the letters come through the sea.
The first two, although homogeneous, are incorrect,
the proper termination in both cases being *graph*,
representing γραφη (*graphé*), a writing, and not
gram, from γραμμα (*gramma*), a character; and in
the third there is not only the same error, but the
incongruous union of the Teutonic *cable* with the
Greek *gramma*. The last is not worth serious consideration. Such words as *cablegram* and *thalagram* are only deplorable and ridiculous examples
of what is produced when men who are unfit to
work in language undertake to make a word that
is not wanted. There is no more need of such
words as *cablegram* and *thalagram* were meant to
be, than there is of a new name for bread-and-but-
ter. A telegraph is the thing which sends words
from afar, and *telegram* is in general use to mean
the word or words so sent; and whether they
come across land or water, what matter? what is it
to any reasonable purpose? A telegram from Europe, or from California, or from China, is all the
same, whatever may be the route by which it is
sent. Whether it comes by an iron cable, or a
copper wire, over land or through water, what
difference? There could not be a finer specimen
of an utterly superfluous monster than this English-
Greek hybrid *cablegram*.

TIME AND TIDE WAIT FOR NO MAN.—This proverb, one of the oldest in the language, one of the
most commonly used, and one which cannot be
expressed with its full force and point in any other
tongue, may be noticed here without impropriety,
because it is probably not understood by one in a
thousand of its users. The word misunderstood is
tide, which, contrary to almost universal apprehension of the adage, does not here mean the ebb and
flow of the ocean. *Tide* has here its original meaning — time. Thus we find in some Middle English
Glosses, published in the "Reliquiæ Antiquæ" (Vol.
I. p. 12), "*tempore*=tyda." But *tide* is not a mere
synonyme of *time*; it means *a* time, an allotment
of time, an occasion. It was long used for *hour*,
as in the following Anglo-Saxon statement of the
length of the year: "dis is full yer, twelf monþas
fulle and endlufan dagas, six tida;" *i. e.*, this is a
full year, twelve full months, and eleven days, six
hours. It meant also a certain or an appointed
time; *e. g.*, "Nu tumorgen on þis ylcan tid," *i. e.*,
Now to-morrow on this same time. (Exodus ix.
18.) This sense of an appointed time it had in the
old, and now no longer heard, saying, The tider you
go, the tider you come, which Skinner renders thus
in Latin: *Quo temporiùs discedis, eo temporiùs re-
cedis.* The ebb and flow of the sea came to be
called the tide because it takes place at appointed
seasons. The use of *tide* in this sense, a set time,
a season, continued to a very late period; of which
the following passage from Shakespeare is an
example:

> " What hath this day deserved,
> That it in golden letters should be set
> Among the high tides in the calendar?"
>
> *King John*, iii. 1.,

where "high tides" has plainly no meaning of peculiar interest to mariners and fishermen. Chaucer says, in "Troilus and Cressida:"—

> " The morrow came, and nighen gan the time
> Of mealtide."

This use of the word is still preserved in the names of two appointed seasons, the church festivals Whitsuntide and Christmastide, or Christtide, which are more in vogue in England than in this country. *Tide* appears in this sense in the word *betide*. For example: Woe betide you! that is, Woe await you; May there be occasion of woe to you. *Tide* was thus used before the addition of the prefix *be*, as in the following lines from a poetical interpretation of dreams, written about A. D. 1315:—

> " Gif the see is yn tempeste
> The *tid* anguisse ant eke cheste " (*i. e.*, strife).

Our proverb, therefore, means, not time and the flow of the sea wait for no man, but time and occasion, opportunity, wait for no man. The proverb appears almost literally in the following lines, which are the first two of an epitaph of the fifteenth century, that may be found in the "Reliquiæ Antiquæ" (Vol. I. p. 268):—

> " Farewell, my frendis, the tide abideth no man;
> I am departed fro this, and so shall ye,"

where, again, there is manifestly no allusion to the flow of water. There is an old agricultural phrase still used among the Lowland Scotch farmers, in which *tide* appears in the sense of season : "The grund's no in tid," *i. e.*, The ground is not in season, not ready at the proper time for the earing.

The use of *tide* in its sense of hour, *the* hour, led naturally to a use of *hour* for *tide*. Among the examples that might be cited of this conversion, there is a passage in "Macbeth" which has long been a puzzle to readers and commentators, and upon which, in my own edition of Shakespeare, I have given only some not very relevant comments by the Rev. Mr. Hunter. Macbeth says (Act i. scene 3), —

"Time and the hour runs through the roughest day."

As an hour is but a measured lapse of time, there has been much discussion as to why Shakespeare should have written "time *and* the hour," and many passages have been quoted from Shakespeare and other poets by the commentators, in which *time* and *hour* are found in close relation ; but they are all, as such quotations are apt to be, quite from the purpose.

"Time and the hour" in this passage is merely an equivalent of time and tide — the time and tide that wait for no man. Macbeth's brave but unsteadfast soul is shaken to its loose foundations by the prophecies of the witches, and the speedy fulfilment of the first of them. His ambition fires like tinder at the touch of temptation, and his quick imagination sets before him the bloody path by which he is to reach the last and highest prize, the promised throne. But his good instincts — for he has instincts, not purposes — revolt at the hideous prospect, and his whole nature is in a tumult of conflicting emotion. The soul

of the man that would not play false, and yet would
wrongly win, is laid open at a stroke to us in this
first sight we have of him. After shying at the
ugly thing, from which, however, he does not bolt,
at last he says, cheating himself with the thought
that he will wait on Providence, —

> "If chance will have me king, why, chance may crown me
> Without my stir."

And then he helps himself out of his tribulation,
as men often do, with an old saw, and says it will
all come right in the end. Looking into the black,
turbulent future, which would be all bright and clear
if he would give up his bad ambition, he neither
turns back nor goes forward, but says, —

> "Come what come may,
> Time and the hour runs through the roughest day."

That is, time and opportunity, time and tide, run
through the roughest day; the day most thickly
bestead with trouble is long enough, and has occasions enough for the service and the safety of a
ready, quick-witted man. But for the rhythm,
Shakespeare would probably have written, Time
and tide run through the roughest day; but as the
adage in that form was not well suited to his verse,
he used the equivalent phrase, time and the hour
(not time and *an* hour, or time and the *hours*);
and the appearance of the singular verb in this line,
I am inclined to regard as due to the poet's own pen,
not as accidental.

CHAPTER VIII.

FORMATION OF PRONOUNS. — SOME. — ADJECTIVES
IN EN. — EITHER AND NEITHER. — SHALL AND
WILL.

FORMATION OF PRONOUNS.

TWO correspondents have laid before me the
great need — which they have discovered —
of a new pronoun in English, and both have suggested the same means of supplying the deficiency,
which is, in the words of the first, "the use of *en*,
or some more euphonious substitute, as a personal
pronoun, common gender." "A deficiency exists
there," he glibly continues, "and we should fill it."
My other correspondent has a somewhat juster
notion of the magnitude of his proposition, or, as I
should rather say, of its enormity. But, still, he
insists that a new pronoun is "universally needed,"
and as an example of the inconvenience caused by
the want, he gives the following sentence : —

"If a person wishes to sleep, they mustn't eat cheese for
supper."

"Of course," he goes on to say, "that is incorrect :
yet almost every one would say *they*." (That I
venture to doubt.) "Few would say in common
conversation, 'If a person wishes to sleep, he or
she mustn't eat cheese for supper.' It is too much

trouble. We must have a word to take the place
he or she, his or hers, him or her, etc. . . .
As the French make the little word en answer
great many purposes, suppose we take the sam
word, give it an English pronunciation (or any oth
word), and make it answer for any and every ca
of that kind, and thus tend to simplify the la
guage."

To all this there are two sufficient replies. Firs
the thing can't be done; last, it is not at all nece
sary or desirable that it should be done. And
consider the last point first. There is no suc
dilemma as the one in question. A speaker
common sense and common mastery of Englis
would say, "If a man wishes to sleep, he must n
eat cheese at supper,"* where man, as in the wor
mankind, is used in a general sense for the specie
Any objection to this use of man, and of the rel
tive pronoun, is for the consideration of the ne
Woman's Rights Convention, at which I hope
may be discussed with all the gravity beseeming i
momentous significance. But as a slight contribu
tion to the amenities of the occasion, I venture
suggest that to free the language from the oppre
sion of the sex and from the outrage to its dignit
which have for centuries lurked in this use of ma
and he, it is not necessary to say, "If a perso
wishes to sleep, en mustn't eat cheese for supper
but merely, as the speakers of the best English no
say, and have said for generations, "If one wish
to sleep, one mustn't, etc." One, thus used, is

---

* Unless we mean that the supper consisted entirely or chiefly of cheese, we shou
not say cheese *for* supper, but cheese *at* supper.

good pronoun, of healthy, well-rooted growth. And we have in *some* another word which supplies all our need in this respect without our going to the French for their over-worked *en;* e. g., *Voici des bonnes fraises. Voulez-vous en avoir?* These are fine strawberries. Will you have some? Thus used, *some* is to all intents and purposes a pronoun which leaves nothing to be desired. With *he*, *she*, *it*, and *we*, and *one*, and *some*, we have no need of *en* or any other outlandish pronoun.

Or we should have had one long ere this. For the service to which the proposed pronoun would be put, if it were adopted, is not new. The need is one which, if it exists at all, must have been felt five hundred years ago as much as it can be now. At that period, and long before, a noun in the third person singular was represented, according to its gender, by the pronouns *he*, *she*, or *it*, and there was no pronoun of common gender to take place of all of them. In the matter of language, popular need is inexorable, and popular ingenuity inexhaustible; and it is not in the nature of things that, if the imagined need had existed, it should not have been supplied during the formative stages of our language, particularly at the Elizabethan period, to which we owe the pronoun *its*. The introduction of this word, although it is merely a possessive form of *it*, was a work of so much time and difficulty, that an acquaintance with the struggle would alone deter a considerate man from attempting to make a new pronoun. Although, as I have said, it is a mere possessive form of a word which had been on the lips of all men of Anglo-Saxon blood

for a thousand years, and although it was introduced at a period notable for bold linguistic innova-
tions, and was soon adopted by some of the most
popular writers, Shakespeare among them, nearly
a century elapsed before it was firmly established
in the English tongue.

For pronouns are of all words the remotest in
origin, the slowest of growth, the most irregular and
capricious in their manner of growth, the most
tenacious of hold, the most difficult to plant, the
most nearly impossible to transplant. To say that
I, the first of pronouns, is three thousand years old,
is quite within bounds. We trace it through the
Old English *ich* to the Anglo-Saxon *ic*, and the
Gothic *ik*. It appears in the Icelandic *ek*, the Danish *jeg*, the Old German *ih*, the Russian *ia*, the
Latin and Greek *ego*, and the Sanscrit *aham*. Should
any of my readers fail to see the connection between
ah-am and *I*, let him consider for a moment that
the sound expressed by the English *I* is *ah-ee*.

The antiquity of pronouns is shown, also, by the
irregularity of their cases. That is generally a trait
of the oldest words in any language, verbs and
adjectives as well as pronouns. For instance, the
words expressing consciousness, existence, pleasure, and pain, the first and commonest linguistic
needs of all peoples, — in English, *I*, *be*, *good*, *bad*;
in Latin, *ego*, *esse*, *bonus*, *malus*, — are regular in
no language that I can remember within the narrow
circle with which I have been able to establish an
acquaintance. *Telegraph* and *skedaddle* are as
regular as may be; but we say *go*, *went*, *gone*; the
Romans said *eo*, *ire*, *ivi*, *itum*; and the irregular-

ities, dialectic and other, of the Greek ιημι (*eimi*), are multitudinous and anomalous. English pronouns have real cases, which is one sign of their antiquity, the Anglo-Saxon having been an inflected language; but not in Anglo-Saxon, in Latin, or in any other inflected language, are the oblique cases of *I* derived from it more than they are in English. *My, me, we, our, us,* are not inflections of *I;* but neither are *meus, mihi, me, nos, nostrum, nobis,* inflections of *ego.* The oblique cases of pronouns are furnished by other parts of speech, or by other pronouns, from which they are taken bodily, or composed, in the early, and, generally, unwritten stages of a language. Between the pronoun and the article there is generally a very close relation. It is in allusion to this fact that Sir Hugh Evans, putting William Page to school ("Merry Wives of Windsor," Act IV. Scene 1), and endeavoring to trip the lad, — though he learned the trick of William Lilly the grammarian, — asks, "What is he, William, that doth lend articles?" But the boy is too quick for him, and replies, "Articles are borrowed of the pronoun, and be thus declined: *singulariter, nominativo, hic, hæc, hoc.*"

A marked instance of this relationship between the pronoun and the article, and an instructive example of the manner in which pronouns come into a language, is our English *she,* which is borrowed from the Anglo-Saxon definite article *se,* the feminine form of which was *seó;* and this definite article itself originally was, or was used as, a demonstrative pronoun, corresponding to *who, that.* For *se* is a softened form of the older *the;* and *Ic the, he the*

are Anglo-Saxon for I who, he who. The Anglo-
Saxon for *she* was *heó;* the masculine being, as in
English, *he*. And as a definite feminine object was
expressed by the article *seó*, it has been supposed
that the likeness in form and meaning between the
two caused a coalition, so that from *heo* and *shee*
came *she*. But this must have been in the North,
if at all. For *sco* or *scho*, the Northern equivalent
to *heo* seems to have been the direct ancestor of
our *she*. And in Gothic *si* or *se=she;* where, however, there is again the kindred likeness between
the feminine pronoun and the article, *sa, so=the*.

Our possessive neuter pronoun *its*, to which reference has been made before, came into the language
last of all its kin, in this manner: As *heó* was the
feminine of *he*, *hit* was the neuter. From *hit* the
h was dropped by one of the vicissitudes which
have so often damped the aspirations of that unfortunate letter. Now in *it*, the *t* — half the word — is
no part of the original pronoun, but the mere inflectional termination by which it is formed from
he. But by long usage, in a period of linguistic
disintegration, the *t* came to be looked upon as an
essential part of the word, one really original letter of which, *h*, had been dropped by the most
cultivated writers. This letter, however, long held
its place; and in the usage of the common people,
and in that of some writers, the Anglo-Saxon *hit*
was the neuter pronoun nearly down to the Elizabethan period. Of both the masculine *he* and the
neuter *hit*, the possessive case was *his*, just as *ejus*
is the genitive of both *is* and *id;* and so *his* was
the proper lineal possessive case of *it*, the succes-

of *hit*. If *his* had been subjected to a depriva-
n like to that of the nominative, by an elision of
: *h*, and made into *is*, there would have been nc
parent reason to question its relationship to *it*.
t this was not to be. The *t*, not the *h*, had come
be regarded as the essential letter of the word;
was looked upon as belonging to *he*, and not to
and to the latter was added the *s*, which is a
n of possession in so many of the Indo-Euro-
an languages. But there lingered long, not only
ong the uneducated people who continued to use
, but among writers and scholars, a consciousness
t *his* was the true possessive of *it*, and still more
eeling that *its* was an illegitimate pretender.
d, indeed, if ever word was justly called bastard,
one deserves the stigma. But like some other
tards, it has held the place it seized, and justified
usurpation by the service it has rendered.*

his is the history of a pronominal form which
excluded from our English Bible (A. D. 1611),
h was used but nine times by Shakespeare, and
ad of which we find *his*, *her*, and even *it* late in
venteenth century. A singular idiom, *the own*,
ssing reflective possession, was in use between
and 1600. Here *the* does not stand for *its*;
l possessive *hit* having been in general use as
1500. Besides, *the own* expressed plural as
singular possession.

oubt yet prevails as to the origin of the use of *his* as a sign of the posses-
John his book. May it not have come in thus? *Es* or *is*, the possessive
s first separated from the noun; *e. g.,* —

eetest tyring that is to gosshawke & sperhawke is a pigge *is* tayle."
e hawke *is* erys with oyle of olive," etc.
Book of Hawking (tem. Henry VI.), *Relig. Antiq.* I. 296, 301.

effected, *is* was aspirated, and supposed to be the pronoun. A pigge
John his book are not easily distinguishable from a pigg-es tayle and
Hence the confusion of the two.

The formation of certain other possessive
nouns is somewhat like that of *its*. These are
absolute possessives *hers, ours, yours*, and *theirs*
of which are made by adding the singular posses
suffix *s* to an already possessive form, which in
last three is plural — a striking irregularity. Th
absolute possessive pronouns are thus double
sessives. The others, *mine* and *thine*, are only
possessive forms which have been set apart for
absolutely. It is in analogy with them that the
gar absolute possessives *hisn, hern, ourn, yourn*,
theirn are formed. Remarkably, in the femin
personal pronoun, and in no other, both the pos
sive and objective relation are expressed by the s
form, *her*. This results from the fact that the An
Saxon *hire*, the genitive and dative of *heo*=*she*, t
the place of the accusative *hi*. It has long been
tablished that the objective of English pronouns
formed upon the Anglo-Saxon dative. In the cas
heo, however, not only were the genitive and da
identical, but *hire*, in both the genitive and da
use, went through the same changes, *hire, heore, h
hir* in passing into *her*, upon which *hers* was form
and which has long been used provincially a
nominative. This identity of the feminine genit
and dative is common in Anglo-Saxon pronoun

To these illustrations of the way in which
nouns find their way into a language, I will add
other example of this taking of a part of an o
nal word as a stem. Had we lived three hund
years ago, we should have said about the sea
July, when I am writing, that we liked pison for
ner. But by this we should not have meant
fluid which is sung, cold, in the touching ballad
" Villikins and his Dinah," but simply peas

we should have pronounced the word, not *py-son*, but *pee-son*. *Pison* or *pisen* is merely the old plural in *en* (like *oxen*, *brethren*) of *pise* — pronounced (*peese*) — the name of the vegetable which we call pea. Our forefathers said a pise, as we say a pea. When the old plural in *en* was dropped, *pise* (*peese*) came to be regarded as a plural in *s* of a supposed singular, *pi* (pronounced *pee*); and by this backward movement toward a non-existent starting-point, we have attained the word *pea*.

To return to our subject. The British Parliament is called omnipotent, and a majority may, by a single vote, change the so-called British Constitution, as a majority of Congress may, if it will, set at naught the Constitution of the United States. But neither Parliament nor Congress, not both of them by a concurrent vote, could make or modify a pronoun in the language common to the nations for which they legislate.

I shall endeavor to answer another and a difficult question which has been lately asked as to the formation of pronouns. Why do we say *myself, yourself, ourselves*, using, as it appears, the possessive form of the pronoun, and yet *himself, themselves*, using the objective? No reason has been discovered for this anomaly; but its history is traceable.*

* The question was asked by Mr. Edward S. Gould, author of "Good English," a book full of counsel and criticism that justifies its title. His communication appeared in "The Round Table" of April 10; and the above reply, forming the remainder of the present chapter, appeared April 24, in the same paper, under date of April 10. An explanation, substantially the same, was subsequently given in "The Round Table" of June 5 by Mr. Thomas Davidson, of St. Louis, an accomplished scholar and etymologist, who thus introduced his remarks: —

"Mr. Gould's other difficulty is one which he shares with a very large number of scholars. It is a real one, and I have never seen in any book a definite solution of it. I will, therefore, ask leave to state, at some length, the results of my own researches

The emphatic compound pronoun has come directly down to us from the Anglo-Saxon, in which it was formed by the union, although not the compounding, of the pronoun *ic* (I), and the pronominal adjective *sylf* (self). The adjectival force of the latter word continued long unimpaired. In the *Cursor Mundi*, a Middle English metrical version of parts of the Bible, Christ says, "For I am *self* man al perfite," *i. e.*, I am *very* man all perfect; and even in *Twelfth Night* Shakespeare wrote, "with one *self* king," which the revisors of the text for the folio of 1632, not apprehending, altered to "with one self-*same* king." But the Anglo-Saxon *ic* (I) and *sylf* (self) were both declined; and when they were united they still were both declined. So, as we have *res-publica*, *rei-publicæ*, *res-publicæ*, *rerum-publicarum*, and so forth, in Latin, we have *ic sylf*, *min sylfes*, *we sylfe*, *ure sylfra*, in Anglo-Saxon; the third person being, in the singular, — nom. *he sylf*, gen. *his sylfes*, dat. *him sylfum*, acc. *hine sylfne*, and in the plural, — nom. *hi sylfe*, gen. *hira sylfra*, dat. *him sylfum*, or *heom sylfum*, acc. *hi sylfe*. But by the process of phonetic degradation these double-case inflections were broken down, and a compound emphatic pronoun was formed, not from either the nominative case or the accusative, but

and conclusions in regard to it, acknowledging, at the same time, my indebtedness to the works of Koch, Mätzner, Grein, and other German scholars."

I am thus led to believe that my own solution of this question is the first that was given. For what Mr. Davidson does not know of philological literature can be hardly worth knowing; and I refer to his article, not to imply that he took any hint from mine (than which hardly any supposition could be more presumptuous), but to claim for the latter the support of a judgement formed by his acumen and research, and resting on the labors of the learned German philologists whom he mentions, and with whose works I am unacquainted.

from the dative or the genitive; the result being, not *I-self*, *we-selves*, *he-self*, *they-selves*, etc., but *my-self* (*me sylfum*), *our-selves* (*ure sylfrum*), *him-self* (*him-sylfum*), *them-selves* (*heom sylfum*), and so forth; but *us-selven* appears in Henry III's proclamation A. D. 1258. Later we find such forms as *ich-silf* and *me-silf*, *thu-silf* and *the-self* alternating. Within a century, however, we find the modern form fully established. Thus, in the romance of *Sir Perceval of Galles*, about A. D. 1350 : —

> " Sone thou hast takyne thy rede
> To do *thiselfe* to the dede."

> " His stede es in stable sett
> And *hymselfe* to the haulle fett."

> " The sowdane sayse he will her ta,
> The lady wille *hir-selfe* sla,
> Are he that is her maste fa [i. e., greatest foe]
> Solde wedd hir to wyfe."

> " Ane unwyse man, he sayd, am I
> That puttis *myselfe* to siche a foly."

What determined the selection of the case form for preservation can only be conjectured. It may have been accident; but mere accident has little influence upon the course of language; and the notion that *self* expressed an identity possessed by or pertaining to the subject of the pronoun may have led to the choice of the genitive or the dative case, and this selection may have been helped by considerations of euphony, or ease of utterance.

The vulgar use of *his-self*, as, for example, " Sam was a-cleanin of his-self," springs from the notion of the substantive character of *self*, and is not an

error that illiterate people have fallen into, b
remnant of an old usage; educated people, as
as the uneducated, having very early framed
speech upon this notion. Thus in Bishop B
"English Votaries:" "But Marianus sayth
was a presbyteresse, or a prieste's leman, to
the honour of that ordre, bycause he was a monk
selfe" (fol. 91, ed. 1560, *et passim*); and Tyn
in his version of the Bible has (Job xxii. 24), "
the Allmightie *his own selfe* shall be thy harve

I have called this use of the pronoun an idion
our language; but it has a parallel in the Fr
use of *moi*, *toi*, and *lui*. The French do not
je même, *tu même*, *il même*, but *moi même*,
même, *lui même*, in which the pronouns are da
forms, the remnants of the Latin *mihi*, *tibi*, and
But in old French the nominative was used.
have carefully examined early French *chansons*
romans, including the *Chanson de Roland* and
Roman de Tristan, and have found not a sir
instance of *moi*, *toi*, or *lui* used other than ob
tively, and generally after a preposition.
modern Frenchman says *ni moi*: his forefath
eight hundred years ago, said *ne io*, where the
noun is a degraded form of *ego*, which became
and finally *je*; so that, according to correct li
descent, the modern French should be *ni*
Louis XIV. said, *L'état, c'est moi*; Hugh Ca
would have said, *est jo*; as the King of Spain
signs himself, grandly, *Yo el Rey*. Is it not
sible, therefore, that in the phrase, not enti
vulgar, *It is me*, which Dean Alford has defen
on insufficient grounds, and Mr. Moon has

tacked without sufficient knowledge, the pronoun
is not a misused accusative, but, as in the exactly
correspondent French phrase, a remnant of the
dative? *It is me* is not Anglo-Saxon certainly, in
which language we have *Ice com hit*, a form preserved by early English writers of repute.   But if I
remember rightly, the phrase in question may be
traced back to a very respectable antiquity.

  We find, then, that *himself* and *themselves* are
not objective or accusative forms, but remnants of
a dative form, which, by phonetic degradation, have
become, so to speak, the nominative cases of inde-
clinable emphatic pronouns of the third person.   So
herself is not possessive, but a like remnant of a
dative form.   *Itself*, notably, is not possessive, not
a compound of *its* and *self*, it having been used
for centuries before the appearance of *its* in the language.   And until a very late period, after A. D.
1600, it was written separately, *it self*.   We do use
self with a possessive, as "Cæsar's self;" and our
Anglo-Saxon forefathers joined it to proper names,
as *Petrus sylf*, *Crist sylf*.   But here I must stop,
not only to avoid prolixity, but because the etymology and relations of *self* is one of the most difficult
and least understood subjects in the history of our
language.

SOME.

  Several correspondents have asked me, in the
words of one of them, "not to forget the word
that is more misused than any other in our language — *some*.   Thus," my correspondent continues, "people say (writers as well as speakers)

there were some six or seven hundred persons p
ent, there are some ninety vessels, when they m
about, or when *some* is entirely superfluous."
use of the word has also been recently denoun
by some British writers on language, who, h
ever, have given no good reasons for their ob
tions, although one of them calls attention to
fact that some of our best writers are using
word carelessly. Let us look a little into the
tory and the radical signification of this word,
trace this use of it.

We hear all around us, among well-educ
people of good English stock, but who give th
selves no care about their use of words, speak
their mother tongue merely as they have lear
it from the mouths of their kinsfolk and acqua
ance, such phrases as some three or four, s
few. Oliver Wendell Holmes, whose English,
well as whose thought, merits the attention and
miration of his readers, says " some fifty " in a
sage in "The Guardian Angel." Thacker
in one of his lectures on the Queen Anne Wits,
this passage : —

"And some five miles on the road, as the Exeter fly co
ling:ing and creaking onwards, it will suddenly be brought
halt by a gentleman on a gray mare," etc., etc.

Prior closes his epigram on "Phillis's Age"
the line —

"And Phyllis is some forty-three."

Bacon is quoted by Dr. Johnson (not upon
point, however) as using not only the phrase " so
two thousand," but " some good distance," " so

good while;" and Raleigh, in one of his letters, has the following passage:—

"Being encountered with a strong storm some eight leagues to the westward of Sicily, I held it office of a commander to take a port."

Shakespeare, in "Richard III.," writes,—

"Has she forgot already that brave prince,
Edward her lord, whom I, some three months since,
Stabbed in my angry mood at Tewksbury?"

and in "Twelfth Night,"—

"Some four or five attend on him:
All, if you will."

If a man sin against the English language by using *some* in the manner in question, he will do it in very good company; and is it not better to sin with the elect than to be righteous with the reprobate? But in the determination of such a question as this we must not defer to mere usage. I repeat that there is a misuse of language which can be justified by no authority.

Some is one of the oldest simple, underived, uncompounded, and unmodified words in the English language, in the Anglo-Saxon part of which it can be traced without change, as *som* or *sum*, generally the latter, for a thousand years. Its meaning during that whole period seems not to have been enlarged, diminished, or inflected, in the slightest degree, in either popular or literary usage. That meaning is — an indeterminate quantity or number, greater or less, considered apart from the whole existing number. *Some* is separative; it implies others, and contrasts with *all*. It is segregative, and sets apart, either a number, though indefinite, from another and generally a larger number, or an individual person or thing not definite. It corresponds not only to the Latin *aliquantum*, but to *quidem* and *aliquis*, and to *circiter*. Such has been its usage always in English and in Anglo-Saxon. Let us, for instance, examine the passage in the Gospels about the centurion and his sick servant. It begins in the modern version (Luke vii. 2), "And a *certain* centurion's servant, who was dear unto him, was sick." But in Wicliffe's English version, made about A. D. 1385, we find, "Sothli, a servant of *sum* man centurio hauying yvel." In the Anglo-Saxon version, made about A. D. 995, it is, "Dá wæs *sumes* hundred mannes þeowa untrum." Again, in the same Gospel (ix. 19), "Others say that *one* of the old prophets is risen again;" which, in the Anglo-Saxon version, is "Sume þæt *sum* witega of þam ealdum aras." Here the Greek word translated *some* is τις, which the Vulgate renders *quidam*; and the meaning is, clearly enough, an indefinite individual of a certain class. But the word may be used to set apart indefinitely two, or five, or fifty individuals, as well as one. We may say, a certain five, or a certain fifty, as well as a certain one; and so, some five or some fifty. And such, we find, was the very best and oldest Anglo-Saxon usage. King Alfred, first in scholarship as well as in the state, and the writer of the purest Anglo-Saxon that has come down to us, translated, from the Latin, Bede's account of Caedmon, the Anglo-Saxon sacred poet, which begins (in English) thus:—

"In this abbess's minster was a *certain* brother ('*quidam frater*') notably glorified and honored with a divine gift," etc.

his Alfred renders thus : —

On þisse abbuddissan mynstre wæs *sum* broðor synderlice
godcunde gyfe gemæred et geweorþad."

i his translation of Boethius (I cite here from
worth) he has the following passage : —

" Þa woeron hi *sume* ten gear on þam gewinne."

hat is, Then they were some ten years in the
.   I find, also, in the Anglo-Saxon Chronicle
passage, which relates to the year 605, but was
ten about A. D. 805 : —

þær man sloh eac cc preosta þa comon ðider þæt her scoldan
ddan for Walana here.   Scromail wæs gehaten hyra ealdor,
t bæerst ðonou fiftiga *sum*."

hat is, "There they slew, also, two hundred
sts, who came thither that they might pray for
British army.   Their prince was named Scro-
l, at whose hands some fifty were slain."   But
word, in this sense of a separated, although in-
nite number or individual, goes far back beyond
Anglo-Saxon, to the Gothic, spoken by the peo-
who broke into Dacia, and settled there in the
nd century.   They became Christians very
y — so early that Ulphilas, their bishop, a man
reëminent learning and ability, made a transla-
of the Gospels for them about A. D. 360, which
ts in a superb manuscript, written in silver and
len letters upon a light-purple parchment, and
wn as the Codex Argenteus.   Referring to the
passages from Luke, quoted above, we find that
about the centurion begins thus : —

Hundafade þan *sumis* skalks siukands, swultawairþbya;"

that about John the Baptist thus : —

Sumai þan þatei praufetus *sums* þize airizane usstoþ."

That is, some centurion, some prophet; as we might say, some one centurion or other, some two or three centurions. So that the Gothic Ulphilas used *some* just as it was used by the Anglo-Saxon Alfred and the English Wycliffe. Returning to the Anglo-Saxon, we find that where Moses tells us, according to our modern version (Genesis xlvi. 37), that "all the souls of the house of Jacob which came into Egypt were threescore and ten," the Anglo-Saxon translator tells us that there were "some seventy" of them — "seofontigra *sum*." Our examination proves, then, that this use of *some*, which is objected to, in so many quarters, as inelegant and incorrect English, conforms strictly to the meaning which the word has had among speakers and the best writers ever since it came out of the darkness a thousand and half a thousand years ago; that it can be traced from Holmes and Thackeray, through Shakespeare, and Bacon, and Wycliffe, and King Alfred, to Ulphilas, the Goth, on the Dacian banks of the Danube; where, we may be sure, the Emperor Julian heard it, as, during the life of Ulphilas, and before Alaric came upon the stage, he led his victorious legions down that river, after his splendid campaign against the Germans, which so revived the somewhat tarnished lustre of the Roman arms. In fact, this idiom, as well as this word, is found, without variation, in the oldest Teutonic dialect known to us, and is, at least, a thousand years older than the modern English language, in which it has been preserved, without change, both in the writings of scholars and in the common speech of the people. There can be no higher authority, no better reason, for any word or form of language, than that it springs from a simple native germ, and is rooted in the usage of fifteen hundred years. And it would be difficult to find in any tongue another word or phrase which has such simplicity of origin and structure, and such length of authoritative usage in its support, as this, which has offended the ears of some half a dozen of my correspondents and some three or four British critics.

It is not my purpose to enter here upon the defence of good English words and phrases; but I have gone somewhat at length into the history of this phrase, not only because I hoped it might be interesting to my readers, but because the denunciation of the usage is a noteworthy example of the mistakes that may be made by purists in language. When a word, a phrase, or an idiom is found in use both in common speech and in the writings of educated men, we may be almost sure that there is good reason for the usage. But cultivated and well-meaning people sometimes take a scunner against some particular word or phrase, as we have seen in this case, and they flout it pitilessly, and think in their hearts that it is the great blemish upon the speech of the day.

And, by the bye, one of my critics, and one who I fear rates my judgment and my knowledge much above their desert, finds fault with my own English (which I am far from setting up as an example, having neither time nor inclination to "Blair-up" my sentences), because I use the phrase *first rate* as denoting a high degree of superiority, which he says " will hardly be found in that sense

17

in serious English composition, certainly not until
within a comparatively recent period." This
brought to my mind the following passage from Sir
Walter Scott's "Monastery" (chapter xxviii.) : —

"The companion of Astrophel, the flower of the tilt-yard of
Feliciana, had no more idea that his graces and good parts could
attach the love of Mysie Happer than a *first-rate beauty* in the
boxes dreams of the fatal wound which her charms may inflict
on some attorney's apprentice in the pit; "

and this also from Fielding's "Tom Jones" (chapter
iv.) : —

" — and she was indeed a most sensible girl, and her understanding was of *the first rate."*

and this from Farquhar (" Poems, Letters and Essays," A. D. 1700, p. 14) : —

" No *first-rate* beau with us, drawn by his six before and his six
behind," etc.

But I had, I need hardly say, no thought of
these precedents when I wrote, and should have
used the phrase without scruple, even were I sure
that it had never been used before. Too much
stress is generally laid upon the authority of mere
previous usage, which is not at all necessary to the
justification of a good word or phrase. A lawyer
of distinction once said to me that, before a jury, he
had needed, and on the spur of the moment, had
made and used, the word *juxtapose*, adding that he
had no business to do so, but that it was a pity that
there was no such word in the language, or, as he
said, in the dictionaries. But no man needs the
authority of a dictionary (even such authority as
dictionaries have), or of previous usage, for such

a word as *juxtapose*. It is involved in *juxtaposition* as much as *interpose* and *transpose* are in *interposition* and *transposition*. The mere fact that it had not been used before this occasion, or rather that no maker of dictionaries had happened to notice it, is of no moment whatever. Any man has the right to use a word, especially a word of such natural growth and so well rooted as *juxtapose*, for the first time, else we should be poorly off for language. But he must be wary and sure of his ground; for an innovator does his work at his own proper peril.

ADJECTIVES IN EN.

Unless a stand is made by the writers and speakers who guide the course of language (I mean not only scholars and men of letters, but the great mass of well-educated and socially-cultivated people), we shall lose entirely a certain class of words — adjectives in *en* formed from nouns — which contribute much to the usefulness and beauty of our language. *Threaden* is hopelessly gone, and, rarely needed, will be little missed. *Golden*, *brazen*, *leaden*, *leathern*, *wheaten*, *oaten*, and *waxen* are in more or less advanced stages of departure. They all appear in poetry, but are not often used for the every-day needs of life, except in figurative language. Most people would say, a gold candlestick, a brass faucet, a lead pipe, and so forth; but a golden harvest, a brazen face, a leaden sky. The most untaught or the most eccentric person would hardly say, a brass face, or a lead sky. The adjective in *en* seems to be restricted to the

expression of likeness; whereas it was formed
express substance, of course including likene
Golden, meaning made of gold, and, of cour
like gold, now is generally used to mean the lat
only; and for the former sense the noun g
is used as an adjective. This is to be deplored,
only because the formation in question is one of
oldest in our language, but because its loss is a r
impoverishment of our vocabulary, compelling us
put one word to two uses, and also because we
thereby deprived of what we much need — d
syllables the last syllable of which is unaccent
In proportion as a language is without such wor
it lacks one of the chief elements of a flowi
rhythm, and becomes stiff and chalk-knuckl
Compare the sound of a golden crown, a lead
weight, a wheaten loaf, with that of a gold crow
a lead weight, a wheat loaf. To a person who
an ear for rhythm the former is agreeable,
latter harsh and offensive. To any one the forn
phrases are easier of utterance than the latt
The adjectives in *en* can be saved if we will,
they are well worth saving. If those who
strong enough do not stretch out their hands
them, we shall soon be wearing wool clothes;
shall not know the difference between a wood
house and a wood-house; we shall be talking
the North States and the South States, the East
the West States; and when we go back to the
well, we shall find there, not the old oaken buck
but an oak bucket, which, in losing half its disti
tive epithet, will have lost half the association,
all the beauty, of its name. In an old invent

before me, which was made about the year 1600,
there are these items: "A tynnen quart, 10*d.*; a
square tynnen pot, 6*d.*" Overbury, in his "Characters," writes of "pellets in eldern guns;" Tubervile
of "a pair of yarnen socks." And in the "Apology
for the Lollards," supposed to have been written by
Wycliffe, is this passage, which contains a cluster
of adjectives in *en* formed from substantives, and
used by our forefathers five hundred years ago.

"As the hethun men hed sex kyndis of similacris clayen,
treen, brasun, stonun, silveren, and golden, so have lordis now
sex kyndis of prelatis."

It is difficult to see why *silveren* should have
been dropped, and *brazen* and *golden* retained.
Better return to *stonen* and *clayen* and *yarnen*, than
lose *golden* and its fellows.

EITHER AND NEITHER.

Either is a singular word. It expresses, and from
Anglo-Saxon times has expressed, in the best usage,
one of two and both of two. As *both* means two
taken together, so *either* means two considered separately. Thus, "On either side of the river was
the tree of life," means that the tree grew on both
sides alike; but, "Take either side of the river,"
means that one or the other of the two sides may
be taken. It is well to assert this claim for *either*, because it has been questioned by some purists. It is almost impossible to explain how this
word means both one and two, and how it can
yet be used without causing any confusion for intelligent people. *Either*, being compounded of the
Anglo-Saxon æg, every, and hwæper, which of two,

and so meaning every which, or one, of two, sh
strictly, be used only with reference to two obj
Neither, being but the negative of *either*, conf
to like usage. But for a very long period, t
particularly the latter, have been used by our
writers in relation to more than two objects.
example, —

" Which of them [the ancient Fathers] ever said that n
kings, nor the whole clergy, nor yet all the people together ar
to be judges over you?"— Bishop Jewell's *Apology*. Part V

" — their main business [that of sacred writers] is to ab
man from this world, and to persuade him to prefer the bare
of what he can neither hear, see, nor conceive, before all pi
enjoyments this world can afford." — Hobbes's *Liberty an
cessity*, Epistle.

"Independent morals are to be neither Catholic, Evan
Buddhist, nor Atheistic." — *Saturday Review*, October 31,

" — this new and ambitious organ attacks neither Prote
like M. Guizot, Catholics like its orthodox readers, Israelite
M. Rothschild, nor Atheists like M. Prudhon." — *Idem*.

This use of these words, although not defen
on any other grounds than those of convenience
custom, seems likely to prevail, and it were
if no graver errors had been sanctioned by the
thority of eminent writers. *Either*, used separa
is responded to by *or*, and *neither* by *nor ;* thu
either this or that, neither this nor that. This r
which is absolute, is frequently violated. S
people, not uneducated, seem to think that if *e*
has been preceded by a negation, it should be
lowed by *nor*. They would write, for instanc
passage in Bacon's " New Atlantis" thus: "
never heard of any ship that had been seen to ar
upon any shore of Europe; no, nor of either
East *nor* the West Indies." But Bacon wrote,

rectly, " nor of either the East *or* the West Indies."
The introduction of a second *nor* in such sentences
involves the use of two negatives in the same assertion. It is like, He hadn't none.

The pronunciation of *either* and *neither* has been
much disputed, but, it would seem, needlessly. The
best usage is even more controlling in pronunciation
than in other departments of language; but usage
itself is guided, although not constrained, by analogy. The analogically correct pronunciation of
these words is what we call the Irish one, *ayther* and
nayther; the diphthong having the sound which it
has in many words in which *ei* is, and apparently
has always been so pronounced — *weight, freight,
deign, vein, obeisance,* etc. This sound, too, has
come down from Anglo-Saxon times, as we have
already seen, the word in that language being
ægper; and there can be no doubt that in this, as
in some other respects, the language of the educated
Irish Englishman is analogically correct, and in
conformity to ancient custom. His pronunciation
of certain syllables in *ei* which have acquired in
English usage the sound of *e* long, as, for example,
conceit, receive, and which he pronounces *consayt,
resayve,* is analogically and historically correct. *E*
had of old the sound of *a* long, and *i* the sound of
e, particularly in words which came to us from or
through the Norman French. But *ayther* and *nayther,* being antiquated and Irish, analogy and the
best usage require the common pronunciation *eether*
and *neether.* For the pronunciation *i-ther* and *ni-
ther,* with the *i* long, which is sometimes heard,
there is no authority, either of analogy or of the

best speakers. It is an affectation, and in this country, a copy of a second-rate British affectation. Persons of the best education and the highest social position in England generally say *eether* and *neether*.

SHALL AND WILL.

The distinction between these words, although very clear when it is once apprehended, is liable to be disregarded by persons who have not had the advantage of early intercourse with educated English people. I mean English in blood and breeding; for, as the traveller found that in Paris even the children could speak French, so in New England it is noteworthy that even the boys and girls playing on the commons use *shall* and *will* correctly ; and in New York, New Jersey, and Ohio, in Virginia, Maryland, and South Carolina, fairly educated people of English stock do the same; while by Scotchmen and Irishmen, even when they are professionally men of letters, and by the great mass of the people of the Western and South-western States, the words are used without discrimination, or, if discrimination is attempted, *will* is given the place of *shall*, and *vice versa*. It is much to be regretted that an English scholar of Mr. Marsh's eminence should have expressed the opinion that the distinction between these words " has, at present, no logical value or significance whatever," and have ventured the prediction that "at no very distant day this verbal quibble will disappear, and that one of the auxiliaries will be employed with all persons of the nominative, exclusively as the sign of the future, and the other only as an expression of purpose or authority."

The distinction between *shall* and *will*, as auxiliary verbs to be used with various persons as nominatives, is a verbal quibble, just as any distinction is a quibble to persons too ignorant, too dull, or too careless for its apprehension. So, and even yet more, is the distinction between *be, am, art, is*, and *are*, a quibble. All these words express exactly the same thought — that of present existence. Why, therefore, should not the distinction between them, which assigns them to various persons as nominatives, be swept away, so that, instead of entangling ourselves in the subtle intricacies of *I am, thou art, he is, we are, you are, they are*, which are of no logical value or significance, we may say, with all the charm and the force of simplicity, *I be, thou be, he be, we be, you be, they be?* — as, in fact, some very worthy people do, and manage to make themselves understood. Why, indeed, should we suffer a smart little verbal shock when the Irish servant says, "Will I put some more coal on the fire?" And why should we be so hard-hearted as to laugh at the story of the Frenchman, who, falling into the water, cried out, as he was going down, "I vill drown, and nobody shall help me"? But those who have genuine, well-trained English tongues and ears are shocked, and do laugh. The reason of the distinction is regarded by most writers upon language as very difficult of explanation. Essays have been written upon the question; Sir Edmund Head even made a little book about it; but no one has yet traced the usage to its origin so clearly as

to satisfy all philologists. Without pretending to
do what so many others have failed to do, I shall
give the explanation that is satisfactory to me.

The radical signification of *will* (Anglo-Saxon
willan) is purpose, intention, determination ; that of
shall (Anglo-Saxon *sceal*, ought) is obligation. *I
will do* means, I purpose doing — I am determined
to do. *I shall do* means, radically, I ought to do ;
and as a man is supposed to do what he sees he
ought to do, *I shall do* came to mean, I am about
doing — to be, in fact, a mere announcement of
future action, more or less remote. But so *you shall
do* means, radically, you ought to do ; and therefore
unless we mean to impose an obligation or to
announce an action on the part of another person,
over whom we claim some control, *shall*, in speaking of the mere future voluntary action of another
person, is inappropriate ; and we therefore say
you will, assuming that it is the volition of the
other person to do thus or so. Hence, in merely
announcing future action, we say, I or we *shall*,
you, he, or they *will ;* and, in declaring purpose on
our own part, or on the part of another, obligation,
or inevitable action, which we mean to control,
we say, I or we *will*, you, he, or they *shall*. Official orders, which are in the form *you will*, are but
a seeming exception to this rule of speech, which
they, in fact, illustrate. For in them the courtesy of
superior to subordinate, carried to the extreme even
in giving command, avoids the semblance of com-
pulsion, while it assumes obedience in its very
language. *Should* and *would* follow, of course, the

fortunes of *shall* and *will;* and, in the following short dialogue, I have given, I believe, easily-apprehended examples of all the proper uses of these words, the discrimination of which is found by some persons so difficult. [A husband is supposed to be trying to induce his reluctant wife to go from their suburban home to town for a day or two.

He. I shall go to town to-morrow. Of course you will ?

She. No, thanks. I shall not go. I shall wait for better weather, if that will ever come. When shall we have three fair days together again?

He. Don't mind that. You should go. I should like to have you hear Ronconi.

She. No, no; I will not go.

He. [*To himself.*] But you shall go, in spite of the weather and of yourself. [*To her.*] Well, remember, if you should change your mind, I should be very happy to have your company. Do come; you will enjoy the opera; and you shall have the nicest possible supper at Delmonico's.

She. No; I should not enjoy the opera. There are no singers worth listening to; and I wouldn't walk to the end of the drive for the best supper Delmonico will ever cook. A man seems to think that any human creature would do anything for something good to eat.

He. Most human creatures will.

She. I shall stay at home, and you shall have your opera and your supper all to yourself.

He. Well, if you will stay at home, you shall; and if you won't have the supper, you shan't. But my trip will be dull without you. I shall be bored to death — that is, unless, indeed, your friend Mrs. Dashatt Mann should go to town to-morrow, as she said she thought that she would; then, perhaps, we shall meet at the opera, and she and her nieces will sup with me.

She. [*To herself.*] My dear friend Mrs. Dashatt Mann! And so that woman will be at her old tricks with my husband again. But she shall find that I am mistress of this situation, in spite of her big black eyes and her big white shoulders. [*To him.*] John, why should you waste yourself upon those ugly, giggling girls? To be sure, *she's* a fine woman enough; that is, if you *will* buy your beauty by the pound; but they !

He. O, think what I will about that, I must take them, for politeness' sake; and, indeed, although the lady is a matron, it wouldn't be quite proper to take her alone — would it? What should you say?

She. Well, not exactly, perhaps. But it don't much matter; she can take care of herself, I should think. She's no chicken; she'll never see thirty-five again. But it's too bad you should be bored with her nieces — and since you're bent on having me go with you — and — after all, I should like to hear Ronconi — and — you shan't be going about with those cackling girls — well, John, dear, I'll go.

The only passage in this colloquy which seems to me to need a word of explanation, is that in which the lady says to herself that her friend Mrs. D. Mann " *shall* find " that some one else is mistress of the situation. It would have been quite correct for the wife to say " she *will* find," etc. But, in that case, she would merely have expressed an opinion as to a future occurrence. By using *shall*, she not only predicts with emphasis, but claims the power to make her prediction good. I have given my readers this colloquy, because more can be gained toward the proper use of these words through example than from precept. It seems to be instinctively apprehended — imbibed. Association and early habit cause many people, who are far from being well educated, and who are entirely unconscious as to their speech, to be unerring in their use of this idiom, which, in my judgment, is one of the finest in the language.

It is violated with conspicuous perversity in the following examples. The first is from Coverdale's version of the Bible : —

" And Gedeon sayde unto God, Yf thou wilt delyuer Israel thorow my hande, as thou hast saide, then wil I laye a flese of woll in the courte : yf ye dew be onely upon ye flese, and dry upon all the grounde, then *wyll* I perceaué that thou *shalt* delyver Israll thorow my hande, as thou hast said." — *Judges* vi.

Here, in the last sentence, *will* is used for *shall*, and *shalt* for *wilt*. Gideon meant to express merely a future occurrence in both cases, and to imply no will on his own part, and no obligation on God's. And thus, in the King James version of the same passage, we have "then *shall* I know that thou *wilt* save Israel."

The next example is from a "Narrative of a Grand Festival at Yarmouth," in honor of the victory of Waterloo (Yarmouth, 1815).

"Every individual was requested to take his place at the table, . . . and it was requested that no persons *would* leave their seats during dinner."

Here the right word is *should*, as *would* and *should* follow the regimen of *will* and *shall*, and we request that people *shall* do thus or so, not that they *will* do it. A similar error appears in the following extract from an account published in the "New York Tribune" of the interview between President Grant and a committee of Pennsylvanians who waited upon him to urge the importance of appointing a Pennsylvanian to a place in the Cabinet.

"They intended making no suggestions or recommendations further than that if Pennsylvania was to be represented, the appointment *would* be given to a man who *should* be known as an unflinching supporter of the Republican party."

These disinterested gentlemen meant to say, and perhaps did say, that they recommended that the appointment *should* be given to a man who *would* be known as a thorough-going party-man.

The next passage, which is from an article in

"The World" on the last change in the British embassy at Washington, contains an example of a monstrous misuse of *will*.

"Mr. Thornton was without any *suite*, as it is intended that the staff or legation formerly attached to Sir Frederick Bruce *will* act under the orders of Mr. Thornton until further news from the Foreign Office."

Without doubt, the writer meant that it is intended that the staff *shall* act, etc. The intention was to lay a future obligation upon the members of the legation. We cannot intend what others will do.

Another New York journalist, not improbably an Irishman, exclaims, as these pages are in preparation for the press, —

"When *will* we get through with the everlasting, tedious, unprofitable, and demoralizing Byron controversy?"

He meant, When *shall* we get through with it?

There is a fine use of *shall*, the force of which escapes some intelligent and cultivated readers. An example is found in the following passage from a number of "The Spectator," written by Addison: "There is not a girl in town, but, let her have her will in going to a mask, and she shall dress like a shepherdess." Upon this even the acute and generally sound Crombie remarks in his "Etymology and Syntax of the English Language" (p. 398, ed. 1830), "It should be 'she *will*.' The author intended to signify mere futurity; instead of which he has expressed a command." But mere futurity was not what Addison meant to express, nor did he express a command. He meant to assert strongly; and therefore, instead of the word *will*, which with the third person predicates simple futurity, he used

shall, which implies more or less of obligation, —
here a propensity so strong as to control action.
So in the Urquhart translation of Rabelais, a masterpiece of idiomatic English, we find (Book I.
c. 17), "A blind fiddler shall draw a greater conflu-
ence together than an evangelical preacher." So
Dr. Johnson says, in the Preface to his Dictionary,
that it should be considered, —

"— that sudden fits of inadvertency will surprise vigilance,
slight avocations will seduce attention, and casual ellipses of the
mind will darken learning; and that the writer *shall* often in
vain trace his memory at the moment of need for that which
yesterday he knew with intuitive readiness, and which will come
uncalled into his thoughts to-morrow."

Here *will* is used in three clauses, and *shall* in
one, to express the same relation of time in the third
person; but the latter clause would lose much of its
significance if *will* were to take in it the place of
shall. And in the prophecy of Isaiah, "He shall feed
his flock like a shepherd . . . and shall gently lead
all those that are with young," how much of its
grandeur, as well as of its power of assurance, would
be lost, if *will* were substituted for *shall!* Bishop
Jewell nicely discriminates (but intuitively, we may
be sure) between *shall* and *will* thus used, in the
following passage in one of his sermons : —

"Let us turne to him with an upright heart. So shal he turne
to us; so shal we walke as the children of light; so shall we
shine as the sunne in the kingdome of our father; so shall God
be our God, and will abide with us forever." —Ed. 1583, fol. q. iii.

An example of this distinction, unsurpassed in
delicacy and exactness, and consequent effect, is
found in the following passage, — my memorandum
of the source of which is unfortunately lost, — and

which refers to the assassination of President Lincoln : —

"It justly fastened itself upon the rebellion, and demanded new and severer punishment of the rebels, instead of the magnanimous reconciliation which the beloved president, of whom it had been bereaved, had recommended. Who will say that this sentiment was unnatural? Who shall say that it is even unjust?"

Here, again, *will* and *shall* are used to express the same time in regard to like actions of the same person. *Will* might have been used correctly in the latter question as it was in the former; but some force would thereby have been lost. *Shall* could not have been used with the same fine effect in both questions. *Will* having been used, *shall* intensifies the query. It is as if the questions were, Who can say that this sentiment was unnatural? Who could venture to say that it is even unjust? But we may be sure that no conscious, careful selection of these words was made in this case. And we may be even surer of the unconsciousness with which the following passage was written, in a letter from a lady to a friend from whom she had been alienated, and who sent her a present which she felt delicate about accepting. The subject is commonplace, and the writer expresses in the simplest language a feeling natural, yet not too common. But the passage is so remarkable for its free yet nicely correct use of idiom, that I am sure the writer, as well as the friend to whom I am indebted for a sight of it, will pardon its appearance here. In the last sentence, the use of *may*, instead of *will*, which would have been quite proper, shows a delicate instinct in the use of language, which, as I have said before, is characteristic of the epistolary style of intelligent and cultivated women.

"I thank you sincerely for still thinking of me, and I will keep it just as it is until I hear from you again. If you are willing to become friends with me once more, I shall only be too happy. I will accept it as a seal on the renewal of our friendship. If not, then I will return it and what you gave me before we parted. Perhaps, after you have read this letter to the end, you may not wish to continue our acquaintance; if not, I shall come back to ——, and will keep my engagements there, and then go home."

Such a mastery of idiom belongs only to persons who, having grown up among those who use language correctly, have themselves a delicate and sure sense of the various significance of words. It is not so common even among the educated as to be taken as a matter of course : for instance, see the following note, printed from the original, which was written by a distinguished member of one of the learned professions in New York : —

"I enclose to you a document which your interest in Sanitary matters will doubtless induce an appreciation of the views therein expressed."

"I should feel very obligatory to you if you could find a good appointment for my son ——, to enable him to procure a free living for himself and his family, having a wife and 2 children. He is intelligent, industrious, and perfectly reliable, and would devote all the time required for the necessary duty."

Of the authors of these two specimens of letter writing, the lady is not, I believe, highly educated, and her intellectual pretensions, should she make any, would be scouted by the gentleman; but she could no more fall into his blundering style and incorrect use of words than he could write or speak with her simple clearness and unaffected grace.

18

CHAPTER IX.

GRAMMAR, ENGLISH AND LATIN.

THE first punishment I remember havin[g]
ceived was for a failure to get a less[on]
English grammar. I recollect, with a half pa[in]
half amusing distinctness, all the little incide[nt]
the dreadful scene; how I found myself standi[ng]
an upper chamber of a gloomy brick house, bo[ok in]
hand, — it was a thin volume, with a tea-gree[n pa]
per cover and a red roan back, — before an [awful]
being, who put questions to me, which, for all [I]
could understand of them, might as well have [been]
couched in Coptic or in Sanskrit; how, [when]
asked about governing, I answered, "I don't kn[ow,"]
and when about agreeing, "I can't tell," un[til at]
last, in despair, I said nothing, and choked [down]
my tears, wondering, in a dazed, dumb fas[hion]
whether all this was part and parcel of that [innate]
depravity of the human heart of which I h[ad read]
so much; how then the being — to whom I a[pply]
no harsh epithet, for, poor man, he thought h[e was]
doing God service—said to me, in a terrible v[oice]
"You are a stupid, idle boy, sir, and have negl[ected]
your task. I shall punish you. Hold out [your]
hand." I put it out half way, like a machine

a hitch in its gearing. "Farther, sir." I advanced
it an inch or two, when he seized the tips of my
fingers, bent them back so as to throw the palm
well up, and then, with a mahogany rule, much
bevelled on one side, and having a large, malig-
nant ink-spot near the end, — an instrument which
seemed to me to weigh about forty pounds, and to
be a fit implement for a part of that eternal torture
to which I had been led to believe that I, for my
inborn depravity, was doomed, — he proceeded to
reduce my little hand, only just well in gristle, as
nearly to a jelly as was thought, on the whole, to
be beneficial to a small boy at that stage of the
world's progress.

The carefully-filed and still preserved receipts of
a methodically managed household enable me to
tell the age at which I was thus awakened to the
sweet and alluring beauties of English grammar.
I was just five and a half years old when one Alfred Ely — may his soul rest in peace! — thus gently
guided my uncertain and reluctant steps into the
paths of humane learning.   Fortunately, my father,
when outside the pale of religious dogma, was a
man of sound sense and a tender heart; and as
there was nothing about English accidence either
in the Decalogue or the Common Prayer-Book, he
sent a message to the schoolmaster, which caused
that to be my last lesson in what is called the grammar of my mother tongue.   I was soon after removed to a school the excellence of which I have
only within a few years fully appreciated, although,
as a boy, I knew that there I was happy, and felt

as if I were not quite stupid, idle, and depraved.* Thereafter I studied English, indeed, but only in the works of its great masters, and unconsciously in the speech of daily companions, who spoke it with remarkable but spontaneous excellence.

My kind and courteous readers will pardon, I hope, this reminiscence, in which I have indulged myself only because in some of the comments, private as well as public, which have been made upon these chapters in their original form, I have seen myself called a grammarian. God forbid that I should be anything of the sort! That I am unversed in the rules of English grammar (so called), I am not ashamed to confess; for special ignorance is no reproach when unaccompanied with presumption. And that in which I confess that I have no skill, I have not undertaken to teach. That task I leave to those who are capable of the subject, and who feel its necessity.

If grammar is what it has been defined as being, the science which has for its object the laws which regulate language, the remarks just made cannot be justified; for, in that sense, grammar is as much concerned with words by themselves, with their signification and their origin, and with their rightful use in those regards, as with their relations to each other in the sentence; and it is in that sense but another name for the science of language — phi-

---

* Let me mention with respect and love, which have grown with my years, the names of my two teachers, Theodore Eames and Samuel Putnam, to whom I owe all that I could be taught at school before I left them for college. I know that should any one of my fellow-pupils chance to see these lines, he will declare with me that the boy who could remain even a year under their hands without profit in mind, morals, and manners, must indeed have given himself up to original sin.

lology. But, notwithstanding that definition, and its acceptance by some grammarians and some compilers of dictionaries, such is not the sense in which the word *grammar* is generally used. Nor can the position which I have taken be maintained, if grammar is regarded as the science of the rightful or reasonable expression of thought by language; for grammar extended to these wide limits would include logic and rhetoric. But grammar, in its usual sense, is the art of speaking and writing a language correctly; in which definition, the word *correctly* means, in accordance with laws founded upon the relations, not of thoughts, but of words, and determined by verbal forms. It is this formal, constructive grammar which seems to me almost if not entirely superfluous in regard to the English language. Long ago, before any attempt had been made to write its grammar, that language had worked itself nearly free from those verbal forms which control the construction of the sentence, and therefore free in the same degree from the needs and the control of formal, constructive grammar. And, notably, it was not until English had cast itself firmly and sharply into its present simple mould that scholars undertook to furnish it with a grammar, the nomenclature and the rules of which they took from a language — the Latin — with which it had no formal affinity, to which it had no formal likeness, and by the laws of which it could not be bound, except so far as they were the universal laws of human thought. Allusions to grammar and to its importance as a part of education abound in our early literature. In a rhyming exhortation to a child, written in the fifteenth century, these lines occur : —

> "My lefe chyld I kownsel ye
> To furme thi vj tens, thou awyse ye;
> And have mind of thy clensoune
> Both of nowne and of pronowne,
> And ilk case in plurele
> How thai sal end, awyse the wele;
> And thi participyls forgete thou nowth,
> And thi comparisons be yn thi thowth;
> Thynk of the revele of the relatyfe;
> And then schalle thou the better thryfe;
> And how a verbe schalle be furmede,
> Take gode hede that thou be not stunnede;
> The ablatyfe case thou hafe in mynd,
> That he be saved in hys kynd;
> Take gode hede qwat he wylle do.
> And how a nowne substantyfe
> Wylle corde with a verbe and a relatyfe,
> *Posculo, posco, peto.*
>
> *Reliquiæ Antiquæ,* II. 14.

But, as appears on its face, this exhortation refers not to English, but to Latin grammar, which was the only grammar taught or thought of at the time when it was written. That was the day of the establishing and endowing of grammar schools in England; but the grammar taught in them was the Latin, and afterward a little of the Greek. Chaucer and Wycliffe had written, but in English grammar schools no man thought of teaching English. When, at last, it dawned upon the pedagogues that English was a language, or rather, in their significant phrase, a vulgar tongue, and they set themselves to giving rules for the art of writing and speaking it correctly, they attempted to form these rules upon the models furnished by the Latin language. And what wonder? for those were the only rules they knew. But the construction of the English language was even less like that of the Latin than English words were like Latin words. From this heterogeneous union sprang that hybrid monster known as English grammar, before whose fruitless loins we have sacrificed, for nearly three hundred years, our children and the strangers within our gates.

Of grammar, the essential parts, if not the whole, are etymology and syntax. For orthography relates to the mere arrangement of letters for the arbitrary representation of certain sounds, and prosody to the æsthetic use of language. And, if prosody is a part of grammar, why should the latter not include rhetoric, and even elocution? In fact, grammar was long regarded as including all that concerns the structure and the relations of language; and a grammarian among the ancients was one who was versed, not only in language, but in poetry, history, and rhetoric, and who, generally, lectured or wrote upon all those branches of literature. But it seems to me that in the usage of intelligent people the English word *grammar* relates only to the laws which govern the significant forms of words, and the construction of the sentence. Thus, if we find *extraordinary* spelled *igstrawnery*, or hear *suggest* pronounced *sujjest*, we do not call these lapses false grammar; but if we hear, "She was *hisn*, but he wasn't *hern*," which violates true etymology, or, "He *done* it *good*," which is incorrect syntax, these we do call false grammar.

Etymology, which relates to the significant forms of words, and syntax, the rules of which govern

their arrangement, are, then, from our point of
the great essentials, if not the whole, of gram
Now, the principal Latin words, the noun, th
jective, the verb, the participle, and the adverb,
their forms by a process called inflection, an
Latin sentence is constructed upon the basis of
significant verbal forms. English words do
vary their forms by inflection, and the English
tence is constructed without any dependence
verbal forms. To this remark there are except
but they are so few, and of such small import
that they cannot be regarded as affecting its ge
truth. The structure of the Latin sentence dep
upon the relation of the words of which it is
posed; that of the English sentence, upon the
tion of the thoughts it expresses. In other w
the construction of the Latin sentence is gram
cal, that of the English sentence, logical. A
first offshooting of the English language fron
parent stem, its growth and development bega
once to tend toward logical simplicity — in fact,
tendency was its offshooting; and since then i
gradually, but surely and steadily, cast off in
tional forms, and freed itself from the tramme
a construction dependent upon them. This b
true, how preposterous, how impossible, for
measure our English corn in Latin bushels!
that is what we have so long been trying to do
our English grammar.

In illustration of the foregoing remarks, I
present and compare some examples of Latin
English words and sentences, the former of w
shall be so simple that they can hardly escape

apprehension even of those who have not received the training of a grammar school.

The Latin for *boy* is *puer*. But *puer* stands for *boy* only as the subject of a sentence. When the boy spoken of is the object of an action, he is represented by an inflection of *puer* — the word *puerum*. Boys as the subjects of an action are called *pueri*, but as the objects, *pueros*.

The Latin for *girl* is *puella*, as the subject of a verb, but when the girl is the object of the action, she is not represented in that relation by changing *puella* into *puellum*, as *puer* was made *puerum*, but the word *puella*, being feminine, becomes *puellam*. In the plural it becomes, not *puelli* as the subject, and *puellos* as the object, of an action, but *puellæ* and *puellas*, those being feminine inflections.

Loved is *amabam*, if you wish to say, I loved; but if he or she loved, *amabat*; if they loved, *amabant*. Any of my readers will now be able to translate this little sentence : —

Pueri amabant puellam.

There being no article in the Latin, it of course must be supplied, and we therefore have, —

The boys loved the girl.

In this Latin sentence, and in its English equivalent, the words not only represent each other perfectly in sense, but correspond exactly in place. If, however, we change the relative positions of the English nouns, without modifying them in the least, we not only change, but entirely reverse the meaning of the sentence.

The girl loved the boys.

But in the Latin sentence we may make what

changes of position we please, and we shall not make a shade of difference in its meaning.

Puellam amabant pueri,
Puellam pueri amabant,
Pueri amabant puellam,
Pueri puellam amabant,

all have the same meaning — the boys loved the girl. For *puellam* shows by its form that it must be the object of the action; *amabant* must have for its subject a plural substantive, and which must therefore be, not *puellam*, but *pueri*. The connections of the words being therefore absolutely determined by their forms, their position in the sentence is a matter at least of minor importance. The reader who has not learned Latin will yet, by referring to a preceding paragraph, have little difficulty in constructing a Latin sentence, which represents the reverse of our first example; *i. e.*, the girl loved the boys. For in that the girl is the subject, and the boys are the objects of the action, and the verb must have its singular form, which gives us

Puella amabat pueros.

In the corresponding English sentence, the words are exactly the same as those in the sentence of exactly opposite meaning; in the Latin they are all different. And again, their position has no effect on the meaning of the sentence; for these words, whether given as above in the order, the girl loved the boys, or in the more elegant order,

Puella pueros amabat
[The girl the boys loved],

or,

Pueros amabat puella
[The boys loved the girl],

can have but one construction, and therefore but one meaning; *i. e.*, the girl loved the boys.

If we extend the sentence by qualifying either the subject or the object, or both, the operation of this rule of construction will be more striking. Let the qualification be goodness. The Latin for *good* is *bonus;* but in this form the word qualifies only a subject of the singular number and masculine gender; singular feminine and neuter subjects are qualified as good by the forms *bona* and *bonum*. A singular feminine object is qualified as good by *bonam;* a plural masculine subject by *boni*, a plural masculine object by *bonos*. If, therefore, we wish to say that the boys were good, the sentence becomes

> Boni pueri amabant puellam,
> The good boys loved the girl.

By merely changing the position of the adjective in the English sentence, we say, not that the boys were good, but the girl:

> The boys loved the good girl.

But a corresponding arrangement of the Latin words

> Pueri amabant boni puellam,

means still that the boys were good, and the girl was loved; because *boni*, from its form, can qualify only a plural masculine subject — here *pueri*. If we wish to say that the girl was good, we must use the form of *bonus* which belongs to a singular feminine object, and write *bonam puellam*. Then, wherever we put *bonam*, it will qualify only *puellam*. Thus, in the sentence,

> Bonam puellam amabant pueri,

the order of the words, represented in English, is

      The good girl loved the boys;

but the meaning is, the boys loved the good girl.
It is not even necessary, in Latin, that the adjective
and the noun which it qualifies should be kept
together. Thus, in the sentence,

      Puella bonos amabat pueros,

the order of the words, represented in English, is

      The girl good loved the boys;

and in this arrangement,

      Pueros amabat bonos puella,

the order is,

      The boys loved the good girl;

but the meaning in both is the same, and is quite
unlike that conveyed by the English arrangement — The girl loved the good boys.

The reason of this fixed relation is simply that
bonos, whatever its place in this sentence, qualifies
pueros only, as appears by the number, gender,
and case of each, which are shown by their respective and agreeing forms; that *pueros* must be an
object of action, which is shown by its form; and
that *puella* and *amabat* are subject and predicate,
pertaining to each other, which is also shown
by their forms. *Bonos* cannot belong to *puella*,
because the former is masculine plural, and belongs
to an object; and *puella* is feminine singular, and a
subject; *pueros* cannot be the subject of *amabat*,
because the former is plural in its inflection, and the
latter singular. In Juvenal's noble saying, *Maxima
debetur puero reverentia*, The greatest reverence
is due to a boy, the order of the words is this:

greatest is owed to a boy reverence; and there is nothing in this order to preclude the application of the word meaning greatest to the word meaning boy, which would give us, Reverence is due to the biggest boy. But in Juvenal's sentence, the Latin word for boy has the dative inflection, which shows that the boy is the recipient of something, and is the object of the verb *debetur;* it is also masculine; and as *maxima* agrees in case and in gender with *reverentia*, the feminine subject of the verb, it must qualify that word.

If we should find the following collocation of words, "For thy now sake of my of mistress with weeping swollen redden pretty eyes," we should pronounce it nonsense. It is not even a sentence. And yet it is a translation of the beautiful lines, in the order of their words, with which Catullus closes his charming ode, "Funus Passeris."

> "Tua nunc opera meæ pullæ
> Flendo turgiduli rubent ocelli."

And the words, reduced to their logical or English order, are, For thy sake the pretty swollen eyes of my mistress now redden with weeping. The Latin arrangement is as if we were presented with the figures 172569384, and were expected to read them, not one hundred and seventy-two million five hundred and sixty-nine thousand three hundred and eighty-four, but one hundred twenty-three million four hundred fifty-six thousand seven hundred and eighty-nine; the order 123456789 being indicated by some peculiar and correspondent form of the characters known only to the initiated.

Enough has been said in illustration of the difference between the construction of the Latin and that of the English sentence. The former depends upon the inflectional forms of the words; and its sense is not affected, or is affected only in a secondary degree, by their relative positions. In the latter, the meaning of the sentence is determined by the relative positions of the words, their order being determined by the connection and interdependence of the thoughts of which they are the signs. Syntax, guided by etymology, controls the Latin; reason, the English. In brief, the former is grammatical; the latter, logical. English admits very rarely, and only in a very slight degree, that severance of words representing connected thoughts which is not only admissible, but which is generally found in the Latin sentence; of which structural form the foregoing examples are of the simplest sort, and are the most easily resolvable into logical order.

Milton is justly regarded as the English poet whose style is most affected by Latin models; and the opening passage of his great poem is often cited as a strongly-marked example of involved construction. But let us examine it briefly.

> "Of man's first disobedience [and the fruit
> Of that forbidden tree whose mortal taste
> Brought death into the world, and all our woe,
> With loss of Eden, till one greater Man
> Restore us, and regain the blissful seat],
> Sing, heavenly muse [that on the secret top
> Of Oreb, or of Sinai, didst inspire
> That shepherd who first taught the chosen seed
> In the beginning how the heavens and earth
> Rose out of chaos]."

This, certainly, is not the colloquial style, or even the high dramatic. How many young people, when called upon to "parse" it, have sat before it in dumb bewilderment! And yet its apparent intricacy is but the result of a single, and not violent, inversion. In all other respects the words succeed each other merely as the thoughts which they represent arise. The natural order of the passage is, Sing, heavenly muse, of man's first disobedience; and that simple invocation is the essential part of the sentence. What follows *muse*, between brackets, is a mere description, modification, or limitation of *muse;* what follows *disobedience* is a description of the disobedience, which is the object of *sing*—that is, the subject of the poem. The words between brackets are only a sort of prolonged parenthetical adjectives, qualifying *muse* and *disobedience*. If any intelligent person, bearing this in mind, will read the passage, beginning at *sing*, and turning from *chaos* back to the first line, all the seeming involution will disappear; and in the after reading of it in its written order, he will be impressed only by the grandeur and the mighty sweep and sustained power of the invocation. The two qualifying or adjectival passages, although composed of several elements, each of which is evolved from its predecessor, which it qualifies, being itself a sort of adjective, are written in a style so plain and so direct that no reader of ordinary intelligence can fail to comprehend them as fully and as easily as he can comprehend any passage in a novel or newspaper of the day. Would, indeed, that novels and newspapers were written with any approach to such simplicity and such directness! I do not say such meaning.

Milton's invocation is not the only example of its kind in the opening of a great English poem. Chaucer, writing nearly three hundred years before the blind Puritan, and in an entirely different spirit, thus introduces his "Troilus and Creseide," a poem as full of imagination and of a knowledge of man's inmost heart as any one, not dramatic in form, that has since been bestowed upon the world: —

> "The double sorrow of Troilus to tellen,
> That was Kinge Priamus sonne of Troy,
> In loving, how his aventures fellen
> From woe to wele, and after out of joy,
> My purpose is, er that I part froy:
> Thou, Tesiphone, thou helpe me for t'indite
> These wofull verses, that wepen as I write."

That is clear enough to any intelligent and educated reader who is not troubled by the fact that Chaucer "didn't know how to spell;" but it is really more involved in structure, more like a passage from a Latin poet, than the opening of "Paradise Lost." The sentence, according to the natural order of thought, begins with the fifth line, "My purpose is," etc., and then turns back to the first line, which itself contains an inversion — "The sorrow to tellen" for "To tellen the sorrow." But the whole of the second line is really an adjective qualifying *Troilus*, and this is thrown in between the verb "to tellen" and the phrase "in loving," the latter of which is really an adjective qualifying the object of the action "sorrow." So that the logical order of the sentence is this: "My purpose is to

tell the double sorrow in loving of Troilus, that was
King Priam's son of Troy, how his adventures fell
from woe to weal, and after out of joy." The construction of the passage, however, as Chaucer wrote
it, is not English; and although in a formal opening of a long poem, it is not only admissible, but
impressive, it would, if continued, become intolerable. Inversion has been used with fine effect in a
single clause by Parsons, in his noble lines upon a
bust of Dante, —

> " How stern of lineament, how grim,
> The father was of Tuscan song! "

Here the limiting adjectival phrase, " of Tuscan
song," is separated by the verb from the noun which
it qualifies, and the result is (we can hardly tell why)
a deep and strong impression upon the reader's mind.
Such effects, however, are not in harmony with the
genius of the English language, and are admissible
and attainable only at the hands of those who wield
language with a singular felicity.

The reason why inversions of the logical order
of thought are perilous, and rarely admissible in
English, has a direct relation to the subject under
discussion. For example, in neither of these passages from Chaucer and from Parsons is the construction safely keyed together by etymological
forms, as would have been the case if they had
been written by a Greek or a Latin poet. We have
to divine the connection of the words and clauses —
to guess at it, from our general knowledge of the
poet's meaning — from the drift of his sentence;
and thus, instead of being placed at once in communication with him, and receiving his thought di-

rectly and without a doubt, and being free to assent
or dissent, to like or to dislike, we must give ourselves, for a longer or a shorter time, — in some
cases but an inappreciable moment, — to unravel-
ling his construction; doing, in a measure, what
we are obliged to do in reading a Greek or a Latin
author. In the example quoted from Parsons, the
inversion, although violent, disturbs so little of the
sentence, and produces so pleasant a surprise, and
one which is renewed at each re-reading, that we
not only pardon, but admire. Success is here, as
ever, full justification. But Chaucer loses more in
clearness and ease than he gains in impressiveness
and dignity; and Milton's exhibition of power to
mount and soar at the first essay does not quite
recompense all of us for the sudden strain he gives
our eyes in following him. But the completest
victory over the difficulty of inversion in the construction of the English sentence will not make it
endurable, except as a curious exhibition of our
mother tongue, disguised in foreign garb, and aping
foreign manners. A single stanza, composed of
lines like that of Parsons, on Dante's bust, would
weary and offend even the most cultivated English
reader. Those who are untrained in intellectual
gymnastics would abandon it, upon the first attempt, as beyond their powers.

The most striking example of the destruction of
meaning by the inverted arrangement of thought that
I have met with in the writings of authors of repute is the following line, which closes the beautiful sonnet in Sidney's " Astrophel and Stella,"
beginning, "With how sad steps, O Moon, thou
climbst the night ! "

"Do they call virtue there forgetfulness?"

The meaning of this seems clear; and it is so, according to the order of the words, which ask if, in a certain place, virtue is called forgetfulness. But this is exactly the reverse of Sidney's meaning, as will be seen by the context : —

> "Is constant love deemed there but want of wit?
> Are beauties there as proud as here they be?
> Do they above love to be loved, and yet
> Those lovers scorn whom that love doth possess?
> Do they call virtue there forgetfulness?"

That is, we at last discover, Do they call forgetfulness virtue? But reason ourselves into this apprehension of the sentence as absolutely as we can, familiarize ourselves with it as much as we may, it will, at every new reading, strike us, as it did at first, that the poet's question is asked about virtue. So absolute, in English, is the law of logical order.

The following passages, which I have recently seen given as examples of confusion resulting from a lack of proper punctuation, illustrate the present subject : —

> "I continued on using it, and by the time I had taken five bottles I found myself completely cured, after having been brought so near to the gates of death by your infallible medicine"!

> "The extensive view presented from the fourth story of the Hudson River"!

> "His remains were committed to that bourn whence no traveller returns attended by his friends"!

The fault here is not in the punctuation, but in the order of the words, which, however, although nonsensical in English, might make very good sense in Greek or Latin. The sentences are all examples of the hopeless confusion which may be produced

by an inversion which violates logical order; and
if they were peppered with points, the fault would
not thus be remedied. I shall leave it to my readers to put the words into their proper order, merely
remarking upon the last example, that the form of
the sentence is quite worthy of a man who could
speak of *committing* a body to a *bourn*, and that
bourn the one whence no traveller returns !

The difference between the construction of the
Latin and Greek languages and that of the English
language is not accidental, nor the product of a
merely unconscious exercise of power. It is the
result of a direct exertion of the human will to make
the instrument of its expression more and more
simple and convenient. The change which has
produced this difference began a very long while
ago, and for many centuries has been making more
or less progress among all the Indo-European languages. Latin is a less grammatical language than
its elder sister, the Greek; the modern Latin or
Romance tongues, Italian, Spanish, French, are less
grammatical than the Latin; the Teutonic tongues
are less grammatical than the Romance; and of the
Teutonic tongues English is the least grammatical—
so little dependent is it, indeed, upon the forms of
grammar for the structure of the sentence, that it
cannot rightly be said to have any grammar.

And here I will remark that it is in this wide difference between the etymology and the syntax of
the modern languages — French, Italian, Spanish,
German, and English, and those of the Greek and
Latin — that the incomparable superiority of the
latter as the means of education consists. The
languages of modern Europe, widely dissimilar

gh they seem to the superficial reader, differ
in their vocabularies; and even there much
ir unlikeness is due to the difference of pro-
ition, an incidental variation which obtains to
iderable degree in the same language within
riod of one hundred years. In structure the
n languages are too much alike to make the
of any one of them by a person to whom any
s vernacular very valuable as a means of men-
cipline. They are acquired with great facility
ople of no education and very inferior mental
s: couriers and *valets-de-place*, who speak
rite three or four of them fluently and cor-
, being numerous in all the capitals of the
ean Continent.

cation is not the getting of knowledge, but dis-
e, development; and it is not for the knowledge
otain at school and college that we pass our
years in study. The mere acquaintance with
hat we then painfully acquire, we could, in our
er years, obtain in a tenth part of the time that
ve to our education. Nor is it necessary in
rn days that any one should go for knowledge
eek and Latin authors. All the lore and the
ht of the past is easily attainable in a living
e. And, finally, to the demand why, if boys
study language as a means of education, can
ot study French or German, languages which
ow spoken, and which will be of some practical
money-getting) use to them, the answer is
he value of the classical tongues as means of
tion is in the very fact that they are dead,
hat their structure is so remote from that of
that to dismember their sentences and recon-

struct them according to our own fashion of speaking is such an exercise of perception, judgment, and memory, such a training in thought and in the use of language, as can be found in no other study or intellectual exertion to which immature and untrained persons of ordinary powers are competent. To us of English race and speech this discipline is more severe, and therefore more valuable, than to any people of the Continent, because of the greater distance, in this respect, between our own language than between any one of theirs and the Greek and Latin, and the wider difference between the English and the Greek or the Latin cast of thought. Because, to repeat what has already been insisted upon, the Greek and the Latin languages are constructed upon syntactical principles, which, in their turn, rest upon etymological or formal inflection, and English, being almost without formal inflection, and nearly independent of syntax — without distinction of mood in verbs, and with almost none of tense and person — with only one case of nouns, and with neither number nor case in adjectives — with no gender at all of nouns, of adjectives, or of participles — without laws of agreement or of government, the very verb in English being, in most cases, independent of its nominative as to form, rests solely upon the relations of thought; in brief, because the Greek and Latin languages have grammar — formal grammar — and the English language, to all intents and purposes, has none.

How this is, and why, will be more fully and particularly considered in the next chapter.

CHAPTER X.

THE GRAMMARLESS TONGUE.

IN the last chapter it was set forth that English is an almost grammarless language. The two elements of grammar being etymology, — which concerns the inflections of words; that is, changes in form to express modification of meaning, — and syntax, — which concerns the construction of sentences according to the formal relations of words, — and the English language being almost without the former, and therefore equally without the latter, its use must be, in a corresponding degree, untrammelled by the rules of grammar, and subject only to the laws of reason, which we call logic. We have, indeed, been long afflicted with grammarians from whom we have suffered much, and to whose usurped authority we — that is, the most of us — have submitted, with hardly a murmur or a question. But the truth of this matter is, that of the rules given in the books called English Grammars, some are absurd, and the most are superfluous. For example, it can be easily shown that in the English language, with few exceptions, the following simple and informal relations of words prevail : —

The verb needs not, and generally does not, agree with its nominative case in number and person:

Pronouns do not agree with their antecedent nouns in person, number, and gender:

Active verbs do not govern the objective case, or any other:

Prepositions do not govern the objective case, or any other:

One verb does not govern another in the infinitive mood:

Nor is the infinitive a mood, nor is it governed by substantive, adjective, or participle:

Conjunctions need not connect the same moods and tenses of verbs.

The grammarians have laid down laws directly to the contrary of these assertions; but the grammarians are wrong, and, in the very nature of things, cannot be right; for their laws assume as conditions precedent the existence of things which do not exist. In English, the verb is almost without distinction of number and of person; the noun is entirely without gender, and has no objective case; the adjective and the participle are without number, gender, and case; the infinitive is not a mood, it is not an inflection of the verb, or a part of it; and conjunctions are free from all rules but those of common sense and taste.

No term was ever more unwisely chosen than *government* to express the relations of words in the sentence. It is one of the mysterious metaphors which have been imposed upon the world, generally by tyrants or tricksters, and with which thought is confused and language darkened. In grammar it implies, or seems to imply, a power in one word over another. Now, there is in no language any such power, or any relation which is properly symbolized by such a power.

In Latin, Greek, and other inflected languages, the forms of the words of which a sentence is made up, present outward signs of requirement which give some hint as to what the grammarians mean by one word's governing another. But in English there is no such visible sign; and this arbitrary, mysterious, and metaphorical phrase, government, is, to young minds, and particularly if they are reasoning and not merely receptive, perplexing in the extreme. Even in languages which have variety of inflection, words do not govern each other; but they may be said to fit into each other by corresponding forms which indicate their proper connection, so that a sentence is dovetailed together. In English, however, with the exception of a few pronouns, one case of nouns, and two tenses and one person of the verb, all the words are as round and smooth, and as independent of each other in form, as the pebbles on the sea-shore. The attempt to bind such words together by the links of etymology and syntax, or, in other words, to make grammatical rules for a language in which the noun has only one case, — in which there is no gender of noun, adjective, or participle, — in which distinction of tense, number, person in verbs is almost unknown, and that of voice absolutely wanting, is, on its face, absurd.

In English, words are formed into sentences by

the operation of an invisible power, which is like magnetism. Each one is charged with a meaning which gives it a tendency toward some of those in the sentence, and particularly to one, and which repels it from the others; and he who subtly divines and dexterously uses this attraction, filling his words with a living but latent light and heat, which makes them leap to each other and cling together while they transmit his freely-flowing thought, is a master of the English language, although he may be ignorant and uninstructed in its use. And here is one difference between the English and the ancient classic tongues. The great writers of the latter were, and, it would seem, must needs have been, men of high culture — grammarians in the ancient sense of the word, which I have before mentioned; but some of the best English that has been written is the simple, strong utterance of uneducated men, entirely undisciplined in the use of language. True, they had genius, — some of them, at least; but genius, giving them strength and clearness of imagination, or of reason, could yet not have taught them to write with purity and power a language like the Greek, in which the verb has three voices, five moods, and two aorists, and nine persons for every tense; in which all nouns have three numbers, and each noun a gender of its own; and every adjective and participle three genders and six cases, a copiousness of inflection possessed by the very articles, definite and indefinite. The Greek language may be the noblest and most perfect instrument ever invented by man for the ex-

pression of his thought; but certainly, of all the
tongues ever spoken by civilized men, it is the
most complicated. And I venture to express my
belief, that its complication, so far from being an
element of its power, is a sign of rudeness, and a
remnant of barbarism; that the Greek and Latin
authors were great, not by reason of the verbal
forms and the grammatical structure of their languages, but in spite of them; and that our mother
tongue, in freeing herself from these, has only cast
aside the trammels of strength and the disguises
of beauty.

But I must turn from these general considerations
of my subject to such an examination of its particulars as will sustain the position which I have taken.
And first of the verb. The Greek verb has, for
the expression of the various moods and times of
acting and suffering by various persons, more than
five hundred inflections; and these inflections so
modify, by processes called augmentation and re-
duplication, and by signs of person and of number,
both the beginning and the end of the verb, that,
to the uninstructed eye, it passes beyond recognition. Thus, for instance, τύπτω (*tupto*), (the verb
which occupies in Greek Grammars the place of
to love in English Grammars), assumes, among its
changes, these dissimilar forms: τύπτω (*tupto*), I
strike; ἐτετύφειν (*etetuphein*), I had struck; τυπτέτω-
σαν (*tuptetosan*), let them strike; ἐτετύφεισαν (*etetu-
pheisan*), they had struck; τύψας (*tupsas*), having
struck; ἐτυπτόμεθον (*etuptomethon*), we two were
struck; ἐτυψάμεθον (*etupsamethon*), we two struck

ourselves; τυφθησοίμην (*tuphtheesoimeen*), I might
be about to be struck. These are but specimens
of the more than five hundred bricks which go to
make up the regular Greek verbal edifice. Each
person of each case has its peculiar significant
form or inflection, every one of which must be
learned by heart.

Looking back upon this single and simplest
specimen of its myriad inflections, I cannot wonder
that boys of English race regard Greek as an
invention of the enemy of mankind. But this
variety of inflection has not entirely passed away
with the life of the ancient Hellenic people and
language. It has been shown that the French language has three hundred different terminations for
the simple cases of the ten regular conjugations,
one thousand seven hundred and fifty-five for the
thirty-nine irregular conjugations, and two hundred
for the auxiliary verbs — making a sum total of two
thousand one hundred and sixty-five terminations
which must be learned by heart.* The verbs of
the Greek language must have, I think, in all,
more than ten times that number of changes in
form. Now, the English verb has, in its regular
or weak form, only four inflections; and in its
so-called irregular, or strong, or ancient form, only
five. These inflections serve for the two voices,
five moods, six tenses, and six persons which must
have expression in a language that answers the
needs of a civilized, cultured people. The four
forms of the verb *to love*, for instance, are *love*,
loves, *loved*, and *loving*. The first two and the last

---

* Sinibaldo, quoted by Max Muller.

express action indefinite as to time, the third, definite action. Two others, *lovest* and *lovedest*, are to be found in the Grammars, but they have been thrown out of use by the same process of simplification which has cast off the mass of the Anglo-Saxon inflections during the transformation of that language into English. The present tense indicative of the verb *to love* is, therefore, now as follows:—

I love,	We love,
You love,	You love,
He loves,	They love.

Here are five, and, in effect, six nominatives of two numbers and three persons, but only two forms of the verb. How, then, to return to our rules of grammar, can the verb agree with its nominative in number and person? The truth is, that it does not so agree, because those who use it have found that such agreement is not necessary to the clear expression of thought. *I love* and *we love* are just as exact in meaning as *amo*, *amamus*. The past tense of the English verb has not even one inflection. It is as follows:—

I loved,	We loved,
You loved,	You loved,
He loved,	They loved.

It was not always thus. The Anglo-Saxon verb, although, like the English, it had but one voice and two tenses, had inflection of person and number. The present, or indefinite, and the perfect tenses of *lufian*, to love, were as follows:—

PRESENT.

ic lufige,	we lufiath,
thu lufast,	ge lufiath,
he lufath,	hi lufiath.

PERFECT.

ic lufode,	we lufodon,
thu lufodest,	ge lufodon,
he lufode,	hi lufodon

These inflections appear in what is called the Early English stage of our language, and some of them are found even in the writings of Chaucer and Gower, although in the days of those poets they had lost their old force, and were rapidly passing away. They were dropped almost with the purpose of simplifying the language, of doing away with complications which were found needless. It was seen that as the noun or pronoun always accompanied the verb, the plural form in *ath* or *en* was not necessary for the exact expression of thought, and that *we love* and *we loved* were as unmistakeable in their significance as *we lufiath* and *we lufodon ;* and so as to the other numbers and persons of the two tenses. The plural form in *en* held a place long after other inflections had disappeared; but that disappeared from the written language about the end of the fifteenth century, and at last from the speech of the common people.

The inflections of the singular number had a stronger hold upon the language, probably because the singular number is more frequently used in the common intercourse of life than the plural, and because it is found more necessary to distinguish between the actions, thoughts, and conditions of individuals than between those of masses or groups. The distinctive inflection of the second person singular, *est*, held its own until the Elizabethan period, when it began to disappear. It prevails in the English Bible, but is less common in Shake-speare and the general literature of the period; one reason being that precision of language is regarded as becoming solemnity of occasion or of subject; another being the increasing use of the second person plural for both the singular and plural, which is now prevalent, not only in Eng-lish, but in most European languages.

Again, the change from *thou lovest* and *thou lovedest* to *you love* and *you loved*, seems to have been made merely from the wish to do away with a superfluous inflection. If, in the course of years, the inflection of the third person singular should follow that of the second, and we should say *he love*, the change would be directly in the line of the natural movement of our language. Should it not take place, the preservation of this lonely, unsup-ported inflection will probably be owing to the restraints of criticism, and the introduction of con-sciousness and culture among the mass of speakers. To some of my readers it may seem impossible that this change should be made, and that *he love* would be barbarous and almost incomprehensible. But such is not the effect of identity of form between the third person and the first of the perfect tense; and as it is neither absurd nor obscure to say *I loved, you* [*i. e.*, thou] *loved*, he *loved*, why should it be so to say *I love, you* [*i. e.*, thou] *love, he love*?

To turn now to the first rule of our text-books of English grammar — "A verb must agree with its nominative case in number and person." In this rule, if *agree* means anything, it can only mean that

the verb must conform itself in some manner to its
subject, so that it may be seen that it belongs to that
subject. This is the case in Latin, for instance, in
which language every person of each number of
the verb has a form which indicates that person.

[ego] amo, I love,	[vios] amamus, we love,
[tu] amas, you [*i. e.*, thou] love,	[vos] amatis, you love,
[ille] amat, he loves,	[illi] amant, they love.

But in English, for five of these six persons the
verb has but one form. It has been released from
all conformity to person except in the third person
singular. It has but one form for all the other
persons, and it therefore cannot agree with its
nominative in number and person, except in the
case specified. To say that this one form of the
verb does agree with all those forms of the nominative — that *love* does agree with *I*, and *you*,
singular, *we*, *you*, and *they*, plural is a mere
begging of the question by a childish and stren-
uous "making believe." And, indeed, as I trust
most of my readers now begin to see, nearly all of
our so-called English grammar is mere make-
believe grammar. No more words should be
necessary to show that verbs which have not number and person cannot agree with nominatives,
or with anything else, in number and person.
And yet that they do so agree is dinned into children from their infancy until they cease to receive
instruction, and they are required to cite a rule
which they cannot understand, as the law of a
relation which does not exist.

The Anglo-Saxon language was even charier as
to tenses of the verb than as to numbers and persons.

It had but two of the former, the present, or rather the indefinite, and the past. As it passed into English, this number was not increased. No English verb has more than two tenses. With these and the two participles, present and past, English speaking folk express all the varieties of mood and tense, and also of voice; for in English there is but one voice, the active. The Anglo-Saxon present or indefinite tense expressed future action as well as present. *Ic lufige* (I love) predicated loving in the future as well as in the present time. Nor has this form of speech passed away from the Anglo-Saxon folk. To this day we say, I go to town to-morrow; Do you go to town to-morrow? The form, *I shall go to town*, is rarely used except for emphasis; that, *I will go*, except to express determination. Indeed, I go is the more elegant form; is heard most generally from the lips of speakers of the highest culture. And in fact, the commonest predication of future action is one which expresses action passing continuously at time present — I am going, *e. g.*, I am going to town to-morrow.

This use of the present or indefinite tense is not at all peculiar to the Anglo-Saxon language, or to the English. It appears in many others. "Simon Peter said unto them, I go a fishing; they say unto him, We also go with thee." Two Greek verbs are here translated *go;* but both the first, ὑπάγω (*hupago*), and the second, ἐρχόμεθα (*erchometha*), are in the present tense. In this passage, too, *I go*, *I am going*, *I shall go*, and *we go*, *we are going*, *we will go*, would be equivalents. The peculiarity of the Anglo-Saxon and the English languages in this

20

respect (if they are two languages, which
philologists with show of reason deny, on the
that our present speech is only a lineal desc
of that of our forefathers), — the peculiarity
tongue as to this tense and others is, that whil
others, it uses the present indefinite form
press future action, it has not developed a fo
the verb for the special expression of that acti
in fact, of any other action but that which is
present or past. We say, I *shall go;* but
can no more be a part of the verb *go* than *w*
may, or *can.* We say, I *have loved;* but, again
is no more a part of the verb *love* than *to*
when we say, If I were loving. When we
am loving, we only say, in other words, I
loving; and what connection has *am* with
other than *exist* would have were it used i
place of the former? We, like other people
obliged to express all the different times of a
present, past, and future; but most other peop
this by inflections, that is, by real tenses of the
As English has different words for expressin
time present and time past of the same a
other tongues have different words for expre
all the varieties of the time of action.

In English we say, I love, I have loved, I
have loved; but in Latin the same thought
expressed respectively by the different single v
amo, amavi, amavero. To express what the
man expressed by *amavi,* an inflection of
we use a verb *have,* and the perfect particip
another verb. That participle is an expressi
completed action in the abstract — *loved.* It h

relation to person, whether the person is the subject or the object of the action, — a point to be remembered in our consideration of voice — or to specific time or occasion. The only real verb that we use in this instance is one that signifies possession. We say, I have — have what? possess what? Possession implies an object possessed; and in this case it is that completed action which is expressed in the abstract by the participle. *Loved* is here the object of the verb *have* as much as *money* would be in the sentence, I have money; and *I have loved* is no more a verb, or a part or tense of a verb, than *I have money* is, or *I have to go*. In the first and the last of these, *loved* and *to go* are as plainly objects of the verb *have* as *money* is in the second; nor is this relation at all affected by the mere verbal origin of the participle and the infinitive.

As to the latter, what the grammarians call the infinitive mood is no mood at all, but a substantive, of verbal origin. It is the name of the verb, and so may well be called a substantive. It is not so called for that reason, but because there is no quality of a substantive which the infinitive has not, and but one relation of the substantive — that of possession — which it cannot assume; and there is no distinctive quality of the verb which it does not lack, or relation of the verb which it can assume. For instance, *I have to go* is merely, It belongs to me to go, To go belongs to me — forms of expression not uncommon among the most cultivated and idiomatic speakers, and which are not only correct, but elegant. But that which is expressed by a verb cannot belong to any one. Only a thing, something sub-

... for generations tea
that *to go* is a mood,
that *I have gone* and
verb.

The substantive chara
discovered in those phras
call the future tense in
and imperfect tenses sub
may love, and I might lov
and have no semblance of
or rather complete sentenc
or contingent action.

The formation of the futu
tenses of the subjunctive mo
The Anglo-Saxon infinitive w
and did not admit the preposi
there was a second infinitive, fi
osition, having a dative sense,
dative form of the infinitive, co
of obligation or pertinence to w
given the name dative. Thus æ
Saxon infinitive, meaning to b
used another inf
obli

to know, *i. e.*, it should be known, or ought to be
known. This very phrase (with the mere rubbing
off of the termination during its passage through the
centuries) has come down to us as *to wit*. But
to know itself has been thus used for five hundred
years, as in the following passage in Purvey's
Prologue to the revised Wycliffe Bible, A. D.
1388 : —

"First it is to know that the best translating is to translate
after the sentence, and not only after the words."

And it also appears not infrequently nowadays in
the phrase, You are to know — thus and so, meaning, You should know, You ought to know, It behooves you to know, thus and so ; and constantly in
the colloquial phrases, I have to go here or there, I
have to do thus and so. The phrase, *This house
to let*, which some uneasy precisians would change
into *This house to* be *let*, is quite correct, and has
come down to us, as it will be seen, from the remotest period.

Now, when Anglo-Saxon was becoming English
by the dropping of its few inflections and the laying aside of its light bonds of formal grammar, the
form of the infinitive which remained was naturally the one which was indicated, not by an inflection, but by a preposition. At first, and indeed for
a century or two, the inflected termination was
retained, but it would seem merely from habit,
with no significance attached to it. Thus in the
passage from Chaucer's "Troilus and Cresseide"
quoted in the last chapter, the first line is, —

"The double sorrow of Troilus *to tellen*."

But in Chaucer's day, our forefathers were be-

ginning to drop the *n* and the syllable of which it
was part, and instead of *to loven* and *to liven*, to
write *to live* and *to love*, as we do. But they wrote
to telle, as we do not; the final *e*, which appears
in old, and in some modern forms of certain verbs,
being in its place, not by mere accident, but as a
remnant of the old infinitive. Hence, too, this final
e was sometimes pronounced, as every student of
Chaucer knows. The dropping of old plurals of
verbs and nouns in *en* (a great loss in the latter
case, I think) left many words ending in silent *e*
preceded by a double consonant, — a form which
began to pass rapidly away in the latter part of the
sixteenth century, but which may still be traced in
our orthography; for instance, the very verb in the
line from "Troilus and Cresseide." If we do not
write *tellen*, there is no etymological reason why we
should not write *tel*. The cause of the present
form of the verb is, that in Anglo-Saxon it was a
dissyllable, and that in dropping the last syllable,
only its essentials, the vowel and the following consonant, were removed. The double consonant is
now retained in some words, and the silent vowel
in some others, as *love* and *live*, for orthoepical
reasons.

To return to the formation of what the grammarians call the future indicative tense, and to the
tenses of the subjunctive mood. These, they tell
us, are formed by means of auxiliary verbs. But
that is a very misleading representation of the case,
consequent upon the endeavor to keep up the fiction of formal grammar in English — the make-
believe system. In fact, the auxiliary theory is a

mere clumsy sham. In *I am loved, I will go*, there are no auxiliary or really helping words. Neither word needs the help of the other, except, as other words do, for the making of a sentence, which each of these examples is, completely. In *I am loved*, and *I will go*, *am* and *will* are no more helping verbs than *exist* and *determine* are in the sentences, I exist loved, and I determine to go. *Loved* and *go* will each make a perfect sense with *I* and without any help — I loved, I go. In the sentences I am loved and I will go, *loved* and *go* are not verbs. The former is a participle, or verbal adjective, the latter a verbal substantive. The Anglo-Saxon had not even any seeming auxiliary verbs. Its use of *habban, beon, willan, magan, cunnan* and *mot* (*i. e.*, have, be, will, may, can, might), does not convey the notion of time and contingency, but simply predicates possession, existence, volition, necessity, power; and hence came those phrases by which we speak of action or existence in the future or under supposed circumstances. *I will tell* is in old English, *I will tellen*, and this is merely the verb *I will* joined to the infinitive or verbal substantive *tellen*. From the latter the last syllable has been worn; but none the less *I will tell* is simply I will to tell. The dative pertaining idea is conveyed, *i. e.*, my will is to tell, my will is for telling, or toward telling. Thus *I can love* is merely I can to love, I am able to love; and so it is with the phrases *I might love, I could love, I would love, I should love*. They are all, not verbs or parts of verbs, but phrases formed by the use of the indicative present of one verb with the infinitive or verbal substantive of other.

By this discarding of inflected tenses the E lish language has gained, not only in simplicity in flexibility and variety. The Latin langu for instance, has, for the expression of I might l and also of I could, and of I would, and of I sh — love, only the single inflected form *amar* whereas we are able to express, in regard to same time of action, four very marked and diffe shades of meaning, while we are entirely freed the grammatical restraints and complications posed by inflection. The Latin folk were obl to remember six forms for this one tense, and were able to make no distinction in tense betw the ideas of possibility, power, volition, and gation, in connection with future action.

SINGULAR.	PLURAL.
1. Amarem	1. Amaremus,
2. Amares,	2. Amaretis,
3. Amaret,	3. Amarent.

Whereas in English we, by a simple change the subject, noun or pronoun, say, —

I		
You	might, *or*	
He	could, *or*	
We	would, *or*	love.
You	should,	
They	(according to the meaning to be conveyed)	

But we do not thereby form a tense of the v Could absurdity be more patent than in the as tion, not only that *might* and *should* are a of the verb *to love*, but that several words com

ing thoughts so widely different as *I might love*
and *I should love,* are actually the *same* part of the
same verb? A consideration of the difference in
meaning of those two sentences, of their radical
difference, or rather their absolute opposition, the
one expressing possibility, the other obligation, and
of the fact that, according to the English grammarians, they are equally parts of one so-called
tense, the imperfect subjunctive, which in Latin is
a tense, *amarem,* will make it clear that in English
we have not merely substituted one tense form for
another. We have done away with the tense; we
have done away with all tenses, except the present,
or indefinite, and the past. We have found that
those tenses are all that we need; that with the
forms significant of present and of past action, or
being, or suffering, we can express ourselves in conformity to all the conditions of time, past, present,
and future.

As we have dealt with tenses, so have we with
voices. The English verb has but one voice — the
active. And not only has it no passive voice, but
there is in the language no semblance of a passive
voice. The Greek, who must have three numbers
to his nouns, one for an individual, one, the dual,
for two, and a third for more than two, was also
not content without three voices — the active, the
passive, and one which was in sense between those
two, which has been called the middle voice, but
might better have been called the reflective voice.
Thus we say I wash, I am washed, I washed myself; the Greek, expressing the same facts that
are expressed by these English phrases, said in

three words, λούω (*louō*), λούομαι (*louomai*), ἐλουσάμην (*elousameen*). Now, the English grammarians tell their hapless pupils that *to be washed* is the passive voice of the verb *to wash*. It is no such thing. If *I am washed* is the passive voice of *I wash*, equally is *I wash myself* its middle voice. But no English grammarian known to me, or that I ever heard of, has set forth such forms of speech as *I washed myself* as a middle voice. It is a sentence, as much so as *I washed John*; and if *myself* is no part of the verb *to wash*, no more is *am*; and *I am washed* is no part of any verb, but a complete sentence, with a subject and a predicate consisting of a verb and a participial adjective. The reason why, although *I am washed* is set down by the English grammarians as a part of the verb *to wash*, *I wash myself*, is not, plainly is that the Latin language, upon which our English grammarians have formed their system, and to which their rules have been as much as possible assimilated, has a passive, but no middle voice. Had there been a middle voice in the Latin, there would have been one in the English Grammars, and we should have been told that one part of the verb *to wash* was *I shall have washed myself*, although we could separate this tense thus: *I probably shall* by ten o'clock *have* nearly *washed* or bathed *myself*.

We have done away with the passive voice in all its moods and tenses; and we have no passive form of the verb whatever, not even a passive participle. We express the fact of passivity, or the recipience of any action, by some verb, and the perfect participle of the verb expressing that action; and this

perfect participle we apply to ourselves or to others
as a qualification. In technical language we make
it a participal adjective, that is, a word which qualifies a noun by representing it as affected or modified
by some action. Thus we say, a good man, or,
a loved man; and in these phrases both *good* and
loved are adjectives qualifying *man.* *To be loved*
is no more a verb than *to be good.* According
to the English grammarians, we can conjugate the
former, in all the moods and tenses of their so-
called passive voice. But so we can the latter.

I am good,	We are good,
Thou art good,	Ye or you are good,
He is good,	They are good.

This is conjugation as much as *I am loved, Thou
art loved,* and so forth, is; and it can be carried
out, of course, to I shall have been, or I might,
could, would, or should have been — either good
or loved, it makes no difference which. But that
is not conjugation in either case; it is the mere
forming of sentences. When a Greek boy wished
to express his conviction that at a certain time
future, if he had done what was wrong, or had not
done what was right, certain unpleasant consequences would have followed, he said in one word,
τετύψομαι (*tetupsomai*), which is a tense of the verb
τύπτω (*tupto*). But the English boy uses instead of
this one word a sentence made up of a pronoun,
two verbs, and two participles: he says, I shall
have been beaten. Of the verbs, the first, *shall,*
expresses a present sense of future certainty,
obligation, or inevitableness. Thus Dr. Johnson
says, *I shall love* is equivalent to "it will be so that

I must love." The second verb, *have*, ex
possession. He says, I shall have — what?
thing.

$$I \text{ shall have} \begin{cases} \text{something.} \\ \text{a beating.} \\ \text{been beaten.} \end{cases}$$

Have cannot have one meaning in two o
instances, and another in the third. Of th
perfect or definite participles, the first, *bee*
presses past existence. He says, I shall
been — what? Something, or in some con

$$I \text{ shall have been} \begin{cases} \text{a bad boy.} \\ \text{deficient in my lesson.} \\ \text{beaten.} \end{cases}$$

By what process can, or in consequence of
necessity does, *been* have one meaning in
of these instances, and another in the third?
by the union of the verb of existence with th
fect or definite participle of an active ver
English language can and does express the
ence of action, *i. e.*, existence under action. T
fore the perfect participle of the verb of exi
united to that of an active verb expresse
perfected recipience of action. But, accordi
English idiom, we cannot use *been* without p
the idea of possession between it and the su
To express a completed existence, we say n
been, but *I have been*. Therefore our E
boy, when he says, I shall have been beaten
in other words, It will be so that I must p
the perfected recipience of the action of be
Truly, a long and lumbering equivalent
phrase; but so are, and so must be, all exp

tions and paraphrases of idiomatic or figurative forms of speech. None the less, however, is *I shall have been beaten* a sentence; and this sentence, thus made up of a pronoun, with two verbs and two participles which have no etymological relations, English grammarians call a tense, the future perfect tense of the passive voice of the verb *to beat!* Could there be better proof that the English verb has neither future tense nor passive voice? [*]

The simplification of our language, which has left the English verb only one voice and but two tenses, has given only one case to the English noun, the possessive, or two if we reckon the nominative, which, strictly speaking, is not a case. The English noun has no objective case. English grammarians tell us that it has, and that this case is governed, and agrees, and is put in apposition, and what not. But the truth is, that the English language, although it expresses clearly the objective relation, does it without case, and merely by position, arrangement in logical order. One of the rules of the English grammarians is that, "Active verbs govern the objective case," or, according to another form, "A noun or pronoun used as the *object* of a transitive verb or its participles must be in the objective case; as, William defeated Harold." Here, therefore, we are told Harold is in "the objective case." How, then, is it with this sentence? — Harold defeated William. No change

---

[*] I need not stop to say to the candid scholar that the Latin, like the English, is without a tense corresponding to the Greek third future passive, and also without some other formal tenses in the passive voice. But that is not to my present purpose. Here Latin and Greek concern me only when they can be used by way of illustration. As to some objections which have been made to the theory of our verb formation imperfectly set forth above, see the Note at the end of this chapter.

has been made in the word *Harold;* it is in the same case in both sentences. It has simply changed its position, and so its relation. In the former sentence, Harold is the object, and William the subject, of the action; in the latter, Harold is the subject, and William the object. But what in language could be more absurd or more confusing to a learner than to say that a mere change in the place of a word makes a change in its case? And so, as to the rule, "A noun or pronoun used to explain or identify another noun is put by apposition in the same case; as, William, the Norman duke, defeated Harold, the Saxon king." Here we are told that *duke* is in the nominative case, because it is in apposition with *William*, and that *king* is in the objective case, it being in apposition with *Harold*. But let the words be merely shifted, without any inflection, and let us read, Harold, the Saxon king, defeated William, the Norman duke; which is English, and might have been truth. In what case here are *king* and *duke?* Clearly they are in no case in either example. They are simply subject and object, or object and subject, according to their relative positions.

We are told by one of the latest English grammarians, in his etymology of pronouns, that, "To pronouns, *like nouns*, belong person, number, gender, and case." This is a notably incorrect assertion. Upon two of these points, nouns and pronouns are remarkably unlike; upon one other they are correctly said to be alike; upon the fourth, the assertion is untrue as to both.

Pronouns and nouns have number; pronouns

have person, nouns have not; pronouns have two cases — the possessive and the objective, nouns but one — the possessive. The rules given in English Grammars for the syntax of nouns, apply, with a single exception, to pronouns only, and are founded chiefly upon the persons and cases of the latter — the forms *I, my, me, We, our, us, Thou, thy, thee, You, your, He, his, him, She, hers, her, It, its, They, their, them*, to which there are no corresponding forms in nouns, except the possessive in *es*, which has been contracted to *'s*, as if we were feeling our way towards its entire abolition. Disappear it surely will, if we find that we can do without it, and that, for instance, *John coat* is just as precise and apprehensible as *John's coat*. One of the pronoun cases is visibly disappearing — the objective case *whom*. Even in the fastidious "Saturday Review" we sometimes find *who* as the object of a verb. Our pronouns, however, are still inflected, and have cases; and of pronouns, active verbs do govern, or rather require, the objective case. To our few pronouns, then, may be applied all those rules of construction which rest upon case-form, which, borrowed from the Latin language and thrust upon the student of English, are announced in our Grammars as the laws for the syntax of the vast multitude of nouns.

Thus far, as to the positive likeness and unlikeness of nouns and pronouns. They have also a negative likeness, as to which they are misrepresented in all English Grammars, as in the one above cited. Both nouns and pronouns are *without gender*. There is no gender in the English language. Distinctions of sex are expressed by English folk; but this fact does not imply the existence of gender in the English language. Sex is generally, although not always, expressed by gender; but distinction of gender rarely implies distinction of sex. There are thousands of words in Greek, in Latin, and in French, which are masculine or feminine, and which are the names of things and of thoughts that can have no sex. The Latin noun *penna*, a pen, is feminine; and so is the French *table*, a table. These words have gender, although the things they signify have no sex. The corresponding English nouns are said in English Grammar to be of "the neuter gender." But they are of no gender at all.

Gender in language belongs, not to things, but to words. It is one of the most barbarous and foolish notions with which the mind of man was ever vexed. One or two examples shall make this plain. *Beau* is the French adjective expressing masculine beauty; its feminine counterpart is *belle;* so that a fine man has come to be called a *beau*, and a beautiful woman a *belle*. But, notwithstanding this, women, as the fair sex, are called in French *le beau sexe* — the reason being that in French, sex, the word *sexe*, is masculine! All languages afflicted with gender are covered with such irritating absurdity; so that this distinction of words is the bane and the torment of learners, whether to the manner born or not. For instance, in French, one is in constant dread lest one should commit such blunders as to speak of masculine breeches — the name of that garment in France being, with fine satire, feminine. And

with all this complicated provision of gender —
rather by reason of it — these languages are
letimes unable to distinguish sex A case in
it is this passage from "Gil Blas:" —

Je fis la lecture de mon ouvrage, que sa majesté n'entendit
sans plaisir. Elle témoigna qu'elle était contente de moi." —
VIII. Chap. 5.

This passage tells us that Gil Blas read his work
monarch, who was pleased and who expressed
sfaction. But although every word in the two
tences, except the participles and the verbs, has
der, it is impossible to learn from this passage
ther the monarch was male or female; as im-
sible as it is to do so from my paraphrase, which
urposely made without distinction of sex. The
r of the two sentences is bewildering to the
mon sense of an English reader who knows
context. It is, *She* showed that *she* was satis-
with me. Now, the she was a man — King
lip IV. of Spain. But in defiance of sex, the
inine pronoun is used because majesty, not the
lity or the condition, but the word *majesté*, is
inine! Here sex is not expressed by gender;
the lack of necessary connection between sex
gender is manifest.
n English we express only sex; that is, we
ely have different words to express the male
the female of living things. The human male
call man, the human female, woman; so we
boy and girl, father and mother, brother and
r, uncle and aunt, bull and cow, horse and
e, bullock and heifer, buck and doe, cock and
, and so forth. But even in cases like these,

21

woman, for instance, is not the feminine form
word *man*, or *girl* of *boy*, or *doe* of *buck*, or
cock. (In Anglo-Saxon *wer* = man is masculin
wif = woman is of neuter gender!) And altho
such instances as *actor, actress, hunter, huntress*
tigress, the name of the female is a feminine
of the name of the male, this has no effect up
construction of the sentence; the distinction
is still one purely of sex, and not of gender.
further: in pronouns, although they represent
belonging to the two sexes, there is no disti
of gender whatever; and, what is the mor
markable, considering the ado grammarians
about gender, none even of sex, except in one
ber of one person. *I, thou, we, you, they,*
and all the rest, except *he, she,* and *it*, refer to
culine and feminine persons alike. In the pr
of the third person singular we have a relic o
forefathers' inflected tongue. The Anglo-S
pronoun was masculine *he*, feminine *heó*, neute
which are respectively represented by our *he*
it. But here, again, the distinction is of se
of gender, and would be so even if it were c
through all the persons. *He, she,* and *it* are m
words that stand for male, female, and se
things, and their forms are not affected by
"governing" or requiring power of the other
in the sentences in which they appear. The
then, no gender in the English language, but
distinction of sex; that is, merely, we do not
woman a man, a hen a cock, or a heifer a bul
This being true, it is impossible that there c
agreement in gender of nouns or of pronouns.
The one case of English nouns, the posses

is equally without power in the sentence, upon the
structure of which it has no effect whatever. It
merely expresses possession, and its power, confined
to that expression, "governs" nothing, requires
nothing, "agrees" with nothing. The reason of
which is, that English adjectives and participles are
without case, as they are without number and without gender. In Latin every word qualifying a
noun in the genitive or possessive case, or closely
related to it, must be also in that case. Thus we
see upon the title-pages of the classics, sentences
crammed with genitives like the following: Albii
Tibulli, Equitis Romani Elegiarum aliorumque Car-
minum, Libri IV. ad optimos codices emendati,
curâ Reverendissimi, Doctissimi, Sanctissimi Caroli
Bensonis; that is, Four books of the Elegies and
other poems of Albus Tibullus, a Roman knight,
restored according to the best manuscripts, by the
care of the most reverend, learned, and holy Carl
Benson. Here, in Latin, because Tibullus is in
the genitive or possessive case, the words meaning
Roman and knight must also be in that case; so
with the word meaning other, because that meaning poems is in the genitive; and of course so with
those meaning most reverend, most learned, and
most holy, that these may agree with Carl Benson.
This is syntax or grammatical construction. We English folk have burst all those bonds of speech forever.

It must have been with some reference to this
topic that Lindley Murray has vexed the souls of
generations by proclaiming as the tenth law of
English grammar, that "One substantive governs
another signifying a different thing in the possessive
case." Truly an awful and a mysterious utterance

It is about substantives and the possessive cas
what about them? I can believe that the A
lypse is to be understood — hereafter ; I will
take to parse "Sordello" — for a consideration
I admit that before the Yankee Quaker's tent
I sit dumbfounded. I cannot begin, or he
begin, to understand it, or believe that it has
is, or will be understood by any man.

The assertion that it is a law of the Englis
guage that conjunctions connect the same
and tenses of verbs, may be confuted by a
example to the contrary, such as, " I desire
have pursued virtue, and should have bee
warded, if men were just." That sentence is
English ; and yet in it the conjunction *and* con
what are, according to Murray and the other
lish grammarians, two moods and three tenses

But I must bring this chapter to an end ;
may well do so, having shown my readers
government, and agreement, and apposition
gender have no place in the construction of
English sentence, that tense is confined to
necessary distinction between what is passin
may pass, and what has passed, and case, t
simple expression of possession. This bein
condition of the English language, gramma
the usual sense of the word, — *i. e.*, syntax ac
ing to etymology, — is impossible ; for infl
forms and the consequent relations of words a
conditions, *sine qua non*, of grammar. In spe
or writing English, we have only to choose the
words and put them into the right places, resp
no laws but those of reason, conforming to no
but that which we call "logical."

NOTE.

THE views set forth in " The Grammarless Tongue "
as to the English verb have met with an opposition which
I looked for, and which, indeed, has been less general
and' violent than I expected it would be; for the reason,
I am inclined to think, that the article in question had
the good fortune to express the opinions to which many
silent and unprofessional thinkers on language — among
whom I was until I began these articles — had been led,
independently of authority, and by the mere force of right
reason.

My assertion that the English verb has but two tenses,
that it generally does not agree with the nominative in number and person, and the like, bring upon me the charge,
not of error, but of blundering, misstatement, ignorance,
and impertinent self-assertion. (I take some pleasure in
the recapitulation.) As to the general non-agreement
of the English verb with its nominative case, it is too
manifest to need a word of argument. And as to whether
a man in taking this position may justly be held guilty
of ignorant and impertinent self-assertion, I cite the following passage from Sir John Stoddart's " Universal
Grammar."

"The expression of Number is another accidental property of
the verb, and belongs to it only in so far as the verb may be combined with the expression of person. . . . The verb is equally
said to be in the singular or plural whether it has or has not
distinct terminations appropriated to those different numbers;
we call *I love* singular, and *we love* plural; but it is manifest
that in all such instances the expression of number exists *only
in the pronoun*." — p. 155.

Now, it is the calling of things what they are not, in
order that the terminology of English Grammar may

correspond to that of the Greek and Latin languages, which I think pernicious.

Upon some of the points in question, I cite the following passages from Crombie's " Etymology and Syntax of the English Language."   Dr. Crombie, an Oxford Doctor of Laws, and a Fellow of the Royal Society, is one of the profoundest, and closest, and least pedantic thinkers that have written on our subject; and his work (from the third and last edition of which — London, 1830 — I quote), was made a text-book for the class of English literature in the London University.   Dr. Crombie is examining the argument of an English grammarian, which is to this effect.   If that only is a tense which in one inflected word expresses an affirmation with time, we should in English have but two tenses, the present and past in the active verb, and in the passive no tenses at all,—the very position that I have taken.   " But," the writer, Dr. Beattie, adds, " this is a needless nicety, and, if adopted, would introduce confusion into the grammatical art.   If *amaveram* be a tense, why should not *amatus fueram?*   If *I heard* be a tense, *I did hear*, *I have heard*, and *I shall hear* must be equally entitled to that appellation."   This argument Crombie thus sets aside : —

" How simplicity can introduce confusion I am unable to comprehend, unless we are to affirm that the introduction of Greek and Latin names, *to express nonentities in our language,* is necessary to illustrate the grammar and simplify the study of the language to the English scholar. . . . Nay, further, if it be a needless nicety to admit those only as tenses which are formed by inflection, is it not equally a needless nicety to admit those cases only which are formed by varying the termination?   And if confusion be introduced by denying *I had heard* to be a tense, why does not the learned author simplify the doctrine of English nouns by giving them six cases — *a king, of a king, to* or *for a king, a king, O king, with, from, in,* or *by a king?*   This, surely, would be to perplex, not to simplify.   In short, the inconsistency of those grammarians who deny that to be a case which is not formed by inflection, yet would load us with moods and tenses not formed by change of termination, is so palpable as to require neither illustration nor argument to oppose it. . . . Why do not these gentlemen favor us with a dual number, with a middle voice, and with an optative mood? Nay, as they are so fond of tenses as to lament that we rob them of all but two, why do they not enrich us with a first and second aorist and a *paulo post futurê*" (pp. 118, 119.) "Whether *amatus fueram* be or be not a tense is the very point in question; and so far am I from admitting the affirmative as unquestionable, that I contend it has no more claim to the designation of these than Ἔσομαι τετρὰς, — no more claim than *amandum est mihi, amari oportet,* or *amandus sum* have to be called moods. Here I must request the reader to bear in mind the *necessary distinction* between the *grammar* of a language and its *capacity of expression.* . . . Why not give, as English cases, *to a king, of a king, with a king,* etc.? The mode is certainly applicable, whatever may be the consequences of that application. A case surely is as easily formed by a noun and a preposition as a tense by a participle and an auxiliary." (p. 121.) "What should we think of that person's discernment who should contend that the Latins had an optative mood because *utinam legeres* signifies, I wish you would read? It is equally absurd to say that we have an imperfect, preterpluperfect, or future tense; or that we have all the Greek varieties of mood, and two voices, because by the aid of auxiliary words and definitive terms we contrive to express these accidents, times, or states of being. I consider, therefore, that *we have no more cases, moods, tenses, or voices in our language* — as far as its *grammar,* not its capacity of expression, is concerned — than we have *variety of termination* to denote these different accessory ideas." — p. 127, 128.

But upon this point I cite also the following passage from a yet higher authority, — Bosworth, — in the front rank of the Anglo-Saxon and English scholars of the world, who speaks as follows upon the subject, at p. 189 of the Introduction to his Anglo-Saxon Dictionary. The passage, it will be seen, touches what I have said, and upon voices and cases as well as upon tenses.

"What is generally termed the passive voice has no existence in Anglo-Saxon, any more than in modern English. The Anglo-Saxons wrote, *he is lufod,* he is loved. Here *is* is the indicative indefinite of the neuter verb *wesan,* and *lufod,* loved, is the past participle of the verb *lufian,* to love. In parsing, every word

should be considered a distinct part of speech. *To a king* i
called a dative case in English, as *regi* in Latin, because the
lish phrase is not formed by inflection, but by the auxiliary w
to a. If auxiliaries do not form cases in English nouns,
should they be allowed to form various tenses and a pa
voice either in the English, or in its parent, the Saxon? 'I
Ic maeg beon lufod, I may be loved, instead of being callec
potential mood passive, *maeg* is more rationally consider
verb in the indicative mood, indefinite tense, first singular,
the neuter verb in the infinitive mood after the verb *maeg ;*
is the perfect participle of the verb *lufian.*"

This view is exactly the same, it will be seen, as
which is taken of the subject by Crombie; and, ind
it is hard for me to understand how any man of com
sense, who thinks for himself, can take any other.
worth here supports the main position taken in "
Grammarless Tongue," which is in effect, to use
worth's words, that in analyzing the English sentence
ery word should be considered a *distinct* part of speec
every word, auxiliary verbs as well as auxiliary prej
tions, as he regards them in his analysis of what Eng
grammarians call the first person singular, present
dicative, potential mood, passive voice of the ver
love — I may be loved. That is the point of
whole question.

Against the position taken in the foregoing cha
as to the so-called tenses which are formed by the un
of a verb and a participle, — that the verb retains
proper meaning; *e. g.,* that in *I have loved, have*
presses possession, — a position impregnable, I think
argument, — two of my critics have directed the shaft
feeble ridicule. One says, " He, therefore, who
loved, has, in his possession, an abstract completed act
bearing the name ' loved.' Such a person may wel
excused for inquiring with some anxiety what he s
do with it." Another flouts the pretensions of a
who dared to write about language, and yet " thou
that a participle could be the object to a verb."

Now, in the first place, Bosworth's dictum — say rather his primal law of English construction — that, in parsing, every word should be regarded as a distinct part of speech, covers this ground entirely. The case of a verb followed by a participle is no more than any other excluded from the operation of that law, which, indeed, as we have seen, Bosworth himself illustrates by an analysis of the so-called tense *I may be loved*. What I have written upon this point is therefore merely an expression and particular enforcement of a general law recognized by the *facile princeps* of British Anglo-Saxon scholars. But I am not left without a particular justification of my view of the relation of the auxiliary verb to its participle. Dr. Crombie, explaining the difference between the tenses which some grammarians have called the preterite definite, *I have written*, and the preterite indefinite, *I wrote*, furnishes me with the following opinion in point : —

"When an action is done in a time continuous to the present instant, we employ the auxiliary verb. Thus, on finishing a letter, I say, I have written my letter, i. e., *I possess* (now) *the finished action of writing a letter*. Again, when an action is done in a space of time which the mind assumes as present, or when we express our immediate *possession* of things done in that space, we use the auxiliary verb. 'I have this week written several letters,' *I have now the perfection of writing several letters* finished this week. These phraseologies, as the author last quoted justly observes, are harsh to the ear, and appear exceedingly awkward; but a little attention will suffice to show that they correctly exhibit the ideas implied by the tense which we have at present under consideration." — *Etymology*, etc., p. 166.

Upon the same subject, one of my critics has the following passage, which is useful in enabling me to illustrate my position : —

"All participles are adjectives, and cannot, without being made substantives by the prefixing of the article, or in some similar way, be used as objects to transitive verbs. We can, of course, say, *He posits the conditioned*; but we cannot say, *He posits conditioned*, or, *He possesses conditioned*. In the third place, suppose we admit that a participle could be the object of a transitive verb, and that *I possess conditioned* expressed what we mean by *I have conditioned*; is there not one respect in which *I have conditioned* or *I have loved* differs from *I have money?* We can certainly say *I have loved the ocean*; but can we also say *I have money the bank?* *I have hunted the fox* does mean something; *I have a hunt the fox* means nothing."

Clearly all participles are adjectives when they are predicated of the subject, or used to qualify a noun. That is so obviously true that it hardly needs to be asserted. Thus, in *I am good* and *I am loved*, *good* and *loved* are equally adjectives, as in *a bad man* and *a hated man*, *bad* and *hated* are also adjectives. But I am not so sure that the prefixing of an article, or the like, is the condition and sign of use as an object of a transitive verb. I am overwhelmed with such a tremendous illustration of the use of participles, as *He posits the conditioned*. It takes me back, however, to the days when Tappan and Henry led my youthful steps through the flowery paths, and fed my downy lips with the sweet and succulent fruits of metapheezic. Of this experience I retain sufficient memory to admit, with shame and confusion of face, that we can say, *He posits the conditioned*, and that we cannot say, *He posits conditioned*, or *He possesses conditioned*. But when, stepping down from the sublime of the conditioned, I reflect that although we may say of Paddy, *He bolts the pratie*, we may not say, *He bolts pratie*, or, *He possesses pratie*, and yet that we may say, *He bolts praties*, and even, *He likes bolting praties*, I am comforted. I admit that although we may say, *I have loved the ocean*, we may not say, *I have money the bank*, unless we would talk nonsense. But that is because *loved the ocean*, which in one case is the object of the verb *have*, is sense, and *money the bank*, which is its object in the other case, is not sense. As a phrase or sentence may be the subject of a verb, so it may be its object. For example, in the sentence, *He likes bolting*, the participle, although no article is prefixed to it, is the object of the transitive verb *likes;* but in the more complex, fully-developed, and well-rounded sentence, *He likes bolting praties*, the object of the verb is *bolting praties*.

I have called English the grammarless tongue; but it merits that distinction only because it excels in its superiority to inflections, and its regard for the logical sequence of thought, all other languages of civilized Christendom. Compared with Greek and Latin, the French, Italian, and Spanish languages, and even the German, may be called grammarless. Indeed, the tendency to the laying aside of inflections showed itself early in the Latin tongue, in the very Augustan period of which we find in the best writers the germ of our method of expressing action in combination with the idea of time, by the use of the verbs signifying existence and possession, in combination with participles. Cicero, instead of De Cæsare satis dixi, said, " De Cæsare satis *dictum habeo*" — I have said enough of Cæsar; and Cæsar himself wrote, " copias quas *habebat paratas*," instead of *paraverat* — the forces which he had prepared.* Now, will any one pretend that when Cicero said *habeo dictum* — I have said, he used the word *habeo* without the idea of possession, and yet that he used it with that idea when he said *habeo pomum* — I have an apple? I think no one will do so who is competent to write on language at all; and should there be such a person, I confess at once that I cannot argue with him. We do not approach each other near enough to clash. And as to the questions whether English verbs have real tenses, and what is the force of " auxiliary " verbs in all cases, I shall leave them without further discussion, merely giving my readers an example upon which to ruminate. If *I shall have*

* These examples I find to my hand, among others of the same sort, in Bracnet's "Grammaire Historique de la Langue Française."

followed is a tense, the future perfect tense of the
to follow, in which the verb *shall* does not express
rity, and the verb *have* does not express possession.
becomes of that tense, and what is the meaning of
verbs, when, instead of saying, I shall have followe
so long to-morrow, we say, I shall to-morrow ha
lowed him so long, or, I shall to-morrow have s
followed him, or, I shall have so long followed h
morrow? If a tense may be split in pieces and sca
about in this way, and its component parts, each of
a word in constant and independent use, may ret
their divided condition the same modified meani
lack of meaning which they have in combinati
would seem that the construction of English, acc
to the grammarians, is so absolved from the laws o
son, which hold on all other subjects, that any d
sion of it in conformity with those laws must b
tirely superfluous and from the purpose.

A volume like this is not the place for contro
even were I inclined thereto; but I will notice o
two of the remarks elicited by the foregoing ch
from writers who, I am sorry to say, were not prete
ignoramuses, but men of sense and some philolo
acquirement, because these examples will show the
and temper of even the ablest of my opponents.
of them sneered at the views set forth in that ch
because, among other things, they were those of
who " could make τετύψομαι a future perfect," mean
shall have been beaten. As to that point, I cite th
lowing passages from a grammarian of authority : -

" The third future, or paulo post future, of the pas
respect to signification (§ 139), and form is derived fro
perfect passive, of which it retains the augment, substi
εομαι for the termination of the perfect passive. It is the
only necessary to take the ending of the second person
passive in σαι (ψαι, ξαι), and change the αι into ομαι — τέτυψαι
ψαι), τετύψομαι." — *Buttman*, § 99.

" The third, or paulo post future, is properly, both in
and in signification, compounded from the perfect and

It places what is past or concluded in the future; *e. g.*, *ἡ πόλιϛ τελέωϛ κεκοσμήσεται ἐὰν ὁ τοιοῦτοϛ αὐτὴν ἐπισκοπῇ φύλαξ* — The city will ha[ve] been perfectly organized if such a watchman oversee it; *i. e.,* *disposita erit*, not *disponetur*." — *Ibidem,* § 139.

This is Greek, as I learned it. I do not pretend [to] write a new Cratylus, or profess to be able to do so[.]

Another of my censors is facetiously severe upon [a] man who ventures to write on language, and yet himse[lf] uses such phrases as " a young-eyed cherubin," ar[d] " poning the gutter." This writer, although he figur[ed] in the Philological Convention at Poughkeepsie, seem[s] not to know that *cherubin* came into our language fro[m] the Italian *cherubino*, and that until a very late perio[d] the form *cherub* was not known. And as to the pa[r]ticular phrase I used, if my very scornful censor w[ill] take a poor mariner's advice, and overhaul his litt[le] Shakespeare, he will find, in a passage famous (amor[g] the ignorant) for its beauty, the following lines : —

> " There's not the smallest orb which thou beholdest
> But in his motion like an angel sings,
> Still quiring to the young-eyed cherubins."
> *Merchant of Venice,* V. 1.

Now, if very learned and scornful professors of ph[i]lology will not, before criticising a poor layman like m[e,] and before figuring at philological conventions, make them selves acquainted with such familiar passages of poetry [as] that, why, all the worse for me — and for Shakespeare.

As to " poning the gutter," that is a city boy's name f[or] a city boy's amusement. In winter, when a hard frost ha[s] filled the gutters with ice, boys make slides on then[,] and as they dash down the slide and run up again to tal[ke] a start from the head, they cry out one to another, " P[o]ne the gutter." Therefore, although the origin of the fir[st] word is unknown to me, I said of my young-eyed che[r]ubin, that " five years ago he, rustic, was milking th[e] cow, or urban, was poning the gutter."

With this answer I shall leave my critics in charge [of] my reputation, and their own.

CHAPTER XI.

IS BEING DONE.

TO a man who has reached what Dante the middle of the journey of our life, the outside world is more remarkable than conscious freedom with which people ten or years younger than himself adopt new fashion fangles of dress, of manners, and of speech, perhaps, their persistence in these novelties the absurdity thereof has been fully set forth explained. His difficulty is, that for a long he does not see—does not unless he combines usually, quickness of penetration and reading reflection—that what seems so new and strange him seems to younger people neither strange new. The things *are* new, indeed, to them only in that they are not yet old; they are not elties that disturb their peace as they disturb He wonders that that beautiful girl of seventeen about in public unconcerned, and in fact unnoticed,—that is the strangest feature of the case,—in such amazing apparel as would two ago have made her mother the laughing-stock whole town, and which yet she wears as calm if from Eve's day down the sex had known

garments. Why should she not? The fashion of
to-day is all that she knows of fashion, and she
cares to know no more, except for the sake of
curiosity. All the rest is to her in the keeping of
history, where she may, perhaps, in an idle moment, look at it, and find it food for wonder or for
laughter. In it there is nought to her of personal
concern.

When does a fashion cease to be new? When
does it become old? when obsolete? Before these
questions can be answered, we must know the
measure of time used by him who asks them.
What would be new to a young elephant of thirty
or forty years would be old to an aged cony of nine
or ten; what to the butterfly of a meadow and a
summer would date from the beginning of all things,
would hardly be a memory to an eagle that had
soared for half a century above half a continent.
What is new to one man may be old to men only
five years younger than he, and to men ten years
younger, obsolete. Few truths are more difficult
of apprehension than this, apparently so obvious
Few mental faculties are rarer than that which gives
to a mature man the prompt, intuitive recognition of
the fact that there are human beings whose opinions
and habits, if not worthy of consideration, must yet
be considered, to whom that which is to him a part
of the present is not merely unfamiliar, but shut out
among the things of the past as completely as the
siege of Troy, or the building of the Pyramids.
Five thousand years ago, five hundred, fifty, five —
what is the difference as to that which is beyond
the grasp of consciousness, out of the record of ex
perience?

This elasticity of the standard ... measured, is in no respect more ... ation than in that of language. Unless ... monster of pedantry and priggishness, ... deed, not then, — the words and the forms ... he uses are not made, or even chosen, by ... The first condition of language — that it sh... means of communication between men— for ... near approach to a vocabulary or a constr... which is, even in part, the work or the choice ... one man. As we get our food and our breath... the earth and the air around us, so we get our l... guage from our neighbors — not the langua... which we work out and discuss questions in ... in art, or in letters, but that which serves th... of our daily life. A little comes to us from ... but this is mere spicery, much of which is n... wholesome nor appetizing.

A fastidious precisian in language might ... his nicety so far as to leave himself almost ... less. A man must speak the language of ... ple and his time. As to the first, there can ... doubt; but what is his time? Generally ... If A hears B use a word or a phrase to-day ... although it is entirely new to him, has a ... that he readily apprehends, and that saves ... and "will do," he will use it himself, if he ... to-morrow. And so it will go on from ... mouth, until within a year it may pervade a ... borhood; and in these days of railways and ... papers, a year or two may spread it over ... country. The child that was in the cradle ... the new word first was spoken, on going to ...

finds it a part of the common speech. For that child it is neither new nor old; it simply is. And that impression of its far-off, unknown origin — for "I am" expresses the eternal — the child will carry through life, although he may afterward learn that it was new when he first heard it. But to him who was a man when the word came in, and who reflects at all upon the language that he uses, it will always have upon it the stamp of newness, because it is one of the things of which he remembers the beginning.

In bad eminence, at the head of those intruders in language which to many persons seem to be of established respectability, but the right of which to be at all is not yet fully admitted, stands out the form of speech *is being done*, or rather, *is being*, which, about seventy or eighty years ago, began to affront the eye, torment the ear, and assault the common sense of the speaker of plain and idiomatic English. That it should be pronounced a novelty will seem strange to most of my readers; for we have all heard it from our earliest childhood. But so slow has been its acceptance among unlettered people, so stoutly has it been resisted by the lettered, that we have heard it under constant protest; yet it is so much used, and seems to suit so well the mental tone of those who now do most to mould the common speech, that to check its diffusion would be a hopeless undertaking. But to examine it may be worth our while, for the sake of a lesson in language.

Mr. Marsh says of this form of speech, that it is "an awkward neologism, which neither convenience, intelligibility, nor syntactical congruity de-

22

mands," and that it is the contrivance of
grammarian.   But that it is the work of any
marian is more than doubtful.   Grammarians
all their faults, do not deform language with
tastic solecisms, or even seek to enrich it with
and startling verbal combinations.   They
resist novelty, and devote themselves to formu
that which use has already established.   I
hardly be that such an incongruous and ridic
form of speech as *is being done* was contrived
man who, by any stretching of the name, shou
included among grammarians.   But, neverth
it is a worthy offspring of English gramma
fitting, and, I may say, an inevitable conseq
of the attempt to make our mother tongue
herself by Latin rules and standards.   Some
cise and feeble-minded soul, having been t
that there is a passive voice in English, and
for instance, *building* is an active participle
builded or *built* a passive, felt conscientious scr
at saying, The house is building.   For what
the house build?   A house cannot build; it mu
built.   And yet to say, The house is built, is
(I speak for him), that it is finished, that
"done built."   Therefore we must find some
that will be a continuing present tense of this
sive verb *to be built;* and he found it, as he tho
in the form *is being built;* supposing that, b
introduction of the present participle, expressi
continued existence, between *is* and *built,* he
modified the meaning both of the former an
latter.   Others, like him, half taught and
taught, precise and fussy, caught up the p

which seemed to them to supply a deficiency in their passive voice, and so the infection spread over England, and ere long into this republic. It was confined, however, to the condition of life in which it had its origin. Simple-minded common people and those of culture were alike protected against it by their attachment to the idiom of their mother tongue, with which they felt it to be directly at variance.

To this day there is not, in the Old England or the New, a farmer's boy who has escaped the contamination of popular weekly papers, who would not say, While the new barn was a-building, unless some prim schoolma'am had taught him to say, was being built; and, at the other extreme of culture, Macaulay writes, " Chelsea Hospital was building," " While innocent blood was shedding," " While the foulest judicial murder that had disgraced even those times was perpetrating."

Mr. Dickens writes (Sergeant Buzfuz's speech), " The train was preparing." In the " Atlantic Monthly " for May, 1869, I find, " Another flank movement was making, but thus far with little effect;" and in the " Brooklyn Eagle " for June 13, 1869," St. Ann's Church, which has been building for nearly two years on the corner of Livingston and Clinton Streets." I cite these miscellaneous writers to show modern and common usage, meaning to set up neither the " Brooklyn Eagle " nor Mr. Dickens as a very high authority in the use of language.

And thus, to go no farther back than the Elizabethan period, Bishop Jewel wrote, " Some other

there be that see and know that the Church of
is now a building, and yet, not onely refrain t
selves from the worke, but also spurne downe
other men have built up." (Sermons, Ed.
fol. F. vii.) "After the Temple was buylded
was in building, and rearing, Esdras the pr
read the Law of God." (*Idem.* G. vi.)
Bishop Hall, "While my body is dressing, not
an effeminate curiosity, nor yet with rude neg
my mind addresses herself to her ensuing ta
and Shakespeare,

> "and when he thinks, good easy man,
> His greatness is a-ripening."
>
> *Henry VIII.*

Thus Milton wrote, "While the Temple of
Lord was building;" Bolingbroke, "The n
had cried out loudly against the crime which
committing;" and Johnson wrote to Bos
" My 'Lives' are reprinting." Hence we see
the form *is being done, is being made, is b
built*, lacks the support of authoritative usage
the period of the earliest classical English to
present day. That, however, it might do wit
if it were consistent with reason, and confor
to the normal development of the language,
there would be no growth of language. But
very consistency and conformity it lacks. L
see why and how.

The condition sought to be expressed by *is
done* is not new in any sense. It is neither a
shade of thought nor a new-born idea. On
contrary, it is one of the first conditions that
expression. It has been expressed in many

guages from remote ages, and very completely in English for centuries. At best the phrase is merely a new name for an old thing already well named. Those who use it seem to me to disregard the fitness of the forms of speech by which the thought which they would present has been uttered by our best writers and speakers. For example, Hamlet says to the king, of the slain Polonius, that the latter is at supper, "not where he eats, but where he *is eaten;*" and the words fully express — there has never been a doubt suggested by the most microscopic commentator that they express — just what Hamlet meant, that the eating of Polonius was going on at the time then present. "Is eaten" does not mean *has been eaten up.* It is in the present tense, and expresses what has been called "the continuous recipience of action," as much as *I eat* expresses continuous action. Hamlet goes on to say, "A certain convocation of politic worms *are* e'en at him." So Hotspur says, —

> "Why, look you, I am *whipp'd* and *scourg'd* with rods,
> *Nettled* and *stung* with pismires *when I hear*
> Of this vile politician, Bolingbroke."

It was not necessary for Hotspur, although he spoke of time present, to say, "I am being whipped, being scourged, being nettled, being stung, when I hear," or for Hamlet to say that Polonius was being eaten, although the worms were at him while the prince was speaking.

It will be of some interest to observe how this idea has been expressed in various languages, including English. It may be, and has been, expressed, both participially and verbally. In the New Testament

(1 Peter iii. 20) there is the following passage in the original : ἐν ἡμέραις Νῶε, κατασκευαζομένης κιβωτοῦ, which, in our English version, is translated thus : "In the days of Noah, while the ark was *a-preparing*." Here the last clause represents the Greek passive participle present used absolutely with the substantive, according to the Greek idiom. In the translation of 1582 we find, "when the ark was *a-building;*" in that of 1557, "while the ark *was preparing;*" but in Wycliffe's translation, made about A. D. 1380, "In the days of Noe, when the ship *was made.*" The last form, which corresponds to Hamlet's "not where he eats, but where he *is eaten,*" represents the imperfect subjunctive passive, "*cum fabricaretur arca*" of the Vulgate, from which Wycliffe made his translation. In the account of the building of Solomon's temple is another passage (1 Kings vi. 7), which serves in illustration : "And the house, when it was *in building, was built* of stone made ready before it was brought thither ; so that there was neither hammer, nor axe, nor any tool of iron heard in the house while it was *in building.*" Here, "when it was in building" is represented in the Septuagint version by ἐν τῷ οἰκοδομεῖσθαι αὐτὸν (the infinitive passive), and in the Vulgate by "*cum ædificaretur*" — again the imperfect subjunctive passive. The German translation gives in the first instance, "*da man die archa zurüstete,*" when they prepared or fitted out the ark ; in the second, "*und da das haus gesetzt ward,*" and when the house was founded ; at the end of the verse, "in building" of the English version has its exact counterpart in "*im bauen.*" The

French version gives, in the first instance, '*pendant que l'arche se bâtissoit*," which, according to the French idiom, is, while the ark was built; and in the second instance, both at the beginning and the end of the verse, *en bâtissant la maison*, that is, in building the house. In the Italian version we find, in one passage, "*quando la casa fù edificata*," which is, literally, when the house was built; and "*mentre s' edificava*," while it built itself, an idiomatic form for while it was built; and in the other, according to the same idiom, "*mentre s' apparecchiava l' archa*," while the ark was prepared. Now, all these versions express the same facts completely, not only each one of them to those to whom the respective languages are vernacular, but completely to every man who has acquired a knowledge of all these tongues; and in all of them we find either the verbal substantive form, *was in building*, *was a-preparing*, *was preparing*, or the imperfect verbal form, *was built*, *was prepared*. In no one of them, not even in the Greek with its present passive participle, is there an approach to such a phraseology as *is being done*, *is being built*, which in Latin, for instance, could be represented only by the use of the obsolete participle present *ens*, and the monstrous construction *ens factus est*, *ens ædificatus est*.

In the form *is a-doing*, *is a-making*, the *a* is a mere degraded form of *on* or *in;* as in ten o'clock *o'* represents *of the*. Such words as *doing* and *making* are both participles and verbal nouns. When we say, I am doing thus, I am making this, they are real participles. When we say, It was

long in the doing. It was slow in the making, they
are verbal nouns. For example, in the following
passage from Ascham's "Schoolmaster," it is plain
that *weeping, learning*, and *misliking*, are nouns
no less than *grief, trouble*, and *fear* : —

"And when I am called from him I fall on weeping, because
whatever I do else but learning is full of grief, trouble, and fear,
and whole misliking unto me."

So in the following passage from Barrow (Sermon XIII.), *on going*, which we nowadays cut
down into *a-going*, is as much a noun as *rest* is in
"put at rest:" —

"Speech is indeed the rudder that steereth human affairs, the
spring that setteth the wheels of action on going."

In the Anglo-Saxon, the participle and the verbal
noun were distinguished in sense and in form; the
participle ending in *ende*, the verbal noun in *ung*.
In the lapse of time, and by the simplifying process which I have before mentioned, these two terminations were blended in the form *ing*, which
represents them both. Hence has arisen the difficulty of those precise people who were not content
to speak their mother tongue as they learned it from
their mothers, and who undertook, not only to criticise, but to take to pieces and put together in a
new shape, something the structure of which they
did not understand. If, in their trouble about the
active present participle, they had looked into Ben
Jonson's Grammar (for he, like Milton, was a scholar
as well as a poet, and wrote an English grammar, as
Milton wrote a Latin accidence), they would have seen
that he said that, "Before the participle present, *a*,

an, have the force of a gerund ;" and a gerund, they might have learned, was a Latin verbal noun (taking its name from *gero,* I bear, I carry on), used to express the meaning of the present infinitive active, under certain circumstances. Jonson cites, in illustration of his law, this line from Norton, " But there is some grand tempest *a-brewing* towards us," which they would have done well to consider before making their improvement; for I think that, even now, one of their sort would hesitate to look up into a lowering sky, and say, There is a storm *being brewed.* He would be laughed at by any sensible Cape Cod fisherman or English countess. To this day we say, — every man and boy of us who is not fitter for Bedlam than many who are sent there, — There is a storm a-brewing, as our forefathers have said for centuries. So, in "The Merchant of Venice" (Act II., Scene 5), Shylock says to Jessica, —

> " I am right loath to go :
> There is some ill *a-brewing* toward my rest;
> For I did dream of money-bags to-night."

This *a,* which represents *in,* is said, by Mr. Marsh, to have been dropped (by writers, I suppose he means) about the beginning of the eighteenth century. It might better not have been dropped at all; but it began to disappear before that time. Witness this passage in Cotton's translation of Montaigne's Essays, a masterpiece of idiomatic English, which was produced about the year 1670 : —

" A slave of his, a vicious ill-conditioned fellow, but that had the precepts of philosophy often ringing in his ears, having, for

some offence of his, been stript, by Plutarch's command
he was whipping muttered at first that he did not deserve
etc." — Book II. "Of Anger."

That the suppression of the *a* is a loss v
clear, from consideration of this example. It
deniable, that the phrase "whilst he was whip
might be misunderstood as meaning, whi
he was whipping a him. Its meaning is
mined only by the context. But so is the m
of nearly half the words in any sentence
however, Cotton had written "whilst he w
whipping," there would be no opportunity f
mistaking of the verbal noun *whipping* f
present participle *whipping*. The distinctic
tween these two intimately-related parts of s
may be clearly exemplified by the following
tence: Plutarch was whipping a slave, and
the slave was a-whipping he told his maste
in this whipping, he set at nought his own
principles. Here no one can fail to see at onc
the first *whipping* is a participle, and that th
is a noun; and a moment's consideration will
to any intelligent person that the second *whi*
is also not a participle, but a verbal noun. If
in "a-whipping" were the article, that woul
cide the question; for the article, definite or i
nite, can be used only with a substantive. T
illustrated even by the phrase "a go," whi
sometimes heard; for, when a gentleman rem
"Here is a rum go," without meaning any all
to spirituous liquors, or if, with such all
speaks of "a go of gin," the anguish that
flicts upon the well-regulated grammatical

is caused merely by his placing the first person present indicative of the verb *to go* in the relation in which it can be properly parsed only as a noun. But the *a* in the phrases, While the slave was a-whipping, While the house was a-building, While the thing was a-doing, is not the article, as I have said before, but a mere corruption of *in*, or *on*, the change of which to *a* was caused, clearly, by that lazy carelessness of speech that tends so much to the phonetic degradation of language. Either *on* or *in*, however, determines the substantive character of the words to which it applies. As, for example, if the gentleman just referred to speaks of "going on a bust," the preposition, no less than the article, shows that he is so reprobate, so lost to Murray and to Moon, as to treat the verb *burst* as if it were a noun; and his omission of the *r* from the perverted word is not only a striking instance of the addition of insult to injury, but a warning example of the phonetic degradation of language, and of man.

The nature of this noun of action, and of the simple, strong construction which it admits, is finely shown in this pregnant passage from Hobbes (" De Corpore Politico," Part II., chap. 2) : —

"In the making of a Democracy there passeth no covenant between the sovereign and any subject; for, while the Democracy is a-making, there is no sovereign with whom to contract."

Here the word *making* is, in both instances, the same part of speech, the representative of the same idea, and in the same relation; and the writer who would change the latter to, While the democracy is *being made*, must also, that his language may not be at variance with itself in one sentence, change the former, and read, In the being made of a democracy, or, what is the same thing, In a democracy's being made.

The latter course of this idiom of *in, on,* or *a* with the verbal noun may be traced, and the period of the concoction of *is being* may be approximated by a comparison of the heading of chapter xxii. of "Don Quixote," as it appears in the principal English translations. The original is as follows:—

"De la liberdad que dió don Quixote á muchos desdichados que mal de su grado los llevaban donde no quisieran yr."

Shelton, in 1612, rendered it thus: "Of the liberty Don Quixote gave to many wretches who *were a-carrying* perforce to a place they desired not." Motteux, A. D. 1719, gives, "How Don Quixote set free many miserable creatures who *were carrying*, much against their wills, to a place they did not like." Jarvis, whose translation was published in 1742, has it thus: "How Don Quixote set at liberty several unfortunate persons who *were carrying* much against their wills where they had no wish to go." But in the edition of Jarvis's translation published A. D. 1818 "carrying" is changed to "being carried."

This change indicates the latter part of the seventeenth century as the birth-time of *is being.* And in fact the earliest known instance of its use occurs in a letter by Southey dated 1795. Coleridge used it, and Lamb, and Landor; yet after three-quarters of a century it is pronounced a novelty and a nuisance. It made no little stir when it was first brought here, and it was adopted at once by many people — of course those who wished to be elegant. I have heard of an instance of its use, after it had become in vogue among such people, which illustrates one of the objections to which it is obnoxious — that it represents an act as going on (*is being*) and as completed (*done*) at the same time. A gentleman called early in the evening at a house with the ladies of which he was intimate. The door was opened by a negress, a bright, pompous wench, in one of the Madras kerchief head-dresses commonly worn at that time by such women. She needed not to wait for his inquiry for the ladies, but welcomed him at once; for he was a favored guest. "Good evenin', sar! Walk in, sar. De ladies bein' done gone to de uproar." "Gone to the opera! Thank you, I won't come in. I'll see them there." "No, sar, I didn't say dey done gone to de uproar," but, with a slight toss of the Madras kerchief and a smile of superior intelligence, "dey *bein'* done gone. Walk in, sar. Ole missus in de parlor; young missus be down stairs d'recly." My grandmother told me that story, which she heard from the gentleman himself, in my boyhood, neither of us thinking that it would be thus used to expose the absurd affectation in speech at which she laughed. From the negress's point of view, — that is, the "done gone" point, she was as right in her "bein' done gone" as those whose speech she aped were in their "is being done," and "is being built." To her, *done gone* expressed a going that was finished, a completed going. But the ladies were in process of going, not going or "gwine;" that

would have expressed an act too much in th
according to the new light she had seen c
language; and so she boldly dashed at he
uing present of a completed action —" b
gone." She was more nearly right in her
than some learned linguists are in their
For the phrase under consideration is not
tinuing present of the passive voice." T
ciples *done*, *built*, etc., are not passive, bu
perfect participles, as we have seen befc
being is merely a present participle. Th
of the two, therefore, cannot express an
and continuing passivity; it merely brings p
ously together the ideas of the present and

The combination of *do* and *go* by th
whites and the negroes of the South, chief
forms *done gone* and *gone done*, is not w
logical and absurd; nor is it without so
like respectable precedent in English li
Witness these passages from Chaucer :—

> " That ye unto your sonne as trewly
>   *Done her been* wedded at your home cor
>   This is the final end of all this thing."
>   *Legend of Good Women,*

> " And I woll geve him all that fals
>   To his chamber and to his hals;
>   I *woll do paint* with pure gold
>   And tapite hem full manifold."
>   *The Duchess,* l.

> " Bid him creepe into the body
>   And *do it gone* to Alcione.
>   The queene, there she lieth alone."
>   *Ibid.,* l. t.

And indeed the Southern provincial use of
go is capable of formulation into tenses, wh

were not for the prejudice in favor of other — in the present delicate condition of the country, I will not say better — usage, might claim the attention, and even the adhesion, of people like those who adopt *is being done* — who shun an idiom as they would be thought to shun a sin, and who must be correct, or die. For example: —

INDICATIVE MOOD.

PRESENT AND IMPERFECT TENSE.

Singular.	*Plural.*
1. I done,	1. We uns done,
2. Yer done,	2. You uns done,
3. He done,	3. They uns done.

PERFECT.

1. I gone done,	1. We uns gone done,
2. Yer gone done,	2. You uns gone done,
3. He gone done,	3. They uns gone done.

PLUPERFECT.

1. I done gone done,	1. We uns done gone done,
2. Yer done gone done,	2. You uns done gone done,
3. He done gone done,	3. They uns done gone done.

FUTURE.

1. I gwine done,	1. We uns gwine done,
2. Yer gwine done,	2. You uns gwine done,
3. He gwine done,	3. They uns gwine done.

FUTURE PERFECT.

1. I gwine gone done,	1. We uns gwine gone done,
2. Yer gwine gone done,	2. You uns gwine gone done,
3. He gwine gone done,	3. They uns gwine gone done.

Cætera desunt.

Here, I submit, is as regular and symmetrical a form of conjugation as can be found in any English grammar. In some respects it is more so. For instance, the ambiguity of the singular *you* and the plural *you* is obviated by the use of *yer* for the second person singular, and *you uns* for the same person plural. Of these two persons, on this system, there can be no confusion. *I gwine gone done* is as reasonable a part of the verb *to do* as *I shall* or *will have done*.

But the full absurdity of this phrase, the essence of its nonsense, seems not to have been hitherto pointed out. The objection made to it is, that it unites a present with a "passive," or rather a perfect participle. But this combination is of frequent occurrence, and, of itself, is quite unobjectionable. For instance, "He, *being forewarned* of the danger, fled." And there is a combination of the same participles which seems yet nearer in meaning to the one under consideration. A lady will say to her servant, Why can't you set the table thus, or so, *without being told* every morning? That is good sense and good English. In Cotton's translation of Montaigne's "Apology for Raimond de Sebonde" is this passage, which contains a like construction: "There is more understanding required in the teaching of others than in *being taught*." Here we have also sense and English; and that being admitted, it will seem to some persons a full justification of the phrase, "while the boy is being taught." It is not so, however. Florio, writing nearly a hundred years before Cotton, translates the same passage thus: "More discourse is required to teach others than to be taught," using the infinitive in both parts of the sentence. The likeness between the infinitive and the verbal noun is so close that the latter may almost always be used for the former, although the former may not be used for the latter. Montaigne used the verbal noun in both instances. His sentence has merely an elision of the article before the last verbal noun, and in full is, "There is more understanding required in the teaching of others than in *the* being taught." This elision is common, and appears in the lady's question to her servant, which in full is, Why cannot you set the table thus without [what? some *object*]— without *the* being told?

What, then, is the fatal absurdity in this phrase, which has been so long and so widely used that, to some people, it seems to be an old growth of the language, while it is yet in fact a mere transplanted sucker, without life and without root? It is in the combination of *is* with *being;* in the making of the verb *to be* a complement, or, in grammarians' phrase, an auxiliary to itself — an absurdity so palpable, so monstrous, so ridiculous that it should need only to be pointed out to be scouted. *To be* — called by Latin grammarians the substantive verb — expresses mere existence. It predicates of its subject either simple absolute existence or whatever attribute follows it. *To be* and *to exist*, if not perfect synonymes, are more nearly so, perhaps, than any two verbs in the language. In some of their meanings there is a shade of difference, but in others there is none whatever; and the latter are those which serve our present purpose. When we say, He, being forewarned of danger, fled, we say, He, existing forewarned of danger, fled. When we say that

23

a thing is done, we say that it exists done. When
we say, That being done I shall be satisfied, we
say, That existing done I shall be satisfied. *It
being done* is simply *exists existing done.* To say,
therefore, that a thing is being done is not only
to say (in respect of the last two participles) that a
process is going on and is finished, at the same
time, but (in respect of the whole phrase) that
it exists existing finished; which is no more or
other than to say that it exists finished, is finished,
is done; which is exactly what those who use the
phrase do not mean. It means that if it means
anything; but in fact it means nothing, and is the
most incongruous combination of words and ideas
that ever attained respectable usage in any civilized
language.

This absurdity is cloaked by the formation of *to be*
from parts of three verbs, which gives us such
dissimilar forms as *is* for the present tense, *was*
for the past, and *being* for the present participle.
It seems as if in *is being* there were two verbs.
We may be sure that if the present participle of
to be were formed like that of *to love* (*loving*)
we should never have heard the phrases *bes being
done* or *is ising done, bes being built* or *is ising
built.* This nonsense is hidden from the eye and
deadened to the ear by the dissimilarity in form of
is and *being.* We may rightly use *to have* as a
complement to itself, and say *have had*, or even *had
had*, because we *can* have having, possess possession. But we cannot be being, exist existence.
To be being is merely to be; nothing more or less.
It is being is simply equal to *it is.* And in the

supposed corresponding Latin phrases *ens factus est, ens ædificatus est* (the obsoleteness of *ens* as a participle being granted), the monstrosity is not in the use of *ens* with *factus*, but in that of *ens* with *est*. The absurdity is in Latin just what it is in English, the use of *is* with *being*, the making of the verb *to be* a complement to itself.

But it is strongly urged, and speciously maintained, that *to be* and *to exist* are not synonymes when the former is used as a so-called auxiliary verb. In the words of one critic, "The verb *is*, as a *copula* between a subject and a predicate, is no synonyme with the verb *exist*. It does not affirm the existence of either subject or predicate. It is *simply* the sign of connection, the coupler, directing the reader to think subject and predicate in unity."

That there is a difference between the signification of a verb used independently, and that which it has as a so-called auxiliary, seems to me, with my present light, a mere fiction of the grammarians, whose rules are, in my judgement, valuable only in those rare instances in which they conform to reason and common sense, in behalf of which I have dared to do battle.

This very notion that the verb is a copula, fulfilling the functions of a coupler in a sentence, is one of those against which, in boyhood, I beat my inapprehensive head in vain. Now, apprehending it, I believe it to be the merest linguistic fiction with which man ever was deluded. The verb is the life of the sentence. A sentence is an assertion, direct or hypothetical; and it is the verb, and the verb only,

which asserts. Assertion is its peculiar an
sive characteristic. True, in asserting it n
nect subject and predicate: but this is an in
and we might almost say an unessential,
of the verb, whose office is to move the sen
be the engine that propels the train of thou
not the coupling that keeps it together.

The substantive verb *to be* expresses ex
and whether used by itself or in connectio
participle or an adjective, it does nothin
But existence may be simple and absolute, c
be modified by the relations of its subject
condition or quality. In the sentence "Soc
simple existence is predicated of Socrates
this, "Socrates speaks," a certain act, tha
istence together with a certain condition (
tence, is predicated of him. For it is as t
as it was when Aristotle said it, as true of
as of Greek, that the assertion "Socrates s
is equivalent to the assertion "Socrates is spe
Now, it seems to me clear that the differe
tween "Socrates is" and "Socrates is speak
merely that the former predicates simple e
of Socrates, and the latter, existence and sor
more. The participle *speaking* modifies, l
limitation and expansion; the assertion of t
is. "Socrates is speaking" is equivalent to
rates exists speaking." So when we say
man is loved, is hated, is condemned, we say
that the loved, hated, or condemned cond
that in which he exists. And even the s
"the man is dead" is equivalent, neither m
less, to the other, "the man exists dead."

last example should provoke, even in those who accept its predecessors, a smiling doubt, and a suspicion that this example is fatal to my view of the meaning of *to be*, it must be by reason of a misapprehension of the meaning of the verb *exist* as it is used in this construction. If *exist* must mean literally is alive, and nothing else, we cannot accept the sentence "the man exists (is alive) dead," as the equivalent of "the man is dead." But an objection resting upon this assumed ambiguity can be quickly set aside. The existence predicated by the substantive verb *to be* is not necessarily one of life, but one that is predicable alike of things animate and inanimate. We say that a planet, a country, a town exists, or that it does not exist, *i. e.*, that it is, or is not; as Virgil made Æneas say *fuit Ilium*, or as we might say, using the verb *to be* in two tenses to express the same fact, The man was, and is not; in which sentence *was* predicates an existence past, and *is not*, a negative existence present; a negative existence being no more a contradiction in terms than a negative affirmation. So when we say, The man is dead, we merely predicate of him a dead existence, which so far as he is concerned is no existence at all in this world, as far as we know; but so far as we are concerned with him as the subject of speech, is a mere change in the condition of his existence. With a ruined city or a dead man before us, the existence of either palpable, though changed in its condition, we say, The city exists no more, or, The city is (exists) ruined, The man exists no more, or, The man is (exists) dead. To this sense of the word *exist*, life is not

more essential in the one case than in t
This construing may easily be ridiculed,
quite sure that it will outlive any ridicu
may provoke, and that it affords the only
ble explanation of the intimate significatio
phrases as those which have just been
illustration.

Horne Tooke, as if to leave an example
set aside of the identity of *is* and *exist*, v
following remarkable sentence in his dialo
Prepositions." B. asks whether good-bre
policy dictated a certain sharp criticism u
Johnson and Bishop Lowth.   H. replies,—

"Neither. But a quality which passes for brutal
nature; and which, in spite of hard blows and heav
would make me rather chuse in the scale of beings
mastiff or a mule than a monkey or a lap-dog." — *Di*
I. 370, ed. 1798.

Now, can any man who has preserved
senses doubt for a moment that "to exist a m
a mule" is absolutely the same as " to be a
or a mule?"   And can such a person believe
the phrases, *to be a mule, to be stubborn*, a
beaten, there is the least shade of differenc
meaning of the verb *to be?* that it has one
ing when it is followed by the noun, *mule*,
same when it is followed by the adjective, *st*
but another when it is followed by the par
beaten, which is but a kind of adjective? If
such a difference, then the verb must have the
meaning before the adjective *afraid* in the se
He is afraid.   But *afraid* is merely the
participle of the verb *affray* — affrayed, afray

same as the old participle *afeared*, from the Anglo-Saxon *afaeran*, and how and when did the verb *to be* change its meaning by the mere contraction of *affrayed* into *afraid*?

But it is said that the use of *is* with *being* involves no absurdity, because here *being* does not mean existing, but continuing. In illustration of which, the phrase, *The anvil is being struck* is given. That, we are told, is equivalent to, The anvil is continuing struck. "*Being struck* implies a process, a continuity of some sort beyond a simple instant. *Is* affirms the *being struck* of the anvil." Let us examine that position, and see if it relieves us of confusion and ambiguity. Keeping to Noah's ark, let us say, The ark being finished, the hippopotamus declined entering it. Does that mean, the ark continuing finished, etc.? The bond being given, Shylock lent the money. Does that mean the bond continuing given, etc.? Plainly it does not, cannot mean, in either case, that, or anything like that. We find ourselves landed in the confusion and the ambiguity of assuming that in, "The ark being prepared," *being* has one meaning, and in, "The ark is being prepared," another. But if we hold to reason, and regard *being* as always meaning existing, and *preparing*, *building*, as verbal substantives that *mean a process*, we have no confusion, neither ambiguity nor absurdity. The ark being prepared, means the ark existing prepared; and, While the ark was in preparing, or was preparing, means while the ark was in process of preparation. Is there a man of sense who can speak English, who does not understand, *In the building of the house* to mean in the process of the erection of the house? It is safe to say, not one. The verbal substantive in *ing*, or, if you please, the present participle used substantively, expresses, to the apprehension of all men, a process. And such phrases as *being built, being done*, must be used absolutely, in a participial sense, as, The house being built, he went into it; The thing being done, it could not be helped; or they must be used substantively. For example, the following passage from the first book of Young's " Night Thoughts : " —

> " Of man's miraculous mistakes this bears
> The palm : That all men are about to live,
> Forever on the brink of being born."

Here *being born* is a substantive, equivalent to *birth*, as much a substantive as any single word in any language. Which may be shown thus : —

$$\text{Forever on the brink of} \left\{ \begin{array}{l} \text{an abyss.} \\ \text{ruin.} \\ \text{being born.} \\ \text{birth.} \end{array} \right.$$

We can say, His being born at that time was fortunate, as well as, His birth at that time was fortunate. But, to meet the last and most specious suggestion which has been made in favor of the *is-being* or *to-be-being* phraseology, that *is* merely predicates of its subject the *being* and the following participle — we cannot say, He was birth; and no more can we correctly say, He was being born. And so we may say, The anvil's being struck was evident; in which *being struck* means the blow which the anvil received, and which thus is the anvil's blow; but we cannot correctly (*i. e.*, logically, in accordance with reason and common sense) say, The anvil was being struck, any more than we can say, The anvil was blow. If we wish to say that the anvil is in the continued recipience of blows, and do not wish to say substantively, The anvil is in striking, or a striking, or striking, we may with perfect propriety and clearness of expression say, The anvil is struck, as Hamlet said Polonius "is eaten." *Is struck* does not mean has been struck, as *is eaten* does not mean has been eaten: both express present continuous recipience of action.

These comparisons and this reasoning are pertinent to the consideration of what has been said in defence of the phrase *is being done*, because that phrase is not an idiom which came into the language in its unconscious formative stages, but the deliberate production of some pedantic writer of the last generation, who sought to make, in the words of one of his apologists, "a form of expression which should accurately represent the form of thought," that thought being one which has been fully expressed among all civilized peoples for thousands of years; and the result of his labors is, as might have been expected, a monstrosity, the illogical, confusing, inaccurate, unidiomatic character of which I have at some length, but yet imperfectly, set forth. The suggestion has been made that, in the phrase under examination, *is* means becomes, and that *the house is being built* means, the house is becoming built. Now, if any man chooses to say, The house is becoming built, I, for one, shall make no objection other than that he is setting aside a healthy and sufficient idiom, which has grown up naturally with the language, and is, in fact, coeval with its birth, for a new phrase which has nothing of force or of accuracy in its favor. But that *is* does, or by any possibility can, *mean* becomes, that the verb of existence, the substantive verb, can in any way represent or be represented by another verb, the radical thought in which is motion toward, entrance into, is, I confess, beyond my comprehension.

The question is thus narrowed simply to this: Does *to be being* (*esse ens*) mean anything more or other than *to be?* Does it so mean logically, according to the common sense of men, and the spirit and analogies of the language? For as to what it may be made to mean, what men may agree to accept it as meaning, there is nothing to be said. *Beef*, for a good reason, means the flesh of the ox, and *steak*, for a like reason, flesh in large slices; and therefore *beefsteak* means the flesh of the ox in large slices. But there is no telling whether by the labors of those who wish to "slough off" old, uncouth forms, and to make "the form of expression accurately represent the form of thought," people may not be led to agree that it shall mean plum-pudding.

What then should we do? Should we say, While the boy was whipping, The room was sweeping, The dinner was eating, The cow was milking, The meat is cooking? Yes: why not? Why not, as well as, The bell is tolling, The grain is ripening, The bread is baking? Could there be a more absurd affectation than, instead of, The tea has been drawing five minutes, to say, The tea has been being drawn five minutes? *Been being* — is that sense, or English? — except to children, who say that they have been being naughty, thereby saying only that they have been naughty. Yet the tea draws nothing, it is drawn ; the bread bakes nothing, it is baked ; the grain ripens nothing, it is ripened. But when we say that, The tea is drawing, we do not say that it is an agent drawing anything, but that it is itself in drawing. And so with regard to all the other examples given, and all possible examples. In Goldsmith's "Citizen of the World" (Letter XXI.) is the following passage, descriptive of a play : —

"The fifth act began, and a busy piece it was; scenes shifting, trumpets sounding, drums beating, mobs hallooing, carpets spreading, guards bustling from one door to the other; gods, demons, daggers, rags, and ratsbane."

Read the second clause of the sentence according to the formula *is being done.* "Scenes being shifted, trumpets being sounded, drums being beaten, mobs hallooing, carpets being spread," and so forth. By this change the very life is taken out of the subject. No longer a busy piece, it drags its wounded and halting body along, and dies before it gets to rags and ratsbane.

If precise affectation can impose upon us such a phrase as *is being done* for *is doing,* it must needs drive all idioms kindred to the latter from the language. Our walking sticks, our fishing rods, and our fasting days, because they cannot walk, or fish, or fast, must be changed into to-be-walked-with sticks, to-be-fished-with rods, and to-be-fasted-on days; and our church-going bells must become for-to-church-go bells, because *they* are not the belles that go to church. Such ruin comes of laying presumptuous hands upon idioms, those sacred mysteries of language.

CHAPTER XII.

A DESULTORY DENUNCIATION OF ENGLISH DICTIONARIES.*

A DICTIONARY is an explanatory word catalogue; and a perfect one will contain the entire literary and colloquial vocabulary of a language; that is, every simple word, and every compound word with a single and peculiar meaning, having the authority of usage respectable for antiquity, generality, or the eminence of the user. It would seem that such a catalogue could be certainly made, patient research and a not very remarkable degree of learning being the only requisites to its making. But, in fact, an absolutely perfect dictionary of any living language does not exist, and perhaps will never exist, for the reason that it cannot be produced.

* In the first sentence of this chapter as it was originally published (in the "Galaxy" for May, 1869), I mentioned that, but a short time before the writing of it, I had heard, for the first time, of Trench's pamphlet, "On some Deficiencies in our English Dictionaries," of which I had until then in vain sought a sight, either as a buyer or a borrower. Since that time — owing to the kindness of one of the proprietors of Brotherhead & Company's Library — I have had an opportunity of reading the dean's criticism. The differences between my reverend predecessor's presentation of the subject and my own arise chiefly from the difference of the ideals we each had in mind. His dictionary is a philological history of the language, with illustrative examples; mine, a hand-book of every-day reference for the general reader. I have modified none of my opinions since reading Archbishop Trench's pamphlet; but I have obtained the advantage of citing his judgement in support of my own on several important points.

Bailey's "Universal Etymological English Dictionary" was the first worthy attempt at the making of a word-book of our language; and it was a very creditable work for the time of its publication, A. D. 1726. For those who care to do more about language than to see how "the dictionary" says a word should be spelled, or what it means, Bailey's work has never been entirely superseded. There was some reason that the compiler should say that he had enriched his book with "several thousand English words and phrases in no English dictionary before extant; " for the English dictionaries that preceded his were so small and deficient, that, as representations of the vocabulary of our language, they were of little worth. But the boasting of subsequent dictionary-makers, like most other boasting, is empty and ridiculous in proportion to the magnitude of its pretensions. When we are told that Webster's Dictionary contains sixteen thousand words not found in any similar preceding work, and then that the Imperial Dictionary contains fifteen thousand words more than Webster's, and yet again that the Supplement to the Imperial Dictionary contains twenty thousand words more than the body of the work, we might well believe that our language spawns words as herrings spawn eggs, and that a mere catalogue of its component parts would soon fill a shelf in an ordinary library, were it not that when we come to examine these additions of thousands and tens of thousands of words thus set forth as made in each new dictionary, and in each new edition of each dictionary, we find that not one in a hundred of the added words, hardly

one in a thousand, is really a before uncatalogued
item of the English vocabulary.   Our estimate of
the worth of an addition that proceeds by columns
of four figures is further lowered by the discovery
that these dictionaries, with all their ponderous bulk
and verbal multitudinousness, do not fully represent
the English of literature or of common life; that
they give no aid to the reading of some of our
standard authors; that while they set forth, with
wearisome superfluity and puerile iteration, that
upon which every one who has sense and knowledge enough to use a dictionary at all, needs no
information, they pass by as obsolete, or vulgar,
or colloquial, or what not, that upon which people
of intelligence and education do need instruction
from the special students of language; and that,
while they spot their pages with foreign words and
phrases, the use of which by some writers has
shown, with a superficial knowledge of other
tongues, a profound ignorance of their own, — they
neglect home-born words that have been in use
since English was written or spoken.

That works to which the foregoing objections can
be justly made — as they may be, in a greater or
less degree, to every existing English dictionary —
can have no real authority, is too plain to need
insisting upon with much particularity.   As to
dictionaries of the present day, that swell every
few years by the thousand items, the presence
of a word in one of them shows merely that its
compiler has found that word in some dictionary
older than his own, or in some not low and
indecent publication of the day; the absence of

a word from any one of them showing merely that it has not been thus met with by the dictionary-maker. Its presence or its absence has this significance, and no more. Word-books thus compiled have the value which always pertains to large collections of things of one kind, even although the things may be intrinsically and individually of little worth; but the source of any authority in such word-collections it would be difficult to discover. Upon the proper spelling, pronunciation, etymology, and definition of words, a dictionary might be made to which high and almost absolute authority could justly be awarded. And the first and the second of these points are determined, with a very near approximation to such merit, in the works of Ogilvie, Latham, Richardson, Worcester, and that which is strangely enough called Webster's.

With one exception, Etymology is the least valuable element in the making of a dictionary, as it is of interest only to those who wish to study the history of language. It helps no man in his use of the word *bishop* to know that it comes from two Greek words, *epi*, meaning upon, and *scopos*, meaning a looker, still less to be told into what forms those words have passed in Spanish, Arabic, and Persian. Yet it is in their etymologies that our dictionaries have shown most improvement during the last twenty-five years; they having profited in this respect by the recent great advancement in the etymological department of philology. The etymologies of words in our recently published dictionaries, although, as I have said before, they are of no great value for the purposes for which dictionaries are consulted, are little nests (sometimes slightly mare-ish) of curious and agreeable information, and afford a very pleasant and instructive pastime to those who have the opportunity and the inclination to look into them. But they are not worth, in a dictionary, all the labor that is spent on them, or all the room they occupy. The noteworthy spectacle has lately been shown of the casting over of the whole etymological freight of a well-known dictionary, and the taking on board of another. For the etymological part of the last edition of "Webster's American Dictionary," so called, Dr. Mahn, of Berlin, is responsible. When it was truly called Webster's Dictionary, it was in this respect discreditable to scholarship in this country, and even indicative of mental supineness in a people upon whom such a book could be imposed as having authority. And now that it is relieved of this blemish, it is, in this respect, neither Webster's Dictionary nor "American," but Mahn's and German.

Dictionaries are consulted chiefly for their definitions; and yet, upon this point, all our English dictionaries are more or less misleading and confusing. And they are so in a great measure because the desire to multiply words has its counterpart in the desire to multiply definitions, in defiance of simple common sense. Minuteness of division and variety of signification have been sought, that the book might be big, and its definitions be styled copious. They have been marshalled one after the other in single file, that their array might be the more imposing; and to increase the impressiveness of the spectacle, they are solemnly numbered.

And so, at last, we are seriously told that, for instance, *fall*, as a verb, has twenty-eight meanings, and as a noun nineteen — all as well-defined and several as the two-and-seventy stinks that Coleridge found in the City of Cologne — besides thirty-eight which it has in established phrases! But this simple word is far over-passed, in the multitude and variety of the meanings assigned to it, by another, *run*, which would seem to express always one simple thought, as clearly and absolutely as is possible in language. We are actually told that *run*, as a verb transitive, has fifty-six distinct meanings, thirteen as a verb intransitive, and fourteen as a noun, besides twenty-seven in current phrases. To each one of these a special paragraph is given, so that the line stretches out like that of Banquo's progeny in the witches' cave; and by the tenuity of its sense, it vanishes away into nothing, like the receding figures in a perspective diagram. Here are some of these definitions of *fall*, as they are given in Webster's Dictionary. Of the verb, —

5. To die, particularly by violence.
6. To come to an end suddenly, to vanish, to perish.
7. To be degraded, to sink into disrepute, etc., etc.
8. To decline in power, wealth, or glory, to sink into weakness, etc., etc.
26. To sink, to languish, to become feeble or faint.
10. To sink, to be lowered.
11. To decrease, to be diminished in weight or value.
17. To happen, to befall, to come.
18. To light on, to come by chance.
20. To come, to arrive.
21. To come unexpectedly.
27. To be brought forth.
28. To issue, to terminate.

24

Of the noun, —

3. Death, destruction, overthrow.
4. Ruin, destruction.
5. Downfall, degradation, loss of greatness.
6. Declension of greatness, power, or dominion.
7. Diminution, decrease of price or value, depreciation, as the fall of prices, the fall of rents, the fall of interest.
8. Declination of sound [whatever that may be], a sinking of tone, cadence, as the fall of the voice at the close of a sentence.

Of *run* we find the following among the fifty-six meanings given of it as a transitive verb : —

3. To use the legs in moving, to step, as children run alone or run about.
4. To move in a hurry — The priest and people run about.
8. To contend in a race, as men and horses run for a prize.
13. To be liquid or fluid.
14. To be fusible, to melt.
15. To fuse or melt.
18. To flow, as words, language, or periods.
21. To have a course or direction.
24. To have a continued tenor or course.
29. To proceed in succession.
31. To proceed in a train of conduct.
36. To extend, to lie in continued length, as veins.
37. To have a certain direction — The line runs east and west.
46. To pass or fall into fault, vice, or misfortune, as to run into vice, to run into mistakes.
48. To have a general tendency — Temperate climates run into moderate governments.
51. To creep, as serpents run on the ground.
52. To slide, as a sled or sleigh runs on the ground.
53. To dart, to shoot, as a meteor in the sky.
54. To fly, to move in the air, as the clouds run from N. E. to S. W.

Of *run*, the noun, we have these among other discriminated meanings : —

2. Course, motion, as the run of humor.
3. Flow, as a run of verses to please the ear.
4. Course, process, continued series, as the run of events.

Words would be wasted in showing the absurdity of a system of definitions which gives such results as this; which not only sets forth mere metaphorical uses of words as instances of their use in different senses, but in the metaphorical use, regards the application of a word in one sense to two objects as its use in two senses; as, for instance, *to fall*, to die by violence, and, also, to come to an end suddenly; *run*, to pass or fall into vice, and, also, to have a general tendency. Let the reader, who wishes to see to what lengths this mania for copious definition can lead those upon whom it seizes, examine the words *work, turn, free, live, life, light, wood, head, make, lay, break, cast, cut, give, go, have, heart, heavy, high, hold, put, raise, serve, set, so, stand, take, to,* and almost any other such simple words in Webster's Dictionary. Let him turn to Johnson's, and see that *wooden* is defined first as "made of wood," and next as "clumsy, awkward," two passages, of which the following is one, being quoted as support for the latter definition:—

"When a bold man is out of countenance, he makes a very wooden figure on't."

But *wooden* does not here *mean* clumsy or awkward; it only *suggests* clumsiness and awkwardness; and it verily has that suggestion in its power, because it means made of wood, and means, and can mean, nothing else. The use of *wooden* in this instance brings vividly to mind how like a wooden figure, a figure-head, a man appears who has lost his self-possession. Its very value as an epithet consists in that it does *not* mean clumsy and

awkward. In the following passage in "
Crusoe," Defoe furnishes an example of tl
the same word more pertinent than eitl
two which have been cited in dictionaries

> " Well, this I conquered by making a wooden sp
> but this did my work in a wooden manner."

A wooden spade could, of course, serv
son Crusoe's needs only in a wooden man
saying this in the person of his hero, D
artfully suggests the clumsy insufficien
homely tool ; and his meaning is conve
pletely and impressively, because it is s
and not literally told. Defoe's use of this
here worthy of Shakespeare himself, wh
many of his happiest reaches of languag
manner. He makes, in "The Tempest," a
of the very word in question, when F
carrying logs, says, —

> " [I] would no more endure
> This wooden slavery, than to suffer
> The flesh-fly blow my mouth."

Here *wooden* at once expresses literally t
of the speaker's labor, and suggests its dul
siveness ; and it does the latter at the wi
poet, just because without that will it does
former.

If we may say that *wooden* means clum
ward, dull, oppressive, we may as well
oak means courage, because of the phrase
of oak," or that *gold* means innocence, bec
speak of "the age of gold," or that *iro*
hard or hardness, because *iron-hearted* is
the sense of hard-hearted, unfeeling, crue

Webster is not wholly responsible for the vicious system of definition upon which he labored with such conscientious thoroughness. This system originated with Dr. Johnson; and it is mere justice to say that, although Webster carried it to an extreme which is both extravagant and injurious, he improved upon his model, and displayed a power of discrimination, and an ability for the exact expression of nice distinctions, much surpassing that of "the great lexicographer."

Johnson's Dictionary was not only a work of great research — it was a work original in its design and its execution; and it is the model of the great English dictionaries, except Richardson's, that have been since compiled. They are all founded upon Johnson's; but his was founded upon no other: it was the result of a critical examination of a range of English literature wider than had ever before been examined by one man for any purpose. It was almost inevitable that a dictionary made in such a manner should, with its great merits, have all the faults by which those merits are counterbalanced, and particularly this one of superfluous, over-subtle, misleading definitions. Johnson undertook to present a full vocabulary of the language gathered from the writings of its principal authors in all departments of literature, and to define each word of that vocabulary according to the various senses in which he found it used. Considering the end in view, the method adopted was the best, if not, indeed, the only one, for its attainment; and the labor was gigantic. But, it was hardly avoidable that, in compiling and defin-

ing a vocabulary in this manner, the various applications of words used by various authors in the
same sense should be accepted as uses of those
words in different senses; and particularly that
various metaphorical applications of words having
but one real meaning should be discriminated by
different definitions. The collection of passages
for the illustration of definitions would naturally
lead to this false distinction of significations. And
as to the remainder of his task, Johnson, although
a scholar, and a thinker of singular clearness and
force, was not a philologist, even according to the
crude and rudimentary philology of his day; nor
was his mind so constituted as to fit him for the
quick perception of analogies and the patient
tracing of verbal vestiges hidden by the drift of
centuries, which are necessary to the successful
prosecution of philological inquiry. The consequence was, that he produced a work that was at
once very convenient and very pernicious. I will
not say, with him who yet remains the greatest
philologist that has made the English language his
peculiar study, Horne Tooke, that Johnson's Dictionary is a disgrace to the English people; but there
seems to be no reason for disputing Tooke's judgement, that Johnson's system was unscientific and
vicious, and that a dictionary ought to be made
of a very different kind from anything ever yet
attempted anywhere. ("Diversions of Purley," i.,
401.) Now, all that has since been done in the
making of English dictionaries is merely to build
upon Johnson's foundation, and to work on his plan,
with the increased materials and the larger knowl-

edge provided by the development of the language and by the investigations of modern philology.

In one respect, the makers of later dictionaries have followed, to a monstrous extreme, a fashion set by Johnson — that of introducing compound words, and words formed from others simple and well known, by the addition of the prefixes *dis*, *un*, *mis*, *re*, etc., the meaning and force of which are as generally understood as that of *s* in the plural and in the possessive case. The catalogues of these words, with which our dictionaries are blown up into a bloated emptiness of bulk, are an offence to the common sense of any reader, even the humblest, and cause him to pay for that which he does not need, while they fill five times the room that would be required by that which he does need. Open almost any dictionary, the Imperial, Webster's, or Worcester's, — but Webster's is the most superfluous and obtrusive in this respect, because it carries to the furthest extreme the vicious plan of vocabulary-making and definition introduced by Johnson, — open it at random, and see how it is loaded down with this worthless lumber. Of words formed by joining *milk* and some other word together, there are twenty-two, of which number are *milk-pail*, *milk-pan*, *milk-porridge*, *milk-score*, *milk-white*. And yet *milk-punch*, *milk-train*, and *milk-poultice* are omitted! *Straw* furnishes twelve compound words, so called, of which are *straw-color*, *straw-colored!* *straw-crowned*, *straw-cutter*, *straw-stuffed!* and even *straw-hat!* Yet in vain will Margery Daw look for *straw-bed*, or Recorder Hackett seek the word *straw-bail*.

Of words, so called, made by the union of *heart* with another, there are acutally sixty-nine paraded, *heart* itself having sixteen distinct meanings assigned to it simply, and eleven in established phrases. Among these compounded words are *heart-ache*, *heart-appalling*, *heart-consuming*, *heart-corroding* (why not *heart-destroying*, and *heart-crushing?*), *heart-expanding*, *heart-shaped* (which we are informed means "having the shape of a heart"), *heart-piercing* (which means "piercing the heart"), *heart-sick* (which means "sick at heart"), *heart-thrilling*, *heart-whole*, and the like; and yet *heart-entrancing*, *heart-enticing*, and *heart-bewitching*, as well as *heart-blood*, are omitted. Why? Gentle Webster, tell us why! Surely a dictionary, of all things, should be "in concatenation accordingly."

After being told that *head*, simple of itself, has thirty-one distinct meanings (it has but one of the thirty-one), we are presented with it in combination with other simple words thirty-seven times; of which manner of dictionary-making here are a few examples: *head-ache* (which the inquirer will learn means "pain in the head"), *head-dress*, *head-first* (which we are told means "with the head foremost." Why not "with the head first?" that would be more in keeping), *headless* (of which we not only learn that it means "without a head," but for which we are given the high authority of Spenser as warranting us to say a headless body, neck, or carcass); *head-strong*, *head-work*, and *head-workman* also appear. We find sixty-seven compounds of *horse*, such as *horse-breaker*, *horse-deal-*

er, *horse-flesh*, *horse-jockey*, *horse-keeper*, *horse-race*, and (important) *horse-racing*, *horse-shoe*, *horse-stealer*, *horse-thief*, and *horse-stealing*, *horse-whip*, *horse-whipped;* and *horse-whipping* twice. Why were there not sixty-eight compounds? for *horse-marine*, alas! is absent.

Sea is repeated in combination with other words one hundred and fifty-seven times! the combined words being all printed at full length, each in a line by itself, with definitions to use them withal. Else, indeed, how could a man, after being told what *sea* means, compass the meaning of *sea-bank*, *sea-bar*, *sea-bathed*, *sea-breeze*, *sea-captain*, *sea-coast*, *sea-man*, *sea-resembling* (which means " like the sea "); *sea-shell*, *sea-shore*, *sea-side*, *sea-thief*, *sea-water*, or *sea-weed?* And yet, in defiance of Cooper and Marryatt, and Admiral Farragut and the Navy of the United States being set at nought, *sea-cook* is not to be found, nor yet *sea-lubber*. Again why? Webster, why? for you give us *cook* and give us *lubber*, as you give us *bank*, and *breeze*, and *captain*, and *shell*, and *shore*, and *side*, and *thief*, and *water*. Why, therefore, *sea-captain*, and not *sea-cook?* why *sea-thief*, and not *sea-lubber?* We are told what *ear-deafening* means, but are left in ignorance as to *ear-stunning*. *Tooth-drawer* is deemed worthy of explanation, but *tooth-filler* pines in neglect. *Dining* having been defined, and *room*, we are nevertheless told that *dining-room* is a room to dine in; and yet we are heartlessly left to our own resources to discover the meaning of *breakfast-room*, *breakfast-time*, *tea-*

room, *tea-time*, *supper-room*, and *supper-time*; and although we are told what *banquet* means, and what *room*, and also (perhaps therefore) what a *banqueting-room* is, and what a *hall* is, yet as to what those *banquet-halls* are, visions of which float through the stilly night, we are left to guess from the poet's context, or to evolve from the depths of our own moral consciousness. We are told the meaning first of *apple*, and then gravely informed of that of *apple-harvest*, of *apple-john*, *apple-pie*, *apple-sauce*, *apple-tart*, and even of *apple-tree*. But we learn nothing about *apple-butter*, *apple-dumpling*, *apple-pudding* and *apple-slump*, as to two of which information is more needed than of any other compounds of *apple*, the only words of all these compounds which have properly a place in a dictionary being *apple-john*, *apple-butter*, and *apple-slump*. Thus, and properly, we have *cranberry*, but we do not find *cranberry-sauce*; *currant*, but not *currant-jelly*; *strawberry*, but not *strawberry-iced-cream*, or *strawberry-short-cake*; *short-cake* being a good example of the sort of compound word that should be given in dictionaries. Perhaps the most audacious of all these presentations of simple words in couples as words with individual claims to places in an English vocabulary, is the array in which *self* is shown in conjunction with some noun, adjective, or participle. Of these there are actually in Webster's Dictionary one hundred and ninety-six. Not one, of all this number, from the first, *self-abased*, to the midmost, *self-denial*, and the last, *self-wrong*, has a right to a place in an English dictionary; for in every case *self*, in the simple, primitive sense it always preserves, is a mere adjective, qualifying the word that follows it; and there is no reason why, if the combinations thus detailed should appear in a dictionary, all other possible combinations of *self* should not also be presented. The list is either entirely superfluous or very defective. In fact, such an array is an affront to the understanding of English-speaking people.

But what need of the further working of a mine of absurdity so rich that its product is not worth taking out, and so homogeneous that one specimen is just like another? Let the reader turn the pages himself, and think as he turns. Besides such compounds as those just cited, let him remark the array of words joined to the common adverbs and adjectives that come correctly from the lips of the most ignorant man a hundred times daily. Of *ever*, thirty-four. (Why not three hundred and forty?) *Ever-active* is present, and *ever-silent*, absent: we have *ever-living*, but why not *ever-running*? Of *out*, *over*, *less*, *after*, *counter*, *all*, *back*, *free*, *foot*, *fore*, *high*, and the like, the compounds swarm upon the page. Finally, let him, not inspect, but take a bird's-eye view (for life is short) of the hordes that troop under the standards of *dis*, and *mis*, and *in*, and *inter*, and *un*, and *re*, and *sub*, and *ex*, and the like, not one in a hundred of which has any more right to a place in a dictionary than one man has to enlist under two names and draw two rations; or than a Fenian has to stir up insurrection in Ireland as an Irishman, and to vote (twice) in New York as what he calls an "American citizen." Upon this point

Johnson's successors have bettered his instructions with a vengeance; for they have more than doubled his array of words with particle prefixes. Rather, they have bettered Johnson's practice, and set at naught his instructions. For on this point he taught much more wisely than he practised. It is one upon which a few examples will serve our purpose. For instance, *agree, agreeable, appear, approve, arm*, being given in a dictionary, upon what supposition or pretence of need can *disagree, disagreeable, disappear, disapprove*, and *disarm* be given? We are properly told all about *trust*; and could there be a better reason why not a word is needed upon *distrust?* And yet we have, in all such cases, not only the simple word, and also the simple word with the prefix, but all the inflections and derivatives of both: *trust, trusted, truster, trustful, trustfully, trustfulness, trustily, trustiness, trusting*, and *trustingly*, and then soberly *distrust, distrusted, distruster, distrustful, distrustfully, distrustfulness, distrustily, distrustiness, distrusting*, and *distrustingly*. In like manner are paraded the combinations of all the other particle prefixes. Of words compounded with *dis* Johnson gave 637, Webster gives 1334; of words compounded with *un* Johnson gave 1864, Webster gives 3935; these two prefixes heading a catalogue of more than 5000 words, so called, and such compounds as *unwitty, unsoft*, and *unsuit*, going to make up the multitude.* In Webster's Dictionary,

---

* The counting for this statement, and some others in this chapter, was carefully made for me by one whom I have learned to rely upon; and although it may be not exactly correct, I am sure that it is nearly enough so for our purpose.

the Imperial, and Worcester's, compounds like
those previously noticed comprise one tenth of the
vocabulary, from which, nevertheless, words used
by English authors of repute, and by English-
speaking people the world over, are omitted. If
we did not know by what contrivances dictionaries
are sold, and how thoughtlessly they are bought
and consulted, we might well wonder that books
thus made up had not long ago been scouted out
of use and out of sight. Here is page after page,
from the beginning of the book to the end, filled
with matter that is worse than worthless, the very
presence of which is an affront to the common
sense of common people. For no man who has
intelligence enough and knowledge enough to need
a dictionary at all, or to know what one is, requires
one in which *arm* and *disarm*, *armed* and *unarmed*,
take and *retake*, *bent* and *unbent*, *bind* and *unbind*,
and the like pairs, are both given. To say the
least, the latter are mere superfluity, cumbering the
pages on which they appear. And yet it is largely
by the insertion of compound, or rather of double
words (for they are few of them really compounded), like *dining-room*, *heart-consuming*, and *tooth-
drawer*, and of words with particle prefixes, that
dictionary-makers sustain their boasts that their
books contain so many more thousand words than
those of their predecessors, or than their own of
previous editions. Dictionaries made in this manner are the merest catalogues of all possible verbal and syllabic combinations, — notably and necessarily incomplete catalogues, too; for there is no
end to word-making of this kind. The compound-

ing of the words already in the language may go
on *ad infinitum*, and on such a plan of lexicogra-
phy the introduction of a new verb or noun would
have consequences too numerous, if not too serious,
to mention.[*]

Another way of increasing the bulk, impairing
the worth, and diminishing the convenience of dictionaries, is the hauling into them — as with a drag-
net — of all the technical words that can be cap-
tured. Johnson began this vicious practice. In
his work we find *polysyndeton, ecphractick, stria,
vocle, quadriphyllous*, and many of like sort. His
successors and imitators have improved upon him —
Webster, as usual, far outdoing all. " His Dictionary," — as Archbishop Trench remarks, " while
it is scanted of the barest necessaries which such
a work ought to possess, affords, in about a page
and a half, the following choice additions to the
English language : *zeolitiform, zinkiferous, zinky,
zoophytological, zumosimeter, zygodactylous, zy-
gomatic*, with some twenty more." Thus far
Trench. But it should be added that such words
as these, and those given from Johnson, are no
part of the English language. They belong to no
language. They are a part of the terminology

---

[*] " Again, there is a defect of true insight into what are the proper bounds and
limits of a dictionary, in the admission into it of the innumerable family of compound epithets, such as *cloud-capped, heaven-saluting, flower-enwoven*, and the
like. ... Here is, in a great part, an explanation of the twenty thousand words which
he [Webster] boasts are to be found in his pages, over and above those included in
the latest edition of Todd. Admitting these transient combinations as though they
were really new words, it would have been easy to have increased his twenty thousand by twenty thousand more.

" Richardson very properly excludes all these : where he errs, it is, perhaps, in the
opposite extreme, in neglecting some true and permanent coalitions." — Trench,
" *On Some Deficiencies in our English Dictionaries*."

common to science and to scientific men of all
tongues and nations. When technical words, like
zenith and *nadir*, have passed from technical into
general use, they may claim a place in an English
dictionary, but not before.

I have spoken of the book called "Webster's
American Dictionary" in terms that are not applied
to a thing that is a model of its kind. But as
I have already said, in its present form, its objectionable traits are due merely to the fact that in it
a radically vicious plan is followed to an absurd extreme. Whatever was once peculiar to a book bearing its title was bad in itself and pernicious in its
effects. But as the years have gone on during
which the book has been forced into use by business combinations of publishers and printers,
adroitly and ceaselessly employed, it has been
modified, piece by piece, here and there, and always in its characteristic features, until now those
features have altogether disappeared. As it laid
aside its peculiar traits it ceased to have peculiar
faults; its offensiveness passed away with its indi-
viduality. When it was Webster's, and was "American," it was a book to laugh at and be ashamed of;
but now, having, by the protracted labors of able
scholars in both hemispheres, been purged of its
singularities in orthography and etymology, and
partly in definition, and having ceased to be Webster's (except in regard to definitions) and American (except as to the place of its publication), it
has become as convenient and trustworthy a com-
pilation of its kind as any other now before the
public. For between such dictionaries as Worces-

ter's, the Imperial, and Webster's in the last edition,
there is not a choice worth the toss of a copper.
In their labor-saving, thought-lulling convenience,
as in their serious faults, their many and grave deficiencies, and their needless, inconvenient, and
costly cumbrousness, they are alike.

It is always easier to criticise, and particularly to
find fault, than to make or to plan that which will
bear criticism. Yet we all must criticise, and we
all do find fault, from our uprising to our down-
lying, from birth to death, or else what is bad would
never be good, and what is good would never be
better. Nor is it necessary that we should be able
to cook our dinners, to make our clothes, or to com-
pile, or even plan, our dictionaries, that we should
know and declare whether they are well cooked,
made, or planned. As to a dictionary, I will venture to sketch the plan of one; such a one as has
not been made, and as I presume to hope Horne
Tooke had in mind when he wrote the passage
which I have quoted.

A dictionary, or better, a word-book, made for
the use of those to whom its language is vernacular, should be very different in its vocabulary and
in its definitions from the lexicon of a foreign
tongue. So a grammar written for the use of those
born to its language-subject, should omit countless
items, great and small, that must be carefully set
forth for the instruction of foreigners. But one
great vice of our dictionaries, as of our grammars,
is, that they are planned and written as if for men
who know nothing of their own language; the fact
being that the most ignorant of those who take up

dictionary and grammar have a kı owledge of
their mother tongue that a life's study of both books
can neither give nor take away. In making a lexicon of a foreign tongue, it must be assumed that
the person consulting it is ignorant of the combinations, the idioms, the inflections, contractions, and
all the minute variations of its simple words, which
are matters of the earliest knowledge to those to
whom the language is vernacular. This difference
between what is needed in a vernacular word-book
and a foreign lexicon being constantly borne in
mind, the first end sought in making a dictionary
should be the inclusion of all simple English words
used by writers of repute since the formation of the
language, at about A. D. 1250, beginning with the
works of Wycliffe, Chaucer, and Gower. The
omission of any such word would be a defect in the
dictionary. The plea of obsoleteness is no justification for such an omission. There is no obsoleteness in literature.* The old, irregular orthography
is not to be followed, nor need the old inflections
be given; but a professed dictionary of the English
language which does not contain all the simple
words and their compounds of deflected meaning,

* "In regard of obsolete words, our dictionaries have no certain rule of admission
or exclusion. But how, it may be asked, ought they to hold themselves in regard
of these? This question has been already implicitly answered in what was just said
regarding the all-comprehensive character which belongs to them. There are some,
indeed, who, taking up a position a little different from theirs who would have them
contain only the standard words of the language, yet proceeding on the same inad-
equate view of their object and intention, count that they should aim at presenting
the body of the language as now existing; this and no more; leaving to archaic
glossaries the gathering in of words that are current no longer. But a little reflection will show how untenable is this position; how this rule, consistently carried out,
would deprive a dictionary of a large part of its usefulness. . . .
"It is quite impossible, with any consistency, to make a stand anywhere, or to
admit any words now obsolete without including, or at least attempting to include
all." — Trench, "On Deficiencies," etc.

25

which are used by an English poet of such eminence as Chaucer, is not what its name pretends it to be. The addition of such of these words as are now omitted from our dictionaries would not increase their bulk appreciably, as may be seen by an examination of the glossaries to our authors from Chaucer to Spenser. And besides, it is to be remembered that the voluminousness of the dictionary, as it is at present known to us, is to be abated materially by the next provision of our plan, which is, that of compound or double words and words formed by particle prefixes only those have a proper place in a dictionary in which (1) the combination has acquired a meaning different from that of the mere union of its elements, or (2) one of the elements is known, or used, only in combination. Thus, if *disease* had continued to mean only *dis* and *ease*, or the negation of ease, as it does in the following lines from Chaucer's " Troilus and Creseide," —

> " And therewithall Creseide anon he kist,
> Of whiche certain she felt no disease." —

there would be no need of it in an English dictionary made for men to whom English is their mother-tongue. But it has acquired a modified and an additional meaning, and therefore should be given as a distinct word. So should *disable*, because *able* is unknown as a verb; and, for a like reason, Howell's *dister* (Letters, Book I., Sec. 3, Letter 32); but in an English dictionary in which *inter* appears, *disinter* has no proper place. So *breakfast*, having come to mean something less, or more, or other than the mere breaking of fast, must be given. But to give *breakfast-room*, or *dining-*

room, is as absurd as to give *joint-stock-company*, which Webster does; and why *joint-stock-company-limited* should not as well be given, it would be as difficult to discover, as why we are instructed upon *fiddle-string* and *fiddle-stick*, but are left in our native ignorance as to *fiddle-bow*, and in utter darkness upon the subject of the fitting tail-piece of this list — *fiddle-stick's-end*. Words like *after-thought*, *counter-act*, and *un-sound* have no place in a dictionary, except, perhaps, in a list of compounds under *after*, *counter*, and *un ;* but words like *aftermath*, *counterfeit*, and *uncouth*, in which one element is known only in composition, should of course be defined. Double words, like *black-smith* and *white-smith*, in which one of the elements has a deflected or perverted signification, should be given; but what good end, for any human creature with wit enough to find a word in a dictionary, is gained by giving such double words as *silver-smith*, *gold-smith*, *copper-smith ?*

Nor does vulgarity more than obsoleteness justify the omission of any English word. Dictionaries are mere books of reference, made to be consulted, not to be read. In the bear-baiting days of Queen Elizabeth it might be said, without offence of a vile, dull man, that he was "not fit to carry guts to a bear." Nowadays a man who used, in general society, the simple English word for which some New England "females" elegantly substitute *in-'ards*, would shock many of his hearers. But this is no good reason for the omission of the word from a dictionary. Through mere squeamishness, words, once in general use, are shunned more and more.

until at last they are regarded as gross and low,
when the things and thoughts of which they are the
mere names are, and always must remain, on the
same level. If need be, no one hesitates now to
speak of intestines. Horne Tooke has well said,
"It is the object for which words are used and the
manner of their use that give that use its character;"
and also that what are called vulgar words are "the
oldest and best authorized, the most significant and
widely-used words in the language." No man need
use them or seek them in a dictionary unless he
chooses to do so.*

Although words obsolete in the speech of the
day should be given, provincial words are out of
place in a dictionary of standard and established
English.†

Proper names are no part of language; and
whether words formed upon proper names, such as
Mohammedanism, Mormonism, Swedenborgian,
have claim to recognition as a part of the English language is at least very doubtful. Their inclusion in a
dictionary might be defended on the ground that it
would be convenient to have them there; but on the

---

* "A dictionary, then, according to that idea of it which seems to me alone capable of being logically maintained, is an inventory of the language; much more or-
deal, but this primarily; and with this only at present we will deal. It is no task
of the maker of it to select the *good* words of language. If he fancies that it is so,
and begins to pick and choose, to leave this, and to take that, he will at once go
astray. The business which he has undertaken is to collect and arrange all words,
whether good or bad, whether they commend themselves to his judgement or otherwise, which, with certain exceptions hereafter to be specified, those writing in the
language have employed. He is an historian of it, not a critic." — Trench. "*On
Some Deficiencies,*" etc.

† "Let me observe here, that provincial or local words stand on quite a different
footing from obsolete. We do not complain of their omission. In my judgement
we should, on the contrary, have a right to complain if they were admitted; and it
is an oversight that some of our dictionaries occasionally find room for them, in
their avowed character of provincial words; when, indeed, as such, they have no
right to a place in a dictionary of the English tongue." — Trench, "*On Some
Deficiencies,*" etc.

same grounds a chronological table, a list of post-
offices, or the best recipes for curing corns, might
well be given. A dictionary of the English language
is not an encyclopædia of useful information.[*]

Definitions, unless we would have them sprout
into the multitudinous absurdities which have been
already held up to the light in this chapter, must be
formed upon the principle, which is axiomatic in
language, that a word can have but one real meaning. Of this, all others—the all being few—are
subsidiary modifications; and of this meaning, the
metaphorical applications being numberless, un-
ascertainable, dependent upon the will and the taste
of every writer and speaker in the language, have
no proper place in a dictionary. This renders quotation in support of definition generally superfluous.
The maker of a dictionary for general use, *i. e.*, a
hand word-book, is not called upon to give a brief
history and epitome of his language, with the purpose of illuminating his pages or of justifying his
vocabulary.

Figures, diagrams, and the like (first used, not
in this country, but in England by Bailey), are not
only superfluous in a dictionary, but pernicious.
Language is the subject-matter of a dictionary; its
function is to explain words, not to describe things.
The introduction of a figure or a diagram is a con-

* "It is strange that Johnson's strong common sense did not save him from falling
into this error; but it has not. He might well have spared us thirteen closely printed
lines on an opal, nineteen on a rose, twenty-one on the almug-tree, as many on the
air-pump, not fewer on the natural history of the armadillo, and rather more than
sixty on the pear. All this is repeated by Todd, and in an exaggerated form by
Webster, from whom, for instance, we may learn of the camel, that it constitutes the
riches of the Arabian, that it can sustain abstinence from drink for many days, and if
all, twenty-five lines of its natural history."—Trench, "*On Some Deficiencies*," etc.

fession of an inability which does not exist. The
pictorial illustrations with which dictionaries have
lately been so copiously defaced, merely to catch
the unthinking eye, are entirely out of place. They
pertain to encyclopædias. And, indeed, the dictionaries of the last crop, such as the Imperial,
Worcester's, and the so-called Webster's, are too
much like encyclopædias to be dictionaries, and too
much like dictionaries to be encyclopædias. Their
pictures are as much in place as a fall of real water
would be in a painting of Niagara; which, doubtless, would also be pronounced "a very popular
feature."

In giving the etymology of an English word it
is not necessary, and is rarely proper, to trace it
beyond the Anglo-Saxon, Norman-French, Latin,
Greek, or other word from which it is directly derived. A dictionary is a word-book of reference,
not a treatise on general philology. To what purpose is it that a man who consults a dictionary for
the meaning, the form, or the sound of a word in
the English language, is informed that before the
existence of his language, or since, a word with
which the object of his search has possibly some
remote connection, had, or has, in another language,
the same, a like, or a different meaning? Whether
the word should be traced from its primitive meaning down to that which it has in present usage, or
from the present usage (which is that for which a
dictionary is chiefly consulted) up to its primitive
meaning, is not quite clear. The latter arrangement seems to be the more natural and logical.

In orthography the usage of the best writers,
modified, if at all, by a leaning toward analogy, is

the only guide to authoritative usefulness, as even the publishers of Webster's Dictionary have at last been obliged in practice to admit.

In pronunciation the usage of the most cultivated people of English blood and speech is absolute, as far as their usage itself is fixed. But the least valuable part of a dictionary is that which is given to orthoepy. Pronunciation is the most arbitrary, varying, and evanescent trait of language; and it is so exceedingly difficult to express sound by written characters, that to convey it upon paper with certainty in one neighborhood for ten years, and to the world at large for one year, is practically impossible.*

Upon the plan thus lightly sketched, an English dictionary might be made which would give a vocabulary of the language from its formation, with full and exact definitions, etymology, and pronunciation, and which yet would be a convenient handbook, in clear typography, and which could be sold at half the price now paid for "the best," whichever that may be.

* With the request that I should give some attention to the subject of elocution — a request made chiefly by readers who seem to suffer under the stated preaching of the gospel — I cannot comply. According to my observation, elocution cannot be taught; and systems of elocution are as much in vain as the physicians immortalized on the gravestone that fascinated the young eyes of David Copperfield. The ability to speak with grace and force is a gift of nature that may be improved by exercise and observation, but very little, if at all, by instruction. What can be profitably said upon this subject has been well said by Mr. Gould in his book "Good English."

CHAPTER XIII.

"JUS ET NORMA LOQUENDI."

WALKING down the Bowery one morning of last spring, I met a lad who took a paper from a package that he carried and thrust it into my unwilling hand. I suspected him of having lain in wait for the purpose; for on looking at the paper I found on it a printed announcement in these words:

Being about to inaugurate my Sample Room at No. — Bowery on the 16th instant, I invite my friends to be present at a Free Lunch on that occasion.

N. B.—Liquors and everything first class.

A— B—.

It is probable that neither this young gentleman nor his employer had given his days and nights to the perusal of the first edition of a certain book, which need not be named upon this page, or they would not have singled out its author for the unexpected honor of an invitation to the inauguration of a "sample-room." And yet possibly, even in that case, they, knowing the proverbial impecuniosity of literary men, might have supposed that, considering the tempting terms on which entertainment was proffered, I might be induced to be present on that occasion. However that might be, I did not scorn the invitation, but, for purposes of my own which have taken me to places even less to my liking than a "sample-room," on the appointed day I was present at the inaugural ceremonies, which I observed were of a very interesting nature to those who took part in them. I will confess, too, as Doctor Johnson once did, that at the early hour at which I made my visit I was *impransus*; but how much I ate and drank, I shall never tell; and as to how many brethren of my craft were also present, I shall ever preserve a discreet silence. Far be it from me to reveal to a curious and unsympathizing world how the priests of literature eke out their scanty means, and supply the wants of nature from the deodands of such inaugural sacrifices.

I remained long enough to discover that, whether the liquors were first-class or not, the language was. Among the choice morsels with which I was regaled was the remark of a gentleman with a pallid face, and a heavy mustache very black in the mass and very red just at the roots, who wore a dirty shirt confined by a brilliant pin worth at least five thousand dollars. Evidently disgusted with either the quality or the quantity of his entertainment, he said as he swaggered out, "Blessid is them wot don't expect nawthin'; for them's the ones wot won't git disappointed." Another gentleman, who as plainly was better pleased with his luncheon, replying for himself and a companion to an inquiry as to how he had fared, said, "Other fellers goes in for the fried liver, but me and him comes down orful on the corn beef." I was not surprised to hear another free-luncher assert with emphasis that his host was a perfect gentleman, and that he wished he would inaugurate every day. Soon after which I departed, no less pleased with my entertainment than he with his! I had

17*

gotten all I came for; and at how many receptions at which luncheon is also free (although that, of course, is never thought of), can a man say as much as he goes away, leaving "society" behind him?

Now, if the first mentioned of my *convives* had uttered his apophthegm in the form, Blessed are they who expect nothing, for they will not be disappointed, and if the other had said, He and I come down awfully on the corned beef, and the remainder of the company had discoursed in like manner, I confess that the entertainment would have lacked for me the seasoning that gave it all its savor. Their talk afforded me the enjoyment of an inward laugh. But why was it so ridiculous? Merely because it was at variance with cultivated usage? I think not. It seems to me that the amusing element in such a use of language is absurdity—the absurdity which is the consequence of incongruity. Their meaning was as unmistakable as if their sentences had been constructed by a pedagogue; but with this intelligibility there was a confusion due to the heterogeneous incongruity of the words with their position and their real significance. The combination of singular verbs with plural nouns, the use of words expressing an object in the place of those which express a subject, of those which express the quality of a thing to tell the manner of an act—this incongruity was the cause of the laughable absurdity. To a certain extent, indeed, the violation of usage was at the bottom of this absurdity; for if usage had not made the verb *is* singular, and the pronoun *them* objective, the word *awful* expressive of quality, and *corn* a substantive, and so forth, there would have been no incongruity. But here the point to be observed is, that usage does not act arbitrarily. It is guided, almost governed, by a union of the forces of precedent and reason.

Within certain limits usage has absolute authority in language. To assert this is not to lay down a law, or to set up a standard, but merely to recognize a fact. For as the only use of language, outside of Talleyrandic diplomacy, is to express, and not to conceal, our ideas, and as language which does not conform to the general usage of those to whom it is addressed cannot convey to them the meaning of the speaker or of the writer, such language fails to fulfil the first, if not the only, condition of its being. It has been said that the usage which controls language is that of great writers and cultivated speakers. To a certain extent this is true; but it is not true without important qualification. For the very necessity which controls communication by words, that is, the making of a thought common to the speaker and the hearer by means of a medium which has a common value to both, is binding upon the great writers and the cultivated speakers themselves. A man who uses words that are unknown, or familiar words in senses that are strange, or who, using familiar words in accepted senses, puts them together in an incoherent succession, which jars and interrupts rather than easily leads the train of thought, will fail to convey his meaning, whatever may be his mental gifts or his culture. Ideas and facts may be new or strange; but the language in which they are uttered must be old in fact or familiar in form, or they cannot be imparted.

This is so manifestly true as to be almost truism;
and yet old words do pass out of use; new words do
come into use; the construction of language does
change, although slightly and slowly, in the lapse of
years. Are these changes the work of the great
writers and the most cultivated speakers of a language? It will be found upon examination that
they are not—that the very few writers who can
justly be called great, or even distinguished, and
the comparatively small class of cultivated speakers, contribute to such changes only in proportion to
their actual numbers, even if in that degree. The
disuse of old words, the adoption of new ones, and
changes in phraseology and in the structure of the
sentence are, or thus far have been, an insensible,
unconscious process, going on among the whole mass
of those who speak the language in which they occur.
These changes are made in speech; for writing does
little in this respect; in which its chief, if not its only,
function is to fix and record that which has already
taken place in speech. Upon this point I hope that
I shall be excused for repeating what I said some
years ago, that the student of language, or the mere
intelligent observer of the speech of his own day,
cannot but notice how surely men supply themselves
with a word, when one is needed. The new vocal
sign is sometimes made, but is generally found. A
lack is felt, and the common instinct, vaguely stretching out its hands, lays hold of some common, or
mayhap some forgotten or rarely used, word, and,
putting a new stamp upon it, converts it into current coin of another denomination, a recognized representative of a new intellectual value. Purists may

fret at the perversion, and philologists may protest against the genuineness of the new mintage, but in vain. It answers the needs of those who use it; and that it should do so is all that they require.* It is in a language thus made that all writers, great or small, are obliged to write, that all speakers, cultivated or uncultivated, must needs utter their daily wants, their thoughts and feelings. Indeed, the excellence of speech and writing is in no small measure determined by the taste and judgment with which speaker or writer, yielding to the new and clinging to the old in language, conforms to usage with the discretion insisted upon in Pope's terse injunction:

> In words, as fashions, the same rule will hold,
> Alike fantastic if too new or old;
> Be not the first by whom the new are tried,
> Nor yet the last to lay the old aside.
>> "*Essay on Criticism*," Part II.

Yet Pope himself elsewhere says that great writers, "the men who write such verse as we can read," in the severe selection of their language, will

> Command old words that long have slept to wake,
> Words that wise Bacon or brave Raleigh spake;
> Or bid the new be English ages hence;
> For use will father what's begot by sense.
>> *Second Epistle of the Second Book of Horace.*

Thus Pope himself, who affected preciseness in the use of language (and who yet in this very passage, for instance, was incorrect in his use of it, as precisians often are), on the one hand recognizes not only right but propriety in the use of words that would be classed by lexicographers as obsolete, and

---

* "An Essay toward the Expression of Shakespeare's Genius." 1865.

on the other, sets at naught the purist's horror of
neologism. And indeed there seems to me nothing
weaker than that purism which shrinks from a word
or a phrase merely because it is new. If there are to
be no new words, how can language express more
than the first and lowest needs of human nature.
Without neologism language could not grow, could
not conform itself to the new needs of new generations. The question as to a word is not, Is it new?
but, Is it good? And Pope has given us the test by
which to try new words and phrases. They must be
begotten by sense. But one parent of language must
be precedent. The language of one generation brings
forth the language of the next, as surely as the
women of one generation bring forth the men of the
next. Hence, indeed, the language spoken by a
people is its mother tongue. True and sound language is therefore the product of precedent and reason; in other words, it is the normal development
of germs within itself. All other speech is monstrous
and illegitimate. If an unreasonable and monstrous
change establishes itself, men must needs submit as
to any other effective usurpation. They have no
choice. But in the discussion of a proposed change,
or of one that is beginning to effect itself, our test of
its normality must be reason; because there is no
other by which to determine its conformity to its
proper type. The same rule applies to that which is
in use, and which it is proposed to drop or modify.
For if we make the use of eminent writers and cultivated speakers authoritative, we shall soon find ourselves involved in a conflict not only of use with reason, and of use with precedent, but of use with itself

The gift of judgment, imagination, fancy, humor, or of all these, does not necessarily make a man correct in his use of language, although such use does generally accompany one or more of those intellectual qualities. Great errors in language might be justified by the authority of great writers. The saying that in that case they are not errors, is a mere begging of the question. Words and phrases may have been used by great writers, and yet be out of the line of normal development of the language; and on the other hand, a word or a phrase may have been used only once by a writer without genius and of inferior rank, or may not have been used at all, and may yet be a normal growth in speech, and perfectly good English. An accomplished and thoughtful writer on language recently offered as complete justification of the use of *proven*, as the past participle of *prove*, the fact that it had been used by Mr. Lowell. It implies no diminution of our delight in Mr. Lowell's poetry, in his criticism or his humor, if we admit that his use of language may not be invariably correct. Since the death of Hawthorne probably no writer of our language is more irreproachable in this respect than the author of "Venetian Life," "Italian Journeys," and "Suburban Sketches," which make us long to be more indebted to the same dainty pen; yet Mr. Howell's pages have furnished a few examples of incorrect English—incorrect not because other good writers had not used them, but because they do not conform to the acquirements of reason and precedent in the English language. Mr. Lowell has said that the objection to *illy* is "not an etymological objection,' but that it is inconsistent with good usage. *Illy* is not so violently at variance with etymology as some persons seem to think that it is. But if it were so, good usage would not thereby make it correct ; the usage would only in so far cease to be good (for sometimes it *is* " so much the worse for the facts"), although, like many other strong tyrants, it might force base coin into circulation.

Leaving out of consideration for the present Shakespeare and the dramatists who immediately preceded and followed him—those chartered libertines of language—let us see where the pilotage of eminent usage would land us. And I will say that my examples have not been curiously sought out, but are merely transfers of memorandums made on the margins and fly-leaves of books as I read them.

First, consider the following use of *both* by Chaucer, a poet second only to Shakespeare :

> O chaste goddesse of the woodes greene,
> To whom bothe heven and erthe and see is seene.
>
> *The Knight's Tale, l. 439.*

Now for such a use of *both* the "authority," that is the example, of Chaucer, can be of no more weight than that of an anonymous advertisement in a newspaper. Etymology and usage, including that of Chaucer himself in other passages, make the meaning of *both*, two taken together ; and it is impossible that the same word can mean two and three. If fifty passages could be produced from the works of Chaucer, Spenser, Shakespeare and Milton, in which *both* was applied to three objects, such a use of it by others might be excused, but it could not be justified. The case is extreme, but therefore of value ; it brings the point out sharply ; and by such examples a point to be established has its best illustration. And there it is; *both* used by one of our greatest poets to mean three taken together. It is indeed possible to conceive of *both's* being brought to mean three or three hundred, and the latter as well as the former. For that matter, let the present generation agree that *both* shall mean fifty-six, and the succeeding generation agree to the same, and it will thenceforth so mean until like general consent shall assign to it some other meaning. But such is not the way in which words are fitted to thoughts, even by usage; which itself conforms generally to reason, and follows a line of logical connection and normal growth.

The word *practitioner*, which has already (p. 216,) been remarked upon as abnormal and indefensible, also affords an illustration of the point under discussion. It is not a new word, its use dating back at least three hundred years. Bishop Latimer, according to Richardson, uses it in his sermon on the Lord's Prayer, applying it to Satan: "Consider how long he hath bin a practitioner;" and I find it in "The Gardener's Labyrinth" (Ed. 1586), more than once. For example: "Sundrie practitioners mixed the bruised leaves of the cypress tree, &c." (p. 32.) We have legitimate words with which the formation of this one seems to be analogous. Wicliffe writes, "For how manye weren possessioneris of feldis, &c.," and Sidney, "Having been of old freedmen and possessioners." I venture to say that Wicliffe and Sidney might much better have written *possessors;* but still there is a noun *possession* from which *possessioner* may be properly formed. So from *redemption* we have *redemptioner*, and from *probation, probationer*. But there is no noun *prac-

tition, from which to form *practitioner*, and there-fore even Latimer cannot make it a normal pro-duct of our language. As to my conjecture that it was formed in imitation of the French *practicien*, I have since found the following interesting and con-firmatory passage in Stephen's "World of Won-ders" (A. D. 1616);

"What reason is it then that Lawyers should make them such good sport for nothing? Or that they should be weary of taking before they be weary of giving? And I am easily induced to thinke, that when they were called *Pragmaticiens*, that is, *Pragma-titioners* (by the original word), things were not so out of square; but since that a sillable of their name was clipped away, and they called *Practiciens*, that is, *Practitioners*, they knew well how to make themselves amends for this curtailing of their name, as well upon their purses who were not in fault, as upon theirs who were the authors thereof." p. 129.

I have pointed out in a previous chapter Pope's use of the perfect participle for the past tense, *begun* for *began*, *sprung* for *sprang*, and of the weak pret-erite for the strong, as *thrived* for *throve*, *shined* for *shone*, and the like. An attempt has been made to justify this use, partly on the ground of Pope's authority as an eminent poet, and partly on the ground of usage more or less extensive. What this ple: is worth will appear on comparison of various passages in works of the same author. For instance:

> Not with such majesty, such bold relief,
> The forms august of king or conquering chief,
> E'er swelled on marble, as in verse have *shin'd*
> (In polished verse) the manners and the mind.
> *First Epistle, Second Book of Horace.*

And again, this passage in the "Essay on Man":

> If parts allure thee, see how Bacon *shin'd*,
> The wisest, brightest, meanest of mankind

This would seem to give Pope's authority in favor of—I shined, they shined, the sun shined. But when we read the following passage from the third book of the same essay,

> Alike or when or where they *shone* or shine,
> Or on the Rubicon or on the Rhine,

we see that the evidence of the former passages is merely that when Pope wanted a rhyme he would not hesitate to give a strong verb a weak preterite, regardless of law, analogy, or usage. When that need did not press him, or he wished to gain a contrast of sound, he wrote correctly.

The following couplet from the " Essay on Criticism" I have cited before for its striking use of the participle instead of the preterite:

> A second deluge learning thus o'er*run*,
> And the monks finished what the Goths *begun*.

So in "Windsor Forest" we find,

> And now his shadow reach'd her as she *run*,
> His shadow lengthened by the setting sun.

Shall we then on Pope's authority say, When she came home, I run to meet her? The gentlemen who assisted at the inauguration of the " sample-room" would thus be sustained in a use of language very common with them. But no; for in the ' Essay on Man" we read :

> True faith, true policy united *run ;*
> That was but love of God, but this of man.

And again, in the same poem :

> In each how guilt and greatness equal *run*,
> And all that raised the hero sunk the man.

Thus, as before, we see that Pope's rule in language was rhyme, not reason; usefulness, not usage; as we find that it was in the following passage from the same book of the same essay, where he does not hesitate to use *began* and *begun* interchangeably, caring nothing for correctness, but only for rhyme:

> Till drooping, sickening, dying, they *began*,
> Whom they rever'd as God, to mourn as man;
> Then looking up from sire to sire explor'd
> Our first great father, and that first ador'd;
> Or plain tradition that this all *begun*,
> Conveyed unbroken faiths from son to son.

Pope's writings are so filled with this inconsistency, or rather this consistent disregard of correctness in favor of rhyme, rhythm, or desired assonance or dissonance, that it would be superfluous to follow him further on this track. He writes at pleasure— *you rid* or *you rode, they writ* or *they wrote, you was* or *you were*. His authority is evidently nothing worth in this respect; and the same may be said of poets generally, who, if they can make themselves understood, and get the flow and the sound of their verses to please their ears, shrink little from any perversion of the form, or even of the sense, of language. This is particularly true of the poets who preceded Dryden; but even Tennyson, in his most carefully finished poem, "In Memoriam," writes thus:

> Then echo-like our voices rang;
> We *sung*, tho' every eye was dim,
> A merry song we *sang* with him
> Last year; impetuously we *sang*.
>
> XXX.

To turn to prose writers, there is hardly any con

fusion or mutilation of the preterite or the perfect participle that is not supported by the "authority" of Swift, who, in the "Tale of a Tub," has "they *writ* and *sung*" for they wrote and sang; "if a cruel king had not *arose*," for had not arisen; "the treatises *wrote*," for written; for all of which his authority has just as much weight as it has for such a use of language as "the perfection of writing *correct*," which we find in the same book, and which does not exhibit the perfection of writing correctly. Because Gibbon produces such a passage as this,

Either a pestilence or a famine, a victory or a defeat, an oracle of the gods or the eloquence of a daring leader *were* sufficient to impel the Gothic arms—

and Junius such a one as this,

Neither Charles nor his brother *were* qualified to support such a system—

are we to take their authority as a justification of the use of *either* and *neither* with *were?* Here follow three passages from eminent writers; the first from Macaulay's "Essay on Milton," the second from the same writer's "History of England," the third from Junius's "Letters to Woodfall":

Skinner, it is well known, held the *same* political opinions *with* his illustrious friend.

During the last century no prime minister *has become* rich in office.

This paper should properly *have appeared to-morrow.*

Does the eminence of the writers make such a use of language authoritative? Certainly not. Here reason comes in and sets aside the weight of authority, however eminent. *Either* and *neither* are essentially separative, and therefore they cannot be correctly used with plural verbs. *Same* expresses identity and therefore cannot properly be used in correspondence to *with*, which means nearness, contact, and implies duality, severalness. *The last century* is time completely past, to express events in which, a present perfect verb cannot be logically used. *Have appeared* expresses a perfected action, and therefore it cannot be correctly predicated of something in the future—to-morrow.

The taking of isolated passages from the works of eminent writers, as examples of a use of language which has their sanction, is not to be defended. It is unfair, unreasonable; for writers, like other men, are to be judged by their general practice, not by the occasional lapses to which they, like all other men, are subject. And it is in part to illustrate the unsoundness of conclusions drawn from such rare or solitary instances, that these examples are here brought forward. It is too common to see an abnormal or illogical use of language defended on the ground that it may be found in the writings of some author of deserved reputation.

As the example of eminent writers, when it is inconsistent with reason and analogy, is not authoritative, so good usage, that is, continuous use by writers of repute and people of culture, is not necessary to the recognition of a word or a phrase as good English. A good new word brings its own credentials, and is as good English the first day that it is spoken or written as after a hundred years of the best usage. But it is also true that many a bad word, like many a bad man, is well received and must be recognized merely because it has forced its

way among its betters, and has been adopted for
convenience sake. It is enough if the new word is
normally formed upon a sound stem and conveys its
intended meaning clearly. For example, the word
streeted, which I have previously cited as having
been used by James Howell in his "Letters," and
probably never before or since, is good English, not
because he was a writer of uncommon power or purity, which he was not, but because it is formed according to a law (so to speak) which permits the formation of adjectives participial in form from nouns,
and which has come down to us from the Anglo-
Saxon. Thus, in Wyatt's "Request of Cupid":

> Weaponed thou art, and she unarmed sitteth.

Weaponed, although unheard in these days, is good
English now, was good English when Wyatt used it
three hundred and twenty-five years ago, and would
have been good English then even if six hundred
years before *waepened* had not meant male, *i.e.*, weap-
on-bearing. If it were used to-day for the first time, it
would be as good English, as utterly beyond reproach
or exception, as if it had continued in constant use
these thousand years.

In Mr. Lowell's "Cathedral" a word occurs,
undisprivacied, which when the poem appeared was
made the occasion of many sneers from philological
witlings. It probably had never been used before,
and therefore those purists denounced it as a neologism. So it is, in the newness of its form, but not in
the essence of its formation. It is good English;
but not because Mr. Lowell used it. His use would
not make *undisprivacied* English any more than it

could do the same for *proven*. It is English because
its meaning is clear and its formation normal. Its
meaning is,—has not been robbed of privacy; and
it is as correctly formed as *undisturbed*. I do not
know whether Mr. Lowell hesitated to use the word
in question; but I am pretty sure that he did not.
No man who felt in him any mastery of language
would be likely to hesitate a moment over such a
word. But the fact is, that he approached it gradually. He did not begin with *privacied*, which,
although unknown to dictionaries, is perfectly good
English, meaning possessed of privacy. But assuming *privacied*, he wrote in the "Fable for Critics":

> But now, on the poet's *disprivacied* moods,
> With *do this* and *do that* the pert critic intrudes.

Disprivacied is as unknown to dictionaries as *privacied* or *undisprivacied*; but its meaning — having
had privacy taken away—is clear, and its formation
is as normal as that of *disprized* or *disgusted*. Then
came the double prefix in the "Cathedral"—

> Play with his child, make love, and shriek his mind,
> By throngs of strangers undisprivacied.

It may be asked, As *un* here merely cancels the
dis to which it is prefixed, how does *undisprivacied*
differ from *privacied*, and what necessity justifies the
use of the former? To this the reply is, that although
the *un* merely cancels the *dis*, there is in *disprivacied*
a suggestion of an active and unpleasant taking away
of privacy, and that therefore an *undisprivacied* man is
one who has escaped that injury from those who are
willing to inflict it, while in *privacied* there is no such
implication. All this comes at once by intuition to

men who are masterful in language, or ready and true in its apprehension.

Another author of high and well-deserved repute, Mr. Charles Reade, affords an example of the unique use of a word apparently formed in a mood similar to that which led Mr. Lowell to *undisprivacied*, but which is really formed upon an exactly opposite principle. In that charming story, "Peg Woffington," there is this passage:

> Mrs. Vane . . . wore a thick mantle and a hood that concealed her features. Of these Triplet disbarrassed her.—*Chapter XIII.*

Now *disbarrassed* is not English, and never could be, except in virtue of a usage to which it quite surely will never attain. The word is made on the assumption that as *em* (*i. e., in* or *on*), combined with *barrass*, conveys the idea of personal encumbrance, *dis* (*i. e.,* away, from) prefixed to the same stem would convey the opposite meaning. But the fault in this formation is that there is no such English stem as *barrass*, nor can such a stem be properly assumed, as in the case of *privacied*. Our word *embarrass* is adopted, as a whole, directly from the French; and it, as a whole, conveys a simple idea, that of encumbrance, the reverse of which must be expressed by *disembarrassed*. Not because it is new, but because it is obscure and badly formed, *disbarrassed* must be rejected, although it is found in perhaps the best book of an English novelist whose vivid style and creative genius will secure his works a fame that will endure when the memory of men who use language much more correctly will be forgotten. *Undisprivacied* would be English if, instead of being first used by the author of the "Commemoration Ode" and the

"Biglow Papers," it had been introduced in the reporting columns of a penny newspaper. These two neologisms, similar in kind and purpose, brought forward by two writers of eminence, under similar circumstances, have a directly diverse fate.

A finer example of the introduction of a sound, good, new, and purely English word, could not be found than in the following passage in Doctor John C. Peters's paper on "Pathology and Therapeutics":

Again, to a starving person we would first administer homœopathically such small quantities of food as would enhunger, if not almost starve a hearty person.

Dr. Peters has such well-won eminence as a physician that he can afford to have it said that, notwithstanding the generally clear and correct style of his medical writings, he has not the authority in literature that he has in medicine. *Enhunger* receives no literary sanction from his use of it; but although it seems (strangely, I must confess) never to have been used before, it has as robust an English constitution as any word in the Bible or in Shakespeare.

It is chiefly to those debauchers of thought and defilers of language, the newspapers, that we owe the verbal abominations that are creeping—nay, rather rushing into common use—use unhappily not always confined to those who inaugurate "sample-rooms" or assist at those solemn rites. Nor are these hideous excrescences upon our mother tongue confined to the reporter's columns. In the correspondence of a paper of high position—correspondence not without evidence of fine appreciation and of some literary taste—that is the worst of it—I met with this sentence about Pompeii:

Even now, when the city has been dead, buried eighteen hundred years, and *resurrectionized*, one is startled by an air of gayety that clings to it.

This is bad enough, worse if possible than its forerunner, *resurrected*; but what shall be said of the sin of the writer of the following passage in a leading article in a journal of the very highest position in the country:

And what are the *misnomered* Republicans doing but seeking to perpetuate in the Southern States the social nuisance of class distinctions?

What social nuisance could be greater than a newspaper which deliberately sets before fifty thousand readers—unsuspecting, receptive, and confiding —the printed example of the use of such an execrable compound as *misnomered !* By what process did a man who has been able to command the right to use a pen in the leading columns of a first-rate journal reach that depth of degradation in language, compared to which cant is classical and slang elegant? He meant misnamed; nothing more or less. But because he must have "finer bread than is made of wheat," and because there is a noun *misnomer*, he makes from it that hideous verb. Now again it is to be observed that *resurrectionised* and *misnomered* are not outcasts because they lack the sanction of usage or the authority of eminent writers. They are no newer, nor less sanctioned by use, good or bad, rude or cultured, than *undisprivacied* or *streeted* or *enhungered*, no stranger to the common ear than *weaponed*. But the latter are sound and healthy growths; the former are fungi, monstrous and pestilent.

18

Long established usage not being an essential
condition to the recognition of a word or a phrase as
correct English, does such usage of itself make that
correct which will not bear the tests of reason and
analogy? Observation justifies the answer that it
does not. Latham's judgment, that as whatever is,
in language, is right, whatever was and is not, was
wrong, is unsound; not only unsound in its conclusion, but incorrect in its premise. In language, as in
every other manifestation of man's intellectual and
moral nature, that which is may be wrong; and that
which was and is not, may have been right. Owing
to the peculiar function of language as the only
means of communication between man and man,
whatever is, must be accepted, in a certain degree at
least. A writer or speaker cannot be justly censured,
as for a personal fault, because he uses words and
phrases which are current in his day. But custom
has thus sanctioned not a little, in all languages, the
incorrectness of which is discernible, and has been
discerned, not only by the critical and the highly
cultured, but by men of ordinary intelligence and of
not more than ordinary carefulness or carelessness in
speech. The mere fact that a word or a phrase has
long been in good and in general use is presumptive
evidence in its favor, and therefore a complete justification of its use by any individual, but not proof
that it is a normal product of the language of which
it practically forms a part. Words and phrases
come into being, we hardly know how; and quickly
caught up from one to another, they pass into use
unchallenged, and good or bad, right or wrong, soon
become fixed as recognized parts of speech. Rarely

is there such reluctance as there was two hundred and fifty years ago in regard to *its*, or such protracted aversion and discussion as there has been of late in regard to *is being*.* But in this way, words and forms of speech creep into use which, although they are not idioms, cannot be justified by either reason or analogy.

Neologism is not reprehensible if the deviation from precedent is in the line of normal movement; which is a very different matter, for instance, from

---

* This "continuing passive present" seems to be fastened upon us; those who inaugurate "sample-rooms," or who report the proceedings on those occasions, being instant in its use, and seizing every opportunity of airing their precision. In the report of a case of a forlorn damsel, I have met "while she was being paid attention to," instead of while she was made love to, or, while she was courted; elsewhere, "while this narrative was being proceeded with," instead of while this story was told; and, "the Democrats of Kentucky are being much exercised at a prospective failure," etc., and even in the London *Spectator*, "Precisely the same scene in a milder form is being witnessed before Paris." The following passage from a leading article in a New York journal clearly illustrates the peculiar absurdity of this phrase:

"History has never moved with strides more gigantic than she has done during the six weeks just closed, and behind the encircling walls and bristling cannon of Paris there may at this moment be transacting a more momentous drama than has been seen there since the *coup d'etat* of 1851, and a more imposing one than has been witnessed since the head of a king went down as the gage of battle to a confederation of kings. 'What will they say in Paris?' is to-day in every one's mouth, while the answer is being flashed across to serve for to-morrow's admiration or blame."

The writer felt that it became him to say "is being flashed across" but just before he had written "there may be transacting," and not, there may be being transacted, which, according to the formula, is absolutely required. *Is being* was very well, and more than well, it was fine; but he instinctively shrank from *be being*; and yet in that is the gist of this whole question.

the substitution of one part of speech for another.
The preterites and participles of the strong verbs
again furnish us with apt illustrations. The original
formation of the past participles of those verbs is in
en, as *ride*, *rode*, *ridden*; but the language in its tendency to contraction and simplification has been
steadily, although very slowly, dropping this syllable.
For example, *fight*, *fought*, *fought(en)*, *drink*, *drank*,
drunk(en), *get*, *gat*, *got(ten)*, *begin*, *began*, *begun(nen)*, to
which category might consistently be added *write*,
wrote, *writ(ten)*. Therefore, *I have writ* is normal;
and the question between *writ* as a past participle
and *written* is merely one of usage. But the use of
writ as a preterite, and that of *wrote* as a participle,
have no such justification. Both are abnormal and
monstrous. Yet those perversions have the support
of such eminent writers as Addison and Pope, Swift,
Prior and Sterne. Addison has, " I remember two
young fellows who *rid*," etc. (*Spectator*, No. 152);
and Pope, " statesmen farces *writ*"; and of course
the Pope-lings all wrote in the same fashion, which,
indeed, was very prevalent in the last century among
the most eminent writers and cultivated people.

But there are phrases and forms of expression
which have been in use for centuries among both
the learned and the ignorant, the cultured and the
rude, and which have passed or are passing out of
use, not by way of an unthinking conformity to
capricious fashion, but because of a perception that
they are at variance with reason. One of these is
the double negative which, by Anglo-Saxon and
early English speakers and writers, was universally
used to strengthen a negation. It may be that the
change was in a measure due to the attempt to

construct a grammar of the English language upon that of the Latin, in which two negatives were equivalent to an affirmative. But it seems to me that it was chiefly owing to a deliberate conformity to the requirements of logic, which in the process of time was inevitable, and which, once attained, will never be abandoned until language comes to be informed by the rule of unreason. If "There is not any reason," predicates the entire absence of reason, surely "There is not no reason," predicates exactly the reverse. The case, instead of being at all high, subtle or mysterious, seems to be one of the simplest that can be put before any reasonable creature. It is even stronger than that as to the double superlative, which went out in company with the double negative about the beginning of the seventeenth century. For as to the double superlative the question is almost one of mere superfluity. Look for a moment at this passage in Bishop Tunstall's Palm Sunday Sermon (A. D. 1539), a piece of English well worth study:

"It was harde suffering that He suffered for wicked men. It was more harde that He suffered of wicked men. And the most hardest of all was that He suffered with wicked men."

When Tunstall wrote it was the custom to double the comparative as well as the superlative. But here we have "more hard," and yet "most hardest." Now can there be a doubt that if *more hard* expresses the comparative degree, *most hard* equally expresses the superlative? and, *vice versa*, that if the learned and clear-headed Tunstall was right in writing *most hardest*, he was wrong, or at least in-

sufficient, in writing *more hard?*   We may be sure
that it is owing to such perception and such reasoning, first on the part of careful and thoughtful
writers—who generally do, in very deed, evolve
their language from the depths of their own consciousness, although some are content with fishing
theirs from the shallows of usage—and afterwards
on the part of the cultivated, and then of people in
general, that the use of the double comparative and
superlative, as well as of the double negative, disappeared from English speech.

Under a like influence of reason another old usage
has given up its hold on the language, and we may
be sure forever—the separation of the limiting
adjective from the word which it modifies.   Thus
Bunyan makes Interpreter's minstrel sing, "The
Lord is only my support."   Now Bunyan meant
not that the Lord was nothing but a support to the
singer, but either that the Lord and none other was
his support, or that the Lord was his single and
sufficient support.   Nowadays we write more correctly, The Lord only is my support, or The Lord is
my only support; both of which phrases express
one fact indeed, but not the same conception of the
fact.   The former use of *only* and similar adjectives,
was the general one, even in literature, until a comparatively recent period, and a remnant of it still
exists in common speech.   Shakespeare even makes
a page in "As You Like It" say that hawking and
spitting and saying we are hoarse are "the only
prologues to a bad voice," an assertion seeming so
absurdly at variance with the fact that I was
tempted to transpose *only* and read "only the prologues to a bad voice."   But Shakespeare, I am

sure, wrote "the only," etc., according to the inexact usage of his time. So we hear now sensible,
educated, farmer folk say, "That is most an excellent apple" (I heard it but a short time ago), or
"That was most a capital sermon," instead of a
most excellent, a most capital. And in old sermons
and moral essays phrases like "so oft to wallowe
in such his wickednesse" are common. Modern
usage, which requires that the adjective, or modifying word or phrase, shall not be separated from the
word or phrase which it modifies, is a deliberate
conformity to the characteristic logical structure of
the English sentence.

Another phrase "sanctioned" by universal usage
is disappearing under our eyes at this day before
the advance of reason—*whether or no*. It is now
seen, to cite for instance an old story, that there
will be Divine service at this meeting-house on
next Wednesday evening whether [it rains] or
[rains] *not ;* and therefore *whether or no* is doomed.
Now fifty or a hundred or two hundred years ago
whether or not would have been the correct form
and good English, just as it is now, although *whether
or no*, being in universal use, was admissible.

Yet another example of the so-called authoritative
misuse of language is the use of *had* in the phrases, *I
had rather*, *You had better*. This has the sanction of
usage for centuries, not only by the English-speaking
people generally, but by their greatest and most
careful writers. Nothing, however, among the few
enduring certainties of language is more certain than
that *had* expresses perfected and past possession.
How, then, consistently with reason, and with its
constant and universally accepted meaning, in every

other connection, can it be used to express future
action? A perception of this incongruity, and a consequent uneasiness as to the use of these phrases, is
becoming common, and it is safe to say that they
will, ere long, begin to be dropped in favor of a more
logical and self-consistent phraseology. *Had rather*
will probably yield to *would rather*, and *had better*
to *might better*. In like position is the use of the
present perfect and the perfect infinitive, thus: If
I had have done, I was ready to have gone, which
is supported by the best usage of centuries. Bishop
Jewell writes, "the church was ready to have fallen."
There seems to be no doubt that this is logically incorrect. Jewell meant that the church was ready to
fall; we should say, If I had done, I was ready to
go; and we may be sure that, ere long, this phraseology will be deliberately substituted for the other
on logical grounds.

I pass over *right away* in the sense of immediately, which is in common use here among the most
cultivated people, merely with the mention of it as
altogether unjustifiable on any ground, and as having no affinity whatever with *straightway*. It is an
undoubtable Americanism, one of the very few words
or phrases, not slang, which can be properly so
called. *Different to* is as exclusively British. It has
come into use since the Commonwealth and the
Restoration, and it pervades British speech and literature even of the highest class, producing such combinations as the following:

The words *la maniere Gottica* appear to have been first applied by
the Italian writers, to distinguish the previous style of architecture to
that then in vogue.—London *Athenæum*, Nov. 9, 1859.

It is true that England stands to America, in point of power, some

ing different to that of Athens to the Rome of Cicero.—London
pectator Nov 25, 1865.

A word used in both countries, but more commonly with us, *lengthy*, is a marked example illustra-
ing my present position. It is illogical, at variance
ith analogy, and it is entirely needless, as it has
surped—who knows how or why?—the rightful
lace of a good and well-connected English word,
hich does properly express that which *lengthy* ex-
resses only on sufferance, and by reason of general
ut unjustifiable usage. And yet even Mr. Lowell
ot only uses it but speaks well of it, as a word "civ-
ly compromising between *long* and *tedious*," which
ve have "given back to England." It is true that
English does need such a word, and therefore had it
efore there could have been Americanisms. For
id not Puritan sermons precede Presidents' mes-
ages? Adjectives expressing likeness in quality are
ormed in English from immaterial nouns, by a suffix
hich would have at once occurred to Mr. Lowell if
e had used, instead of the Romance word *tedious*,
he Anglo-Saxon *wearisome* or *tiresome*. The family
s numerous—*lonesome, wholesome, irksome, handsome,*
loathsome, frolicsome, burdensome, and the like. And
o from Anglo-Saxon times to very modern days we
ave had the analogous word *longsome*, meaning, so
ong as to be almost wearisome or tedious. It is
ommon with the Elizabethan writers, so well known
o Mr. Lowell, and Prior is cited for its use by Web-
ter. Bishop Hall, in his "Defence of the Humble
Remonstrance," writes: "They have had so little
mercy on him as to put him to the penance of their
ongsome volume." It is manifest that writers who

use *wearisome*, *irksome*, and *burdensome* can have no
consistent objection to *longsome*, which has long and
eminent usage in its favor, and which Mr. Lowell
might well bring up again, as Tennyson has brought
up *rathe*. The objection to *lengthy* seems to be well
taken. As to our having given the latter back to
England, it may be said that an instance of the use
of the word before England gave her people and
her language to America has not yet been produced,
and, according to my observation, does not exist.

Another error common among cultivated writers
and speakers is the use of adverbs with the verb to
look, as, He looked wretchedly, She looked beautifully. It might as well be said that the grass looks
greenly, or the man looks bluely. A man who lives
wretchedly will probably look wretched ; a woman
who is formed and dressed beautifully will look
beautiful. The error is the consequence of a confusion of *look* in the sense to direct the eye, and *look*
in the sense of to seem, to appear. The same persons who say that a man looked wretchedly, or a
woman looked beautifully, would not say that he
seemed wretchedly, or she seemed beautifully. In
the phrases, He looked well, She seemed ill, *well* and
ill are not really adverbs. Such phrases as, I had
rather, You had better, Had have done, Ready to
have fallen, Right away, Different to, and Looked
wretchedly, have, it need hardly be said, nothing in
common with such as, We made the land, The ship
stood up the bay, He took his journey (Jewell writes
"tooke his progresse"), They came in thick, He took
her to wife, A house hard by, He took up with her,
He did it out of hand, I won't put up with it,

Given to hospitality, Stricken in years. The latter are truly idiomatic, and generally metaphorical; and, although they defy analysis, they are not, like the former at variance with themselves and defiant of reason.

This healthy tendency toward logical correctness in language is liable to perversion; a perversion to which we owe such phrases as "is being built," and "written over the signature." The former is due to an inability to perceive that a word formed upon a verb by the suffix *ing* (*e. g., building*) may be either a verbal noun or a participle, and have a passive or an active signification according to its place in the sentence and the words with which it is connected, and that the combination of the present participle with the perfect, (*e.g., being built, having been*), logically expresses action or being which is complete at the time spoken of. The latter is the product of a prim and narrow righteousness of mind incapable of sympathy with that free, figurative use of words which gives strength and richness to much of the daily speech of simple folk, and which is so characteristic of the nervous and vivid phraseology of the Elizabethan period. Both these incapacities are illustrated in the following dialogue. It is said to have taken place somewhere in Massachusetts, and it was published in the newspaper from which I quote it "for the benefit of grammarians."

Old Gentleman.—"Are there any houses building in your village?"

Young Lady.—"No, Sir. There is a new house being built for Mr. Smith, but it is the carpenters who are building."

Gentleman.—True; I sit corrected. To be building is certainly a different thing from to be being built. And how long has Mr. Smith's house been being built?"

Lady.—(Looks puzzled a moment, and then answers rather abruptly.) "Nearly a year."

Gentleman.—'How much longer do you think it will be being built?"

Lady.—(Explosively.) "Don't know."

Gentleman.—" I should think Mr. Smith would be annoyed by its being so long being built, for the house he now occupies being old, he must leave it, and the new one being only being built, instead of being built as he expected he cannot—"

At this point, it is said, the young lady disappeared; and here I return from my digression. If, then, novelty is not a tenable ground of objection to a word or a phrase, and long usage is not in itself full justification, and if the example of writers eminent for the instruction or the pleasure they give is not authoritative when they disregard reason and analogy, what is the rule or standard by which language may be tested, and the appeal to which is final? The question is answered in the putting of it. There is no such absolute rule. Usage gives immunity to use; but the court that pronounces judgment upon language is a mixed commission of the common and the critical, before whom precedent and good usage have presumptive authority, on the condition that they can bear the test of criticism, that is, of reason. To that test they are continually subjected, and before it they are compelled frequently to give way. Usage is not a guarantee of correctness; criticism is incapable of creation. By the former, acting instinctively, language is produced and has its life. By the latter, it is wrought toward a logical precision and symmetrical completeness, which it constantly approximates, but which, owing to its unstable nature and the uncontrollable influences to which it yields, it can never perfectly attain.

CONCLUSION.

It is not for lack of material at hand that I here end this series of articles, which has stretched out far beyond the not very definite limits of my original design. I have passed by some subjects unnoticed that I purposed to take in hand, but I have also been led whither I did not think of going when I set out. If my readers have lost anything, they have also gained something in the event. That it should be so was hardly to be avoided. To go directly to a fixed point, which is the only object of one's journey, is easy; but a tour of observation is generally brought to an end with some proposed object left unattained, through the failure of time and means, and often by the weariness of the observers. If those who have gone with me, in some cases as my confiding fellow-students, in others as my sharp and vigilant censors, — a sort of linguistic detective police, — do not rejoice at the termination of our word-tour for the latter reason, I have been more fortunate, either in my subjects or in their treatment, than I could have reasonably hoped to be. If I have seemed to neglect the important for the trivial, and to ask my readers to give time and attention to the consideration of minute distinctions which they have thought might better be occupied with the discussion of great principles, or at least with

the investigation of the laws of speech, it should be
remembered that linguistic discussion, from its very
nature, must be minute; that the widest difference
in the meaning of words and of sentences may be
made by the slightest changes; that the wealth of
language is a sum of trifles; that that which is in a
great measure determined by arbitrary usage cannot be judged upon general principles; and that that
cannot be tried by its conformity to law for which
no law has yet been established. This, true of all
languages, is particularly true of English, which is
distinguished among the outcomings of Babel for its
composite character and its unsystematic, although
not unsymmetrical, development. It is, I suspect,
less a structure and more a spontaneous growth
than any other language that has a known history
and a literature. Through all languages, as through
all connected phenomenons, there may be traced
certain continuous or often-repeated modes of general development, which may be loosely called
laws; and upon those there have been attempts,
more or less successful, to found a universal grammar or system of speech formation. But upon this
field of inquiry I have not professed to enter; having
devoted myself to the consideration of what is peculiar to our mother-tongue, rather than to what she
has in common with others. Even in this respect,
what I have written is at least as far from being
complete as my object in writing was from completeness.

The series has been honored by an attention that
gratified and cheered me as I wrote. I owe much
to my critics; not only to those who have given me

a favorable hearing and insured it for me from others, but to those who have endeavored to sting me with sneers and overwhelm me with ridicule, partly from a sense of duty to their language and their kind, and partly that they might show their readers that, with all my deficiencies, I had the merit of being the occasion of the display of superior knowledge, if not of superior courtesy, in others. To the latter, indeed, I stand more indebted than to the former; for it is not from our friends that we learn, but from our enemies. They show us where we are weak. And, besides, few of mine have failed, while giving me instruction in English, to furnish me with the most valuable means of improvement in the use of language — examples of false syntax for correction. Of these, however, I have not availed myself publicly for the instruction of others, although I might have crucified most of my critics upon crosses made out of their own heads. And, indeed, in my search for examples I have generally turned from the writings of my immediate contemporaries and countrymen to those of other generations and other countries, or to the anonymous pages of public documents and newspapers.

Many letters have come to me with welcome questions, objections, suggestions, of which I have had time and opportunity to notice very few, to my regret. Among the remarks I have made, none was so fruitful of letters of information as my mere passing allusion to the slang phrase "a continental damn." The number of "The Galaxy" in which it was made was hardly published before I received a letter informing me of the existence in this country, at the remote period of seventy or eighty years, of a paper currency called continental, and that this currency was worthless, and that hence — and so forth, and so forth. This was soon followed by others to the same effect, their numbers increasing as the time wore on. They came to me from the north, south, east, west, and middle; from Passamaquoddy and the Gulf; from Squam Beach and Lower California. I might almost say or sing that they were sent from Greenland's icy mountains, from India's coral strand, to tell me that there had been Continental money in this land. They came to me at "The Galaxy" office, at my own office, at my house. Like Pharaoh's frogs in number and in pertinacity, they climbed up into my bed-chamber, and I have the satisfaction of knowing that, like the frogs, some of them went into my oven. I dreaded meeting my friends in the street; for I felt that there was not one of them that did not long to lead me quietly aside, even if he did not do so, and say, "About that continental damn, I think I can set you right. After the Revolution there was a vast amount of paper money circulating through the country. This was called the Continental currency, and, as it proved to be worthless —" and so forth, and so forth. Really, I hope my friends will not misapprehend me when I say that it is generally safe to assume that the court knows a little law. I had heard, before the coming of this year of grace 1869, that, after the Revolution, there was a vast amount of paper money circulating through the country; that this was called Continental currency; that it proved worthless — and so forth, and so forth.

Yet I do not incline to the opinion that hence comes our "continental damn." The phrase seems to me a counterpart, if not a mere modification of others of the same sort — a tinker's damn, a trooper's damn; and as the troops of the colonies were called Continentalers, or Continentals, during the war, and for many years afterward, it seems to me much more probable that the phrase in question was, at first, a Continental's damn, from which the sign of the possessive was gradually dropped, than that an adjective was taken from money and used to qualify a curse; and still more probable that the epithet was added in that mere disposition toward the use of vague, big, senseless phrases that moulds the speech of such as use this one.

Among the propositions and requests that have been elicited by the articles embodied in this volume, is one which comes to me from many quarters, and which one correspondent puts in the following attractive form to the editors of "The Galaxy": "Could not he [*i. e.*, the present writer] be induced to prepare a book for schools which would embody his ideas and all that it would be necessary for scholars to learn in regard to the use and construction of language, and so save many cries and tears that go out over the present unintelligible books that pass for grammars? I am sure that a future generation, if not the present, would rise up and bless his name." This request is made by a teacher, as it has been by others of the same honorable profession. I answer, that I would gladly act on this suggestion if it were probable that any responsible and competent pub-

lisher would make it prudent for me to do so. It
would be delightful to believe that the next generation would rise up and call me blessed; but I am
of necessity much more interested in the question
whether the present generation would rise up and
put its hand in its pocket to pay me for my labor.
Any one who is acquainted with the manner in
which school-books are "introduced" in this country knows that the opinions of competent persons
upon the merits of a book have the least possible
influence upon its coming sufficiently into vogue to
make its publication profitable; and publishers, like
other men of business, work for money. One of
the trade made, I know, — although not to me, — an
answer like this to a proposition to publish a short
series of school-books: "I believe your books are
excellent; but supposing that they are all that you
believe them to be, after stereotyping them I should
be obliged to spend one hundred thousand dollars
and more in introducing them. I am not prepared
to do this, and therefore I must say, No, at once.
The merit of a school-book has nothing to do with
its value in trade." And the speaker was a man of
experience. Provoked by the ineptness of a school-
book which fell into my hands, I went once to an
intelligent and able teacher, in whose school I
knew it was used, and calling his attention to the
radical faults in the book, — faults of design which
I knew there was no need that I should point out to
him in detail, — I asked him why he used for elementary instruction a book so fitted to mislead his
scholars. His answer was, "All that you say is
true. I know that the book is a very poor one; but

we are ordered to use it. What can I do?" Now, one of the body that gave this order was, at that time, a neighbor of mine — a coarse, low-minded, entirely uneducated man, who was growing rapidly rich. He was about as fit to pronounce upon the merits of a school-book as Caligula's horse was for the consulship. The publication of elementary school-books and dictionaries is one of the most profitable branches of the trade, if books can be "introduced" into general use; but otherwise it is not so; and publishers manage this part of their business just as railway companies and other corporations do — with a single eye to profit. A railway company, managed by men of respectable position, finds itself threatened with a law restraining its privileges, or desires the passage of a law increasing them. Its agents make a calculation somewhat in this form: To submit to the threatened law, or to do without the one that is desired, will involve the loss of so much money; to defeat the law in one case, or to obtain it in the other, by spending money to influence votes, will cost so much less. The latter course is taken, without scruple or hesitation. With the company it is a mere matter of business; the morals of the question are the concern of the other parties to the arrangement.*

* That these strictures made in "The Galaxy" of May, 1869, were just and timely, is shown by the following articles, which subsequently appeared in "The American Booksellers' Guide" (January, 1870), and "The Evening Mail" (March 3, 1870).

"A PROTEST ADDRESSED TO PUBLISHERS OF SCHOOL-BOOKS.

"In the last number of the GUIDE we reprinted from the Brooklyn "Eagle" the list of school-books adopted by the Board of Education of that city, and the prices at which the books were furnished by the publishers. These prices were about one third of those at which the books are regularly sold. They were furnished at the reduced prices to influence the Board of Education of Brooklyn to adopt them over

Now, were such a grammar and such a dictionary published as some readers of these articles would like to have, and should they be received with

other books that were offered, and thereby to secure their introduction into the schools.

'This case is only one example of what is being done all over the country by the agents of the school-book houses. The prices of the books sold to Brooklyn, though much less than first cost, are better than are obtained in the majority of cases of what is called 'first introduction.' Introduction is usually effected by exchanging new books for the old ones in use. The house whose books are thus thrown out naturally seeks the first opportunity in any quarter to exchange its books for those of its rival.

"The introduction of school-books has become a source of bribery and corruption, which is paralleled only in the municipal politics of our largest city. Boards of Education are completely demoralized. Cases are known of exchanges of books being made in some cities as often as once a year. We shall not refer to the damaging effect of such changes upon the progress of education. Pupils are little more than made acquainted with the rudiments of a study as presented in a text-book, and prepared to follow out the method of the author, when, lo! another text-book is put into his hands, and he is compelled to discard the old and take up a new system. But a few changes of this kind is required to muddle the clearest intelligence.

"It is because of its effect upon the trade that we desire to protest against this system of bribery, and the damaging reduction of prices all over the country. In the first place, it causes a direct loss to publishers; and, secondly, it ruins the business in school-books of the local booksellers.

"It is estimated that the loss caused to publishers by this unscrupulous and corrupt competition annually amounts to over five hundred thousand dollars. Nothing is really gained by this wasteful expenditure, as the same books would be sold in about the same proportion if it was entirely discontinued. What is gained in one place by unfair means is lost in another by the same means. Whether publishers confine themselves to fair methods or foul, as the same agencies are open to all, the effects will in general be about equal. If this vast sum were saved to be employed in legitimate channels, better prices could be paid to authors and better work obtained, more could be spent upon the mechanical execution of books, they could be offered lower, and, lastly, publishers would realize more money, and their business would rest upon a securer basis.

"But the greatest injury is done to the local booksellers, who sell the larger portion of the books. By publishers offering their books through periodical travelling agents at one half the retail prices, the trade of the booksellers is not only taken out of their hands at particular times, but their customers are dissatisfied to pay the regular retail prices at any time. This has become such a source of dissatisfaction that we almost wonder at retail booksellers undertaking to supply school-books at all. They might compel publishers to deal directly in all cases with the schools, and we doubt if the ruinous prices would, if this were done, be long continued.

"We advise some honorable combination among the leading houses to put an end to this great and growing evil, which is subversive not only of educational progress, but of commercial integrity. Such a combination is possible, and such penalties might be assessed against offenders, by mutual consent, as would redeem the business from its present repulsive aspect." — *American Booksellers' Guide.*

".... Next to the copyright reform, the one thing needed by the publishing trade is the abolition of the present outrageously wasteful system of "introducing" school

favor, they would at once provoke the hostility —
cool, vigilant, business-like — of men who have
many hundreds of thousands of dollars invested in
books — in whole systems of books — planned
upon radically different principles. Until some man
on horseback comes and purges the commonweal,
it always will be necessary to fight these men with
their own weapons. And even then there is the
fight in newspapers, by articles, advertisements,
and opinions from eminent gentlemen. I have
been behind the scenes enough to know thoroughly
how all this business is managed, and I would tell
on very slight provocation. Why, even already
the priests of the present idols have begun to de-
nounce a certain pestilent fellow, and their crafts-
men to cry, Great is Diana of the Ephesians!

To publish, with any chance of success, a book
intended for use in public schools has become a
serious commercial and political undertaking; and,

books. As our readers probably know, it is the almost universal custom of school-
book publishers, for the sake of getting their series used and ousting books of rival
houses, to furnish the former — at least the first lot — at even below cost price, and to
take the old books in part pay, sending them to the junk dealers. Teachers are induced, by the smooth-tongued agents of these houses and the large commissions
which they offer, to change books so frequently that their pupils are in a constant
state of perplexity, while the waste of books is terrible, and all the publishers have
their profits more than half eaten up by the necessary outlays and recriminations.
There are two houses in this country each of which loses probably between two and
three hundred thousand dollars a year in this way, while the total loss to publishers
cannot be much less than a million dollars. We are glad to be able to state that a
movement is now on foot, which bids fair to succeed, toward doing away with this
great evil. Representatives of such houses as Barnes, Harper, Appleton, Sheldon,
etc., of this city, have issued an invitation to twenty-one firms in New York, thirteen in Philadelphia, ten in Boston, and sixteen elsewhere, to send representatives to
meet in this city the 16th of March, and continue in session until some arrangement
is made, looking to more sensible and profitable relations between school-book publishers." — *Evening Mail.*

The proposed meeting was held, and measures were taken which may possibly put
an end to this reproach to the book trade, and to the schools, public and private,
throughout the country.

if nothing more is expected for it than its introduction into private schools, even then it should be in
the hands of publishers sufficiently wealthy and
adroit to make it the interest of teachers to adopt
the book in their schools.   For if it were left to go
upon its mere merits, it would, if good, of course
meet with a certain sale among intelligent and honorable teachers ; but this would be too small to cause
it to be regarded by any enterprising publisher as
profitable investment of money and labor.   For these
reasons I fear that I must be content with dropping
what I have written as seed into the ground, hoping
that it may have life enough to grow and bring forth
fruit, although in that case others will reap the harvest. *Sic vos, non vobis.*

APPENDIX.

I.

HOW THE EXCEPTION PROVES THE RULE.

THE few people who care to say only what they mean, and who therefore think about what they say and what others say to them, must sometimes be puzzled by the reply often made to an objection, " Well, he, or that, is an exception, and you know the exception proves the rule." This is uttered with calm assurance, as conclusive of the question at issue, and is usually received in silence — with an air of indifferent acquiescence on the part of the thoughtless, but on the part of the more thoughtful with a meek expression of bewilderment. The former are saved from the trouble of further mental exertion, and they are content; the latter feel that they have been overcome by the bringing up of a logical canon which always stands ready as a reserve, but the truth of which, admitted as indisputable, they would like very much to be able to dispute. In fact, this pretentious maxim infests discussion, and pervades the every-day talk of men, women, and children. It appears in the writings of historians, of essayists, and of polemics, as well as in those of poets, novelists, and journalists. A legislator will use it to destroy the effect of an instance brought forward which is directly at variance with some general assertion that he has made. " The case so strongly insisted upon by the honorable gentleman does apparently show that all women do not desire the passage of a law permitting them to wear trousers. I admit the preference of Miss Pettitoes for petticoats. But, sir, her case is an exception, and we all know that the exception proves the rule." It enters even into the word-skirmish of flirtation. " How dare you assert," says Miss Demure to Tom Crœsus, defiance on her lip and witchery in her eye, "that women nowadays are all mercenary! Don't you know that is an insult to me?" "Ah, but, Miss Demure," replies the weakly-struggling Crœsus, "you're an exception; and you know the exception proves the rule." Whereupon the lady submits with charming grace to the conqueror, having within her innocent breast the consoling conviction that she is playing her big fish with a skill that will soon lay him gasping at her feet. There is no turn which this maxim is not thus made to serve; and this use of it has gone on for a century and more, and people submit to the imposition without a murmur.

An imposition the maxim is, of the most impudent kind, in its ordinary use; for a mere exception never proved a rule; and that it should do so is, in the very nature of things, and according to the laws of right reason, impossible. Consider a moment. How can the fact that one man, or one thing, of a certain class, has certain traits or relations, prove that others of the same class have opposite traits and other relations? A says, "I, and C, and D, and X, and Y, and Z are white; therefore all the other letters of the alphabet are white." "No, they are not," B answers, "for I am black." "O, you are an exception," A rejoins, "and the exception proves the rule." And A and most of his hearers thereupon regard the argument as concluded, at least for the time being. The supposed example is an extreme one, but it serves none the less the purposes of fair illustration. For of what value, as evidence, upon the color of the alphabet, is the fact that B is black? It merely shows that one letter is black, and that any other may be black, except those which we know to be of some other color. But of the color of the remaining twenty-three letters it tells us nothing; and so far from supporting the assertion that because A, C, D, X, Y, and Z are white, all the other letters are white, it warrants the inference that some of them may be black also. And yet day after day, for a hundred and fifty years,* men of fair intelligence have gone on thoughtlessly citing this maxim, and yielding to its authority when used exactly as it is used in the case above supposed.

For instance, the following passage is from a leading article in the " New York Tribune : " —

" The business of printing books is now leaving the great cities for more economical and more desirable locations. The exceptions rather prove the rule than invalidate it."

How do the exceptions either prove or invalidate the rule? In what way does the fact that there are some printing offices in Boston, New York, and Philadelphia prove that printers generally choose the smaller towns or the country? Plainly, one of these facts has no relations whatever to the other.

In "Lothair," Mr. Disraeli makes Hugo Bohun say that he respects the institution of marriage, but thinks that "every woman should marry, but no man," and to the objection that this view would not work practically, reply, —

" Well, my view is a social problem, and social problems are the fashion at present. It would be solved through the exceptions, which prove the principle. In the first place, there are your swells, who cannot avoid the halter — you are booked when you are born; and then there are moderate men, like myself, who have their weak moments," etc., etc.

* The date of its first appearance in literature or the records of colloquial speech I do not profess to know; but I cannot recollect an instance of its use earlier than the days of the Queen Anne essayists.

Perhaps Mr. Bohun or Mr. Disraeli could explain how the fact that the natures or the circumstances of some men are such that they are likely to marry " proves the principle" that men should not marry. But to the eye of unassisted reason, it is merely evidence in favor of the positive proposition, that whatever men should do, some will marry: it does nothing toward showing that other men should, or should not, either marry or do anything else. If the proposition were that only men of certain natures and circumstances should marry, and it were found that in general only they did marry, there would at least be a connection between the facts and the proposition; which, in Mr. Bohun's argument, there is not.

The London "Spectator," in one of the few discriminating judgements that have recently been published of Dickens's genius, thus supports the opinion that he was unable to express the finer emotions naturally : —

"In the delineation of remorse he is, too, much nearer the truth of emotion than in the delineation of grief. True grief needs the most delicate hand to delineate [it] truly. A touch too much, and you perceive an affectation, and therefore miss the whole effect of bereavement. But remorse, when it is genuine, is one of the simplest of passions, and the most difficult to overpaint. Dickens, with his singular power of lavishing himself on one mood, has given some vivid pictures of this passion which deserve to live. Still, this is the exception, which proves the rule. He can delineate remorse for murder, because there is so little real limit to the feeling, so little danger of passing from the true to the falsetto tone."

Now, in what way does the fact that Dickens had the power of delineating one of the simple passions prove that he had not the power of delineating the more complex? Plainly, it does nothing — can do nothing of the sort, unless by the introduction, as a premise, of the postulate that writers who can delineate simple passions cannot delineate the complex; which is not true, and which is not implied. Such passages as this are mere examples of the habit into which the most intelligent writers and critics have fallen of regarding an exception not merely as an exception, a phenomenon which is the consequence of exceptional conditions, and there an end, but as a proof of the rule which they wish to establish, and which the "exception" would otherwise seem to invalidate.

This habit has arisen, it would seem, out of a slight perversion of a word. For, although an exception does not and cannot prove a rule, the word *exception* being used in its ordinary sense, the exception does prove the rule, the word being used in its proper sense. The fallacious use of the maxim is based on the substitution of a real substantive, that is, a substantive meaning a thing, for a verbal substantive, that is, a substantive meaning an act. The maxim, as we have it, is merely a misleading translation of the old law maxim, *Exceptio probat regulam*, which itself is, if not mutilated, at least imperfect. Now, *Exceptio probat regulam* does not mean that the thing excepted proves the rule, but that the excepting proves the rule. *Exceptio* was translated, and rightly enough, exception. But what was the meaning of that word when the translation was made? What is its primitive meaning now? It is the act of excepting or excluding from a number designated, or from a description. *Exceptio* in Latin, *exception* in English, means not a person or a thing, but an act; and it is this act which proves a rule. But we, having come to use *exception* to mean the person or the thing excepted, receive the maxim as meaning, not that the excepting proves the rule, but the person or thing excepted; and upon this confusion of words we graft a corresponding confusion of thought. The maxim, in its proper signification, is as true as it is untrue in the sense in which it is now almost universally used.

I have said that, if not mutilated, it is at least imperfect. I am unable to cite an instance of its use in any other form than that under which it is now known; but it exists in my mind, whether from memory or from an unconscious filling up of its indicated outlines, in this form : *Exceptio probat regulam, de rebus non exceptis*; i. e., the excepting proves the rule concerning those things which are not excepted. The soundness of the maxim in this form, and the reason for its soundness, will be apparent on a moment's consideration. Suppose that, in a book of travels, we should find this passage: "Here I saw large flocks of birds in the cornfields cawing and tearing up the young corn. In one flock, two of these birds were white." The conclusion warranted by this account would be, that there were crows, or birds like crows, in the country visited by the writer, and that these crows were generally black. The writer would not have said that the birds were black, but his exception of two which were white would go to prove that, "as a rule" (according to our idiom), the birds were black, or at least not white. His exception of the two would prove the rule as to the others. *Exceptio probat regulam, de rebus non exceptis*. Again, if we knew nothing about the elephant, but were to learn that the King of Siam, when he wished to ruin a courtier, distinguished him by sending him a white elephant, — a present which he could not refuse, although the provision for the proper lodging of the beast and attendance on him was sure to eat up a private fortune, — we should be told nothing about elephants in general; yet we should know, without further information, that they were dark colored, because of the implied exception of the white elephant.

The maxim in question is akin to another recognized in law : *Expressio unius, exclusio alterius*; i. e., the expression of one (mode or person) is the exclusion of another. This maxim is no legal fiction or refinement :

it is dictated by common sense, and is a guide of action
in daily life. If we see on the posters of a museum or a
circus, "Admission for children accompanying their parents, Fifteen cents," we know at once that children without their parents are either not admitted at all, or m..st
pay full price. Children themselves act intuitively upon
the reasoning embodied in this maxim. If a parent or a
teacher should go to a room full of children, and say,
"John may come and take a walk with me," they would
know, without the telling, that all except John were expected to remain. They know this just as well as any
lawyer or statesman knows that, when a constitution provides for its own amendment in one way, that very provision was meant to exclude all other methods. The child
and the statesman both act in accordance with the maxim,
Expressio unius, exclusio alterius. Both this maxim
and the one which is the subject of the present article are
founded upon the intuitive perception common to men
of all times and races, and which is developed, as we
have seen, in the very earliest exercise of the reasoning
powers, that an exclusive affirmation implies a corresponding negation.

A rare modern instance of another and really logical
use of the maxim, that the exception proves the rule, is
furnished by Boswell in one of his trivial stories about
Doctor Johnson. It was disputed one evening, when the
Doctor was present, whether the woodcock were a mi-
gratory bird. To the arguments in favor of the theory
of migration, some one replied that argument was of
little weight against the fact that some woodcocks had
been found in a certain county in the depth of winter.
Doctor Johnson immediately rejoined, "That supports
the argument. The fact that a few were found shows
that, if the bulk had not migrated, many would have
been found. *Exceptio probat regulam.*"

Johnson himself affords another example of the same

use of the maxim. In the Preface to his edition of Shakespeare's works, he opposes and ridicules those critics who have supposed that they discovered in Shakespeare imitations of ancient writers, and that these were evidence of great learning. He says, —

"There are a few passages which may pass for imitations, but so few that the exception only confirms the rule. He obtained them from accidental quotation or by oral communication, and, as he used what he had, would have used more if he had obtained it."

Yet another instructive example of the use of this maxim is found in the following passage from Cowper's "Tirocinium, or Review of Schools:" —

"See volunteers in all the vilest arts,
  Men well endowed with honorable parts,
  Designed by Nature wise, but self-made fools:
  All these, and more like these, were made at schools.
  And if by chance, as sometimes chance it will,
  That, though school-bred, the boy is virtuous still,
  Such rare exceptions, shining in the dark,
  Prove rather than impeach the just remark.
  As here and there a twinkling star descried
  Serves but to show how black is all beside."

According to the common use of the maxim, the inference from this passage would be, that a few virtuous school-bred men prove, not what they are evidence of, that virtuous men may be bred at school, but that the rule is, that school-breeding is dangerous to virtue! But they prove that, if they prove it at all, by "shining in the dark;" that is, the surrounding vileness points them out as peculiar and solitary: it excepts them; and this excepting (*exceptio*) as to them proves the rule as to the mass.

The common use of this maxim is worthy only of idiots, for it involves idiotic reasoning; a good example of which would be the application of the maxim to the following criticism of two political conventions : —

"We dare say, if the truth were all known, there would be little to choose between the two conventions in point of morals or manners. Doubtless there were high-minded and able gentlemen in both, but we fear such were the exception, and not the rule."

Now, if the exception proves the rule, those exceptions, that is, those high-minded and able gentlemen would of themselves be evidence that the rest were not able and high-minded. Another characteristic example would be the following : — It is declared that all men are totally depraved. But we find that A is not totally depraved. But this only shows that A is an exception, and his not being totally depraved proves the rule of total depravity. That such an application of the maxim should be made day after day for generations among people of moderate sense is striking evidence, on the one hand, of the way in which the modification of meaning in a word may cause a perversion of an established formula of thought ; and, on the other, of the supineness with which people will submit to the authority of a maxim which sounds wise and has the vantage-ground of age, particularly if they cannot quite understand it, and it saves them the trouble of thinking. Let any man invent such a maxim, and use well good opportunities of asserting it, and he may be pretty sure that his work, if not himself, will attain a very considerable degree of what is called immortality. The failure of such a maxim to be accepted as conclusive would be a sign of the decline of that peculiar mode of reasoning which would insist upon this failure itself as an exception that proved the rule to which it did not conform, and of the reëstablishment of that other mode which claims that, in general, the excepting proves the rule concerning that which is not excepted.

II.

CONTROVERSY.

PERHAPS the following letter, which was published in "The Round Table" of February 27, 1869, and the reply, which appeared in the next number of the same paper, may interest, or at least amuse, some of the readers of this volume. I may say here without impropriety, I hope, that the articles on Words and their Uses which appeared in "The Galaxy" were, as is customary with me, written in haste and under the pressure of a cry for copy from the printing office. Although the series extended through two years, not one of them was begun before that cry was heard, or was ready one hour before the last minute when the article could be received; and the manuscript was sent off to the printer with the ink damp upon the last page. It was put in type that day, and the next was stereotyped. Throughout the whole series I did not rewrite a single page, or, I believe, a single sentence. I generally saw a proof, which I corrected at my business office within the hour of its receipt; but sometimes I did not. One of those cases in which I did not see a proof was made the occasion of the following communication. I do not offer this confession as an excuse or defence of any essential error. A critic can concern himself only with what is produced: he cannot take into consideration the circumstances of its production, even if he knows them. It would have been well if the articles had been written more deliberately, and corrected more carefully; but had I waited till I could do that, they would, in all probability, not have been written at all; which alternative is doubtless the one that would have been preferred by my censor. In choosing a specimen of the attacks to which these articles subjected me (from all of which I tried to learn something, but to only two or three of which I made any reply), I have taken his, because he was very much the ablest and most learned of my critics:—

STAND-POINT, ETC.

To the Editor of the Round Table.

Sir: I noticed in your issue of January 9 a letter from "J. B." upon the word *stand-point*, condemning it as an exploded heresy, and moralizing upon the "total depravity of human nature" which after such an explosion could still countenance the heresy. Your correspondent informs the world that "Mr. White recently in the "Galaxy," and Mr. Gould, at greater length, in "Good English," have thoroughly analyzed and exposed" "the literary abortion." Such language, so unlike that of a man of scholarship or culture, led me to think that perhaps your correspondent did not know very much of etymology after all, and that his pitying contempt might be nothing more than a cloak for sciolism or ignorance. So, being somewhat interested in the fate of the word *stand-point*, I gave "J. B.'s" letter a second reading, and found my suspicions verified. He says,—

"The two words *stand* and *point* cannot be grammatically joined together; the first word must be changed to a participle in order to make them legally united. Stand*ing*-point is English."

From this it is evident that "J. B." thinks the former half of the word *standing-point* to be a participle; so also of *turning-point*, *landing-place*, etc. What will he say when it is suggested to him that in each of these compounds the former element is a substantive, and not a participle, and that a participle placed before a noun in

English, whether to form a compound or not, always qualifies the noun — becomes, in fact, an adjective! *Jumping-jack, dancing-girl,* are examples of compounds formed of a qualifying participle and a noun, for *dancing-girl* means a girl who dances. *Stumbling-block,* on the contrary, does not mean a block that stumbles, nor does *turning-point* mean a point that turns, or *landing-place* a place that lands. The words mean respectively a block which causes stumbling (*stumbling* is used as a noun 1 John ii. 10), a point at which turning (or a turn) takes place, a place for landing (=disembarkation). On the same analogy is formed the word *standing-point,* which means not a point which stands, but a point where one takes his stand, *standing* being a noun, and not a participle. But *stand,* as the phrase "takes his stand" shows, is as good a noun as *standing,* and has the additional advantage of not being ambiguous, as the latter is. "J. B.," however, evidently thinks that in the word *stand-point, stand* must necessarily be part of a verb, inasmuch as he talks about turning it into a participle. Now he must know, for he has read Mr. White's remarks in the *Galaxy,* that *stand-point* is an Anglicized form of the German *Standpunkt.* If he were acquainted with German, he would know that in that word the former element, *Stand,* is a noun; were it a verb, the word would be *Stehpunkt,* on the analogy of *Drehbank, Wohnzimmer,* and so forth. This being so, why, if we may say *play-ground, bath-room, death-bed,* may we not say *stand-point?* Even supposing the former half were a verb, why might we not admit the compound on the analogy of *go-cart, wash-tub, thresh-old, dye-house?* So much for the form of the word. But "J. B." proceeds : —

"Standing-point is English; but the difficulty with that is, that nobody can be fooled into believing that it means 'point of view.' Hence it cannot replace *stand-point,* which people fool themselves into believing *does* mean 'point of view.'"

Now, it is well to remark that *point of view* is not an indigenous English expression any more than *stand-point* is. It is simply a verbal translation of the French *point de vue*, and cannot plead analogy in justification of its adoption to the same extent as *stand-point* can View-point or *viewing-point* would be more correct. I am aware that we can say *point of attack;* but that, also, is a translation of the French *point d'attaque.* So far, then, as the origin and form of the expressions *stand-point* and *point of view* are concerned, *stand-point* has a decided advantage. It is also the more convenient expression, and the only thing, therefore, that remains to be decided with regard to it is, whether it gives any intelligible signification. When I say, "Viewed from a scientific stand-point, it is false" (*Vom wissenschaftlichen Standpunkt angesehen, ist es falsch*), what do I mean? Simply, "Viewed from the position occupied by science, it is false." Here *stand-point* has not the meaning of *point of view;* and, indeed, I doubt whether it ever has precisely. There is no other word in the English language that will exactly express the meaning of *stand-point*, as any one may convince himself by trying to express otherwise the phrase, "The stand-point of philosophy is different from that of science." "The philosophical point of view is different from the scientific" has quite a different signification.

After convincing myself of the inaccuracy of "J. B.'s" remarks on the word *stand-point*, I thought I should like to know what Mr. White had to say about it. Accordingly, I procured a copy of the number of the *Galaxy* containing the article in which his remarks on the word occur. These I found very temperate, and I regretted that I could not agree with him. But when I came to read the rest of his article, I found so many indications of want of profound knowledge and scholar-like accuracy, that I bade my regrets farewell. To give an instance or two. In speaking of the word *telegram*, which he does not seem to know is altogether an incorrect formation, he says, —

> "If *engrave* (from *en* and *grapho*) gives us rightly *engrave* and *engraving*, *photograph* or *photograve* should give us *photographer* and *photographing*, and *telegraph*, *telegrapher*, and *telegraphing*."

This would be true if *engrave* did come from *ἐν* and *γράφω;* but it does not, and only a person profoundly ignorant of English etymology could have supposed that it did. In the first place, the existence of the verb *grave* as a verb (see Chaucer, "Troilus and Creseide," Book II. Proeme, line 47, "Eke some men *grave* in tre, som in stone wall." Ibid, Book III., line 1468, etc.) and the form of the participle *engraven* might have sufficed to convince Mr. White that the word *engrave* was of Saxon origin. A very common verb in Anglo-Saxon is *grafan* (conj. *grafe*, *gróf*, *grafen*), *e. g.,* Psalm lxxvii. 58 [English version lxxviii. 58] : —

> "Svâ hi his yrre oft âveahtan,
> þonne hí oferhydig up-âhófan
> and him vohgodu vorhtan and *gráfan*."

The forms *graue* and *igrauen* occur in Layamon, *grave*, *grauea*, *grauen* (and *graued*) in Middle-English, and *grave*, *graved*, *graven* (and *graved*) in Modern English. It is only in comparatively recent times that the compound *engrave* has replaced the simple verb. It is no doubt true that *grave* is from the same root as *γράφω*, but that is quite a different thing from saying that it is derived from *γράφω*. It is the same as the Mœso-Gothic *graban* (see Ulfilas, Luke vi. 48. Galeiks 1st mann timrjandin razn. saei *grob* jah gadiupida, etc.), Old Saxon *bigraban*. Old Frankish *greva* (whence modern French *graver*), Swedish *gräfva*, *graf*, Danish *grave*, German *graban*. Spanish *grabar*. I hope this is sufficient to show that the word *engrave* is not of Greek origin. But apart from these considerations, Mr. White ought to have known at what period Greek words began to be transferred directly into English. In the year 1500 there were probably but four men in all England who knew anything of Greek.

Under the head of *Enquire, Enclose, Endorse*, Mr. White says, —

> "A much-respected correspondent urges the condemnation of these words, and the advocacy of their disuse, because they are respectively from the Latin *inquiro, includo*, and *in dorsum*, and should, therefore, be written *inquire, inclose, indorse*. He is in error. They are, to be sure, of Latin origin, but remotely; they came to us directly from the French *enquirer, encloser*, and *endosser*."

There is, no doubt, a verb *endosser*, but who ever heard of such monstrosities as *enquirer* and *encloser?* Only writers who, in their ignorance of French and of the primary principles of etymology, coin them out of their own brain. The French verbs corresponding to *enquire* and *enclose* are *enquérir* and *enclore*. These are written with various orthographies, it is true, but never as Mr. White writes them. His remark notwithstanding, Chaucer and his contemporaries wrote *enquest, enquere*, seldom *enquyre*.

Mr. White very modestly confesses, —

> "My having in Sanskrit, like Orlando's beard, is a younger brother's revenue — what I can glean from the well-worked fields of my elders and betters."

That he might have said as much, or even more, of his English and French, judging them by the particular article under consideration, I think I have shown abundantly. I am almost tempted to leave his Latin unimpeached, to spare him " the most unkindest cut of all ; " but I cannot. *Il a perdu son latin.* Under the head of the word *Reliable*, he says, —

27

"This view of *laughable* seems to be supported by the fact that the counterpart of that adjective, *risible*, is not formed from the verb *rideo* — to laugh (although, of course, derived from it); but from the noun *risum* — a laugh, or laughter."

I should like to ask Mr. White, first, whether he knows that *rideo* means *I laugh at* as well as *I laugh;* second, whether he does not know that adjectives in *bilis* are sometimes formed from the stem of the supine as well as from that of the present of verbs; third, in what Latin author he ever found the noun *risum*, meaning a laugh or laughter; fourth, what *risibilis* means in Latin.

It would be easy to show ignorance of languages on the part of public instructors by many more examples, but I think the above will suffice to make evident the fact that their knowledge is often of the flimsiest kind. There are, unfortunately, in this country a large number of persons who get a reputation for learning simply because they have the presumption to write on learned subjects; their statements pass among the multitude unchallenged, because the country lacks a learned class, which, by its very presence, might deter sciolists from disgracing themselves by exhibitions of ignorance and presumption. I wait and hope for better things.

Yours very faithfully,　　　Θ Δ

January 30, 1869.

MR. GRANT WHITE CONFESSES.

To the Editor of the Round Table.

Sir: The "Round Table" of February 27, which reached me only this morning, contains a communication, the purpose of which is, first, to maintain that *stand-point* is a nice English compound, and last (this being the gist of the matter), to make the little argument on *stand-point* the start-point of a tilt against me, overthrowing entirely my credit for knowledge of Latin, French, English, and other things in general, and ending in a denunciation of "the public instructors" and "the multitude" of "this country;" which goal, when comfortably reached, is my assailant's sit-point.

That your readers may know whom I mean, I will say that the article to which I refer is signed with the strange characters "Θ Δ," which, as nearly as I am able to discover, are two Greek letters, named *theta* and *delta*. Even to a person less ignorant than I am, these characters would only conceal the identity of an assailant who calls me out by my own name. But perhaps he hid his full terrors in kindness to me, or it did not suit his own purpose to let me know who it is that is hunting me for the amusement of the public; for in the latter case I might have seen that I was what the more learned boys at my school called a " γον κυν," and have come down at once, thus spoiling sport.

As to *stand-point*, I shall have no dispute with him. I shall merely ask to be allowed to say " from a scientific point of view," instead of " viewed from a scientific stand-point," and " the position of philosophy," instead of " the stand-point of philosophy." But I hope that it will not be looked upon by " Θ Δ " as an instance of my presumption, that I protest against his telling "J. B." that he " must know, *for* he has read Mr. White's remarks in the *Galaxy*, that *stand-point* is an Anglicized form of the German *Stand-punkt*." That I said no such thing as to the origin of the compound in question, will be seen by this repetition from the " Galaxy " of what I did say : —

" STAND-POINT. — To say the best of it, this is a poor compound. It receives some support, but not full justification, from the German *Stand-punkt*."

" Θ Δ " may think that because two similar word-combinations or phrases exist in two languages, one must be formed by a mere phonetic change (in this case an Anglicization) of the other. Such is not my view of the formation of language. If your correspondent will consult some elementary philological work, he will learn that like forms of expression are found in languages which are not only without kindred, but without contact; and that such forms, being developed according to mental laws common to the race, are said to support each other.

Your correspondent again misrepresents me by saying that I do not seem to know " that *telegram* is altogether an incorrect formation." Here is what I did say : —

"TELEGRAM. — This word, claimed as an 'American' invention, has taken root quickly, and is probably well fixed in the language. It is convenient, and is correctly enough formed to pass muster."

I have mistaken the force of my language if it did not convey to my readers, every one of them, that in my judgement *telegram* is an incorrectly formed word, but that the irregularity is of a kind not worth making a point about.

" Θ *Δ* " says, in relation to my remarks on the etymology of *enquire, enclose,* and *endorse,* —

"There is, no doubt, a verb *endosser,* but who ever heard of such monstrosities as *enquirer* and *encloser ?* Only writers who, in their ignorance of French and of the primary principles of etymology, coin them out of their own brain."

Certainly I neither heard nor coined them. The mere turning to " Webster's Unabridged " would have saved me from such a blunder. " Θ *Δ*'s " letter seems like the fruit of a frequent consultation of that work, the learning of which may be had by any one in a few minutes for a few dollars, even in a copy, like mine, of the old edition. To say nothing of knowledge, I must have been very lazy, or very imprudent, not to turn to that cheap " cram," if I did nothing more. I wrote *enquerir, enclore,* and *endosser.*[*]

[*] The mode and spirit of this critic's attacks — I will not say their purpose, for I sincerely believe that he did not mean to be dishonest — may be inferred from the fact that he again held me up as a pretentious ignoramus because in the passage quoted

Having ruthlessly shown that I know nothing of English, or French, or "the primary principles of etymology," he is "almost tempted" to let me off without further exposure. But an opinion I hazarded upon the formation of *laughable* is too much for his self-denial, and he says of me, "*Il a perdu son latin.*" I cannot be sufficiently grateful for the tenderness and the delicacy that led him to couch in a language unknown to me the terrors of the sentence it became his duty to pronounce. But the designs of benevolence are sometimes defeated, and the mysteries of learning are not always impenetrable. I have discovered — in what way is my own secret — that the meaning of this awful denunciation is, that I have lost my Latin.* But even here is hidden balm ; even here, benign concession. What I have lost I must once have had. I confess that I have lost something, perhaps without compensating gain, since a body of learned men sent me out from them with a certificate that I was an ingenuous youth, of faultless morals, imbued with humane letters. (If they had but known what they were doing !) But nevertheless I shall endeavor to answer these abstruse questions : —

"I should like to ask Mr. White, first, whether he knows that *rideo* means *I laugh at* as well as *I laugh ;* second, whether he does not know that adjectives in *bilis* are sometimes formed

from "Gil Blas" (p. 321 of this volume) *sans, témoigna, qu', était,* and *contents* were printed in "The Galaxy" *dans, temoigna, q', etait,* and *content.* It would seem that a minute's reflection would have shown him that as I must have written out the passage from the original, I had only to copy the letters that were before me, and be surely correct, even if I were as ignorant of French as I am of the language of the Man in the Moon.

* My judge does not quote the words in which he condemns me, perhaps because he assumed that all his readers would know their origin. Of this, perhaps, I alone among them am ignorant. The earliest use of the phrase that I remember is in the following passage of the "Recueil General des Caquets de l'Accouchée." 1625.

"Que voulez vous ma Commere, dit une Rousse du mesme cartier, ainsi va la fortune, l'un monte, l'autre descend : pour moy ie ne l'ay iamais esprouvé favorable à mes desirs, i'ay dix enfans en nostre logis, dont le plus grand n'a que xij ans, Il me met hors du sens, i'avois fait venir un Pedan de l'Université pour le tenir en bride : mais il y perdu son latin, il [s] seront en fin contraints d'aller demander l'aumosne si le temps dure." — *La Seconde Fournée,* p. 62.

from the stem of the supine as well as from that of the present of verbs; third, in what Latin author he ever found the noun *risum*, meaning a laugh or laughter; fourth, what *risibilis* means in Latin."

I do, or did, know that the secondary meaning of *rideo* is to laugh at, to deride. I do, or did, know that adjectives in *bilis* are not only sometimes, but often, formed upon the stem of the supine; but also that they are sometimes made from nouns. *Risibilis* (which I have heard it whispered is not the best Latin) is, of course, the counterpart of *risible*, or was when I went to school; and as to *risum*, at that time I met with the following line in a Latin author — Horace — who was held up to me as a poet of some repute : —

> "Spectatum admissi risum teneatis amici?"

and this *risum* I translated, without reproach, "laughter;" parsing it as the accusative case or objective form of *risus*. Horace asked the question in regard to the picture of "a meermaiden vot hadn't god nodings on," which some Roman Barnum seems to have exhibited in the Forum; but it has since been applied to other spectacles, as "Θ Δ" may find on the publication of the next "Round Table."

It is upon *engrave*, however, and my passing assumption that its origin is *en* and *grapho*, that your correspondent lays himself most largely out, here seeming to put all that he knows into one article — something I never do if I can help it. To prove, what I cast no doubt upon, that the word *grave* is to be found in Teutonic tongues at a period before the revival of learning, he musters the Anglo-Saxon, the Old Saxon, the Frankish, Swedish, Danish and German forms of the word. Here, indeed, is an immense display of erudition; which, alas! is something quite beyond me, as, again, all this is in that blessed and wonderful book "Webster's Unabridged," which is a

very present help in time of trouble to gentlemen who
wish to appear learned in etymology — a book which I
confess, with tears, that I have shamefully neglected, and
with a painful sense of wasted opportunities, when I see
the prodigious erudition that its perusal has developed in
the other boy. I am also told that Chaucer uses *grave*
in such phrases as " some men *grave* in tre," which, to a
man who, having read Chaucer for pleasure from his boyhood, has within the last six months re-read every word
of him and of Gower carefully and critically, is valuable,
nay, invaluable information.

My executioner also piously finds a *grave* for me in
sacred ground — Ulfilas's Mœso-Gothic translation of the
Gospels — a very interesting and philologically instructive
remnant of early Christian scholarship, the many *lacunæ*
in which are much to be deplored. But the example
cited by " Θ *Δ*," " saei *grob* jah gadiupida," is not the
happiest he might have chosen, as it presents only the
strong preterite of the Mœso-Gothic verb, with a change
of the vowel. The following seems more to the purpose :
" *graban* ni mag, bidyan skama mik " Luke xvi. 3) ; *i. e.*,
I may not dig, to beg shames me. For *grave* seems always to have meant, to dig, to make a hole, to scratch.
Very long before the time of Ulfilas and his Mœso-Goths,
Homer used it in the *Iliad.* First thus : —

" Γράψας ἐν πίνακι πτυκτῷ θυμοφθόρα πολλά."—Z., l. 169.

Here γράψας ἐν πίνακι means, writing upon a tablet ;
but in the next passage in which *grave* occurs, it means,
to scratch deep, to wound :—

" Βλῆτο γὰρ ὦμον δουρί, πρόσω τετραμμένος αἰεί,
  Ἄκρον ἐπιλίγδην· γράψεν δέ οἱ ὀστέον ἄχρις
  Αἰχμὴ Πουλυδάμαντος." —P., l. 599.

Here γράψεν δέ οἱ ὀστέον ἄχρις means, pierced to th-
bone. Thus, even in Greek, to write, *i. e.*, scratch
wax, seems to be only the secondary meaning of *gra*

which has not changed its signification or its form for three thousand years, and which, in my ignorance, I think, went, with other words and some letters, westward and northward through Dacia into Western Europe.

My Greek initialed censor says I "ought to have known at what time Greek words began to be transferred directly into English." I confess I ought, for I learned it long ago; and he tells me that in the year 1500 there were probably but four men in England who knew anything of Greek. In very deed I had heard something of this kind before; and I connected with it the fact that the word *engrave* does not appear in English before that time. The old English-formed participle *graven* I know, but the English-formed participle *engraven* I do not know in literature three hundred and fifty years old. I am inclined to the opinion, not only that *grave* is a direct descendant, as it is a perfect counterpart, of γράφω, but that the appearance of *engrave* in English is a consequence of an acquaintance with the Greek compound ἐγγράφω; just as (to cite an extreme case in illustration), although we find *asperge* in French, *spargen* in Old-German, and *sperage* in English before the year 1500, *asparagus*, not known in English before that date, is a direct descendant and counterpart of the Greek ἀσπάραγος.

The editor of the "Round Table," with courteous justice, offers me the opportunity of defending myself. Far be it from me to do so. Rather, lest I should be justly placed, to use the words of my accuser, among "that large number of persons" who, "in this country," "get a reputation for learning merely because they have the presumption to write on learned subjects," let me at once confess my utter ignorance of the subject on which I have been writing. Yet it was not until I had read the "Round Table" this morning that I fully appreciated the flagrancy, the brazenness, of my imposture. Nevertheless, may it not be accepted as a plea *in misericordiam* that I make no pretension to the "profound learning" of my accuser, but only to some knowledge, yet very imperfect, of the English language?

I have, however, managed to discover, as I think, by the aid of a gentleman who hath the tongues, and whose services I have secured, at an enormous expense, for this occasion only, what the Greek characters of your correspondent's signature "Θ Δ" stand for. They are, probably, I am told, the initial letters of Θάρσος Δύσκολον, meaning fastidious confidence, or, in the simple English, more becoming to one like me, and more to my taste, peevish boldness.

Your correspondent has now the field to himself. Having confessed all that he has accused me of, I assure him that it shall be his fault if I trouble him hereafter. I am, sir, your obedient servant,

RICHARD GRANT WHITE.

BAY RIDGE, THE NARROWS, L. I., March 1, 1869.

INDEX.

A.

A, broad *ah* sound of, 62.
abortive, 85.
accommodated, 34.
accouchement, 178.
accountable, 228.
a-doing, 343.
Adjectives, 203.
Adjectives in *en*, 259.
adopt, 86.
affable, 86.
aftermath, 387.
after-thought, 387.
againbite of inwit, 21.
aggravate, 87.
agree, 380.
agreeable, 380.
agriculturalist, 215.
ah-am, 242.
airs, 171.
ale-house, 154.
alike, 88.
Alford, Dean, 44.
allude, 89.
allow, 90.
a-making, 343.
amenities, 33.
American English, 8, 44.
American style, 47.
anchorable, 225.

and so forth, 209.
animal, 91.
answerable, 228.
antecedent, 91.
appear, 380.
Apple, 378.
apple-butter, 378.
apple-john, 378.
apple-slump, 378.
approve, 380.
apt, 92, 97.
Aristotle, 356.
arm, 380.
armory, 132.
article, 143.
artist, 93.
as, 136.
Ascham's "Schoolmaster," 344
as well, 184.
ate, 143.
authoress, 204.
auxiliary verbs, 310.
available, 227.
aviary, 132.
awful, 162, 185.
axed, 17.

B.

Bad, 242.
bade, 120.

457

distrust, 380.
divine, 106.
do, 120.
dock, 107.
donate, 205, 229.
donation, 229.
done, 120.
done gone, 350.
Don Quixote, 348.
downward, 211.
drank, 121.
dress, 107.
drive, 192.
drunk, 121.

E.

Ecphractick, 382.
editorial, 109.
effectuate, 141.
eg, 242.
eggs, 17.
ego, 242.
either, 261.
either and neither, 261.
electropathy, 212.
en, 239, 240.
enceinte, 177.
enclose, 206.
endorse, 206.
endure, 115.
English, composite character of, 393.
English Dictionaries, 364.
English, pure, 19.
English sentence, 280.
enquire, 206.
enthused, 207.
epigram, 233.
epigraph, 233.
esquire, 109.

L'état, c'est moi, 250.
etymology, 7, 279, 367, 390.
evacuate, 109.
eventuate, 141.
ever, 379.
ever-acting, 379.
evergreens, 216.
ever-living, 379.
ever-running, 379.
every, 110.
ewer, 83.
example, 112.
excellent, 112.
except, 112, 216.
executed, 111.
exemplary, 112.
exist, 306, 353.
expect, 112.
experience, 112.
experienced, 113.
experiment, 113.
experimentalize, 214.
exponential, 217.
extend, 115.
extraordinary, 279.
eyren, 17.

F.

Fall, 369.
fashionable, 223.
father, 62.
female, 179.
female relation, 134.
fellowship, 209, 221.
fetch, 95.
fiddle-bow, 387.
fiddle-stick, 387.
fiddle-string, 387.
figures, 389.
first rate, 257.

THE END.

Ingram Content Group UK Ltd.
Milton Keynes UK
UKHW022125060323
418148UK00005B/183